Policy Implications of Research in Education

Volume 5

Scope of the Series

In education, as in other fields, there are often significant gaps between research knowledge and current policy and practice. While there are many reasons for this gap, one that stands out is that policy-makers and practitioners may simply not know about important research findings because these findings are not published in forums aimed at them.

Policy Implications of Research in Education aims to clearly and comprehensively present the implications for education policy and practice drawn from important lines of current education research in a manner that is accessible and useful for policy-makers, educational authorities and practitioners.

More information about this series at http://www.springer.com/series/11212

Carolyn A. Brown
Editor

Globalization, International Education Policy and Local Policy Formation

Voices from the Developing World

Springer

Editor
Carolyn A. Brown
Educational Leadership,
Administration, and Policy
Graduate School of Education
Fordham University
New York, NY, USA

ISBN 978-94-024-0591-0 ISBN 978-94-007-4165-2 (eBook)
DOI 10.1007/978-94-007-4165-2
Springer Dordrecht Heidelberg New York London

Softcover reprint of the hardcover 1st edition 2015

Printed on acid-free paper

Springer is part of Springer Science+Business Media (www.springer.com)

To Jim, with all my love

Preface

The purpose of this book is to give voice to scholars from developing countries and regions around the world by inviting them to explore how the international educational policy, invariably linked to international aid, influences education policy formation and implementation in their country or region and how this influence does or does not meet the local cultural, social, economic, and political needs.

A relatively recent and small body of research and commentary supports a discourse that questions how well international education policy mandates such as *Education for All* serve the needs of developing countries. Noel McGinn argues that policy mandates should not be tied to funding assistance. He advocates for a separation between "material assistance" and "technical assistance" in education and recommends that donor technical assistance make a shift away from providing international "best practices" to enabling local researchers and policymakers to generate relevant policy alternatives. However, others argue that while donor countries advocate for local government control of development, these countries are inextricably linked to the donor for funding, the result being that donor money continues to drive policy formation. Kenneth King from a 2011 contribution to the Norrag website claims that "It would be easy to show that they have been valuable for the politics of the Northern international development community…but very much harder to prove that they are genuinely and widely owned by the South" (para 4).

In addition, while international education scholars have developed illustrious careers and vast knowledge in the field of education in developing countries, their perspective, however expert, does not always reflect the perspectives of the local scholars. As more and more developing countries—through government grants and nongovernmental organization funding—are providing advanced education for the best and brightest, it seems time to give these scholars a voice in the discourse on educational policy formation.

The intent of this book is to provide these local scholars with a platform to advance this discourse. Historically, these scholars, who observe and study the donor process, have had little influence over the decisions. Decisions are largely negotiated between international donors and local government officials to fund educational programs, with government officials having policy agendas that may be intertwined with donor requirements. It is hoped that this book will give established scholars, emerging scholars, and graduate students in international and comparative education studies an alternative perspective for the study of international educational policy.

The book is divided into two sections, with a concluding chapter: The first section sets the stage for the discussions by providing the background for the genesis of the book along with a historical context for international education policy and the current state of international donor policy for education. The second section consists of chapters written by scholars from around the developing world—Latin America, South Asia, Southeast Asia, Africa, and Eastern Europe. Many, but not all, of the authors were educated in the West, but all have roots in the countries about which they are writing. The book poses these questions to the scholars: Do these policies work for your country? How has the international policy influenced the formation of the local education policy in your country or region? What would you propose for your country or region? The concluding chapter draws together the ideas and perspectives posed by the contributing scholars and attempts to form generalizations about policy but also a theory for framing the development of education policy.

New York, NY, USA Carolyn A. Brown

Acknowledgments

This book was conceived as a vehicle for giving voice to scholars from the developing world on the topic of educational development. Without the insights of the gifted scholars who contributed, this volume would never have been possible. Their hard work, perseverance, and infinite patience with both my demands and my limitations formed the backbone of this book.

Also, my colleagues in the Graduate School of Education supported me through this project with enthusiasm and sometimes by providing me with relief from other duties to write. Special thanks is due to my graduate assistant Cassie Fromowitz, who organized all the documents as they came in and provided extensive editorial assistance. I also want to thank the staff at Springer for their support and patience—Bernadette Ohmer for believing in the project, Marianna Pascale for her logistic support.

Finally, this book was completed because of the help and support of my husband Jim Angelo, who, as a professional editor and publisher, offered me invaluable advice on the publishing process, edited most of the chapters, and consulted on compiling the final copy.

Contents

1 **The Need to Give Voice to Local Scholars in Educational Policy** 1
Carolyn A. Brown

Part I Historical Background and Current Status of International Donor Policy in Education

2 **A Brief History of International Education Policy: From Breton-Woods to the Paris Declaration** 9
James H. Williams

3 **Current Trends in Education & Development** 25
James H. Williams, Carolyn A. Brown, and Sarah Kwan

Part II Voices from the Developing World

4 **Different Policies, Distinct Processes: Three Case Studies of International Influence in Education Policy Formation in El Salvador** 39
D. Brent Edwards Jr., Pauline Martin, and Julián Antonio Victoria

5 **Education for All and the Global-Local Interface: A Case Study of The Gambia** 59
Matarr Baldeh and Caroline (Carly) Manion

6 **Nordic Aid and the Education Sector in Africa: The Case of Tanzania** 81
Zehlia Babaci-Wilhite, Macleans A. Geo-JaJa, and Mwajuma Vuzo

7 **Quality with Equity in Primary Education: Implications of High Stakes Assessments on Teacher Practice in Bangladesh** 107
Jaddon Park and Manzoor Ahmed

8 No Nation Is an Island: Navigating the Troubled Waters Between Indigenous Values and Donor Desire in the Republic of the Marshall Islands 131
Paul Robert Sauer

9 Education and Gender Rights in Latin America 143
Ezequiel Gomez Caride

10 Where to From Here? Analysis of Cambodia's 2009–2013 Information Communication Technologies in Education Plan 157
Jayson W. Richardson, John B. Nash, Lyda Chea, and Chivoin Peou

11 International Aid Influences on South African Policy Development in Education and Training 183
Peliwe Lolwana

12 A View from Latin America: Two Generations of Reforms on Higher Education; Towards a New Decade of Collaboration 201
Jorge Uribe-Roldán

13 Global and Local: Standardized Testing and Corruption in Admissions to Ukrainian Universities 215
Ararat L. Osipian

Part III Toward a Theory of Collaboration

14 Can There Be Real Collaboration Between Donors and Developing Countries in Educational Policy? Conclusions and Recommendations 237
Carolyn A. Brown

Index 249

About the Authors

Manzoor Ahmed is Senior Adviser at the BRAC University Institute of Educational Development (BRACU-IED) in Dhaka, Bangladesh, of which he was the founder-director. He has been Chair of the Bangladesh Early Childhood Development Network (BEN) since 2007 and Convener, from 2003 to 2006, of Education Watch Bangladesh. He served for over two decades in senior positions at UNICEF, including Senior Education Adviser, and was Country Director in China, Ethiopia, and Japan. Earlier, he served as Senior Researcher at the International Council for Educational Development in Connecticut, USA. Manzoor Ahmed is the author of several books on education and development, educational planning, and nonformal education.

Zehlia Babaci-Wilhite is a researcher with a doctorate in Education and Development from the University of Oslo (UiO). Her research interests include Language and Human Rights in Education, Development Aid, and African Higher Education. Currently, she serves as a research assistant in the Department of Educational Research and Intermedia at the Faculty of Educational Sciences at the UiO. She has been a member of the Language of Instruction in Tanzania and South Africa (LOITASA) team of researchers. As a LOITASA member, she has presented her research at workshops in Tanzania and South Africa. Her work has also been presented in international conferences. She has published several peer-reviewed articles and has contributed to book chapters on language and human rights and development aid within the education sector in Africa. She is fluent in Berber, French, English, Norwegian, and Japanese and has taught in several countries including France, USA, Japan, India, and Norway.

Matarr Baldeh For close to 10 years, Matarr Baldeh has been part of global and local efforts to achieve education for all, serving on the executive board of the Education for All Campaign Network, The Gambia, as well as as a member of the Board of Directors for the Fast Track Initiative and the Global Campaign for Education for All. An educator, literacy specialist, and passionate advocate for the educational rights of children, Matarr has worked as a consultant for a variety of nongovernmental organizations and donor agencies throughout his career as well as working as a curriculum developer for the Department of Education, The Gambia. His research interests include equity and social justice in education, adult education and literacy, and nonformal education.

Carolyn A. Brown is an Associate Professor of Educational Leadership and Policy in the Graduate School of Education at Fordham University in New York. She has taught and provided leadership training and consulted in K-12 schools and higher education institutions in the United States and abroad for 25 years. She holds a PhD in Education from UCLA, with a concentration in Social Science and Comparative Education. She has a breadth of knowledge in the field of Education and is most interested in critical analyses of issues in education that are often overlooked and in the confluence between education and political, economic, social, and cultural institutions and issues.

Ezequiel Gomez Caride is currently a PhD candidate in the School of Education at the University of Wisconsin-Madison. He earned his bachelor's degree in Education at the Pontificia Universidad Catolica in Argentina, where he later taught Pedagogy at the School of Education. He has published several articles, most of which use a comparative perspective, and has presented his research in numerous international conferences. He was a Fulbright Scholar in 2008–2010 and is currently the Weinstein Distinguished Graduate Fellow (2012–2013) at UW-Madison. His research is concerned with issues of national identity, educational policy, and cultural studies, with a focus on Latin America.

Lyda Chea is currently completing her master's degree in Development Studies with a major in Social Policy for Development at the International Institute of Social Studies at Erasmus University Rotterdam, Netherlands. Her main research interest focuses on youth and development-related issues. Her recent research accomplishment was to coimplement a research project at the Department of Media and Communication at the Royal University of Phnom Penh. In this 7-month Cambodia Public Policy Research Project granted by Freedom House, she focused on ICT readiness in Cambodian secondary schools and the use of technology by students and teachers. Ms. Chea holds two bachelor's degrees from the Royal University of Phnom Penh, Cambodia: one in Media Management at the Department of Media and Communication and one in English Language Teaching.

D. Brent Edwards Jr. is an Assistant Professor of Educational Administration and International Education at Drexel University. He holds a PhD in International Education Policy from the University of Maryland and a Master of Science in Education from the University of Pennsylvania. He has worked with the University of California, Berkeley; The George Washington University; the Autonomous University of Barcelona; the University of Amsterdam; the University of Tokyo; and the World Bank. While his research examines the political economy of education reform, some of his work can be found in the *Comparative Education Review, Comparative Education, Education Policy Analysis Archives*, and *Prospects*, in addition to a forthcoming book: *The political economy of schooling in Cambodia: Issues of equity and quality* (Palgrave MacMillan).

Macleans A. Geo-JaJa an experienced educator and researcher in the Department of Educational Leadership, Brigham Young University, combines the scholar's critical approach and the experience of an international development adviser. His research analyzes the underlying causes of Africa's economic and education stagnation and the ways in which inclusive development and quality education are critically intertwined. He studies and teaches about education and development especially with the link between the academic community and the world of development practitioners. For the past several years as a Fulbright Specialist Fellow, he has served as technical adviser to universities in different regions of the world, focusing on capacity building in Economics of Education and the international dimension of African education. He is the author of numerous articles and book chapters on Right in Education and internationalization and globalization of development and serves as an Advisory Board member of the International Review of Education and many others.

Sarah Kwan is currently a Doctoral Candidate in School Psychology at Fordham University. Sarah divides her time between New York City and Shanghai, China. She has worked with students in a variety of settings in New York, California, and Shanghai. Most recently, she spent time in Shanghai working with both local Chinese and international school students, conducting psychoeducational evaluations as well as creating and executing interventions. Sarah has previously conducted qualitative research on third culture kids and is currently focusing on the roles of cultural orientation, racial identity, and ethnic identity in the formation of self-esteem in Chinese Americans.

Peliwe Lolwana is the Director of the Centre for Researching Education and Labour (REAL) at the University of Witwatersrand in South Africa. Previously, she has worked for a variety of educational institutions, statutory bodies, and government directorates. She has worked at all levels of education in South Africa and the United States. She has served in many commissions tasked with the transformation of education. She chairs and serves in a number of associations, boards, foundations, and councils in education and training in South Africa. She also consults for international education and training entities like the World Bank, UNESCO, and ILO. She has written and published in the areas of assessment, quality assurance, adult education, vocational education, skills development, and postschool education.

Caroline (Carly) Manion holds a PhD from the Ontario Institute for Studies in Education, University of Toronto (OISE, UT), with a specialization in comparative, international, and development education. She is currently an Instructor in the Department of Leadership, Higher, and Adult Education and the Comparative, International, and Development Education collaborative degree program at OISE, UT. Caroline's broad research interests include global governance and educational multilateralism, equity and social justice, education for social transformation, social movements and civil society, development ethics, feminist transnationalism, postcolonial theory, and sociology of religion.

Pauline Martin originally from the United States, has lived and worked in El Salvador for the past 20 years and has been a professor and researcher in the Department of Education Sciences at the Universidad Centroamericana in San Salvador, El Salvador, since 1999. With a master's degree in Educational Policy and Evaluation from the same university, she has broad experience working on internationally funded educational projects through the Salvadoran Ministry of Education in areas such as in-service teacher training, accelerated education, school directors' training, etc. She has taught a graduate course on gender in educational policy and researched a case study on this topic.

John B. Nash is a specialist in the design and prototyping of innovations in education. He is an Associate Professor in the Department of Educational Leadership Studies at the University of Kentucky, where he is also a Director of CASTLE and the Laboratory on Design Thinking in Education. He teaches courses on design thinking, school technology leadership, and school reform. His research focuses on the methods to design and prototype innovations in education. He is the former Associate Director for evaluation at the Stanford Center for Innovations (SCIL). He was also a grant maker for the Wallenberg Global Learning Network, an arm of the Knut and Alice Wallenberg Foundation of Stockholm, Sweden. He has also served as the Associate Director of Assessment and Research at the Stanford Learning Laboratory, where he directed an interdisciplinary team of research scientists examining the effects of innovative technologies on learning. John holds a PhD in educational administration from the University of Wisconsin-Madison.

Ararat L. Osipian is a PhD candidate in the Department of Leadership, Policy, and Organizations at Peabody College of Education at Vanderbilt. He holds a PhD in Political Economy from Kharkov National University (Ukraine) and an MA in Economics from Vanderbilt University. He is the author of four books; his articles have appeared in many national and international journals of education and economics. His research interests include corruption in higher education and inequalities in access to higher education in international perspective, corporate, property, and land raiding, nexus of education and economic growth, modern welfare states, and political economy of transition.

Jaddon Park Currently, Jaddon works for an education foundation in Kathmandu, Nepal. Since 1998, Jaddon worked in the education sector in Bangladesh. He was an Education Specialist and Lecturer with BRAC University Institute of Educational Development (BRACU-IED) in Dhaka and also conducted research into nonformal education, technical-vocational education and training, teacher education and change, school improvement, and higher education across South Asia. Jaddon has taught at many levels including primary and secondary schools, and he was the principal at an independent school in Sylhet, Bangladesh.

Chivoin Peou is a lecturer at the Royal University of Phnom Penh. His research interests cover social change, young people, new media, and information and communication technologies (ICT). He is now completing his PhD in sociology at the University of Melbourne, focusing on Cambodian social transformation and youth.

Jayson W. Richardson is an Associate Professor in the Department of Educational Leadership Studies and a Director of the Center for the Advanced Study of Technology Leadership in Education (CASTLE). He earned a Bachelor of Science in mathematics education from Indiana University-Purdue University Indianapolis and a master of science from Indiana University–Bloomington in curriculum and instruction with a focus on international and intercultural education. He then earned a PhD in Educational Policy and Administration with a focus on comparative and international development education from the University of Minnesota – Twin Cities. He currently teaches educational leadership, emerging technologies, technology leadership, action research, and qualitative methods at the graduate level. His research and teaching focus on how digital technologies can be used across the globe to create opportunities for individuals and to increase intercultural understanding between individuals. His articles have appeared in many national and international journals of education and technology.

Paul Robert Sauer is the Pastor and Executive Minister of Our Saviour Lutheran Church and School in the Bronx, New York, and adjunct professor of Religion and Education at Concordia College, New York. He and his wife Jessica are the adoptive parents of Katie, Rosie, and Atadrik from the Republic of the Marshall Islands. He is the cofounder of the Marshall Islands Children's Book Project, which produces and distributes Marshallese Language primary-reader books free of charge to schoolchildren in the Marshall Islands.

Jorge Uribe-Roldán is Dean of the Business School at the University Colegios de Colombia (UNICOC) in Bogota, formerly Dean, Faculty of International Relations, Universidad de Bogotá Jorge Tadeo Lozano, and Chancellor International Affairs, Rosario University in Bogotá. His research interests include comparative international education, cross-border higher education and globalization issues and challenges. At present, he is a PhD Candidate in Education at Universidad Pedagógica de Colombia. In government service, Jorge has been Counsellor at the Colombian Embassy in Washington DC, Consul General at the Colombian Consulate General in London, Director of the Colombian Government Trade Office in London, as well as Private Secretary at the Colombian Ministry of Finance and Public Credit in Bogota. His professional experience includes being an advisor for internationalisation of higher education programmes for the Colombian Ministry of Education, Colombian Institute for Sciences, Colciencias, and the Latin American Intergovernmental Organization for science, culture, and education "Convenio Andrés Bello".

Julián Antonio Victoria a psychologist by training, holds a master's degree in Education Policy and Evaluation, the thesis for which focused on values education in El Salvador. Originally from Colombia, he has lived since 2007 in El Salvador, where he has worked as consultant on educational policies for the Organization of Iberoamerican States and the Ministry of Education. In the last 2 years, he has coauthored two books about accelerated education and adult education. He has also coordinated the formulation process of the national education policy for young people and adults in El Salvador. He is currently the Director of the Student Affairs Center at the Universidad Centroamericana in San Salvador, El Salvador.

Dr. Mwajuma Vuzo is currently a lecturer at the University of Dar es Salaam in the School of Education. She holds a bachelor's degree from the University of Dar es Salaam. She also holds a master's degree in International and Comparative Education from the University of Oslo, Norway, where she specialized in Advanced Development Education. She also holds a PhD in Education from the University of Oslo, Norway, where she specialized in Language and Education. She has been a member of the LOITASA (Language of Instruction in Tanzania and South Africa) team of researchers. She has published journal papers and written book chapters. She is interested in language and education research, classroom discourse research, development education matters, and curriculum issues.

James H. Williams is Associate Professor of International Education and International Affairs at the George Washington University. Dr. Williams received his doctorate from Harvard University in international educational planning, administration, and policy. He has done extensive educational development work in sub-Saharan Africa and Asia. He worked at USAID in the Africa Bureau for 2 years, has taught in Japan for a number of years, and currently directs GW's International Education Program. He teaches classes in education and development. His research interests include education and conflict; education for marginalized and conflict-affected populations; decentralization and administrative reform; education and health, equity, and achievement in large cross-national data sets; and the internationalization of higher education. His recent research includes work in Cambodia, Sri Lanka, and Malaysia as well as Japan and, several years ago, the Philippines and Bangladesh. He can be contacted at jhw@gwu.edu

Chapter 1
The Need to Give Voice to Local Scholars in Educational Policy

Carolyn A. Brown

Abstract This chapter outlines the purpose of this book, *Globalization, International Education Policy & Local Policy Formation: Voices from the developing world.* The introduction describes the need for and historical genesis of a book that gives voice to education scholars in developing countries on how policy that is developed by international organizations and carried out by international and bilateral donors affect the development of education policy within their country – for better or for worse. In addition, the chapter provides a preliminary theoretical frame for how the editor approached the topic of international education policy and gives an overview of each chapter.

This book's primary purpose is to give voice to scholars from developing countries and regions around the world by inviting them to explore how the international policy, invariably linked to international aid, influences education policy formation and implementation in their country or region and how this influence does or does not meet local cultural, social, economic, and political needs.

1.1 The Influence of International Policy Mandates on Local Education Policy Formation

A relatively recent and small body of research and commentary supports a discourse that questions how well international education policy mandates such as *Education For All* serve the needs of developing countries. McGinn (2004) argues that policy mandates should not be tied to funding assistance. He advocates for a separation between "material assistance" and "technical assistance" in education and recommends that "the objective of technical assistance shift from providing international

C.A. Brown (✉)
Associate Professor, Educational Leadership, Administration, and Policy,
Graduate School of Education, Fordham University, New York, NY 10023, USA
e-mail: carolyn@cabrownassociates.com

C.A. Brown (ed.), *Globalization, International Education Policy and Local Policy Formation*, Policy Implications of Research in Education 5,
DOI 10.1007/978-94-007-4165-2_1

'best practices' to enabling local researchers and policymakers to generate more relevant policy alternatives" (p. 17).

King (2004) argues that while donor countries advocate for local government control of development, these recipient countries are inextricably linked to the donor because funding is often tied to contingencies for policy changes or trade agreements with donor countries. As a result, in many cases, donor money continues to drive local policy formation. King (2011) further comments on the *Millennium Development Goals* stating, "It would be easy to show that they have been valuable for the politics of the Northern international development community…but very much harder to prove that they are genuinely and widely owned by the South" (para 4). Both the *Millennium Development Goals* (MDG) and the *Education for All* (EFA) goals reflect, in some way, policy priorities, of wealthy countries. The intent of this book is to advance this discourse by giving voice to local scholars, who observe and study the donor process, but often have little influence over the decisions that are made by their governments. This is largely due to the fact that decisions are nearly always made by government officials who negotiate with international donors to fund educational programs, which benefit both the Western policy agenda and the government revenue needs.

1.2 Need to Give Voice to Local Scholars

As education and especially higher education has expanded throughout the developing world, the old model of the Western scholars as the "experts" on education in the developing world is gradually giving way to voices of local actors and scholars. Educational development is a complicated web of social, political, and economic forces. In the current literature and texts on development education, issues of educational development are often bifurcated into ideological "sides", which place the dominance of the West against the empowerment of the developing world. The time is right to hear from educational scholars in the developing world on the question of the relevance and usefulness of international educational policy as a means of opening up the discussion and bringing the multi-dimensional facets of education policy formation to light.

The genesis of this book began when I completed several teaching assignments for a non-profit organization (NGO) in Bangladesh. This large and well-funded NGO[1] operates a network of services including schools from pre-K through higher education. The walls of the NGO's offices are decorated with posters promoting the MDG and EFA goals. Pre-school stood out to me as a high priority for both the NGO and the government. Donor money – both private and institutional – flowed to both for the implementation of pre-school. While pre-school, arguably, forms a

[1]The NGO is funded through donation from bilateral donors, large international NGOs, and the organization's own enterprises.

foundation for basic education, the emphasis on pre-school in a country where both government and NGO resources are inadequate to provide universal primary school enrollment, not to mention effective instruction that would result in universal literacy was confusing. Why was money being given to pre-school when government schools were run down, classes were overcrowded, and teachers were poorly trained? A conversation with several of my Bangladeshi colleagues revealed that pre-school was a funded priority of the West and, therefore, a priority of the Bangladeshi government.[2] But was it a good use of resources? Maybe not. I wanted to hear from the scholars who were thinking about just these kinds of questions, unencumbered, at least to some extent, by political agendas.

One of the people who inspired this book was Dr. Manzoor Ahmed, a senior scholar and former director of the Institute of Education Policy at BRAC University in Bangladesh. Dr. Ahmed, like many of the contributors to this book, has spent years studying the changes in educational policy in his country through the extensive and open lens of having also studied international educational policy. My conversations with him expanded the limited understanding of development education I had gained in my doctoral program. The problems of education in Bangladesh were deep and complex and not as easily solved by Western donor agendas and funds as the government tended to believe.

The contributors to this book, many of whom were educated in the West (which I address in the final chapter), were able to use their broad view of educational policy and knowledge of international development in general as a foundation for interpreting the policy formations in their own country. Scholars in the developing world, much like scholars in the rest of the world are rarely a part of the policy formation process in education, as these decision are made by governments for reasons that are frequently motivated by politics and finance and at odds with research and practice. Scholars are, arguably, not part of the policy power structure; however, as international donor policy, at least rhetorically, moves toward a "cooperation" between the donors and recipient countries, I believe that empowering the local scholars to participate as policy actors may have long term value in improving education. Government officials and development professionals are often too far from the reality of education and too enmeshed in short term political agendas or financial gain to implement realistic, practical, and long term solutions.

The contributors to this book ranged from doctoral candidates to senior scholars, all of whom had specialized in some area of educational policy in their country of origin. They represent a diverse array of opinions, geographical origin, and academic position. All of the chapters are written or co-written by scholars who are either currently teaching and writing in their country of origin or who were completing their doctorate abroad and whose doctoral research focused on issues of education development in their country of origin.

[2] 87 % of children are enrolled in primary school, but only 66 % are recorded as completing grade 5. The youth literacy is listed at 78 %. Thirteen percent of pre-school aged children are enrolled in pre-school programs. These figures are "self-reported" by the government of Bangladesh, and data inflation can improved the country's standing as a good risk for donor funds.

1.3 Theoretical Framework

As a framework for understanding this issue, the book adopts the position that international policy does not have either the ability or the intent to serve the widely diverse needs of development around the world. International education policy has been formed, historically, by wealthy nations and agencies dominated by Western theoretical paradigms. In recent years, donor countries have made an effort to collaborate with developing countries to create international education policy goals; however, this collaboration has been limited. Developing country collaborators are largely government officials, and while these politicians often lack a deep understanding of the educational needs of their country, they do understand the political realities: wealthy countries will not fund projects *they* do not believe are important. While, overall, the contributions to this book assert some element of this theoretical position, the economic, political, and cultural forces that drive international policy decisions varied widely, and the contributors perspectives reflect this diversity. While though, it can be argued, that the spread of globalization, which is driven by accelerating technological capabilities, has affected a substantial change in both the content and influence of international policy on developing countries' education systems, issues of globalization and free-market driven decision-making are not entirely in the forefront of the chapter discussions. A deeper analysis of donor policy will be included in the final chapter where the diverse points of view come together to form a tapestry of perspectives.

1.4 Structure of the Book

The first section of the book sets the stage with an historical context for the discussions. Chapter 2 is devoted to a brief history of international educational policy development from the Breton-Woods agreement to the Paris Declaration, highlighting the impact of the MDG and EFA goals set by UNESCO as the backbone of education policy as it has been adopted and operationalized by the World Bank, bilateral donor agencies, and private donors throughout the Western world. Chapter 3 briefly outlines the current state of international donor policy and new players in the international educational game.

The second section of the book aims to provide a forum for scholars from around the world to openly discuss and critique the impact of international policy on education in their country or region. The goal is to feature indigenous scholars, as opposed to non-indigenous experts, although some chapters are co-authored by non-indigenous scholars.

Each contributor was asked to address these questions: How does international donor policy impact local policy formation? Do these policies work for your country? How are they helping or hindering education and development? What would you propose for your country or region? The second section of the book gives their answers.

In Chap. 4, Edwards, Martin, and Liberos examine three policies that were implemented in the years following the El Salvador Civil War – gender policy, community participation, and the teaching of values in K-12 education. While the authors acknowledge, and indeed, credit the Salvadoran government and local movements for the changes in education policy, they clearly emphasize the role that the international donors played in the determination of the policy – particular gender policy.

Baldeh and Manion, in Chap. 5, use a series of interviews with local policy experts and government officials to illustrate the processes of international donors – both negative and positive – in play in the development of local education policy in basic education in The Gambia.

In Chap. 6, Babaci-Wilhite, Geo-Ja Ja, and Vuzo begin their analysis with a widely critical view of the role of international donors, particularly the World Bank, in using various contingencies to mandate local education policy formation. This critique is followed by a description of a more participatory model used by Nordic donors in Tanzania and how the increased participation of local policymakers results in a more culturally and linguistically sensitive model of development.

Park and Ahmed, in Chap. 7, describe the evolution of basic education and primary school assessment in Bangladesh. They found that the involvement and, indeed, the incentives of international donors placed on the Bangladeshi government were a force for driving positive change in the implementation of primary assessments.

In Chap. 8, Sauer takes a broad view of the cultural, linguistic, and curricular issues that have been impacted by donor funding in the Marshall Island. His analysis reveals the often inextricable link between colonial policies and influences and post-colonial control through international funding in education.

In addressing the rapid implementation of gender policy in education in Chile, Argentina, and Uruguay, Caride in Chap. 9 shows how local NGOs and expanding rhetoric both locally and globally can combine with international donor policy to form local policy.

In Chaps. 10 and 11, the authors point out the failings of local education policy, while placing the blame more squarely on the shoulders of local policymakers. Richardson, Nash, Chea, and Peou, in Chap. 10, delve into the difficulties of the Cambodian government's implementation of widespread technology in education. In Chap. 11, Lolwana uses an historical policy analysis informed by local policymakers to illuminate the failings of the South African education plans since the end of apartheid.

Uribe-Roldàn and Osipian take on various policy formations in higher education. Uribe-Roldàn, in Chap. 12, discusses the progress of higher education in becoming a priority for international donors. He examines the need and desire of Latin American countries to expand higher education and adult education for years while international donors put their priorities and their funds into basic education. He ends with an optimistic view that a new age of collaboration is dawning for higher education expansion throughout the developing world.

In Chap. 13, Osipian takes a hard look at the internal local corruption of the admission examination for higher education in the Ukraine. While he doesn't absolve the Ukrainian government of fault for the lack of accountability, he views the role of the U.S. Agency for International Development as a force in pushing for examination.

The final chapter of this book attempts to find some common themes among the contributors' views and how scholars and policymakers might understand the needs of developing countries and the pressures of international donor, both currently an as an artifact of colonialism.

References

King, K. (2004). The external agenda of educational reform: A challenge to educational self-reliance and dependency in sub-Saharan Africa. *Journal of International Cooperation in Education, 7*(1), 85–96.

King, K. (2011). Global targets, local realities: Rethinking education and training for development. *Norrag News, 31*. Retrieved August 5, 2001, from http://www.norrag.org/issues/31/en/a-status-report-on-new-thinking-rethinking-on-the-different-dimensions-of-education-and-training.html?PHPSESSID=16108aa45f647ceaecb9babf1f270d0a

McGinn, N. F. (2004). An argument for dialogue in definition of national policies for education. *Journal of International Cooperation in Education, 7*(1), 15–25.

Part I
Historical Background and Current Status of International Donor Policy in Education

Chapter 2
A Brief History of International Education Policy: From Breton-Woods to the Paris Declaration

James H. Williams

Abstract This chapter overviews a history of international education policy, beginning with the establishment of the UN and Bretton Woods architectures up to recent efforts to increase the effectiveness and efficiency of donor funding with the Paris Declaration and the Accra Agenda for Action. Education is increasingly viewed as a human right and a core responsibility of governments and is understood as a core component of individual and national development, a requirement for economic growth, and a key factor enabling human capabilities. Participation in schooling has increased everywhere, though rates are lower in low-income countries, especially among girls and marginal populations. International organizations mobilized the global education community to target *Education for All* by 2015. Though not all countries will reach the goal, participation has increased dramatically. A distinguishing feature of the last half of the twentieth century up to the present has been the development relationship between industrialized nations and developing countries. Though targeted to economic and social development, development assistance including that in education, became embroiled both in the international relations of the times and in the fits and starts of understanding how development occurs and can best be fostered.

Depending on how one understands things, there may be no such thing as international education policy. It is true that Article 26 of the *Universal Declaration of Human Rights*, adopted by the United Nations General Assembly on December 10, 1948, discusses education:

1. Everyone has the right to education. Education shall be free, at least in the elementary and fundamental stages. Elementary education shall be compulsory. Technical and professional education shall be made generally available and higher education shall be equally accessible to all on the basis of merit.

J.H. Williams (✉)
Educational Leadership and Policy, Graduate School of Education and Human Development, The George Washington University, Washington, DC, USA
e-mail: jhw@gwu.edu

C.A. Brown (ed.), *Globalization, International Education Policy and Local Policy Formation*, Policy Implications of Research in Education 5,
DOI 10.1007/978-94-007-4165-2_2

2. Education shall be directed to the full development of the human personality and to the strengthening of respect for human rights and fundamental freedoms. It shall promote understanding, tolerance and friendship among all nations, racial or religious groups, and shall further the activities of the United Nations for the maintenance of peace.
3. Parents have a prior right to choose the kind of education that shall be given to their children (United Nations 1948).

And the *Convention on the Rights of the Child*, adopted in 1989, mentions education 20 times (United Nations 1989). However, if policy is understood as requiring an organization or entity where policy is to guide decisions, a policy-maker or policy-making entity, a policy decision, and perhaps a written policy document, the international arena qualifies only tangentially or perhaps episodically, as a place where education policy is made. If, however, the conception of policy can be expanded to include tacit or implicit policy, then a history of international education policy may be possible.

Formally, policy is formulated primarily by entities such as governments with a formally constituted decision-making authority. So with exceptions noted above and a few others, formal international education policies exist only to the extent that governments adopt them. This is not to suggest that governments act freely to enact or adopt (or reject) policies in the best interests of their people (or their elites). Many forces—most not duly constituted to operate as makers of policy—constrain government choices. But international education policy must be understood either as some aggregate of national policies—influenced as they are by global, international, transnational forces on the one hand and indigenous, local, and national forces on the other—or as tacit or implicit policy.[1]

The diffuse nature of international education policy is complicated by the fact that while no one entity has responsibility for formulating policy internationally, a wide range of organizations play an influential role: national governments; development banks and funds; United Nations (UN) organizations; other multilateral development organizations; bilateral development organizations; research, training, and professional organizations, universities; for-profit firms with government contracts; nonprofit international nongovernmental organizations based in high-income countries; and nonprofit groups based in low-income regions (Chabbott 2003) To these we might add faith-based organizations, philanthropic organizations, and business. Of the work these organizations do, the ideas that are circulated and remain in circulation long enough to affect the decisions of other organizations might be considered policy.

[1] Indeed, neither formulation nor adoption is strictly necessary for tacit policy to be in effect and have effects.

2.1 Overarching (Implicit) Policy: The Universalization of, Right to, and Responsibility for Schooling[2]

If tacit policy is possible, then by far the overriding international education policy since World War II has been the "decision" made more or less consciously by most if not all nations in the world to universalize formal schooling. This "policy" can be seen: (1) in the adoption by most countries in the world of the *Education for All* and *Millennium Development Goals* of universal primary education by 2015, (2) by the schools-on-the ground fact of increases in school enrollment in all regions of the world approaching universality at least at the basic level; and (3) by the acceptance of universal schooling as a global norm, a right of all citizens, a responsibility of national governments and of the international community.

To provide some historical perspective, Table 2.1 compares primary enrollment rates by region in 1935–1940 and 2010. It is clear that there has been tremendous growth in primary enrollment over the past 70 years, and that expansion of schooling, particularly in the industrialized "North" was well under way by the beginning of World War II. The post-war "policy" of universalization of

Table 2.1 Estimated primary enrollment rates 1935–1940 and 2010, by region

1935–1940[a]		2010[a]	
Sub-Saharan Africa	19.6 (25)	Sub-Saharan Africa	77.0
Middle East/North Africa	22.5 (13)	Arab States	88.0
Asia	30.6 (13)	Central Asia	94.0
		East Asia & Pacific	96.0
		South and West Asia	93.0
North America & Oceania	79.1 (6)	North America & Western Europe	97.0
Northern Europe	72.0 (12)		
Southern Europe	50.8 (6)	Central & Eastern Europe	95.0
Eastern Europe	48.2 (10)		
South America	40.7 (13)	Latin America & Caribbean	95.0
Central America	33.7 (9)		
Caribbean	59.0 (13)		
World	40.8 (120)	World	91.0

[a]Figures for 1935–1940 are estimated primary gross enrollment rates (see Benavot and Riddle 1988). Figures for 2010 are primary adjusted net enrollment rates based on UNESCO statistics (see UNESCO 2012). Gross enrollment rates include children outside the primary school age range, of which there are many in developing education systems, and so are considerably higher than net enrollment rates, which are calculated on the basis of children of school age. As a result, the differences between initial and current figures are greater, in some cases substantially so

[2]Throughout the chapter, I attempt to use "schooling" to refer to formal graded education offered by the state, to distinguish schooling from other forms of education.

schooling was more of a playing out and affirmation of earlier trends and an extension of those trends to all regions of the world.

Though it is doubtful that all children in the world will be enrolled in school by 2015 as targeted, the expansion of schooling has been remarkable across political regimes and systems, levels of economic production and consumption, languages and cultural systems. The enrollment figures shown are net of quite high rates of population growth in a number of countries during this period. The rate of growth in absolute numbers of children enrolled in school is much higher.

2.2 Explaining the Universalization of Schooling

Empirical investigations of the expansion of schooling have found this expansion statistically unrelated to factors that might be expected to predict it, rates of economic expansion for example (Meyer et al. 1977). Though it is undeniably true that countries with greater national incomes have higher levels of educational participation, the causal relationships are murky and ambiguous, the direction of causality unclear (Hannum and Buchmann 2006). A number of countries with comparatively low levels of national income have also expanded schooling. Some research suggests that high levels of participation in basic education are not dependent on high national income (Caldwell 1986). This and other areas of policy convergence have been explained explicitly by at least two bodies of theory/research, another implicit one, and one that extends and complicates the other two.

First, implicitly, increases in educational participation as well as convergence on other policies can be understood as a result of the "natural" evolutionary process of "modernization" and "development" of human societies. Modernization, while discredited by many scholars in its stronger forms, is remarkably resilient in the discourses of use. Chabbott (2003) quotes James Grant, founder of UNICEF, (1979): "From 1945 to 1990, the development discourse did not so much evolve as accrete. Old ideas did not go away entirely as new ideas were added on top, creating a great amalgam of good and not so good ideas, none of them fully implemented" (p. 36).

Modernization theories have been critiqued by "world culture" theorists (see for example, Meyer and Ramirez 2000; Ramirez 2003) as well as critical theorists (see for example, Ball 2008; Rizvi and Lingard 2006). World culture theorists see universal schooling as part of a dominant "world culture" characterized by the "institutionalization of rationalized myths of Western modernity in the structure of nation-states and the world polity that houses them" (Takayama et al. 2013). These theorists see school as a national and global imperative:

> The hope that education will foster peaceful, rational, compassionate human beings, who will, in turn create peaceful, rational, compassionate societies, is a tenacious one in the modern world. The power of education to incorporate self-actualized citizens into nation-states and into world society remains central to Western notions of development. The notion that some international development activity, such as a few schools, might change the course of a nation-state's history is a cherished one... (Chabbott 2003, p. 162)

Modernization theorists tend to see the nation-state as the primary unit. Modernization, a universal direction, is accepted and not interrogated. The relevant questions relate to why (and how) some countries develop rapidly, while others do not.

By way of contrast, critical theorists see the universalization of schooling less as a world cultural phenomenon that as a manifestation of the increasing incorporation of nation-states into the global capitalist system, with schooling's ultimate purpose being service to the interests of capital (Rizvi and Lingard 2006; Tarabini 2010).

> ...the hegemonic global education agenda of our times is located in the interaction between finance-driven reforms, competitiveness driven reforms and equity-driven reforms. This agenda aims to solve the main problems of the capitalist system by ensuring the compatibility of two major objectives: economic growth and poverty reduction. The new global mandate for education policy since the 1990s has been based on the quest for growth, productivity and competitiveness but in a way that reduces poverty and guarantees social stability (Tarabini 2010, p. 6).

Other scholars see a more complex process of global forces interacting with local politics—national, sub-national and local processes that mediate global trends (Takayama 2007; Steiner-Khamsi 2000, 2004; Carney et al. 2012); the meanings local actors make of national and global imperatives (see, for example, Anderson-Levitt 2003; Vavrus and Bartlett 2012; Gardinier 2012; Worden 2011 as well as Mundy 1998 and others).

Other scholars see convergence as less interesting than the persistence of differences at national and local levels. Cummings (2003), for example, identified six broad historical-structural-cultural patterns that shape policy in different countries, largely within a multiple-routes-to-modernity perspective, but one that rejects convergence on a single model of education or national development.

Still, the notions of progress, improvement, earlier and more advanced stages, in fact the word development itself, even when critiqued, suggest an underlying paradigm of modernization, or something much like it.

2.3 International Education Policy, International Development, and the (Many New) Nation-States

Of course, the development of global international education policy in the post World War II period cannot be considered apart from changes in the political geography of the world and from the emergence and development of international development more broadly.

The independence of nation-states mostly in Africa and Asia resulting from the breakup of European colonial empires after World War II led to the birth of more than 100 new nation-states.[3] In most colonies, colonial powers had established school systems, some more extensive than others, mostly to train a small cadre of

[3] Much of Central and South America had attained political independence earlier.

local elites to manage the day-to-day operations of the colony. Often these systems were of lower quality than schools in the homeland. British colonizers, for example, tended to offer a two-tier system of a small number of elite academic schools with instruction in English and a larger number of local-medium language schools of less academic rigor to serve the larger population. These were supplemented in many cases by schools established by missionaries and faith-based organizations and by locally run community schools. Malawi, for example, is estimated to have had upwards of 5,000 "community schools" prior to Independence in 1964. Almost never was the colonial system intended to serve the entire population, and only a very small proportion of students expected or equipped for higher levels of education. Still, the colonial school systems firmly established the institution of schooling among certain segments of society at least along with the notion of schooling as a path to formal sector work, prosperity, and modernity. The administrative, curricular, linguistic, and selectivity functions colonial school systems established proved enormously influential in setting the direction of post-Independence policy at the national level (Cummings 2003).

At the same time, this imported formal school system lay on top of existing indigenous systems of socialization, training, and often religious instruction. In some cases, indigenous forms of education have largely been subsumed into formal schools. In other cases, traditional and "modern" operate within their own spheres.

At Bretton Woods, the (winning) nations, having just emerged from the most destructive war in human history, and wanting to put an end to war, established the Bretton Woods global architecture for international cooperation. At the time, most of what would come to be called the "developing world[4]" was soon to emerge from colonial rule. The path to improvement seemed to be that of modernization and economic development along the lines of the North and West, and education played a key role. The linkages between education and development were manifested in several assumptions:

1. That modernization would improve the well-being of poor people;
2. That schooling would help countries and individuals modernize or "grow up modern" (Fuller 1991);
3. That provision of schooling would (singly, necessarily) lead to national development;
4. That the central state was capable of providing sufficient schooling (to all);
5. That carefully-designed external assistance could help countries improve their school systems and foster national development in general;
6. That internationally organized and externally-funded education projects would, or at least could, lead to significant improvements in poor countries' school systems; and
7. That the primary policy challenge of schooling was getting children into school.

[4]We use the terms "developing world" and "developing countries" along with "Third World" as a kind of lazy shorthand, aware of the superiority they assign to industrialized nations.

Each of these assumptions or beliefs was challenged over the interim period, though some remain hardy and alive in the current discourse. However, interestingly, even as the core assumptions linking education and development came under scrutiny in some, more academic circles, faith in schooling grew more generally.

With independence, most new governments moved quickly to create national school systems, signaling their modernity, their concern for the needs of the population, and their aspirations for national development. In Malawi's case, similar to that of many nations, the 5,000 existing community schools were nationalized under the administrative authority of the national education ministry, which developed ambitious plans for growing education systems to meet the demands of a newly-independent people and economy.

However, as a consequence of colonialism and underdevelopment, most new nation-states lacked the financial, human, and technical resources to develop educationally and economically as they hoped. Development assistance from industrialized to poor countries, modeled more or less on the U.S. Marshall Plan which aimed to rebuild Europe after the destruction of World War II, became established as a major element of international relations between the "First" and "Second Worlds" on the one hand and the "Third World" on the other, beginning in the late 1940s. Industrialized nations developed bilateral aid relationships with particular countries. International organizations and multilateral development agencies developed technical assistance and funding relationships across a range of countries. Because of the substantial and strategic financial and technical resources made available to low-income countries in education and most other aspects of government, global international education policy cannot be discussed without reference to development assistance. For even as there is no real authority structure to formulate global policy, nation-states, which receive substantial amounts of external funding, however sovereign they may be politically, are not quite independent in their policy-making.

Even so, schooling appeals to individuals who want progress, i.e., to improve themselves, as well as national leaders seeking to develop the nation economically and otherwise, improve the collective well-being, gain international recognition, or be known for these aspirations. Schooling is the institutional form and the residual of the aspirations of modern man, modern woman, and their states.

2.4 Coercion, Borrowing, Cultural Enactment

In discussing the rise of mass schooling, Ramirez (1997) usefully speaks of educational isomorphism as a consequence of coercion, mimetic processes, and cultural enactment.[5] This seems an apt typology of the means by which international education

[5] In Ramirez's words, "...nation-states and nation-state candidates adopt increasingly similar educational activities because they subscribe to a cultural model within which such activities and organizations are keys to national and individual progress." (Ramirez 1997: 49)

policy has been created among the nations of the world. Increased economic linkages and communications have brought peoples into greater contact and inter-dependency in a world of uneven power relationships. Educational ideas from the West and the North carry greater policy weight than ideas from the South, because the model of schooling is Western, and because the West and North have greater coercive, projective, and cultural power.

But it is not necessarily the case that all policies are imposed by outsiders. Many are adopted, because they seem "the right thing to do". Consider for example the case of gender. Virtually every government in the world has agreed to principles of gender equality in schooling. It is true that international organizations, multilateral and bilateral development agencies, and NGOs have promoted gender equity. Still, it does not seem to be the case that so many countries would have adopted gender equity as a policy goal if it were a matter of direct coercion. Of course, indirect means of influence are common, such as donors making funding available for gender-related activities. Nonetheless, many countries adopted gender policies modeled on those of other countries or because the idea was modeled by other countries. Others developed gender policies because they had "subscribed" to a cultural model in which all people, regardless of gender, have the right to school. Researchers have examined the complex interactions of global practices in national and local contexts (see, for example, Anderson-Levitt 2003; Vavrus and Bartlett 2012). Policy ideas and ideals may be Western or global in origin, but they are adopted locally, by individuals and nations for their own reasons. Of course school systems are famously "loosely-coupled", perhaps even more so in poor countries. Official national policy, however global in formulation, is understood and implemented locally, by actors who have particular and often limited resources, whose exposure to global influence is often less direct and less intense, and in any event whose primary reference groups are nearby.

Of course, there are great variations in the formulation of education policy and its content across time and countries. Policies have variously emphasized basic education, vocational and technical education, higher education, non-formal education. Central objectives have shifted from access to equity to quality to learning. Government-led and supply-oriented strategies have largely given way to market-based strategies with a much greater role for "demand-side" policies and interventions. In all of this, however, what is rarely questioned is the underlying policy—based on a fundamental belief that Meyer et al. (1977) would assert is inherent to modern political society—that schooling is a means of improvement for nations and for individuals. The more of it one or one's country gets, the better.

The next section of this chapter provides an overview of developments in international education policy and development since the late 1940s. Subsequent sections discuss trends in: (1) the formulation of international education policy by nation-states in this complex environment of sovereignty, interdependence, and asymmetrical power; and (2) the content of education policy.

2.5 Decade by Decade

From the end of World War II until the 1970s and beyond, more than 90 new nation-states came into being, mostly as a result of decolonization. In many cases, governments moved quickly to nationalize schools, as a matter of national pride; so schools would more actively promote citizenship, identification, and loyalty to the new nation and its leaders; and to maximize use of limited resources. Educational planners, modeling their work on economic planning carried out in the socialist states, developed elaborate plans for expansion of schooling and its linkages with economic development and national development plans. Western universities and international organizations such as UNESCO promoted education and state-led planning as a development activity. It was the heyday of U.S. and Soviet development assistance, which, though relatively modest in education, linked national development, technical and financial assistance, diplomacy, and national interest in an effort to win allies in the larger Cold War. Nonetheless, the belief in modernization, whether capitalist or socialist, the efficacy of the state and the central role of schooling remained unquestioned.

The 1950s were a period of optimism in international development. Comprehensive economic planning was promoted by development specialists in the market and socialist economies alike, at least planning for economic development in low-income countries. The primary focus was on economic development at the national level. With loans for capital investments, technology transfer, appropriate technical assistance, and increased trade, most though not all development agencies and specialists felt that countries would be able to develop. The primary path to development followed a path similar to that taken by the industrial economies of the West and North, from agricultural and natural resource production to industrialization. Despite the general consensus, some economists, sociologists, and others questioned whether conditions were the same for the late arrivals as for the wealthy nations, whether the playing field had tilted or not, and in whose favor.

Educationally, pent-up demand for schooling on the part of new citizens of new nations led to a remarkable expansion of schooling. Ambitious education plans, corresponding to equally ambitious economic development plans, were developed. Attempts were made to use school systems to develop skilled labor according to manpower plans developed in conjunction with economic and national development plans. Managerial resources in the newly independent nations were often scarce. While national staff "capacity" was developed, expatriates occupied many technical positions in the education and other ministries. Often school systems expanded more rapidly than available resources in human terms of students, teachers, administrative officials, and policymakers and in material terms of school buildings and instructional materials. Regardless, the heady days of fresh independence fostered an atmosphere of possibility and promise. UNESCO assumed a major role during this period as the lead UN agency for education.

The 1960s saw an intensification of the Cold War rivalry between the United States, the Soviet Union and their various allies. In part, this rivalry played out in a competition for favor among developing countries, and corresponding allocations of development assistance to the needy, who were also allies. The 1960s represented the high point of modernization theory. With appropriate technology and good economic development policy, national economies should, it was felt, reach the stage of take-off and sustained economic growth through a series of clear steps (Rostow 1960). Failure to take off was hypothesized by some scholars to result from individuals' non-modern attitudes, for example, the extent or lack of achievement motivation (McClellan 1961). At the same time, critical thinkers especially in the Third World began to write about the need for changes not just in the attitudes of people in less-industrialized countries or in the technologies made available to them by industrialized nations, but in the structure of resources and trade in the world economic order.

In education, the 1960s saw emergence of human capital theory, advanced by Theodore Schultz (1963, 1971) and others. Human capital theory argued that economic development in the West could not be explained simply by the accumulation and application of natural inputs and financial capital. A substantial portion of the difference in growth could (best) be explained by differences in human capital, the knowledge and skills acquired through education and training. Schooling thus became an economic investment, not just a cost to the national treasury.

In both development and education arenas, there was the beginning of awareness that the early promises were not being realized. National economies were not growing as fast as projected by development plans. School systems were overwhelmed by persistent shortages of necessary inputs, and expansion of schooling did not necessarily lead to jobs at the individual level or economic growth at the national. Neither development nor schooling was working out as hoped.

The 1970s and the Second Development Decade saw a shift from economic development as a goal in itself to economic development for improved well-being of the population, especially the poor. Participatory, bottom-up, community-based, and grass-roots approaches to development became prominent, along with the language of basic needs and income (in)equality. Women and children began to draw policy attention along with other groups previously marginal to the development experience. "Structural" inequalities both within and across countries were highlighted. Education saw a number of critiques of schooling. Freire saw most schooling as an instrument of "domestication" (1972) while Illich (1970) urged the "disestablishment" of schooling as credential-granting (and thus socially reproductive) institution. Carnoy (1974) portrayed education "as cultural imperialism" (1974). Nonformal education drew attention as an alternative to the regimentation of formal schooling and a solution to the world educational crisis (Coombs 1968). Some countries worked hard to catch up to population growth and the challenges of underdevelopment. Others especially in East and Southeast Asia were beginning to link schooling with skills development and an export-oriented economic development strategy (World Bank 1993). Others such as Cuba, Tanzania, China, etc.

used education to promote a larger social and political transformation of society (Carnoy et al. 1990).

The 1980s saw the debt crisis. Neoliberal economic analysis found that the governments of developing countries were financially over-extended. Implementation of structural adjustment programs by the World Bank and International Monetary Fund were required as the condition for funding. Structural adjustment programs required substantial reductions in the size of government budgets, mostly by reducing government workforces and cutting back on government programs and bureaucracies, and removal of protections to national currencies and national markets. High levels of inflation and unemployment resulted. Education and other social sectors suffered serious cutbacks in funding. Efficiency became a high goal. With the rise of neoliberal thought, market strategies drew considerable attention in the social sectors as well.

There was a general disillusionment with the efficacy of the central state. Manpower planning and economic planning in general fell into disrepute. The World Bank, USAID and other agencies promoted decentralization in education and other sectors—in an effort to improve bureaucratic responsiveness to clients or beneficiaries; to share the burden of finance with local communities and beneficiaries; to downsize the central bureaucracy. At the same time, local authorities often lacked the capacity, training, and resources to manage decentralized units effectively. Decentralized governance generally requires more capacity, in more places, than more centralized governance.

Research found rather remarkable effects of education, especially secondary education of women, on child mortality, child and maternal health, and fertility decline (see for example, Caldwell 1979, 1980). Parallel developments saw a greater emphasis on inclusion of women and other previously excluded groups and a willingness to broaden the groups involved in schooling. A series of rate of return analyses suggested that the social returns to primary education were greater than to secondary and higher education. As a result, many of the major funding organizations shifted their funding to basic education. Still, there was also a general recognition that past attempts to improve access had failed to reach all children. The decade ended with the World Conference on Education for All (WCEFA), organized by many of the major international organizations and actors in international and development education. Modeled in part on UNICEF's successful immunization campaigns of the 1980s, WCEFA's goal was to mobilize and support governments so as to ensure a basic education for all of the world's children by the year 2000.

The 1990s saw an intensification of several earlier trends. Tightening budgets led to increased calls for accountability including results and impacts, for funding agencies, the agencies implementing projects, and countries receiving aid. At the same time, there was growing awareness of unintended dysfunctions of different approaches to development assistance and the limitations of projectized development assistance. There was increasing recognition of the need for ownership and capacity of the development enterprise on the part of recipient countries, and for coordination among funding agencies and across development initiatives.

Increasingly, the effectiveness of aid came to be understood as dependent on good governance on the part of the recipient country. Alternative modalities of technical assistance were developed, including budgetary support and sector-wide approaches (SWAp). Support was also growing for a comprehensive approach to basic development goals, leading to the *Millennium Development Goals* in 2000.[6]

In education at the global level, much of the 1990s was occupied with mobilization around the *Education for All* (EFA) goals. Later in the decade as it became clear that the initial EFA goals were not going to be met by 2000, a subsequent meeting was organized in Dakar in 2000, where the various nations—donors and recipients alike—recommitted themselves to achieving universal basic education by 2015.[7]

In parallel, there was growing participation of non-governmental organizations (NGOs), both international and national, in development activities. Though not without controversy, the idea was that NGOs were able to reach father and deliver services more flexibly than government.

The fall of socialist regimes in the Soviet Union and Eastern Europe ended the Cold War. Surprisingly, conflict increased, though mostly in the form of intra-state conflicts. The notion of "complex humanitarian emergency" was developed—an emergency that is multidimensional, man-made, and politicized. To a greater extent than before, conflict involved non-state actors, to which the established international architecture, composed as it was of nation-states, had difficulty responding. Some political spaces became impossible to govern becoming "failed states". As other countries moved toward greater risk of failure, the notion the "fragile state" was developed, defined as a government lacking the capacity or will to provide basic services to its people and the ability to govern its spaces after dark (Williams n.d.). As the number of such cases arose, it became clear that standard approaches to development assistance, once the humanitarian crisis ended, were not effective, often not possible, sometimes even making bad situations worse. Areas affected by conflict were in greater need of assistance, yet because of instability, weak institutions—the elements of state fragility—received significantly less funding and support.

Other issues have come to the fore: As a result of the moves to implement EFA policies, including abolishment of school fees, enrollments have increased, outstripping in many cases the capacity of school systems to provide. When successful, increasing numbers of basic education completers put pressure on the secondary level to respond. Often, secondary systems lack the capacity to educate all students who wish to enroll. Many secondary school systems lack the curricula to respond to

[6]Goal 1: Eradicate extreme poverty and hunger; Goal 2: Achieve universal primary education; Goal 3: Promote gender equality and empower women; Goal 4: Reduce child mortality rates; Goal 5: Improve maternal health; Goal 6: Combat HIV/AIDS, malaria, and other diseases; Goal 7: Ensure environmental sustainability; Goal 8: Develop a global partnership for development.

[7]The Dakar goals are: Goal 1: Expand early childhood care and education; Goal 2: Provide free and compulsory primary education for all; Goal 3: Promote learning and life skills for young people and adults; Goal 4: Increase adult literacy by 50 %; Goal 5: Achieve gender parity by 2005, gender equality by 2015; Goal 6: Improve the quality of education.

the needs of diverse students, some of whom will continue on to higher levels of education, but many of whom will not, and who need to leave school with a respected credential and skills to earn a living. Provision of education does not necessarily lead to employment if the schooling provided does not meet the needs of employers (UNESCO 2012), or if the economy does not produce enough jobs.

The 2000s opened with the recognition of failures to reach universal goals of development and education outlined above coupled with renewed commitments to achievement of those goals. Soon after the turn of the century, the events on 9/11 focused U.S. attention on terrorism. Development assistance, at least in the United States, became even more closely linked with diplomacy and defense. Funding was shifted to areas felt to be at greatest potential risk for terrorism.

In parallel, there was a trend among development agencies toward the creation of general funds devoted to particular problems, for example the Global Fund to Fight AIDS, Tuberculosis, and Malaria. The educational equivalent, the *Fast Track Initiative*, was established in 2002 and headquartered at the World Bank. Its goal was to bypass the normal aid processes, which were lengthy and bureaucratic, and get funding quickly to countries able to demonstrate the capacity to use the funds well. Initial criteria for effective capacity were challenged as the Initiative developed. A critical external mid-term evaluation led to establishment of a new management structure more independent of the World Bank, and a new name, The Global Partnership for Education. A number of countries have received funding to achieve EFA goals, through preparation of a comprehensive sector plan and other means. But the neediest and most conflict-affected areas have, until recently, been left out.

Concern with accountability, evidence, results and impact led to a focus on evidence-based policy formulation, development planning organized in terms of results frameworks, and impact as explicit evaluation criteria. Ongoing concerns about aid effectiveness led the OECD to promulgate the *Paris Declaration of Aid Effectiveness* (OECD 2008), which detailed five principles for aid effectiveness and established procedures for monitoring implementation of the principles.[8] This was followed up in 2008 by the *Third High Level Forum on Aid* Effectiveness in Accra, and the *Fourth High Level Forum on Aid Effectiveness* in Busan, South Korea, in 2011. The Accra meeting found progress in some areas, but indicated the need for greater efforts in terms of country ownership, building more effective and inclusive partnerships, and achieving development results and openly accounting for them.

Successful at the level of aspirations, international education policy has failed to reach its potential in several important ways. While more children are enrolled in school than ever before, the extent of learning is not clear. Schools still operate with fewer resources than they need, a situation that will only worsen as demand for schooling is likely to increase more rapidly than the resources to fund it. Current models of schooling may be unaffordable and inappropriate for all. Current curricula fail to prepare many for livelihood after school. New demands continue to be

[8] The principles are: ownership; alignment; harmonization; managing for results; and mutual accountability.

placed on schools and on the education policy process, with few demands taken away. The more critiques that emerge, the greater the burden on schools, school systems and governments, some of which will not reach the "minimum" targets of the *Millennium Development Goals*. Then too, funding agencies are working hard to fix problems in development assistance process. But many of the rigidities are inherent. It is difficult to form an equal partnership when inequalities among nations are structural, and one party is funding the other. Economic, social, and political development are poorly understood, difficult to organize and to support, even without the interests of competing states and the challenges of different languages, cultures, traditions, different histories and differences in power. Still, the aspirational success of education as a modern idea and as an individual goal and national project is remarkable, challenged only perhaps, arguably so, by advances in technology. Schooling has become part of the landscape of modern life, a right of individuals and a rite of passage, defining, in part, the life chances of those who get it and those who do not.

References

Anderson-Levitt, K. M. (2003). *Local meanings, global schooling: Anthropology and world culture theory*. New York: Palgrave Macmillan.

Ball, S. (2008). *The education debate*. Oxford: Policy Press.

Benavot, A., & Riddle, P. (1988). The expansion of primary education, 1870–1940: Trends and issues. *Sociology of Education, 61*(3), 191–210.

Caldwell, J. C. (1979). Education as a factor in mortality decline: An examination of Nigerian data. *Population Studies, 33*(3), 395–413.

Caldwell, J. C. (1980). Mass education as a determinant of the timing of fertility decline. *Population and Development Review, 6*(2), 225–255.

Caldwell, J. C. (1986). Routes to low mortality in low-income countries. *Population and Development Review, 12*(2), 171–220.

Carney, S., Rappleye, J., & Silova, I. (2012). Between faith and science: World culture theory and comparative education. *Comparative Education Review, 56*(3), 366–393.

Carnoy, M. (1974). *Education as cultural imperialism*. New York: David McKay.

Carnoy, M., Samoff, J., Burris, M. A., Johnston, A., & Torres, C. A. (1990). *Education and social transformation in the Third World*. Princeton: Princeton University Press.

Chabbott, C. (2003). *Constructing educational development: International organizations and Education for All*. New York: Routledge.

Coombs, P. H. (1968). *The world educational crisis: A systems analysis*. Oxford: Oxford University Press.

Cummings, W. K. (2003). *The InstitutionS of education: A comparative study of educational development in the six core nations*. Oxford: Symposium.

Freire, P. (1972). *Pedagogy of the oppressed*. New York: Herder & Herder.

Fuller, B. (1991). *Growing-up modern: The western state builds third-world schools*. New York: Routledge.

Gardinier, M. P. (2012). Teachers in Albanian educational reform and democratization. *Comparative Education Review, 56*(4), 659–683.

Hannum, E., & Buchmann, C. (2006). Global educational expansion and socio-economic development: An assessment of findings from the social sciences. In J. E. Cohen, D. E. Bloom, & M. B. Malin (Eds.), *Educating all children: A global agenda* (pp. 495–534). Cambridge, MA: American Academy of Arts and Sciences.

Illich, I. (1970). *Deschooling society*. New York: Harper & Row.

McClellan, D. (1961). *The achieving society*. Princeton: D. Van Nostrand.

Meyer, J. W., & Ramirez, F. O. (2000). The world institutionalization of education. In J. Schriewer (Ed.), *Discourse formation in comparative education*. Frankfurt am Main: Peter Lang.

Meyer, J., Ramirez, F. O., Rubinson, R., & Boli-Bennet, J. (1977). The world educational revolution, 1950–1970. *Sociology of Education, 50*, 242–258.

Mundy, K. (1998). Educational multilateralism and world (dis)order. *Comparative Education Review, 42*(4), 448–478.

OECD. (2008). *The Paris Declaration on Aid Effectiveness and the Accra Agenda for Action*. Paris: Author. http://www.oecd.org/development/effectiveness/34428351.pdf. Accessed 13 Jan 2013.

Ramirez, F. O. (1997). The nation-state, citizenship, and educational change: Institutionalization and globalization. In W. K. Cummings & N. F. McGinn (Eds.), *International handbook of education and development: Preparing schools, students and nations for the twenty-first century* (pp. 47–62). Oxford: Elsevier, Pergamon.

Ramirez, F. O. (2003). Toward a cultural anthropology of the world? In K. Anderson-Levitt (Ed.), *Local meanings, global schooling*. New York: Palgrave.

Rizvi, F., & Lingard, B. (2006). Globalisation and the changing nature of the OECD's educational work. In H. Lauder, P. Brown, J. Dillabough, & A. H. Halsey (Eds.), *Education, globalisation and social change*. Oxford: Oxford University Press.

Rostow, W. (1960). *The stages of economic growth: A non-Communist manifesto*. Cambridge: Cambridge University Press.

Schultz, T. (1963). *The economic value of education*. New York: Columbia University Press.

Schultz, T. (1971). *Investment in education: The role of education and research*. New York: Free Press.

Steiner-Khamsi, G. (2000). Transferring education, displacing reforms. In J. Schriewer (Ed.), *Discourse formation in comparative education*. New York: Peter Lang.

Steiner-Khamsi, G. (2004). Blazing a trail for policy theory and practice. In G. Steiner-Khamsi (Ed.), *The global politics of educational borrowing and lending*. New York: Teachers College Press.

Takayama, K. (2007). A Nation at Risk crosses the Pacific: Transnational borrowing of the U.S. crisis discourse in the debate on education reform in. *Japan, Comparative Education Review, 51*(4), 423–446.

Takayama, K., Waldow, F., & Sung, Y. K. (2013). Finland has it all?: Examining the media accentuation of "Finnish education" in Australia, Germany, and South Korea. *Research in Comparative and International Education, 8*(3), 307–325.

Tarabini, A. (2010). Education and poverty in the global development agenda: Emergence, evolution and consolidation. *International Journal of Educational Development, 30*(2), 204–212.

UNESCO. (2012). *EFA global monitoring report, 2012: Youth and skills: Putting education to work*. Paris: Author.

United Nations. (1948). *The universal declaration of human rights*. New York: Author. http://www.un.org/en/documents/udhr/index.shtml. Accessed 31 Jan 2013.

United Nations. (1989). *The convention on the rights of the child*. New York: Author. http://www2.ohchr.org/english/law/crc.htm. Accessed 13 Jan 2013.

Vavrus, F., & Bartlett, L. (2012). Comparative pedagogies and epistemological diversity: Social and material contexts of teaching in Tanzania. *Comparative Education Review, 56*(4), 634–658.

Williams, P. (n.d.) State failure in Africa: Causes, consequences and responses. http://www.europaworld.com/entry/ass.essay.8. Accessed 31 Jan 2013.

Worden, E. A. (2011). The "mock reform" of history education in Moldova: Actors versus the Script. *Comparative Education Review, 55*(2), 231–251.

World Bank. (1993). *The East Asian miracle: Economic growth and public policy*. Washington, DC: Author.

Chapter 3
Current Trends in Education & Development

James H. Williams, Carolyn A. Brown, and Sarah Kwan

Abstract The current state of international donor policy is reflective of changes that have taken place over the past two decades to consider greater participation by developing countries. Current priorities in donor policies continue to mirror Western priorities, including basic education, quality programming, and program accountability. In addition, tertiary education and adult vocational skills have entered the priorities of multi lateral and bi lateral donors, arguably, in response to demands from donor recipient countries. In addition, a new model of development is emerging from China and other countries that have moved from donor recipient to granting countries. This chapter outlines the current priorities of Western donors and the role of new donors in influencing development in education.

As 2015, the year set to meet the *Education for All* (EFA) goals, approaches, it is useful to examine the current situation in the development and implementation of education policy internationally. While, later chapters discuss ways in which international influences on education do or do not facilitate effective education policy formation and implementation, this chapter will: discuss the current status of international education policy actions and mandates, examine several current issues in international education policy, and look at some of the recent players in the international development arena.

J.H. Williams (✉)
Educational Leadership and Policy, Graduate School of Education and Human Development,
The George Washington University, Washington, DC, USA
e-mail: jhw@gwu.edu

C.A. Brown
Associate Professor, Educational Leadership, Administration, and Policy,
Graduate School of Education, Fordham University, New York, NY 10023, USA
e-mail: carolyn@cabrownassociates.com

S. Kwan
Graduate School of Education, Fordham University, New York, NY USA
e-mail: skwan@fordham.edu

C.A. Brown (ed.), *Globalization, International Education Policy and Local Policy Formation*, Policy Implications of Research in Education 5,
DOI 10.1007/978-94-007-4165-2_3

Recognizing the peril in trying to summarize trends, we do see several areas, which are likely to occupy the attention of international education policymakers over the next few years. Somewhat reflective of the direction international multilateral and bilateral donors are taking, USAID's new Education Strategy goals focus on three areas: "(1) improved reading skills for 100 million children in primary grades by 2015, (2) improved ability of tertiary and workforce development programs to produce a workforce with relevant skills to support country development goals by 2015, and (3) increased equitable access to education in crisis and conflict environments for 15 million learners by 2015" (USAID 2011, p. 1). Interestingly, the topics of the last five Global Monitoring Reports produced by UNESCO reflect similar educational themes—Youth, Skills, and Work; Conflict; Marginalization; Governance; and in 2013, Learning and Teaching. Here, we discuss eight trends or themes that we feel capture much of the current discourse in educational development.

3.1 Continued Emphasis on Basic Education

First is the theme of basic education. Basic education has been a priority for different stakeholders—donors and non-governmental organizations (NGO)—for over 40 years (Lockheed and Verspoor 1992). EFA, since its establishment in 2005, has emphasized basic education, an emphasis which has been echoed in donor and NGO initiatives. The first of six EFA goals calls for expansion and improvement of early childhood education to provide support for primary education. A second goal calls for free compulsory primary education "of good quality" for all children regardless of gender, ethnicity, or socioeconomic situation. "Quality" is undefined, but in most cases includes basic literacy and numeracy (see discussion below). The third and fourth goals call to "promote learning and life skills for young people" and "increase adult literacy by 50 %". The fifth goal calls for the elimination of gender disparities in primary and secondary school with a focus on ensuring girls full and equal access to and achievement in basic education (World Bank 2013). The final goal emphasizes accountability for and "measurable outcomes" for all education, especially in literacy, numeracy, and essential life skills.

Basic education is considered a requirement for "economic prosperity, the key to scientific and technological advancement, the means to combat unemployment, the foundation of social equity, and the spread of political socialization and cultural vitality" (Chimombo 2005). Indeed, support for basic education has become institutionalized in international educational donor policy. Virtually all international agencies and organizations working in education emphasize EFA. Even as there has been a shift in educational donor policy toward tertiary education and adult skills development, basic education remains a cornerstone of international funding.

3.2 Emphasis on Youth, Skills, and Work

A second recurrent trend in recent years links youth, skills and work. Worries about the "youth bulge", exacerbated by the "Arab Spring", high levels of youth unemployment, input from the governments and advocates from developing countries, and perhaps fears of youth's potential for destabilizing politics have led to a renewed focus on skills: Agencies and governments are developing comprehensive youth policies. School systems are exhorted to provide young people not just with degrees but also with skills. Alongside these developments, the large multilateral and bilateral funding agencies are shifting away from an almost exclusive focus on basic education. This comes as recognition increases of the need for external support to maintain a high level of quality in secondary and particularly tertiary education, where the global economy places a high value on specialized technical skill. In addition, the two remaining EFA goals call for ensuring that learning needs for young people and adults are met through access to appropriate learning and life-skills programs, and achieving a 50 % increase in adult literacy.

Increasing globalization of labor markets, production, and trade along with increased school participation and completion are likely to lead to greater demand for specialized and work-appropriate skills among young graduates. Secondary and tertiary schools are under pressure to produce graduates with needed skills if they are to remain relevant and competitive in the global markets. However, in most of the developing world, the majority of work opportunities are likely to be in the informal sector, for which schooling, as currently organized, is generally of very little value.

Moreover, blaming schools for students' lack of employment fails to account for other components of successful school-to-work connections—existence and availability of jobs, linkages between students and jobs, elimination of non-skill barriers to lack of employment, e.g., ethnic discrimination and gender.

Aside from calls to build skilled work forces, increasing numbers of voices from developing countries are calling for a greater emphasis on tertiary education. Tertiary education, beyond mere skills development, is being trumpeted as vital to building internal human capital within the developing world, to providing future cohorts of leaders who can advance development, and to improving the integrity of leadership in government. Some of this capacity is developed by bringing students from developing countries to universities in industrialized nations for advanced study. At the same time, some bilateral donors (Scandinavian countries and others) are working to build the capacity of tertiary education institutions in developing countries directly. Historically, the need for advanced education in the developed world has limited these opportunities to a small elite. Arguably, the development of advanced tertiary education institutions may perpetuate education of the elite and exclusion of a broader range of students. However, improved quality of national tertiary institutions is likely to have a substantial impact on the perspective of future leaders and the capacity of national institutions to meet national needs.

3.3 Emphasis on Assessment and Accountability

A third trend relates to the uses of assessment for accountability. Although assessment and accountability are certainly not new, they are becoming increasingly important in education policy from basic education through tertiary education, including teacher education. EFA suggests assessment to ensure attainment of "all aspects of the quality of education, and ensuring their excellence so that recognized and measurable learning outcomes are achieved by all, especially in literacy, numeracy and essential life skills." (UNESCO 2000, para 6). The Dakar Framework proposes that countries "systematically monitor progress towards EFA goals and strategies at the national, regional and international levels" (UNESCO 2000, p. 21).

Possibly reflecting the increasing role of testing for policy purposes in many Western countries, Western donors have increasingly emphasized assessment in their educational activities and have brought this paradigm to recipient countries as a means of maintaining accountability for educational quality and transparency and to "support greater engagement of stakeholders" (Wagner 2011, p. 1).

While assessments may serve learners, teachers, and parents, assessments are more recently used to provide policymakers with information about the "quality" of their educational programs. "The importance of assessment for policy stems, in part, from the wide-spread recognition that educational indicator systems must include not only inputs but also outputs. A 'results agenda' has become increasingly prominent in the planning of international donor agencies" (Braun and Kanjee 2006). These developments are part of a larger shift in emphasis from inputs and process to outputs and outcomes. Increasingly these measure of indicators of outputs and outcomes are being used by donors to improve programs and sometimes even for accountability at the institutional level.

3.4 Renewed Emphasis on Quality

One of the most prominent trends in international education policy is the heightened emphasis on quality. Calls for quality improvement have been common for the past 20 years, perhaps longer, and may be inevitable in the shift from elite to mass or universal systems of education. One of the problems with improving quality has been its multiple meanings—quality of inputs, quality of outputs/outcomes, quality of process, reputation as quality, etc. Nonetheless, the pressures of successful EFA policies coupled with advances in assessment and a growing emphasis on student-level impact and accountability have resulted in a situation where improvements in learning outcomes have become the *sine qua non* of successful education projects.

Indeed, on the face of it, that an education project should result in improved learning seems self-evident. However, attempts to improve learning outcomes by excessive reliance on assessments used to measure learning can have unintended consequences—teachers teaching to the test, narrowing of the curriculum, corruption, and cheating.

Still, some recent formulations of goals for post 2015 have called for "learning" as opposed to (simply) "education for all". In fact, for most of the history of schooling in most places in the world, there was no systematic attempt to measure the effects of instruction on children's knowledge and skills. This amazing lacuna has been masked, we would guess, by the selection function of schooling. Since there were generally fewer places in higher levels of school than there were aspirants, various sorts of exit or entrance examinations kept the focus on who was passing and failing rather than whether children were learning anything. Though we did not know what children did and did not learn in school, some clearly did get it, while others clearly did not.

The shift toward quality is a major challenge for school systems. This is especially so for low-income countries where increasing expenditures for school inputs system-wide are difficult to finance. In contrast to improving quality, increased access is relatively easy for central managers to achieve. Governments can plan schools, organize facilities, post teachers and principals, and supply curriculum, all without entering the classroom except to drop off provisions. However, improving quality requires increasing teacher professionalism along with changes in teacher behavior and teacher-student interactions. Such changes are difficult to prescribe or to organize centrally. They require professional judgment on the part of teachers and practice honing that judgment with substantial local support. In some sense, these changes require that education authorities move from a "teaching" mode to a position of "learning". The question becomes how education authorities can support teachers in improving instruction. Teacher professional behavior is difficult to foster in low-income environments with teachers who themselves have little training or experience of quality instruction. The management challenge entailed in facilitating conditions for the improvement of instruction—both support and accountability—are orders of magnitude greater than provision of spaces in school.

3.5 Different Approaches to Development Assistance

Though not universal, there has been a general shift from a project-based model to a sector-based model for international funding. For many years, donors operated through projects, funded specially, designed to achieve particular purposes, and bounded in time and location. Projects originally served the operational strategies of donors, and appeared to fill educational gaps in developing countries; however, they failed to provide a substantial or sustained impact on the countries they were designed to help. As a colleague noted, after decades of projects to improve teacher training, curriculum, school-based management and community participation, management information systems, and policy formation, the result was often not a complete and functional education system but a hodgepodge of uncoordinated initiatives.

One of the problems was coordination. Each funder had different reporting and data requirements. Keeping up with a dozen or so funders required the time and energy of ministry staff whose time would better be used managing and improving the country's school system. Highly qualified ministry staff members were not so available as to be easily expendable to international projects. All too often, education ministry data efforts became devoted less to meeting the planning needs of the country than to keeping up with reporting requirements of international donors. Donors often took the lead in defining development initiatives, though with various degrees of consultation with the host country government. Rarely, however, did a government define its objectives *a priori* with donors lining up to meet them.

To facilitate implementation, projects were often run through special units rather than through government bureaucracies. Indeed the challenges of working through government channels were sufficiently great to keep donors away, because of donor accounting and accountability needs and the frequent danger of leakage of funds. In such arrangements, funding generally did not flow through developing government systems but was organized by the funder. At their worst, projects were neither coordinated with each other, nor was real sustainability built into the project. Projects addressed the problems defined by project objectives, but did little to enhance government capacity to deal with such problems in the future.

Recognizing the limitations of projects, the development community increasingly moved toward sectoral approaches to education and other development domains (OECD 2008). In its pure form, sectoral strategies are developed by host country governments in collaboration with donors. Planning is carried out by host government officials, though sometimes with technical support from donors, at least initially. Donors then agree to fund different aspects of the sectoral program, which are implemented by the recipient government, sometimes with assistance from donors or implementing partners. Donors provide funding directly to governments, monitoring achievement of mutually defined objectives and accountability requirements. Sectoral approaches develop strategic plans for the entire sector, thus helping counter the fragmentation of multiple uncoordinated projects.

Still, such sectoral approaches are quite demanding. They require an enormous front-loading of plans, often before full information is available. Because of their scale and the need for upfront specification of desired ultimate and intermediate outcomes and processes, they do not foster a learning approach to development assistance. Additionally, they are difficult to change, making mid-course corrections time-consuming. They bring most donors together, a desirable thing in many cases, but one which gives the assembled donors a great deal of weight. Donor consistency may become monolithic, further opening host countries to external influence.

Moreover, many of the problems in development do not lend themselves to top-down resolution. The scale of sectoral planning generally leaves little practical space for tailoring context-specific solutions.

Still, in the final analysis, it is the governments of the countries themselves that must develop and implement education policy. Despite the problems, some version of sectoral planning is likely to continue into the foreseeable future, even as donors and governments tinker with ways to best realize its greater purposes.

3.6 Increasing Private Provision and "Partnership" and the Role of Non-governmental Organizations

Other trends attest to the ascendency of neoliberalism. Recent years, for example, have seen a mushrooming of private enrollment in many countries, even where "free" public options are available. Though poorly understood, the phenomenon of private schooling seems to result from a failure of public school options to provide the minimum learning environment that parents require. In some contexts such as Nepal, high-fee private schools are mushrooming, in response, presumably, to the failure of the public system to provide schooling of sufficient quality. By contrast, in India and Pakistan, low-cost private schools, generally of low quality, are proliferating (Jamil et al. 2012) Other manifestations of private provision include the widespread phenomenon of shadow schooling, or private tutoring (Privatisation in Education Research Initiative 2012). Both of these trends challenge the public school system.

In addition to private schooling, the past 60 years have seen a steady increase in the number and type of actors involved in education policy-making and provisioning internationally. International NGOs play a greater policy-advocating, policy-making and funding role than ever before, approaching levels of influence previously held exclusively by donors and governments. National NGOs (and teachers unions) play a complex role, constituting new civil societies in many countries, and adding new voices to the policy-making table. Philanthropic organizations now play a major role in some areas, targeting funding toward particular issues or demonstration projects that help shape national and international agendas. A broader range of institutional actors are involved in setting the post-2015 agenda than before (Secretary-General High Level Panel of Eminent Persons 2013). Calls for workplace relevance and skills often recommend greater linkages with the private sector.

3.7 Concerns with Excluded Populations and Child-Centered Learning

The ideal of universal schooling as articulated in EFA plays out in moves for greater inclusion. In most places for most of history, schooling has been limited to children of the well-off, and more recently, middle class. This remains true in parts of the developing world. Recent years have seen increasing concern among Western donors and developing governments alike for those children left out of formal education—girls in many contexts, disempowered ethnic and linguistic groups, rural children, children with special needs, and children affected by conflict. Accompanying moves toward greater inclusiveness is a shift, at least rhetorically, in the focus of instruction, from teacher-centered to child-centered.

This drawing of attention to the individual child, his/her cognition and experience has defined the Western educational paradigm for decades. Recent emphasis on child-centered education reflects a growing understanding of the cognitive and social development of children and the conditions that foster that development among non-Western cultures. It parallels a cultural shift as well in the conception of the child and his/her relationship in the family and larger society. To what extent this shift in thinking can be attributed to Western influence is difficult to determine. Children's rights are a relatively new and likely foreign concept to many people raised in traditional cultural and pedagogical environments, but the ideas have gained support among many working in education and development, in developing countries as well as Western capitals.

3.8 Involvement of New Donors and International Influences

Private philanthropy is playing an increasingly larger role, with the Gates Foundation in health, Hewlett in health and education, Soros Open Society Foundation, Aga Khan Foundations, and others in education. In 2013, the MacArthur Foundation announced an investment of $18 million dollars in secondary education in developing countries in collaboration with Master Card Foundation, Elma Philanthropies, and Human Dignity Foundation These large foundations and charities largely allocate funds directly to educational institutions or NGOS and, therefore, bypass government institutions, interference or corruption. Similar to NGOs, philanthropic organizations tend to support projects that are aligned with the EFA plan, largely basic education, girls education, and tertiary education. Some large foundations and private for-profit organizations have been involved in supporting and expanding the private school movement mentioned earlier in this chapter. For instance the Orient Global Fund, a Singapore company, is active in developing low fee private schools in Africa (Growing Inclusive Markets 2010).

The numbers and types of development funding agencies are expanding. New bilateral donors such as South Korea, China, Taiwan, Brazil, South Africa, and

India are playing increasingly greater roles. These countries, some of which were themselves recipient countries in recent decades, have begun to fund their own national development organization. China, Taiwan, and Brazil have all published policy statements announcing their intention to provide development assistance. China in particular has become one of Africa's largest sources of development assistance.

China is an interesting case, illustrating a new direction in donor development. At this point, China's development interests in Africa largely involve expansion of infrastructure in extracting, transporting, and processing Africa's rich natural resources. In contrast to Western firms, for instance, ALCOA, the world's largest aluminum manufacturer, mines bauxite in Guinea and ships it raw to the U.S., where it is processed. Chinese companies also mine bauxite, but these companies have built processing plants in Guinea that not only provide jobs, but have required the building of hydro-electric dams to generate electricity for the processing plants and, incidentally, for the local population (Michel et al. 2009).

While China's current interest in Africa is primarily trade and influence—importing raw and semi processed materials such as oil and minerals and exporting inexpensive consumer goods—China's recent relationship with Africa dates back to its support for African countries during their wars for independence from Western colonial rulers. In some cases such as Angola, China has built schools and hospitals as well as offering the government low-interest development loans. Thousands of Chinese doctors and teachers have been sent to Africa (Krause-Jackson 2011). These relationships between African governments and Chinese companies tend to be built on common trade interests without particular regard for quality of construction or human rights (Smith 2010). While Western funding increasingly demands transparency and assurance of human rights (even if these are not always accomplished), Chinese deals are accomplished with less bureaucracy and fewer conditions, and therefore move more quickly. This appeals to African governments (Smith 2010).

While Western donors are watching China's entrepreneurial activities with some skepticism, the Chinese are developing, at least in some countries, a new model for development aid. A number of Chinese enterprises are developed at the local city, town, or village level where the projects provide jobs, housing, and various forms of local infrastructure such as solar panels for electricity. These projects differ from Western donor projects in that they largely come with few strings attached.[1] The funds bypass the often corrupt national governments and funding is offered as a trade arrangement without typical Western demands that are often perceived as coercive or remnants of colonialism. The Chinese government has "long boasted of its role…as a supporter of African efforts to throw off Western colonialism" (Buckley 2013, p. 1). Such initiatives challenge many of the assumptions and practices that have characterized development work for most of the post-WWII period.

[1] Chinese projects in Africa often use Chinese workers as well as local labor.

While the future of international development aid in education is impossible to predict, a number of priorities—basic education, assessment, and accountability—appear to be enduring across several decades, while priorities are being expanded to include tertiary education, work skills, and access to education for girls and disadvantaged children. In addition, new players are entering the field—private foundations and new countries with expanding economies and different values from the traditional Western donors who have dominated the funding and form of development for decades.

References

Braun, H., & Kanjee, A. (2006). Using assessment to improve education in developing nations. In H. Braun, A. Kanjee, E. Bettinger, & M. Kremer (Eds.), *Improving education through assessment, innovation and evaluation*. Cambridge, MA: American Academy of Arts and Sciences.

Buckley, C. (2013, March 25). China's leader tries to calm African fears of his country's economic power. *New York Times*. Accessed from http://www.nytimes.com/2013/03/26/world/asia/chinese-leader-xi-jinping-offers-africa-assurance-and-aid.html?_r=0

Chimombo, J. P. G. (2005). Issues in basic education in developing countries: An exploration of policy options for improved delivery. *Journal of International Cooperation in Education, 8*(1), 129–152.

Growing Inclusive Markets. (2010). Accessed from http://www.growinginclusivemarkets.org/

Jamil, B. R., Javaid, K., & Rangaraju, B. (2012). *Investigating dimensions of the privatization of public education in South Asia: Case studies from Pakistan and India* (ESP Working Paper Series, No. 43, Privatisation in Education Research Initiative). London: Open Society Institute. Accessed from http://www.periglobal.org/sites/periglobal.org/files/WP43_Jamil_Javaid&Rangaraju.pdf

Krause-Jackson, F. (2011, June 11). Clinton chastises China on internet, African "new colonialism". *Bloomberg*. Accessed from http://www.bloomberg.com/news/2011-06-11/clinton-chastises-china-on-internet-african-new-colonialism-.html

Lockheed, M. E., & Verspoor, A. M. (1992). *Improving primary education in developing countries*. New York: Oxford University Press for the World Bank.

Michel, S., Beuret, M., & Woods, P. (2009). *China safari: On the trail of Beijings' expansion in Africa*. New York: Nation Books.

OECD. (2008). *The Paris declaration on aid effectiveness and the Accra agenda for action*. Paris: Author. http://www.oecd.org/development/effectiveness/34428351.pdf. Accessed 31 Jan 2013.

Privatisation in Education Research Initiative. (2012). *Regional conference report: Globalisation, regionalization, and privatization in and of education in Asia, 28–29 September, 2012, Kathmandu, Nepal*. London: Open Society Foundation. Accessed from http://www.periglobal.org/sites/periglobal.org/files/PERI_OSF%20Conference_ASIA_Final.pdf

Secretary-General High Level Panel of Eminent Persons. (2013). *A new global partnership: Eradicate poverty and transform economies through sustainable development: The report of the high-level panel of eminent persons on the post-2015 development agenda*. New York: United Nations. Accessed from http://www.post2015hlp.org/wp-content/uploads/2013/05/UN-Report.pdf

Smith, D. (2010, December 23). China says booming trade with Africa is transforming continent. *The Guardian*. Accessed from http://www.guardian.co.uk/world/2010/dec/23/china-africa-trade-record-transform/print

UNESCO. (2000). Education for all goals. Accessed from http://www.unesco.org/new/en/education/themes/leading-the-international-agenda/education-for-all/efa-goals/

USAID. (2011). *Education: Opportunity through learning: USAID education strategy*. Washington, DC: Author.

Wagner, D. A. (2011). *Smaller, quicker, cheaper: Improving learning assessment for development countries*. Paris: UNESCO and International Institute for Educational Planning.

World Bank. (2013). *Education for All* website. Accessed from http://web.worldbank.org/WBSITE/EXTERNAL/TOPICS/EXTEDUCATION/0,,print:Y~isCURL:Y~contentMDK:20374062~menuPK:540090~pagePK:148956~piPK:216618~theSitePK:282386,00.html

Part II
Voices from the Developing World

Chapter 4
Different Policies, Distinct Processes: Three Case Studies of International Influence in Education Policy Formation in El Salvador

D. Brent Edwards Jr., Pauline Martin, and Julián Antonio Victoria

Abstract In this chapter, we analyze and compare three cases of education policy formation in El Salvador, a country affected by civil war from 1980 to 1992. The three cases presented here relate, first, to the "Education with Community Participation" (EDUCO) program, second, to the policy for gender equality in education, and, third, to the policy to include the teaching of values in Salvadoran education. These policies began to develop in the early 1990s and would all be incorporated during the 1990s into policy of the Ministry of Education through the Ten Year Plan and, later, the National Women's Policy. In the three cases, we address contextual aspects as well as the influence of international conferences, international trends, and a range of actors from the local, national, and international levels. In so doing, we explain how and why certain policy formation processes reflect "imposition," "negotiation," or "hybridization." From our findings, we also: suggest factors that determine the dynamics of education policymaking, reflect on the ways in which policy formation can be more symbolic than meaningful, and, finally, emphasize that globalization is diminishing the predominance of traditional state channels with regard to the formulation of education policy.

D.B. Edwards Jr., Ph.D. (✉)
Policy, Organization, and Leadership Department,
School of Education, Drexel University, Philadelphia, PA, USA
e-mail: dbrente@gmail.com

P. Martin, M.Ed.
Universidad Centroamericana, José Simeón Cañas, San Salvador, El Salvador
e-mail: pmartin@uca.edu.sv

J.A. Victoria, M.Ed.
Student Affairs Center, Universidad Centroamericana, José Simeón Cañas,
San Salvador, El Salvador
e-mail: jvictoria@uca.edu.sv

C.A. Brown (ed.), *Globalization, International Education Policy and Local Policy Formation*, Policy Implications of Research in Education 5,
DOI 10.1007/978-94-007-4165-2_4

Though the education system in El Salvador has long received attention from international organizations (McGinn and Warwick 2006), this attention increased dramatically in the years following the end of the 12-year civil war, which concluded in early 1992 (Gillies 2010). Evidence of this is the fact that, between 1991 and 2005, the education sector received over $552 million in development assistance and loans from the Inter-American Development Bank, the United States Agency for International Development (USAID), and the World Bank alone (Gillies 2010).[1] While such intense involvement and heightened levels of funding on the part of international donors and financial institutions can have significant effects on the formation and implementation of local education policy, the way in which these effects manifest is not always clear.

Education policy in El Salvador in the post-civil war context of the 1990s is an example of this situation, and it is that case which the present chapter investigates. The purpose is to understand the influence of international actors on the formation of education policy during a key period that extends from the beginning of the 1990s to 2005. We bound the study with the year 2005 because it was at this point that the Ten Year Plan (TYP)—the key policy document that guided post-war education—expired.

Beyond simply investigating how international influence manifested, however, this chapter also seeks to comparatively analyze various instances of that influence in order to explain how the making of national education policy in El Salvador has been affected by it. In order to do that, the focus is on three specific cases. The first is the program known as Education with Community Participation (EDUCO), which decentralized school management to the community level. The second is the stated intention of the government to pursue gender equality in education, both in terms of access and quality as well as curricular materials and school atmosphere (Parker 2000). The third is the policy to include in Salvadoran education a focus on the teaching and learning of values, an effort that was seen as particularly important in the post-war context. We have chosen these polices because each had distinct characteristics and was formulated differently—thereby providing a useful basis for comparison and for the derivation of lessons regarding processes of policymaking and the range of local, national, and international actors that influence them. In that we examine these cases in relation to each other and provide a nuanced analysis of how international involvement is influential in the making of education reform, this chapter represents a contribution to the literature on education policy, both generally and in El Salvador.

In order to accomplish the stated tasks, the chapter proceeds as follows. First, we detail our methodology. Second, we characterize relevant aspects of the context of the 1980s and early 1990s. Third, we flesh out the framework employed to analyze policy formation processes. The fourth section, which constitutes the majority of this chapter, presents our three cases. The fifth section discusses the cases and sheds light on the central issues that this chapter addresses. In the final section, we offer a few concluding thoughts.

---

[1] To put these contributions in perspective, the total budget for education in 1992 was approximately $109 million (MINED 1994).

4.1 Methodology

The results offered in this chapter derive from three separate case studies completed between March 2010 and April 2013. For these case studies, 70 interviews were performed with representatives from such organizations as the Ministry of Education of El Salvador (MINED); the World Bank; USAID; the United Nations Education, Science and Culture Organization (UNESCO); non-governmental organizations (NGOs); and think tanks, in addition to international consultants. We also performed an extensive and systematic analysis of relevant policy documents, legal decrees, technical reports, and other literature on the historical, political, and economic contexts of our cases.

Data analysis involved not only the well-known methods of coding and memoing, but also case study and matrix-related strategies (Edwards 2012a). Edwards (2012a) writes that matrices provide a useful means through which to organize and analyze not only the actors, elements and various forms of influence that characterize processes of policy formation, but also the level at which, or through which, impactful actors and elements manifest. That is to say, the qualitative data analysis strategies on which we relied were selected because they served to clarify, from a structural and organizational perspective, the dynamics of interaction and the attribution of causality in education policymaking processes that involve actors from multiple levels.

4.2 The Context of Education Policy in El Salvador

While each of the cases we discuss in this chapter has their own particular characteristics, they all came on the heels of a particular national and international context at the end of the 1980s and early 1990s. Nationally, the decade of the 1980s was consumed by civil war between the Salvadoran government and the Farabundo Martí National Liberation Front (FMLN), an organization of five rebel groups fighting for social and economic opportunities for the poor majorities as well as political participation and access to the justice system. On the education front, during the years of the armed conflict, the government substantially reduced the budget for education, which led to the closing of schools and a decrease in teachers' salaries with direct consequences on their social value. By 1989, the coverage of primary education reached only 69 % of the national demand, and for those who were in school the repetition rate was 19 % making access and retention two of the greatest challenges of the time (Fernández and Carrasco 2000).

On an international level, in the context of the Cold War, the U.S. presidential administrations of Carter and Reagan financed the Salvadoran armed forces against the FMLN (LeoGrande 2000). In all, by the end of the war, the U.S. government had contributed approximately $6 billion in the form of military aid and economic assistance (Booth et al. 2006). Despite such assistance, it was not until late 1989, with the election of Alfredo Cristiani as President, that an administration open to those free-market economic policies that the United States preferred would assume control of the Salvadoran government (Foley 1996). Importantly, in the years prior to Cristiani's election, due to a lack of support for the preferred economic policies of the United States, USAID established and funded think tanks and NGOs in El Salvador. This was done in order to create conditions favorable to the goals of the U.S. government including neoliberal economic reform, strengthening democratic institutions, and stabilizing social problems (Quán 2005; Sollis 1993). Such institutions, along with USAID and the World Bank, would subsequently play important roles, in particular through their ability to produce reports designed to shape the debate around education policy (Eriksson and Kreimer 2000; MINED 1999).

In early 1992, the Peace Accords were signed. This momentous achievement—combined with international support for dialogue and research on the state of the education system—set off a series of events that would, within a few years, result in a new national education policy (Guzmán 2005b; MINED 1999; Reimers and McGinn 1997). To summarize, this process involved the following:

1. October–December 1993: A USAID-funded education sector assessment was carried out by international and local consultants and was simultaneously discussed by an advisory committee of key actors from across the Salvadoran political continuum. This advisory committee not only helped to inform on-going research but was also important because it helped to build the relationships and consensus that would later make formation of the new national education policy possible. The process of conducting both the sector assessment and the dialogue of the advisory committee were led by the Harvard Institute for International Development (HIID) in conjunction with the Central American University (UCA), a private, Jesuit institution, and the Business Foundation for Educational Development (FEPADE)—a right-of-center non-governmental organization founded and funded with USAID assistance.
2. January 1994: HIID, UCA and FEPADE conducted workshops on results of the sector assessment with key groups of governmental, educational and private-sector stakeholders in the country. For the rest of the year, an inter-institutional promotional committee ("*comité dinamizador*") comprised of individuals from influential political and technical organizations (including unions, private universities, non-governmental organizations, and the MINED) continued to share the study with stakeholders from the education sector who would be integral to implementing changes in policy that resulted from the study.
3. October 1994–June 1995: President Armando Calderón Sol (who took office in June 1994) appointed a diverse group of 12 high profile educational actors to the National Commission on Education, Science, and Development (hereafter, National Education Commission), which spent 7 months elaborating a vision for the development of the education system.
4. January 1995: With financing from USAID and administrative support from FEPADE, the aforementioned inter-institutional promotional committee organized a final "consultative forum" attended by over 200 people from a wide range of institutions, including the National Legislative Assembly, teachers' unions,

donor organizations, women's groups, community-based non governmental organizations, universities and the MINED, among others, in order to share and receive feedback on both the education sector assessment as well as directions for education reform in general.

5. November 1995: The MINED then finalized and published the TYP, taking into account the sector assessment, the process of consultation, and the report of the National Education Commission. The five objectives of the TYP were to improve educational quality; to increase the efficiency, efficacy and equity of the education system; to expand coverage; to create "new modalities of service provision," which referred to the decentralization of education management; and to strengthen "teaching of human, ethical, and civic values" (MINED 1995b, p. 11). Clearly, then, the over-arching, system-wide policy for education reform contained provisions that correspond with two of the policy cases on which we focus—namely EDUCO and values education. Gender equality in education would be contained within a separate policy in 1997.

Given the context of the years following the Peace Accords, in which successful reform of the education system was seen as central to the recovery and reconstruction of the country, the production and existence of the TYP was a significant event that mobilized key actors and instilled high-hopes for the years to come (Bejar 1997). Moreover, the plan itself, after 1995, became a defining characteristic of the education reform context. Yet, as our research will show, while the broad, official process of research, dialogue, and policy-making described above did garner significant attention and was seen as a meaningful exercise at the time because it helped to maintain momentum for the work of rebuilding the education system, it was neither the only attempt at, nor a particularly efficacious instance of, education policymaking in the 1990s.

The case studies we present below thus emanate from the context described above. Each has its roots in—or prior to—the early 1990s and extends through to the end of the Ten-Year Plan. Despite being born of the same context, each came into existence with important differences. Before sharing the results of our study, however, we first present the analytic framework that we employed to characterize policy formation dynamics.

4.3 Analytic Framework

Edwards (2013a) suggests a typology of four characterizations to analyze policy[2] formation, or the dynamics among key actors as issues emerge and solidify on the reform agenda. This typology can be used to analyze and discuss the increased involvement of international actors and ideas that is now common in processes of

[2] In this chapter, we use the term policy to refer to government policy specifically (and, more narrowly, that of the MINED), as opposed to state policy generally (Krasner 1984).

national education policymaking. These characterizations range from policy attraction to policy negotiation, policy imposition and policy hybridization.[3]

Under the first of these, policy attraction, it is suggested that the international realm is relevant to the formation of national education policy to the extent that domestic actors in one country purposively and voluntarily look to another country for a policy to customize and implement at home.

In the second characterization, policy negotiation, both reform-oriented education stakeholders and policymakers engage external references and/or international rhetoric in order to encourage and lend credibility to desired changes in national education policy. By drawing on external legitimacy and international ideas, these domestic actors gain an advantage in the internal negotiation process that typifies educational reform. Often, however, the extra-national sources that are initially employed to gain legitimacy in this process are ultimately "internalized"; that is, traces of the origins are removed to avoid compromising the credibility of the government's policy.

The third classification, policy imposition, places the structural aspects of aid relationships at the center of education reform processes and, within that, focuses on the ability of international agents, but particularly international donor and financial institutions, to influence the formation and content of the education reform agenda, specifically in developing countries. Often times, the imposition of a policy is a result of the overwhelming research capacity of international organizations combined with the numerous—and, for developing countries, frequently daunting or unavoidable—procedures, requirements, rules, and conditions that accompany the receipt of funds from those same institutions.

Policy hybridization, the fourth classification presented by Edwards (2013a), runs counter to the others because it defines education reform as processes that are not uni-linear, have multiple loci of control, and are the result of complex interactions among the global and the local. The implication is that education reform processes are not easily unpacked and cannot be understood in terms of the first three characterizations because they, at once, reflect multiple and multidirectional forces.

While this typology is useful in that it represents a broad range of characterizations of the ways in which the international realm affects national education, we suggest here that the addition of one further characterization would improve upon it. This characterization, which we suggest be labeled policy funding, pertains to those instances in which the role of the international level is restricted to the funding of domestic prerogatives but without the agenda manipulation and conditionalities that accompany the policy imposition classification. Although this form of international influence may receive less attention in the research literature, it is no less legitimate. Indeed, it could, for example, be said to often characterize the role of aid from such donor countries as Japan, the Netherlands, Spain and those in Scandinavia.

[3] See Edwards (2013a, 2014) for further discussion of these perspectives and for extensive citations of the key authors who have written about each of them, including, for example, Gita Steiner-Khamsi, Jurgen Schriewer, David Phillips, Joel Samoff and Thomas Popkewitz, among others.

4.4 Three Cases of Education Policy in El Salvador

This section presents the findings for each of the three case studies at the heart of this chapter. Given space constraints, the findings presented here represent only the most salient aspects of longer case studies.

4.4.1 EDUCO Program[4]

The EDUCO program, begun in the early 1990s, is famous for decentralizing certain aspects of education management from the central to the community level. In that it formally gave the authority for contracting teachers to parents in rural communities, it was the first program of its kind in Latin America, and would go on to inspire similar reforms in dozens of countries around the world. According to the theory of this program, the education system would be more efficient if the central MINED transferred to the community level the responsibility for managing the hiring and firing of teachers, the latter of whom would work on 1-year contracts that were renewable at the discretion of the school council (of five elected, volunteer parents from the community) that hired them. Additionally, it was thought that this arrangement would promote effectiveness because it would lead to more consistent teacher attendance and improved student test scores, a consequence of the fact that teachers were under the scrutiny of community actors.

Very little is known, however, about the dynamics that generated the initial emergence and subsequent growth of the EDUCO program. Although EDUCO officially entered government education policy in the mid 1990s through the TYP, it appeared on the reform radar many years prior due to global reform trends, the country's general circumstances, and the centrality of donor relationships at the time. Consequently, the trajectory of EDUCO's formation reflects policy imposition, as is explained in what follows.

Internationally, in the late 1980s and early 1990s, much attention was drawn to the idea that "participation" was a central component of "good" development strategies, especially when it came to education policy. This was reflected in March 1990 by the high-profile declaration of the World Conference on Education for All (WCEFA), which asserted that "partnerships at the community level … should be encouraged" because "they can help harmonize activities, utilize resources more effectively, and mobilize additional financial and human resources" (WCEFA Secretariat 1990, p. 58, as cited in Bray 2003, p. 32). During this time, international organizations also highlighted the concept of participation. In particular, USAID raised the issue as a means to promote democracy and the effectiveness of public institutions (Montero and Samuels 2004). The World Bank, in addition to emphasizing the issue of effectiveness, honed in as well on the potential of decentralization to

[4] This section is based on Edwards (2013b).

result in more efficient and accountable service provision arrangements (Edwards 2012b). For their part, UNESCO and the United Nations Children's Fund (UNICEF) focused on a version of participation oriented towards the empowerment of communities through literacy programs, for example (Basso 1985; Jones 1990).

Thus, at the moment that development and education professionals around the world were focusing on the concept of participation, the circumstances in El Salvador made it inevitable that the model for its education reform would flow from an international organization. On the one hand, in 1990, President Cristiani and Minister of Education Cecilia Gallardo[5]—both from the core of the extreme right-wing political party, the Republic National Alliance—were set on modernizing the education system, which implied, among other things, the restructuring of service provision along neoliberal lines (Edwards and Klees 2012), with their first priority being to expand the system's coverage. Countrywide, at least 37 % of children ages 7–14 were out of school, and in the conflictive areas government-provided education services were non-existent (MINED 1990). On the other hand, 96 % of the MINED's budget was dedicated to teacher salaries.[6] As such, MINED did not have the funds necessary to increase access, and it was dependent on external funding sources—both to innovate and simply to expand coverage (MINED 1999).

In this context, the MINED faced the challenge of elaborating a new education strategy in 1990. To inform that task, a study was done by a consultant from UNESCO; the study explored the state of education throughout the country for poor children aged 0–14 and recommended that the MINED build upon the "non-traditional" arrangement found in many of the poorest (and conflict-affected) communities where government services were lacking (MINED 1990). Per this arrangement, and often in conjunction with the popular education[7] movement (Hammond 1998), a member of the community (often with only a few years of education) would teach the children under a tree or in someone's house in exchange for donations of money or food.

Subsequent documents published by the MINED (1994) reveal not only that the above-mentioned 1990 report served as the initial inspiration for the EDUCO program, but also that it led to funding from UNICEF for a brief pilot program in January 1991 with six rural schools. Despite the initial idea and financial support from United Nations institutions, it was the World Bank that would be the catalyst for drastically scaling up the program. This is not surprising, as the World Bank in the late 1980s and early 1990s was preoccupied with the idea of decentralization (Edwards 2012b). At that time, it had conceptual models that predicted the increased efficiency and effectiveness of decentralized education systems (Winkler 1989),

[5]It is of note that Cecelia Gallardo, before becoming minister of education, was an education specialist at FEPADE.

[6]It should also be noted that the MINED's relationship with teachers' unions was also dysfunctional, as these unions tended to support the cause of the FMLN.

[7]Popular education is an approach to education where students, in being taught to read, are also taught to critically interpret their contexts to identify structures and policies that contribute to marginalization (see, e.g., Freire (1970) and Kane (2001)).

but it did not have empirical evidence, especially at the community level. (The level of focus for decentralization to that point had been the departmental level.) It was for these reasons that the World Bank was intensely interested in the proposal by the UNESCO consultant to put communities in charge of school and teacher management.

Within El Salvador, the technical and financial capacity of the World Bank was crucial when it came both to securing MINED buy-in to the EDUCO program and to funding its expansion. Without a doubt, once Minister Gallardo saw that this form of decentralization met the constraints and priorities of the government at that time—i.e., increasing educational access, introducing an innovative (read: modern/neoliberal) reform, and weakening the teachers' unions (an ally of the FMLN and key opponent of the government)—the technical assistance of the World Bank played a central role. As a former World Bank team member working in El Salvador explained, "Really, [the Minister of Education] was convinced by the technical arguments that we used. From then on we developed a very, very good relationship…. She really believed in what the Bank was doing because of our technical relationship."[8]

From mid-1991 onwards, the World Bank engaged a number of mechanisms to ensure that the program would be scaled up (Edwards 2013b). These included not only technical assistance but also conditionalities related to increased financing for education on the part of the Salvadoran government and the creation of a legal basis for community-level education management decentralization (so that the foundation of the program would not be in jeopardy). An initial loan which included $10 million specifically for the education sector was also prepared and then approved in 1991 to accelerate the creation of class sections that would operate under the direct control of parents at the community level (Edwards 2013b, p. 233). By 2006, MINED had received no less than $69.3 million through a series of loans from the World Bank and the Inter-American Development Bank designed to finance system reform generally and EDUCO specifically.

By 1994, thousands of communities had been integrated into the EDUCO program. Concretely, while the program began in 1991 with six communities, 3 years later it had 2,316 teachers and served 74,112 students (Cuéllar-Marchelli 2003). Ten years hence, in 2004, these figures had risen to 7,381 and 378,208, respectively.[9] Approximately 55 % of rural public schools, which make up two-thirds of all schools in El Salvador, would operate under the EDUCO program (Gillies et al. 2010). Along with this expansion, the program became the platform through which the education system management was reformed during the 1990s and 2000s.

For our purposes, the above-mentioned dates and rapid expansion are significant for two reasons. First, they are significant because they indicate that, even before the

[8] Interview with INTACT12, October 19, 2011.

[9] While the EDUCO program was initially only intended as a strategy to provide education at the preschool level and in grades 1–3, it was subsequently expanded in 1994 to cover through grade 6 and then again in 1997 to cover through grade 9 (Meza et al. 2004). After 2005, even some high schools became EDUCO schools (Gillies et al. 2010).

Peace Accords were signed, the EDUCO program was already up and running. The process of program development was neither public nor democratic; civil society did not have the opportunity to contribute to the initial formation of this important reform. Second, its early adoption and expansion were significant because it shows that the EDUCO program already had the political backing of the MINED before the TYP was created. With regard to policy formation, then, the implication is that the extensive process of research and consultation that was orchestrated between 1993 and 1995 to produce the TYP (as described in an earlier section of this chapter) was a formality, a process designed to generate legitimacy for the government's reforms. The general support of key MINED actors for EDUCO had already been secured and stemmed from both constraints on the national government and the dependent relationship of the MINED at the time on external organizations.

In the end, expertise, financial resources, and (in the case of the World Bank) loan conditionalities from international organizations were integral to the emergence of the program and the fact that it became the central policy for the reform of education system management. Due to these dynamics—and the underlying relationship of dependence between the MINED and such organizations as UNESCO, UNICEF and the World Bank for resources and technical capacity—the case of EDUCO is best understood as a case of policy imposition.[10] In other words, while MINED actors were responding to the characteristics of the education system at the beginning of the 1990s, the process that led to the development of EDUCO was also significantly influenced by the policy preferences of the staff of the involved international organizations, with whom MINED representatives had to interact at that time.

4.4.2 Gender Equality Policy

In the early 1990s, the need to address gender inequality in El Salvador was obvious. For example, while 25 % of men over the age of 14 had never studied in school, 30 % of women were in that situation. Moreover, at the primary level, reports showed that there was a difference of enrolment between girls and boys of up to 11 %, and similar situations were found at the secondary and university levels (ISDEMU 1997). Against this backdrop, efforts were made throughout the 1990s at developing and implementing a gender policy which would address equality. As will be shown, the process of forming the first National Women's Policy was a long and slow one in which international commitments would play a key role as local women's groups, national non-governmental organizations, and governmental institutions engaged in policy negotiation (Edwards 2013a).

[10] This finding is not meant to negate the vision and ability of MINED officials, for both interviewees and available literature have affirmed these attributes with regard to Cecelia Gallardo and others (Gillies 2010).

In terms of policy formation, there were three distinct forces that pushed gender equality onto the public policy scene in El Salvador in the 1990s. These were international conferences (and El Salvador's participation in them), a new national movement of grassroots women's groups, and the National Family Secretariat. Each of these is discussed below in relation to the formation of gender policy in El Salvador.

El Salvador has since the 1970s participated in nearly every international conference related to women's issues.[11] This trend continued in the 1990s with official delegations attending and endorsing the resolutions produced at the 1990 WCEFA in Jomtien, the 1993 World Conference on Human Rights in Vienna, the 1994 International Conference on Population and Development in Cairo, and the 1995 World Summit on Social Development in Copenhagen. As Stromquist (1997) notes, these conferences were significant because they "unambiguously" brought the need for equal access and quality of education for girls to the forefront of the international education reform agenda. For women's groups in El Salvador, these conferences complemented their own attempts at bringing attention to this issue.

In 1993, those local non-governmental organizations in El Salvador focused on women's issues brought together 40 grassroots-level women's groups that had been working on women's rights in the areas of health, labor and education. Together, through a year-long participatory process, they elaborated an agenda for the country—known as the Salvadoran Women's Platform (SWP)—on issues of gender equality. While the SWP made general socio-economic demands (related to employment, land, credit, salaries) and advocated fundamental feminist ideals (e.g., non-violence, sexuality, maternity, etc.), the SWP's educational demands emphasized non-sexist education (e.g., elimination of sexist content in curricular materials) and additionally called for sex education, national campaigns for eliminating violence against women, and the teaching of self-defense techniques for girls in schools. The date of this proposal's public presentation, September 1993, was particularly strategic, as the first peacetime presidential elections were scheduled for March 1994.

Nevertheless, despite both the SWP and the fact that many of the same gender-related education issues were raised by women's groups who participated in the January 1995 national consultative forum, by the time the TYP was published in late 1995, the content did not address the issue of gender at all. Both the SWP and the 1995 consultative forum are significant, however, because they show that, in the lead up to the finalization of the TYP, the issue of gender equality had been raised in important ways by a cross-section of national NGOs and local women's groups. Ultimately, while Salvadoran non-governmental organizations and associated women's groups were not able to ensure that the TYP contained a focus on gender equality, other national entities—with a boost from a 1995 international conference in China—would soon succeed in formulating such a national policy.

[11] The one exception was the 1980 conference in Copenhagen, in which El Salvador presumably did not participate because a special resolution was presented citing serious human rights abuses in El Salvador, against women and children.

To that end, a particularly important entity has been the National Family Secretariat, an institution which was created in 1989 and which has traditionally been directed by each First Lady with the objective of developing a variety of social programs, including for women and education. In 1995, the significance of this institution for policy formation became apparent when the First Lady, Elizabeth de Calderón Sol, as director of the National Family Secretariat, along with a representative of the non-governmental organization sector in El Salvador, participated in the Fourth World Conference on Women in Beijing, which committed El Salvador to a platform for action.

This platform for action served, in the following year, as the impetus for the creation of the first public office on women's issues, the Salvadoran Institute for the Development of Women (in Spanish, Instituto Salvadoreño para el Desarrollo de la Mujer, ISDEMU). Importantly, its independent structure not only crosscut all the relevant public ministries within the government but also included non-governmental organization representatives in both its board of directors and consultative council. Additionally, the Minister of Education was named as a board member and a technical assistant was assigned who acted as a link between the ISEDMU and the MINED. Key actors working on issues of gender were thus brought into close contact and the relationships among them were improved through the creation of the ISDEMU.

Then, in 1997, the first National Women's Policy (NWP) was finally created through joint collaboration between ISDEMU, women's non-governmental organizations, and governmental officials (Moreno 1997). This type of interaction among these groups was unprecedented at the time. In order to determine the policy's content, which included a chapter on education, thematic workshops were held in which actors from each of the aforementioned groups co-wrote the content. To be specific, the NWP called for, among other things, the following strategic objectives in education: research on guaranteeing equal opportunities for men and women; increasing women's and girls' access to formal and non formal education; implementing training programs that modify discriminatory practices in education settings; and revising national curricula to promote principles of equal opportunities for men and women at all educational levels.

The key to understanding this process of policy formation is recognizing the catalytic role that the 1995 international conference in China played (Moreno 1997). Not only did it sign the government on to a platform for action, which led to the founding of the ISDEMU, but it also helped to strengthen the relationship among those key actors, which would later work together in the formation of the NWP for diverse sectors including education. It is important to mention, however, that the focus of the non-governmental organization, Salvadoran Women's Platform, differs greatly from the approach of the NWP that resulted from the Beijing Conference; the former focused on asserting rights and the latter on the creation of equal opportunities and on improving women's conditions.[12]

[12] For a detailed explanation on the evolution of approaches to issues of women, development and society, see García Prince (2008).

Moreover, for both civil society and governmental officials, the 1995 conference provided the additional leverage necessary to foment the creation of a national policy, which focused on gender equality issues, both within and outside education. In that the involved actors and the underlying process by which the NWP was born both required an extra push from an international conference, this case of policy formulation clearly reflects policy negotiation. National civil society and governmental actors likely would not have been able to arrive at the formation of a policy otherwise.

4.4.3 Values Education

Despite both the popularity of the idea of values education in the post-war context in the early 1990s and the fact that values education would feature centrally in the TYP, the process by which this concept developed into policy reflected dynamics of hybridization. As will be shown, a variety of actors pursued a number of different strategies as a way to consolidate peace and strengthen democracy in El Salvador. Indeed, those national and international actors that focused on the notion of values education in the period leading up to the TYP did so in an uncoordinated way and without a common vision. The actions of the USAID, the German Agency for Technical Cooperation (GTZ), UNESCO and the MINED made this clear.

In the 1990s, USAID financed a series of three projects related to the development of democracy in El Salvador. This is far from surprising, given that the US government—operating during the 1980s and early 1990s from a Cold War mindset—saw the insurgency by the FMLN as a threat to democracy in the region. The first project was a small one (funded by only $7,489 total) that operated from September 1991 (before the signing of the Peace Accords) until 1994 and took as its central purpose "educating in democracy five thousand students between 15 and 18 years of age…initiating a cycle on civic education" (USAID 1991, p. 8). A year later, in September 1992, USAID provided $4 million to finance the Democratic Electoral Processes project, which ran until 1995 and focused, among other things, on the promotion of civic education efforts that would increase "citizen awareness of political rights and responsibilities" and spread information on the electoral process (USAID 1992, p. 13). The last project provided $1.25 million over 2 years, 1994–1995, in order to train civil society organizations to teach "democratic arts" to young people—that is, skills that include negotiation, dialogue, listening, conflict resolution and compromising (USAID 1993).

While USAID was focused on programs that they hoped would instill democratic values in Salvadorans, GTZ took a slightly different route. Beginning in early 1994, GTZ implemented a year-long project geared towards "integrated human development," known as the Program for the Reintegration and Employment of Ex-Combatants. While the goals of the program were broad, one goal in particular was to "impart crucial values, such as personal empowerment, tolerance, responsibility, fairness and a work ethic," as well as solidarity and cooperation, because these values are critical for "personal and societal recovery and reconciliation" (Guzmán 2005a, pp. 159–160).

Then, in February 1994, once the four above-mentioned projects had already begun, UNESCO hosted the first National Forum on Education for a Culture of Peace. This forum—the first of its kind globally—was the result, generally, of UNESCO's recently renewed worldwide commitment to promoting a culture of peace and, specifically, of (a) encouragement by UNESCO's representative to El Salvador for the idea and (b) the fact that this initiative was favored by government officials in the immediate post-war period (Lacayo 1995; Tünnermann 2003). UNESCO's idea was to provide up to $32 million to support a wide range of projects to be carried out by those non-governmental organizations and government ministries working in the areas of education, culture, social science and communications, with one of the main goals being "to promote the institutionalization of a new form of social interaction; that is, to convert the values, concepts, abilities and skills of a culture of peace into laws, norms, habits, customs, institutions and common sense" (Lacayo 1995, pp. 34–35). Ultimately, while specific actions were neither established nor taken as a result of the Forum, and while the definition of a "culture of peace" was not specified, the Forum did raise the profile of an issue—creating a culture of peace—that was of interest to the government generally.

Clearly, then, by 1995, the year in which the TYP was produced, education for values was an issue that had surfaced previously, either as one element in a larger internationally funded project or as the topic of a national forum. This priority was subsequently echoed, first, at the "consultative forum" held in San Salvador in January 1995, at which 25 % of attendants agreed that one priority which should be addressed was the lack of education on civic and moral values (MINED 1995a), and, then, by the National Education Commission in its June 1995 report, which elaborated a series of issues that education reform should address. Thus, a group of prominent Salvadorans whose primary purpose was to provide suggestions for the content of the TYP had suggested that one of the TYP's four strategic lines focus on the question of education in humanistic, ethical, and civic values—and how to incorporate them throughout the education system and the MINED's curricula (MINED 1995b).

It is no surprise, then, that the resultant TYP reflected the emphasis given to values by both the consultative forum and the National Education Commission. For the MINED, however, such a focus should correspond with moral education. By moral education, the MINED meant—primarily—the ability to evaluate and respond to complex life situations (in accordance with religious principles), though it also highlighted the following in the policy: civic preparation, that is, learning about human rights, understanding the functioning of the State, instilling a sense of nationalism, reading about the country's history, and acquiring the ability to tolerate and participate in political dialogue and discussion (MINED 1995b). Importantly, the MINED's interest in moral values stemmed from the Catholic religious orientation and preferences of the governmental actors involved in the TYP's formation.

In terms of policy formation, perhaps the most notable feature of the years 1991–1995 is the fact that a variety of actors engaged with the idea of values education from distinct perspectives and for different reasons, each following their own motivations in the absence of a unifying entity to articulate these initiatives. On the side of NGOs, although USAID was preoccupied with providing Salvadorans with values related to democratic processes and the importance of participating in them, GTZ invested in integrated human development to support personal and societal recovery and reconciliation, while UNESCO emphasized the development of values to support a culture of peace. On the government side, the National Education Commission and the MINED, on the other hand, highlighted particular moral and civic aspects of values education, aspects more related to being a well-rounded and tolerant citizen in a post-war democracy. Given the multiple and multi-directional forces engaged in the issues of values education during and prior to formation of the TYP, the development of this policy is best understood as a hybridization of interests and efforts.

4.5 Discussion

A number of findings emerge with regard to the influence of international actors in the formation of education policy in El Salvador between the early 1990s and 2005. Yet one over-arching finding is that in a single period of 15 years (1990–2005) international influence manifested in three different ways. The first case—that of EDUCO—reflects dynamics of imposition, while in the second (gender equality) and third (values education) cases the nature of international influence in the process of formation reflected policy negotiation and policy hybridization, respectively.

As was shown, the case of EDUCO was ultimately characterized by imposition because of the numerous constraints that the MINED faced at the time, and because of the resultant dependency on international organizations that this produced. That is, not only did the MINED have to increase educational access, weaken the teachers' unions, and subsume FMLN communities and their schools, but it had to do so in a way that would signify modernization of education system management (e.g., through the introduction of neoliberal participatory arrangements that would, in theory, introduce efficiency, effectiveness, and accountability; Edwards and Klees 2012) and would be approved by the World Bank, the entity that was positioned to fund and facilitate education governance reform (as opposed to USAID, for example, which was more focused on such issues as teacher training and curriculum development). EDUCO met the constraints of the context, and, in the end, beyond funding the program, the World Bank relied on conditionalities and the consistent and intense provision of technical assistance to ensure that the program would become a key feature of the MINED's system reform policy. As a result, EDUCO was both a feature of the educational agenda and at the center of system reform in practice even before it entered the TYP, the MINED's official, over-arching policy education reform in 1995.

The case of gender equity clearly contrasts with the experience of EDUCO. Since the 1970s, local and national non-governmental organizations within El Salvador had supported this theme by participating in relevant international conferences. These local efforts then led to the development of the SWP just after the signing of the Peace Accords in 1992 and just before the first post-war presidential elections. While this Platform was a significant step, a key additional action was set in motion two years later, as a result of official and non-governmental participation in the Fourth World Conference on Women in Beijing. This action was the establishment of the ISDEMU in 1996. With a national governmental entity finally in place and with the responsibility to address women's issues, the National Women's Policy was created in 1997. While this policy represented a significant step forward for gender equality (within and beyond the education sector), for our purposes, the above-described sequence demonstrates the importance of external influence in the form of negotiation in that the conference in Beijing was used as an impetus or reference point for the creation of a catalytic national-level entity that helped to develop a policy related to gender issues. Put simply: international influence facilitated national action that led to policy formation. The significance of international influence in this case if clear when one considers that, two years prior, the MINED chose not to include gender equality among its education reform priorities, as reflected in the TYP.

Finally, the case of values education embodied policy hybridization. This was so in that each of the relevant national and international actors pursued their own interests, and without first agreeing upon a common vision or policy for this issue. International organizations promoted values related with democracy (USAID), solidarity (GTZ) and a culture of peace (UNESCO), while the MINED focused on moral values.

Looking across the cases and taking into account their differences, one can also conclude that certain factors influence how a policy is formed. That is, the present cases suggest that the nature of policy formation processes varies depending on: (a) the differential influence that international organizations possess and are able (or willing) to bring to bear on agenda setting and policy development; (b) the role and impact of local and national NGOs, and the way that they are able to invoke international examples, priorities or events to advance certain priorities within their country; and (c) the interest and initiative that the MINED takes in order to move a policy formation process forward. As should be clear, these postulates derive from the experiences of the cases examined in this chapter—namely, EDUCO, gender equality policy, and values education, respectively. Going forward, the transferability of these generalizations should be assessed against experiences of policy formation in other contexts.

4.6 Conclusions

In this chapter, we have dedicated ourselves to explaining the dynamics of policy formation in El Salvador during the period 1990–2005, a period which saw the end of a civil war, the signing of Peace Accords, and an interest by both national and international actors in the reform of the education system. During this period, the three cases we examined were formally included in two separate policies. Both the policy for education management decentralization and the policy for values education were included in the TYP, which was finalized in 1995. Subsequently, the intention of the government to focus on gender equality in education came about in 1997 and was included in the National Women's Policy. Having detailed and characterized the nature of how each of these cases entered MINED policy, our hope is that the findings provided herein prove relevant to future investigations and discussions about the nature of education reform and policy creation in developing countries and the role that various forms of international influence can play. To that end, we offer two concluding points.

First, due to the ability of certain international organizations to position, promote, or enable programs that accord with their preferences, policy formation processes can—at times—be more symbolic than meaningful. This was the case with EDUCO, for as was explained, this program had—much before the finalization of the TYP—already been incorporated into the MINED's policy for the reform of system management in practice. Importantly, however, this is not always the case, with the counter-example being values education. Although various forms of values education were being promoted by USAID, UNESCO and GTZ, the MINED was still able to use the process of formation of the TYP to insert its preferences for what values education should mean. Whether or not a policy formation process is primarily symbolic often depends on the level of dependence—be it political or economic—experienced by a government and, relatedly, the extent to which it can assert its own priorities.

Second, although the TYP and the National Women's Policy were formally developed through concerted action at the national level, their formation was impacted by dynamics—i.e., dynamics of imposition, negotiation and hybridization—that went well beyond the policymaking process itself. To that end, considering the increasing context of globalization—and the diminishing predominance that it implies for formal processes of policymaking that occur through traditional state channels—it is probable that the centrality of these new dynamics will only increase. Thus, in the future, it will be important for researchers to continue to closely examine the impact of international organizations, international conferences, and international trends, as well as the ways that they interact and manifest in the formation of national education policies.

References

Basso, M. (1985). *Nosotras podemos: Guía para las alfabetizadoras*. UNICEF.

Bejar, R. (1997). The dynamics of educational reform in El Salvador, 1989–1996. In Benjamín Álvarez H & Monic Ruiz-Caseres (Eds.) *Paths of change: Education reform under way in Latin America and the Caribbean* (pp. 47–70). Washington, DC: USAID.

Booth, J., Wade, C., & Walker, T. (2006). *Understanding Central America*. Boulder: Westview Press.

Bray, M. (2003). Community initiatives in education: Goals, dimensions and linkages with governments. *Compare, 33*(1), 31–45.

Cuéllar-Marchelli, H. (2003). Decentralization and privatization of education in El Salvador: Assessing the experience. *International Journal of Educational Development, 23*, 145–166.

Edwards, D. B., Jr. (2012a). Researching international processes of education policy formation: Conceptual and methodological consideration. *Research in Comparative and International Education, 7*(2), 127–145.
Edwards, D. B., Jr. (2012b). The approach of the World Bank to participation in development and education governance: Trajectories, frameworks, results. In C. Collins & A. Wiseman (Eds.), *Education strategy in the developing world: Revising the World Bank's education policy* (pp. 249–273). Bingley: Emerald.
Edwards, D. B., Jr. (2013a). International processes of education policy formation: An analytic framework and the case of plan 2021 in El Salvador. *Comparative Education Review, 57*(1), 22–53.
Edwards, D. B, Jr. (2013b). The development of global education policy: A case study of the origins and evolution of El Salvador's EDUCO program. Unpublished dissertation, University of Maryland, College Park.
Edwards, D. B., Jr. (2014). ¿Cómo analizar la influencia de los actores e ideas internacionales en la formación de políticas educativas nacionales? Una propuesta de un marco de análisis y su aplicación a un caso de El Salvador. *Archivos Analíticos de Políticas Educativas, 22*(12). Available at: http://dx.doi.org/10.14507/epaa.v22n12.2014
Edwards, D. B., Jr., & Klees, S. (2012). Participation in international development and education governance. In A. Verger, M. Novelli, & H. K. Altinyelken (Eds.), *Global education policy and international development: New agendas, issues and programmes* (pp. 55–77). New York: Continuum.
Eriksson, J., Kreimer, A., & Margaret, A. (2000). *El Salvador: Post-conflict reconstruction: Country case evaluation*. Washington, DC: World Bank.
Fernández, A., & Carrasco, A. (2000). *La educación y su reforma: El Salvador, 1989–1998*. San Salvador: MINED.
Foley, M. (1996). Laying the groundwork: The struggle for civil society in El Salvador. *Journal of Interamerican Studies and World Affairs, 38*(1), 67–104.
Freire, P. (1970). *Pedagogy of the oppressed*. New York: Herder & Herder.
García-Prince, E. (2008). *Políticas de igualdad, equidad y gendermainstreaming. ¿De qué estamos hablando? Marco Conceptual*. San Salvador: PNUD.
Gillies, J. (Ed.). (2010). *Education system reform and aid effectiveness: The power of persistence*. USAID and Equip 2. http://www.equip123.net/docs/E2-Power_of_Persistence.pdf
Gillies, J., Crouch, L., & Flórez, A. (2010). *Strategic review of the EDUCO program*. El Salvador: USAID.
Guzmán, E. (2005a). Reintegrating excombatants into society in El Salvador. In E. Vargas-Barón & H. Bernal (Eds.), *From bullets to blackboards: Education for peace in Latin America and Asia* (pp. 159–174). New York: Inter-American Development Bank.
Guzmán, J. (2005b). Educational reform in post-war El Salvador. In E. Vargas-Barón & H. Alarcón (Eds.), *From bullets to blackboards: Education for peace in Latin America and Asia* (pp. 43–62). New York: Inter-American Development Bank.
Hammond, J. L. (1998). *Fighting to learn*. Piscataway: Rutgers University Press.
Instituto Salvadoreño para el Desarrollo de la Mujer (ISDEMU). (1997). *Política Nacional de la Mujer*. San Salvador: ISDEMU, Gobierno de El Salvador.
Jones, P. (1990). UNESCO and the politics of global literacy. *Comparative Education Review, 34*(1), 41–60.
Kane, L. (2001). *Popular education and social change in Latin America*. London: Latin American Bureau.
Krasner, S. (1984). Approaches to the state: Alternative conceptions and historical dynamics. *Comparative Politics, 16*(2), 223–246.
Lacayo, F. (1995). *Cultura de paz: Una 'utopía', viable, urgente y necesaria*. El Salvador: UNESCO.
LeoGrande, W. M. (2000). *Our own backyard: The United States and Central America, 1977–1992*. Chapel Hill: University of North Carolina.

McGinn, N., & Warwick, D. (2006). La planeación educativa: ¿Ciencia o política? *Revista Latinoamericana de Estudios Educativos, 36*(1/2), 153–182.

Meza, D., Guzmán, J., & de Varela, L. (2004). *EDUCO: A community-managed education program in rural areas of El Salvador*. Paper presented at Scaling up poverty reduction: A global learning process and conference, Shanghai, May 25–27.

MINED. (1990). *Servicios educativos a niños pobres Salvadoreños de 0 a 14 años*. San Salvador: MINED.

MINED. (1994). *Memoria institucional: Periodo junio de 1989-junio de 1994*. San Salvador: MINED.

MINED. (1995a). *Foro consultivo nacional sobre reforma educativa*. San Salvador: MINED.

MINED. (1995b). *Lineamientos generales del Plan Decenal, 1995–2005*. San Salvador: MINED.

MINED. (1999). *En el camino de la transformación educativo de El Salvador*. San Salvador: MINED.

Montero, A., & Samuels, D. (Eds.). (2004). *Decentralization and democracy in Latin America*. Notre Dame: University of Notre Dame Press.

Moreno, M. E. (1997). *La política nacional de la mujer* (Alternativas para el desarrollo, No. 50). San Salvador: FUNDE.

Parker, C. (2000). Calidad de la educación enfocada en los géneros. Hacia una pedagogía global. In J. Navarro, K. Taylor, A. Bernasconi, & L. Tyler (Eds.), *Perspectivas sobre las políticas educativas en las Américas* (pp. 147–167). Cambridge: HIID-USAID.

Quán, A. (2005). Through the looking glass: U.S. Aid to El Salvador and the politics of national identity. *American Ethnologist, 32*(2), 276–293.

Reimers, F., & McGinn, N. (1997). Conducting a participatory sector assessment in El Salvador. In F. Reimers & N. McGinn (Eds.), *Informed dialogue: Using research to shape education policy around the world*. Westport: Praeger.

Sollis, P. (1993). Poverty alleviation in El Salvador: An appraisal of the Cristiani government's social programme. *Journal of International Development, 5*(5), 437–458.

Stromquist, N. (1997). *Increasing girls' and women's participation in basic education. Fundamentals of educational planning*. Paris: UNESCO.

Tünnermann, C. (2003). *La universidad Latinoamericana ante los retos del siglo XXI*. Mexico.: UDUAL.

USAID. (1991). *Grant agreement: Education for democracy program*. San Salvador: USAID.

USAID. (1992). *Grant agreement: Democratic and electoral processes project*. San Salvador: USAID.

USAID. (1993). *Grant agreement: Democratic initiatives project*. Washington, DC: USAID.

Winkler, D. (1989). *Decentralization in education: An economic perspective* (Population and Human Resources Department Paper). Washington, DC: World Bank.

Chapter 5
Education for All and the Global-Local Interface: A Case Study of The Gambia

Matarr Baldeh and Caroline (Carly) Manion

Abstract In this chapter we examine the significance of global Education for All (EFA) policy and practice in the context of educational development in West Africa, particularly in relation to the concept and goal of country ownership. More specifically, to illuminate key successes, opportunities and challenges at the global-local interface of efforts to achieve quality basic education for all, we present a case study of EFA policy and practice in The Gambia. Our analysis, in addition to being influenced by the authors' decades of professional experiences and observations in the field of education in The Gambia, is based on data drawn from semi-structured interviews with government officials and representatives from civil society involved in EFA policy and advocacy, as well as document analysis. Our findings, set against the backdrop of globalization and its effects on education policy and practice, reveal both tensions and opportunities with respect to EFA in particular and policy ownership more broadly.

Since 1990 the international institutionalization and global reach of the Education for All (EFA) movement has had a significant influence on educational development in countries around the world (Mundy 2006, 2007). In the wake of the 2000 World Education Forum held in Dakar, Senegal, the World Bank and the donor community launched the *Education for All-Fast Track Initiative* (renamed and rebranded the *Global Partnership for Education* (GPE) in September 2011), to help coordinate and provide financial and technical assistance for low-income countries committed to achieving quality education for all. In exchange for producing a "sound" education sector plan, recipient governments gain access to aid through the *Education for All Fast Track Initiative* (EFA-FTI) Catalytic Fund (or the "Fund" as it is now called

M. Baldeh (✉)
Education for All Campaign Network, Banjul, The Gambia
e-mail: matarr.baldeh@gmail.com

C. Manion
Ontario Institute for Studies in Education, University of Toronto, Toronto, ON, Canada
e-mail: carly.manion@utoronto.ca

C.A. Brown (ed.), *Globalization, International Education Policy and Local Policy Formation*, Policy Implications of Research in Education 5,
DOI 10.1007/978-94-007-4165-2_5

under the GPE), as well as through bilateral and multilateral channels.[1] Moreover, driven in large part by the donor community's promotion of partnerships—a move historically rooted in the principle of participation—the historical education service-provider roles of nongovernmental organizations have been expanded within the EFA-FTI funding mechanism context, with such organizations now actively participating in processes of policy formulation, implementation and evaluation (Bray 2000; Mundy et al. 2008; Sifuna 2000). The Global Campaign for Education for All is a further example of a global coalition of nongovernmental organizations (NGOs) playing important advocacy and policy roles, linking global to local education actors (Mundy and Murphy 2001).

An important feature of the contemporary aid context, and informing the evolution of policy discourse and practice of the Global Partnership for Education (GPE), has been the international development community's embrace and promotion of "country ownership" as a guiding principle for improved aid effectiveness and the sustainability of development interventions (OECD 2005, 2008a, b; see also Bashir 2009; Booth 2011a, b). While the goal of country ownership has been the subject of criticism on the basis that it has been weakly conceptualized and operationalized in the public policy arena, its institutionalization suggests recognition of the need to shift away from the top-down and donor dominated character of traditional aid for educational development (OECD 2008b; Pender 2001, 2007; Smith 2005).

In this chapter we examined the significance of global EFA policy and practice in the context of educational development in West Africa, particularly in relation to the concept and goal of ownership. More specifically, to illuminate key successes, opportunities and challenges at the global-local interface of efforts to achieve quality basic education for all, we present a case study of EFA policy and practice in The Gambia, a country among the first to be invited to apply for support through the EFA-FTI in 2003, and first endorsed in 2003/04. Our analysis was driven by two central questions: (1) In what ways has the global EFA agenda (including policy goals and "best practices") converged with and/or diverged from national education policy priorities, goals and practices? (2) How have EFA policies, practices, and funding mechanisms (e.g. Catalytic Fund/GPE) helped and/or hindered educational development in The Gambia? Furthermore, we sought to better understand how different stakeholders (e.g., government officials, civil society representatives etc.) understood the concept of policy ownership and whether or not they felt that this principle was reflected in the relationship between The Gambia and the Global Partnership for Education.

The findings from the Gambian case study suggest that there is a strong degree of ownership of EFA policy and programming, a claim supported by evidence of genuinely participatory policy processes involving civil society and broad-based consultations with citizens throughout the country, alignment between national and

[1] World Bank, *Global Partnership for Education and the World Bank*, available at http://web.worldbank.org/WBSITE/EXTERNAL/TOPICS/EXTEDUCATION/0,,contentMDK:20278663~menuPK:617564~pagePK:148956~piPK:216618~theSitePK:282386,00.html, accessed on December 15, 2011.

global EFA goals, and government's financial commitments to the sector. Our findings also suggest the somewhat mixed implications of EFA assistance through the Catalytic Fund. On one hand our findings suggested that a key benefit of aid is the expanded availability of technical and financial resources in support of educational access and quality. On the other hand, policy actors in The Gambia suggest that procurement procedures mandated by donors slowed down implementation. Additionally, issues of boys' education—a growing concern in The Gambia—appeared neglected within the context of the funding priorities of the GPE, and we also heard concerns that issues concerning youth and livelihoods were not adequately supported in GPE policy and practice, although they were a central concern in the country.

The chapter is organized into four main sections. Following the introduction we discuss theories of globalization and educational change, as well as how ownership has been conceptualized in global development frameworks and pursued in the context of the Global Partnership for Education. We next describe the research methodology, including data collection and analysis techniques. In the fourth section we present the Gambia case, including country and education sector background, and study findings concerning the successes and challenges of EFA policy and practice in the country vis-à-vis internal and external actors and dynamics. We then conclude the chapter with some brief remarks concerning the significance of the study and areas for future research.

5.1 Conceptualizing Globalization, Policy Transfer and Ownership in the Context of EFA Policy Processes

In the post-WWII period, world order has shifted from an "international political economy (1975–1990) to a global political economy (1990-onward) powered by neo-liberalism as an ascendant ideology" (Robertson and Dale 2006, p. 2). The increasing scope and volume of socio-cultural, economic and political transactions commonly associated with "globalization" and the effects of globalized capital, national competitiveness and consumer culture, appear boundless, and as such are perceived to radically transform national policy processes (Dale 1999, 2000). The concept of globalization is highly contested, yet widely used to refer to a range of "post-cold war processes of accelerating economic, cultural, and political interconnections" around the world (Assie-Lumumba and Sutton 2004, p. 345). Citing David Held, Arnove defines globalization as "the intensification of worldwide social relations which link distant localities in such a way that local happenings are shaped by events occurring many miles away and vice versa" (Held 1991 p. 9, cited in Arnove 2003, p. 2). Globalizing trends have made "hegemonic global discourses" (Schweisfurth 2008, p. 71), such as those associated with the Education for All movement, more influential in public policy spaces with the result that it has become increasingly difficult to understand national education policy and practice without reference to globalization processes (Crossley 2000, cited in Vidovich 2004, p. 341).

In the literature there are three main theoretical approaches to understanding the relationship between "globalization" and national education policy and processes: Common World Educational Culture (CWEC); Globally Structured Agenda for Education (GSAE), and hybridization theories. According to world culture theorists working within what Dale (2000) calls the Common World Educational Culture (CWEC) model, globalization is leading to greater institutional and policy isomorphism and convergence according to the script of a single global model of progress and justice (Boli and Thomas 1999; Meyer et al. 1997). Within the CWEC model, the autonomy of the state in directing education policy change is viewed as diminishing, with the imperatives of a universal model of education, state, and society taking precedence over nationally defined education priorities and strategies. Succinctly describing the CWEC approach, Dale states, "Very simply, the proponents of this view argue that the development of national educational systems and curricular categories is to be explained by *universal* models of education, state, and society, rather than by distinctive *national* factors" (2000, p. 428, italics in original).

In contrast to this "globalist" perspective (Held and McGrew 2000), "internationalists" working within the Globally Structured Agenda for Education (GSAE) model (Dale 2000) use an international political economy approach to analyze locally-mediated responses to globalization and global economic pressures. Within the GSAE, globalization is a set of political-economic arrangements for the organization of the global economy, driven by the need to maintain the capitalist system rather than by any set of values. Adherence to its principles is brought about by political economic leverage and perception of self-interest (Dale 2000, p. 436).

Thus, whereas CWEC proponents emphasize the significance of so-called universal values, norms and beliefs as structuring the policy choices of states, including in the area of education; from the perspective of GSAE policy choices are made by states based on their interpretation of what will help the country be more competitive in the global economy—that is, assessments of material conditions and opportunities are just as important, if not more so, than the supranational "world culture" in explaining patterns of seeming education policy convergence.

Others, however, view globalization not as a singular process, but as multidimensional "globalizations", the impacts of which are equally diverse and multiple (Pieterse 1995, p. 45; Appadurai 1990). In contrast to ideas that the world is becoming more "uniform and standardized" as a consequence of "a technological, commercial and cultural synchronization emanating from the West", it is argued that globalization is a process of "hybridization" which gives rise to a "global melange" (Pieterse 1995, p. 45; see also Anderson-Levitt 2003; Appadurai 1990; Pieterse 1995; Steiner-Khamsi 2004; Steiner-Khamsi and Stolpe 2006). As Steiner-Khamsi (2006) and Steiner-Khamsi and Stolpe (2006) suggest, borrowed policies do not always replace existing ones; rather, selected elements are incorporated within existing practices and norms, based on the specificities and imperatives of particular socio-political contexts.

The above theoretical perspectives each suggest, to varying degrees, that governments and other non-state policy actors remain important agents in public policy processes, even in this so-called age of globalization.

5.2 The Principle and Pursuit of Policy Ownership

Given that three chapters of this book have already traced and analyzed the historical evolution of and contemporary issues and questions facing the field of international education policy, including the global EFA movement, we have chosen to focus our discussion in this section on how "ownership" has been defined and pursued within global EFA policy processes, and particularly within the *Global Partnership for Education* (formerly the EFA-Fast Track Initiative). To contextualize the discussion of ownership in relation to EFA policy, we must first recognize the importance of two contemporary frameworks that have strongly influenced—at least at the level of policy discourse—the evolving aid architecture: the *Paris Declaration on Aid Effectiveness* (2005), and the *Accra Agenda for Action* (2008). With the goal of improving the quality and effectiveness of aid, these two frameworks aim to promote a different kind of aid relationship, that is, one based on partnership, donor harmonization, and mutual accountability. Within this new aid context we have seen the institutionalization of the partnership norm (e.g., partnerships between government, civil society, and donors); the emergence of global funds to support sector specific programming, including education, for example, the Global Partnership for Education's Fund; and, the rise of new aid and development actors such as foundations (e.g. Hewlett, Soros, Gates) and transnational civil society organizations (e.g. Action Aid International, Oxfam International; Save the Children, and Sight Savers International, among others) (Bashir 2009; Mundy 2009).

Box 5.1: Paris Declaration Donor & Partner Commitments in the Service of Country Ownership

Partner countries commit to:

- Exercise leadership in developing and implementing their national development strategies through broad consultative processes.
- Translate these national development strategies into prioritised results-oriented operational programmes as expressed in medium-term expenditure frameworks and annual budgets (Indicator 1).
- Take the lead in coordinating aid at all levels in conjunction with other development resources in dialogue with donors and encouraging the participation of civil society and the private sector

Donors commit to:

- Respect partner country leadership and help strengthen their capacity to exercise it

Source: (OECD 2005/2008, p. 3)

As previously embodied in the 1990 *World Declaration on Education for All* (UNESCO 1990) and the 2000 *Dakar Framework for Action* (UNESCO 2000), a key shared feature of the Paris Declaration and the Accra Agenda for Action, is the inclusion of country ownership[2] as a guiding principle (Bashir 2009; McCormick 2012; OECD 2008a, b). In the *Paris Declaration*, ownership is defined as "Partner countries [exercising] effective leadership over their development policies, and strategies and [coordination] of development actions" (OECD 2005/2008, p. 3). Box 5.1 identifies the commitments made by donors and country partners to support country ownership goals, as per the *Paris Declaration*.

Reflective of the contemporary aid zeitgeist, the *Education for All-Fast Track Initiative,* now (GPE) emerged in 2002 as a global partnership between donors and recipient governments to achieve the goal of universal primary education (Bashir 2009). According to the EFA-FTI Charter, there are six priority areas for partnership action: (1) Expand early childhood education; (2) Provide free and compulsory basic education for all, (3) Promote learning and life skills for young people and adults, (4) Increase adult literacy by 50 %, (5) Achieve gender parity by 2005, and (6) gender equality by 2015 (Global Partnership for Education 2011, p. 1).

According to the GPE website, there are ten areas of focus for the partnership: aid effectiveness; children with disabilities; conflict-affected and fragile states; early childhood care and education; early grade reading; girls' education; learning outcomes; numeracy; and, out-of-school children (GPE 2012).

The GPE concludes that country ownership entails developing country partners taking the lead on designing, implementing, and monitoring education plans, and importantly, that "partner governments provide adequate domestic financing for education and improve their country systems" (GPE 2012). Box 5.2 presents a summary of the GPE compact. Distilling from key global development and education aid frameworks the essence of "country ownership" reveals that political commitment, leadership, broad-based and meaningful participation of state and non-state actors, and increased governmental funding to the education sector are understood to be both cornerstones and indicators of EFA policy ownership.

[2]The five guiding principles are, (a) Ownership by countries; (b) Alignment with countries' strategies, systems, and procedures; (c) Harmonisation of donors' actions; (d) Managing for results; and, (e) Mutual accountability (OECD 2005; Wood et al. 2008).

Box 5.2: The Global Partnership for Education Compact: Mutual Accountability to Deliver the Following:

Developing country partners commit to:

- Develop and implement a sound and sustainable education plan (comprehensive sector plan or interim plan) through broad-based consultation
- Provide strong and increased domestic financial support to education
- Demonstrate results on key performance indicators

Donors, multilateral agencies, civil society organizations and private foundations and the private sector commit to:

- Increase support to the education plan, including financial support
- Assist in mobilizing resources and aligning them with the priorities of developing country partners
- Harmonize procedures as much as possible

Source: (GPE 2011)

The GPE operates at two levels: country and global (Global Partnership for Education 2011). The promotion of the principle of country ownership is intimately connected to the partnership principle, and this is clearly seen in the governance structure of the GPE. At the country-level, the Local Education Group (LEG) serves as the "foundation for partnership governance", and is constituted by government, donors, multilaterals, civil society organizations (CSOs), and the private sector (GPE 2012). Ideally, each partner plays a role in education policy processes, including development, appraisal, endorsement, implementation and monitoring and evaluation. While governments are expected to take the lead in the development and implementation of national education plans, such efforts must, as dictated by GPE policy, include the participation of civil society organizations (CSOs). Expectations for country-led and participatory education planning were supported at the 1999 African Regional Conference on EFA in Johannesburg, South Africa, as reported in the Dakar Framework for Action:

> We recognize that governments have the principal responsibility for ensuring adequate financing of basic education. Included in this responsibility is the leadership that government shall play in facilitating partnership at all levels with civil society, agencies, the private sector, NGOs, religious groups, communities, parents and teachers' associations, teachers' trade unions, families. We seek partnership with stakeholders, not simply in cost-sharing, but for the whole education process, including decision-making, management and teaching (UNESCO 2000, p. 28)

> To achieve genuine partnership, the Dakar Framework for Action suggests that, Learners, teachers, parents, communities, non-governmental organizations and other bodies representing civil society must be granted new and expanded political and social scope, at all levels of society, in order to engage governments in dialogue, decision-making and innovation around the goals of basic education (UNESCO 2000, p. 18)

The expectation that CSOs will "advocate and dialogue with governments and local donor groups to keep education high on the development agenda" represents a shift from their historical roles as service providers (GPE 2012; see also Manor et al. 1999).

The Local Education Group (LEG) and the Coordinating Agency (CA) round out the governance structure of the GPE at the country-level. LEGs are comprised of country-based representatives of bilateral, multilateral and other donors (e.g. transnational NGOs, philanthropic foundations, and in some cases, the private sector). Members of the LEG "support" the development, endorsement, and implementation of national education plans. And finally, the CA in each country acts as a communications conduit between government partners, the LEG and the GPE Secretariat (GPE 2012).

At the global level, the GPE governance structure is comprised of the Board of Directors (BoD) and Committees, with these bodies comprised of representatives from all partner groups: developing countries, donors, multilateral agencies, and CSOs, private sector, private foundations and other stakeholders (EFA-FTI 2011). Every 2 years a Partnership Meeting is convened, serving as a "high level forum for mutual accountability, enabling a review of progress, challenges and bottlenecks, lesson sharing, consultation and advocacy" (EFA-FTI 2011, p. 7). The BoD is the "supreme governing agency", setting policies and strategies, reviewing and approving annual objectives for the GPE, and making funding decisions (EFA-FTI 2011, p. 9). The composition of the BoD includes, six representatives from low-income, GPE endorsed developing country partners; six donor representatives; one representative each from UNESCO, UNICEF, and a regional development bank; one representative each from a northern CSO, southern CSO, and a representative from a teaching profession organization (i.e. teachers' union); and, finally, one representative from a private sector or foundation (EFA-FTI 2011). Supporting the work of the BoD is the GPE Chair (non-voting) and Secretariat (EFA-FTI 2011, pp. 11–13).

Through the GPE Fund, countries eligible for financing through the International Development Association (IDA), but lacking sufficient support for policy and program development and implementation, can apply and receive 3-year grants:

Education Plan Development Grant provides up to $250,000 to all low-income countries interested in joining the Global Partnership to help develop or revise their education plans; Program Development Grant provides $200,000 (up to $400,000 in exceptional cases) for the design of education programs (planning for implementation); Program Implementation Grant provides funding for the implementation of a 3-year program that reflects the strategies of the education plan, including things like schools, books, teacher training, school meals, etc. (GPE 2012).

5.3 Methods

This chapter drew primarily on qualitative research, with the study findings based on data collected from primary and secondary sources. There were four main sources of primary data: (1) First hand experience of the co-authors in the field of transnational and regional education advocacy, and national-level EFA policy processes[3]; (2) Interviews with key state and non-state policy actors in The Gambia[4]; (3) Governmental and donor education planning and project documents[5] (e.g. national education policy documents, funding proposals, and donor program documents); and, (4) Budget and statistical reports concerning governmental allocations to the education sector, aid flows, and education system performance (i.e. gender disaggregated enrollment and completion rates, quality of education etc.). Our desk reviews of global and local EFA policy and practice engaged secondary sources, including empirical studies, technical reports, and program evaluations from a variety of governmental, non-governmental, donor, and scholarly sources.

Data were analyzed using discourse and content analysis techniques. Primary data analysis focused on the EFA goals and strategies identified in national education policy statements, how these were framed—including attention to language and discourse, in relation to broader development goals. In addition, primary data was used to trace the growth (or otherwise) of government education expenditure. Non-governmental reports and advocacy material were used to triangulate the findings from official government and donor statements (documents, policies, and interview manuscripts), as well as to evaluate, from the perspectives of these non-state groups, the degree and nature of their participation in EFA policy processes as "partners" (with government and donors).

---

[3] Mr. Matarr Baldeh is the National Coordinator for the Education for All Campaign Network (EFANET) in The Gambia, and is a sitting member of the Local Education Group (LEG). He has also been actively involved in global and national-level EFA policy and practice advocacy by being a member of the GCE and EFA/FTI boards, as well as UNESCO's CCNGO/EFA. In addition to ten years of research experience on issues of gender and education policy in The Gambia, Dr. Caroline Manion has been actively involved in global EFA advocacy and research.

[4] In total, six interviews were conducted with high-level government officials, representatives from various civil society organizations, and professional associations active in the education sector.

[5] Since the mid-1990s there have been several policy documents that have detailed sector priorities and programmatic strategies for educational development in the country, and as such were included in our analysis: National Education Policy 1988–2003; Education Master Plan 1998–2005; National Education for All Action Plan; National Education Policy 2004–2015; and, Education Sector Strategic Plan 2006–2015. The recently completed mid-term review of the current National Education Policy (NEP) 2004–2015 and new Education Sector Strategy Plan 2013–2022 (please note this is still in draft form) represents the most up to date document representing the government's intentions in the sector, and has been recently been endorsed by the Local Donor Group as the basis for further funding through the GPE Fund.

5.4 Education for All in The Gambia: A Case Study

The Gambia case illustrates some of the successes and potential opportunities and challenges for EFA global-national (and often regional, and local) policy flows (e.g. financial and technical assistance). We start by offering some important contextual information about The Gambia, and then move to present the findings concerning the global-local interface of education for all policy and practice.

5.4.1 Country Background

The Gambia, a country amongst the poorest in the world, is located in the Sahel region on the West coast of sub-Saharan Africa. It is ranked 168 out of 205 countries in the UNDP's 2011 Human Development Index (UNDP 2011). The Gambia has an ethnically, linguistically, and religiously diverse population of around 1.7 million (UNESCO 2010). The country's annual growth rate of 2.6 %, positions it as one of the most densely populated countries on the continent (UNESCO 2010). The population is youthful, with 67 % of Gambians being under 25 years of age (Gambia Bureau of Statistics 2003). The majority of the population has historically lived in rural areas; however, this has changed in recent times, with just over 50 % of the population living in urban or peri-urban areas (Central Statistics Department 2003). A mere 10 % of the labor force is employed in the formal sector, and an estimated 40 % of youth are unemployed (Republic of The Gambia n.d.).

During the early 2000s the country experienced a period of economic instability; however, the situation has stabilized in recent years as a result of the sound macroeconomic policies adopted by the government (The Gambia Ministry of Basic and Secondary Education 2011). For example, between 2007 and 2009 real GDP increased to 6.0 % per year on average, which outpaced growth in many other countries in the sub-region (The Gambia Ministry of Basic and Secondary Education 2011). Even during the global economic crisis, real GDP growth has remained high, for example, reaching 6 % in 2009; however, despite this growth and the fact that the country has received extensive debt relief under the Highly Indebted Poor Countries and Multilateral Debt Relief Initiatives in 2007, Gambia continues to face a heavy debt burden and is classified as being at high risk of debt distress (African Economic Outlook 2012; International Monetary Fund 2011; World Bank 2012a).

The government principally finances the first 9 years of schooling, constituting the basic education cycle. Secondary school education (grades 10–12), extending for 3 years, is primarily provided by the private sector with grant-aided schools assisted by government and managed by school boards. Basic education statistics are presented in Tables 5.1 and 5.2.

Framed as evidence of policy ownership and government commitment to EFA goals and practices, a recent local donor appraisal report points out that "budgetary allocations to the education sector rose from 14.4 % in 2008 to 19.5 % in the 2009 estimates" (World Bank 2012d, p. 1).

Table 5.1 Basic education statistics in The Gambia at the lower basic level

Gross enrollment (%)	Net enrollment (%)	Completion rate (%)	Gender parity (female/male)	Teacher/ pupil ratio
87 (2011)	72 (2011)	71 (2011)	1.02 (2011)	1.38

Source: World Bank (2011)

Table 5.2 Basic education statistics in The Gambia at the upper basic level

Gross enrollment (%)	Net enrollment (%)	Completion rate (%)	Gender parity (female/male)	Teacher/ pupil ratio
66 (2011)	39 (2011)	63 (2011)	1.04 (2011)	1:39

Source: World Bank (2011)

Numerous bilateral and multilateral donors currently support the implementation of The Gambia's education policy and programs through technical and financial assistance to government and NGOs.[6] Given the country's longstanding relationship with the World Bank, reflected in International Development Agency (IDA) support of three major education sector projects since the 1970s, it is unsurprising that The Gambia was among the first ten countries invited by the World Bank to submit proposals for EFA-FTI/GPE support. Following the participatory development of a national EFA action plan proposal, and submission to the EFA-FTI Board of Directors, The Gambia was endorsed as an EFA-FTI beneficiary country in 2003. Since that time, the country has been allocated a total of US$41.4 million, with US$38.37 million disbursed as of the end of 2011 (World Bank 2012b, c).

It is important to note that organizations that would fall under the broad category of "civil society" have been active in The Gambia for decades, working in education and other formal and informal sectors. In addition to providing education services, non-governmental organizations have been participating as partners with government and donors in education policy processes, including in design, implementation and evaluation phases. A good example of an organization active in formal policy processes is the Education for All Campaign Network, the Gambia (EFA/Net), which serves as the national chapter of the transnational Global Campaign for Education for All (GCE), and has been actively engaged in research and advocacy work, training, support, administrative and leadership services in the context of EFA policy and practice in The Gambia. EFA-Net and other organizations liaise with various governmental departments and personnel, as well as with teachers' unions and school management committees.

[6] Key education sector donors include UNICEF (lead in-country donor until 2009), World Food Programme (current lead in-country donor representing the Local Education Group), the UK's Department for International Development (DfID), the African Development Bank (AfDB), the Islamic Development Bank (IDB), the African Bank for Economic Development in Africa (BADEA) and the other UN Funds and Programmes, and the World Bank (IDA) (World Bank 2009b).

5.4.2 Global-Local EFA Policy Convergences and Divergences

The focus of this section is on the points of convergence and divergence we found between Gambian education policy goals and those promoted within the context of the Education for All movement generally and the Global Partnership for Education more specifically. Overall, our findings suggest a great deal of convergence between the education policy priorities and programming of the Gambian government and those of the GPE, specifically with respect to the promotion of a quality basic education for all. While difficult to state unequivocally, we suggest that our findings concerning policy convergence help confirm, to varying degrees, elements of both Global World Education Culture (GWEC) and Globally Structured Agenda for Education (GSAE) models.

First, in accordance with the GWEC model the Government of The Gambia and its non-governmental partners share with their global EFA and GPE counterparts a strong belief in the value and importance of education for social, economic and political development. However, in accordance with the GSAE model, material conditions (and not merely so-called "universal" values and ideas circulating supranationally) and the state's interpretation of their implications for the country are key factors in understanding the behaviour and educational policy choices of the Government: Given The Gambia's weak natural resource base, it has long been recognized that the country's citizens, and more specifically the education of its citizens is the key to national development. The country's constitution provides for equality of educational opportunity, at all levels, to all citizens, and national development policy documents, including Vision 2020: Gambia Inc., and successive poverty reduction strategy papers in The Gambia, have emphasized that the elimination of poverty and progress towards sustainable development can only be realized with increased and improved levels of education (Republic of The Gambia 1996, 1997/revised 2001, see also Republic of The Gambia 2002, 2006; Republic of The Gambia/Department of State for Education 2006).

In addition to sharing with the country's global counterparts a general belief in the importance of education, since the 1990s successive national education policies have also demonstrated convergence on the primacy of basic education, as articulated at the first EFA conference in Jomtien, Thailand[7] in 1990 and reconfirmed at the World Education Forum in Dakar, Senegal in 2000. For example, while vocational and technical education, as well as tertiary and higher education are named as priority policy areas, the current National Education Policy 2004–2015—the theme of which is "Rethinking Education for Poverty Reduction"—maintains a focus on basic education, and in particular with respect to access, quality, and relevance considerations (Republic of The Gambia/Department of State for Education 2004). Moreover, aligning with tenets of the CWEC perspective, The Gambia has adopted the EFA-GPE endorsed expanded vision of basic education, which includes early childhood development, Grades 1–9, adult and non-formal education.

[7] A delegation of Gambian officials participated in the conference.

Another line of convergence between the EFA agenda and The Gambia's education sector development plans is found in the priority accorded to the promotion of girls' educational opportunities (Republic of The Gambia/Department of State for Education 2003). Other vulnerable groups targeted in national education policy frameworks include children in remote areas and children with disabilities, again, aligning with global EFA priorities areas for action and suggestive of the type of policy isomorphism discussed in the CWEC perspective; however, it is possible to also make the case that promoting equity in educational access is reflective of the state's concern with economic competitiveness and poverty reduction (Republic of The Gambia/Department of State for Education 2003, 2004).

The most recent policy framework endorsed by the GPE and paving the way for a second phase grant from the Catalytic Fund is the Education Sector Medium Term Plan 2008–2011. While the policy priorities remain the same as the 2003 EFA-FTI proposal (i.e., equity, access, quality, relevance, capacity-building/sector management), the quality of education is identified as the most pressing challenge to realizing the sector goals (Republic of The Gambia/Department of State for Basic and Secondary Education 2008). Thus, the central project objective in the second phase of Catalytic Fund funding, and converging with GPE priority areas, is "to improve conditions for teaching and learning in basic education including early childhood development" (World Bank 2009b: iv).

We noted an emerging policy divergence in the area of gender and education. While gender equity in education has been a development priority for decades, at both global and local levels, there is growing consensus that boys face educational challenges as well in The Gambia, as in many other parts of the world. A key issue, of course, is to better understand which boys are vulnerable in relation to what facets of the schooling process (i.e., access, retention, output, outcome, see Farrell 2003), and why? In the more remote regions of The Gambia, some communities are experiencing declining enrolment, and increasing dropout rates for boys (Republic of The Gambia/Department of State for Basic and Secondary Education 2007). However, while issues of boys' education have become more prominent in educational debates in the Global North, it is only very recently that such concerns are making their way onto the global EFA agenda, and boys' education remains an under-studied and under-resourced area: The emphasis for over two decades has been on girls' and women's educational opportunities, experiences, and outcomes. Thus, in The Gambia, where boys education is a growing concern, there has been little support from donors, including through the EFA Catalytic Fund, for research into the nature and scope of the problem or financial or technical assistance to assist in the implementation of appropriate measures to promote and enhance the educational opportunities of those boys who are not in school or have left school early (Manion 2010). We propose that this global-local policy divergence on the issue of boy's education, combined with the fact that the Gambian policy community is currently working to develop effective remedial strategies to address the problem outside of external aid from the GPE or other sources, but under the rubric of "gender and education", supports the central hypothesis offered by hybridization theorists. That is, while the government and its civil society partners have adopted the goal of gender equity in education, growing interest in boys' educational problems and early remedial efforts suggest that contemporary "gender and education" policy and practice in The Gambia reflects nationally-defined priorities and interests, shaped by particular values *and* material conditions.

5.4.3 Supporting Educational Development in The Gambia: The Role of the Global Partnership for Education

Based on interviews, document review, and statistical analysis, we were able to identify a number of areas of strength as well as several key successes realized in relation to the government's promotion of quality basic education for all in The Gambia in partnership with civil society and donors. First, the technical and financial assistance provided through the EFA/FTI, and more recently the GPE, has contributed to increasing access to and equity in basic education, especially for vulnerable groups such as girls, the poor and marginalized, and those with disabilities and other special needs. Support from the Catalytic Fund monies have helped the government build more schools and repair and/or retrofit others as a means of attracting out-of-school children. The government has also sought to promote girls' education through the provision of educational subsidies and scholarships for needy girls and has waived school fees for girls at the basic cycle. In another example, the Gambia Chapter of the Forum for African Women Educationalists (FAWEGAM), together with its government, civil society, and donor partners, has been actively engaged and supported in its efforts to create model schools (Centers of Excellence) based on the principles of gender sensitivity and inclusivity. Broader community sensitization campaigns concerning girls' education have been undertaken in close collaboration with numerous national and transnational NGOs and multilateral donor agencies working in the country, including, Action Aid The Gambia, UNICEF, Gambia Teachers Union, EFANet and FAWEGAM. GPE-supported policy interventions aimed at improving access to education for people with disabilities have ensured that newly built public schools include ramps for children using wheelchairs. This is also as a result of sustained campaign by EFANet and Disable Persons Organization. However, as yet, older schools have not been retrofitted, and the need for accessible toilet facilities has not yet been addressed.

A further key Catalytic Fund-supported reform movement geared to extending educational access has been the formalization and integration over the past decade of madrassa (Muslim education institutions) within the national education system. The reform effort has been framed in national education policy documents and funding proposals as necessary for achieving EFA and Millennium Development goals (Republic of The Gambia/Department of State for Education 2004). Over 15 % of Gambian families enroll their children in madrassa and there are indications that this number is growing as more madrassa are established to meet parental demand for this form of schooling for their children, on moral and religious grounds, as well as the perception that the quality of education in madrassa is superior to that of "secular" and/or government schools. Madrassa reform in The Gambia has benefitted from Catalytic Fund support. For example, Action Aid The Gambia collaborated with the General Secretariat for Islamic and Arabic Education through the Commonwealth Education Fund and the Department of State for Basic and Secondary Education in the production of national curriculum resources for classroom use (e.g., teacher guides) and the translation of these into Arabic (Manion 2010).

Through the Catalytic Fund-supported measures discussed above, significant progress has been made in increasing enrolment in basic and secondary education. The number of children enrolled in early childhood education programs grew between 2000 and 2010 from 29,910 to 62,145; at the lower basic cycle from 181,835 to 227,668 students; and, at the upper basic cycle from 41,493 to 75,613. Over the last decade, senior secondary school enrolment more than doubled from 15,554 to 36,141 students, mainly due to expansion of madrassa and private schools (The Gambia Ministry of Basic and Secondary Education 2011).

There have been several successes realized in terms of improving the quality of basic education in The Gambia. Funding and technical assistance from the GPE has supported the revision and development of curriculum and teaching and learning materials, teacher training, and sector management capacity, particularly in the area of monitoring and evaluation systems. As an example of how GPE funding has supported improvements to education quality, in March 2012, a Gambian delegation comprised of government (e.g., Department of State for Basic and Secondary Education) and civil society actors (e.g., Gambia Association of Teachers of English, Future in Our Hands, nominated by the Local Education Group, participated in a GPE-sponsored, All Children Reading conference in Kigali, Rwanda. Early grade reading ability is a priority for the GPE, as part of its broader concern for improving educational quality. Presentations by the Gambian delegation revealed seven programmatic areas that have been pursued as part of the country's early grade reading ability efforts between 2007 and 2012: Instructional material development; in-service teacher training; review of policies to give more emphasis to reading; pilot of teaching reading through use of mother tongue; sensitization of stakeholders; development of effective monitoring and evaluation mechanisms and tools; and, promoting collaboration among government and non-governmental agencies and organizations (The Gambia Country Delegation, Team One 2012). Accomplishments noted at this presentation included an increase in the availability of assessment results; improved monitoring mechanisms; increased and predictable budget allocations; high commitment and leadership; development of reliable assessment tools; and more time and emphasis on teaching reading in schools and teacher training colleges (The Gambia Country Delegation, Team One 2012).

Reflective of the Globally Structured Agenda for Education (GSAE) model, improving the internal efficiency (e.g., retention, drop-out and completion rates) of the Gambian education system has been an ongoing effort in the country. Funding and technical assistance from the GPE has supported the revision and development of curriculum and teaching and learning materials, teacher training, and sector management capacity, particularly in the area of monitoring and evaluation systems. A particularly successful reform noted by participants and in donor, civil society and government reports and appraisals, has been the provision of hardship allowances for teachers in remote areas of the country. This particular Catalytic Fund-supported reform appears to have helped address teacher shortages in some regions.

In our interviews with relevant government officials the procurement process for goods and services paid for with GPE funds was identified as a challenge. In Phase 1 of funding through the EFA-FTI Catalytic Fund, procurement processes were based on the country's own system; however, in Phase 2, money received through the GPE Fund had to follow World Bank procurement procedures. The effect of this change was not benign,

> So the challenge is in terms of the heavy bureaucracy when it comes to the World Bank managing the process. When we first got the FTI, it was really a fast track initiative because we were given the funds and we did the work, but in the second phase we were kind of really implementing a World Bank project. So things can be really slow because we have to follow the World Bank procurement procedures, which at times are really heavy and time-consuming. (Participant #1)

The changes to the procurement process meant, to the above quoted individual, that "we are not in control of the funds fully" (Participant #1), and using World Bank procurement methods were perceived to negatively affect the efficiency and effectiveness of the implementation of some projects; however, the participant concluded by noting that "we cannot say that it's only the Bank that has to been at fault for delays, but also the government in terms of meeting the requirement that is expected as its share of the responsibility" (Participant #1).

5.4.4 Assessing "Ownership": National and Local Stakeholder Perspectives

To dig more deeply into the issue of policy ownership, we first asked various education stakeholders how they conceptualized "ownership". All of the answers we received repeated the assertion that broad-based participation and communication were central to the realization of policy ownership. For example, a civil society representative suggested that, "First of all knowledge of the policy is critical for ownership, as it facilitates buy-in and support. Thus the policy must be communicated for people to take ownership and engage" (Participant #9). Taking a slightly different tack, but maintaining the importance of communication, a government official working in the Project Coordinating Unit (PCU) suggested that,

> … ownership starts from the fact that the government and all those involved in education—be it civil society, NGOs, bilateral and multilateral organizations—come together and make sure that the policies we are talking about are developed by the locals, so that the objectives that we set our are common objectives; that is, not only government coming up with policy and these other [stakeholders] buying it. (Participant #3)

Another civil society organization representative suggested that EFA policy and practice was decidedly "owned" in The Gambia, particularly given the country's longstanding commitment to universal basic education, since country representatives participated in the 1990 Education for All Conference in Jomtien, Thailand:

> Yes, [ownership] is part of the donor discourse, but they had already met people who had already owned the process anyhow. So for us, it was not as if we were pushed to own the process…we had already owned the process. It was now [after Dakar] left to us to come back and convince our constituencies and communities to own the process. And if you come to The Gambia, you will find that EFA is a household word: Everyone talks about EFA. (Participant #2)

Overall, there was a strong sense of ownership expressed by the participants we spoke with, and this is supported by the authors' own experiences and knowledge of education policy processes in The Gambia. In almost every case, participants linked ownership to the high-level engagement of country delegations in the development of global EFA policy, as well as the adoption of participatory policy processes that have opened up spaces for civil society voices and the national and sub-national levels. According to one government official,

> That is why whenever we are developing our policies and our strategic plans, we ensure that there is local participation; we start from the grassroots. We make sure that the process is really owned by everybody, not just by the government officials; we are all involved in the policy development, from the write-up, to the validation and to dissemination. So at the end of the day…we feel that this is a Gambian policy. I think really, for us, ownership comes to that level—that there is real participation and equal information being shared. We try to involve as much as possible, all those involved in the education sector. (Participant #7)

The sense of ownership expressed by the governmental and non-governmental actors we spoke with (as well as our own professional experiences and findings from previous research) support a positive assessment of EFA policy and practice in The Gambia in relation to this important principle and goal. Thus, in its recent Project Appraisal Document for a funding proposal under the EFA-FTI/GPE partnership, the World Bank (2009a) notes, "With strong Government leadership and ownership of the process, harmonization of procedures and alignment of interventions is showing real progress" (p. 6). The World Bank project information document for a 2009 Catalytic Fund proposal from The Gambia notes, with respect to the sustainability of interventions begun in an earlier phase of funding, that many have "been incorporated into the Government budget, including more than half of the teacher allowances, all pre- and in-service teacher training activities, scholarship support for girls (though some may remain under ongoing operations), operations and maintenance including a significant share of vehicle costs, among others" (World Bank 2009b, p. 4).

5.5 Concluding Remarks

As detailed at the beginning of this chapter, two key questions guided our analysis of ownership in the Gambian case: First, we were interested in documenting patterns of convergence and/or divergence between national and global education goals (discourse or policy talk). Second, we asked how global EFA policies, practices and funding mechanisms have contributed, or otherwise, to educational development in The Gambia. An additional line of questioning directed at national and local-level policy actors (government and non-governmental) concerned their perceptions of ownership in the context of EFA policy and programming. In this section we summarize the findings and suggest areas for future research.

EFA/FTI endorsement and technical and financial assistance has represented a unique and valuable opportunity for The Gambia. This was a point that was made by all participants in the study and was demonstrated by the positive trends in almost all statistical indicators used to measure education system efficiency and output (see World Bank 2012c, d). The financial assistance received from the EFA-FTI/GPE helped fill the funding gap for implementation of the country's ambitious education sector development plans and programs. In addition, the achievement of sector management goals has been effectively supported through technical assistance.

Overall, the Gambia case study highlighted the extent to which the country had attained impressive achievements in terms of enrollments, primary completion rate, gender parity, and the development of a more holistic approach to education delivery and system reform and capacity building. Education indicators continued to show progress, and government leadership and commitment appear high. The active participation of NGOs and other civil society associations in education service delivery, policy advocacy, and monitoring and evaluation roles, was widely perceived as adding value to the sector, especially in the basic education sub-sector.

In terms of policy ownership, based on document analysis, interviews and the authors' personal and professional experiences, we assert that EFA policy and practice was, for the most part, "owned" by the Government and civil society in The Gambia. It was truly a success story in the sense that there was strong evidence of broad-based commitment to achieving universal basic education of good quality—demonstrated in levels of public expenditure on education, sector leadership and reform, and the inclusion and participation of a broad cross-section of development NGOs.

The question of what and whose knowledge was legitimized in policy processes, goals and strategies was central to our analysis of power relations in the context of multi-level EFA partnerships as played out in The Gambia. Considered in relation to the theories discussed earlier in the chapter, of globalization and educational development that sought to explain transnational policy transfer, the Gambia case as explored herein suggested that the government and civil society have long contributed to and thus shared the goals and practices associated with the global EFA movement. In such a context, it is unsurprising that the government has been able to strategically align with and meet FTI and GPE requirements as a means of securing the financial and technical assistance necessary for successfully implementing and achieving the goals of its national education policies.

It seemed clear that the EFA-FTI in the past, or the GPE in the current moment, have not been experienced as a coercive force by the Gambian government, nor its non-governmental partners to accept particular goals and prescriptions associated with the global policy model—rather, policy actors and other stakeholders were emphatic in stating that they are part and parcel of this global model—they were not outside of it, or objects of it, rather they and the country's education system were subjects of it. Ultimately, while external influences on policy development had been strong, national and local-level stakeholders had exhibited considerable policy agency in terms of setting objectives, developing plans, and implementing and evaluating them.

It was also clear that context, as everywhere, was critically important in determining the issues, debates, and needs of different jurisdictions. It appeared that in The Gambia, the participatory policy processes, including widespread local, regional, and national consultations had contributed to the production of educational development plans that in large part reflected the needs and interests of the various constituencies in the country. While participatory policy planning had become a cornerstone (read: requirement) of the international aid architecture, in The Gambia the use of such approaches had been embraced. Participatory processes, with support from the donor community, and civil society more broadly, had helped build capacity within the system. Thus, all of the above seemed to bode well for the future and sustainability of country ownership of education goals, strategies, and program evaluation.

In terms of future research, we would suggest that two major lines of inquiry are necessary in order to develop a comprehensive and critical analysis of global-local EFA policy dynamics. First, we call for more macro-level research that includes the perspectives and experiences of external and in-country/embedded donors vis-à-vis their country and local development partners. For example, such research could usefully explore the motivations and strategies of global actors informing the promotion of the goal of country ownership and sustainable educational development. Second, more micro-level research is needed on the ways in which national EFA policy goals and programs impact and shape the activities and perceptions of subnational education stakeholders, including regional and local education authorities, administrators, teachers, students, and parents. Our case study of The Gambia focused primarily on national-level policy ownership and global-national policy flows and dynamics; however, such analyses would benefit from critical explorations of national-regional, and national-local policy dynamics and flows.

References

African Economic Outlook Organization. (2012). The Gambia. http://www.africaneconomicoutlook.org/en/countries/west-africa/gambia/. Accessed 14 June 2012.

Anderson-Levitt, K. M. (Ed.). (2003). *Local meanings, global schooling: Anthropology and world culture theory*. New York: Palgrave MacMillan.

Appadurai, A. (1990). Disjuncture and difference in the global cultural economy. In M. Featherstone (Ed.), *Global culture: Nationalism, globalization and modernity* (pp. 295–310). London: Sage.

Arnove, R. F. (2003). Introduction: Reframing comparative education: The dialectic of the global and the local. In R. F. Arnove & C. A. Torres (Eds.), *Comparative education: The dialectic of the global and the local* (2nd ed., pp. 1–23). Oxford: Rowman & Littlefield Publishers, Inc.

Assie-Lumumba, N. D., & Sutton, M. (2004). Global trends in comparative research on gender and education. *Comparative Education Review, 48*(4), 345–352.
Bashir, S. (2009). Catalyzing country ownership and aid effectiveness: Role of the Education for All-Fast Track Initiative Catalytic Fund. *Prospects: Quarterly Review of Comparative Review, 39*(2), 147–161.
Boli, J., & Thomas, G. M. (Eds.). (1999). *Constructing world culture: International nongovernmental organizations since 1875*. Stanford: Stanford University Press.
Booth, D. (2011a). Aid, institutions and governance: What have we learned? *Development Policy Review, 29*(s1), s5–s26.
Booth, D. (2011b). *Aid effectiveness: Bringing country ownership (and politics) back in*. London: Overseas Development Institute.
Bray, M. (2000). EFA thematic study: Community partnerships in education: Dimensions, variations and implications. Retrieved July 4, 2008, from http://www.paddle.usp.ac.fj/collect/paddle/index/assoc/Dmisc002.dir/doc.pdf
Central Statistics Department. (2003). *The Gambia population and housing census*. Banjul: Central Statistics Department.
Crossley, M. (2000). Bridging cultures and tradition in the reconceptualization of comparative and international education. *Comparative Education, 36*(3), 319–332.
Dale, R. (1999). Specifying globalization effects on national policy: A focus on the mechanisms. *Journal of Education Policy, 14*(1), 1–17.
Dale, R. (2000). Globalization and education: Demonstrating a "Common World Educational Culture" or locating a "Globally Structured Educational Agenda". *Educational Theory, 50*(4), 427–442.
EFA-FTI Secretariat. (2011). *EFA-FTI Catalytic Fund quarterly financial update for the quarter ending 31 March 2011*. Washington, DC: World Bank.
Farrell, J. P. (2003). Equality of education: A half-century of comparative evidence see from a new millennium. In R. F. Arnove & C. A. Torres (Eds.), *Comparative education: The dialectic of the global and the local* (pp. 146–175). Oxford: Rowman and Littlefield Publishers, Inc.
Global Partnership for Education (GPE). (2011). Charter of the global partnership for education. http://www.globalpartnership.org/media/docs/publications/CharterDocument_English-ts%20edits.pdf. Accessed 23 Aug 2013.
Global Partnership for Education GPE. (2012). Aid effectiveness. http://www.globalpartnership.org/about-us/aid-effectiveness/. Accessed 15 May 2012.
Held, D. (Ed.). (1991). *Political theory today*. Stanford: Stanford University Press.
Held, D., & McGrew, A. (2000). The great globalisation debate. In D. Held & A. McGrew (Eds.), *The global transformation reader*. Cambridge: Polity Press.
International Monetary Fund. (2011). *The Gambia: Staff report for the 2011 article IV consultation: Debt sustainability analysis*. Washington, DC: Author.
Manion, C. (2010). *Girls' education as a means or end of development? A case study of gender and education policy knowledge and action in The Gambia*. Ph.D. dissertation, Ontario Institute for Studies in Education, University of Toronto, Toronto.
Manor, J., Robinson, M., & White, G. (1999). Civil society and governance: A concept paper. http://www.ids.ac.uk/ids/civsoc/public.doc. Accessed 14 Nov 2004.
McCormick, A. (2012). Whose education policies in aid-receiving countries? A critical discourse analysis of quality and normative transfer through Cambodia and Laos. *Comparative Education Review, 56*(1), 18–47.
Meyer, J. W., Boli, J., Thomas, G. M., & Ramirez, F. (1997). World society and the nation-state. *American Journal of Sociology, 103*(1), 144–181.
Mundy, K. (2006). Education for all in the new development compact. *International Review of Education, 52*, 23–48.
Mundy, K. (2007). Education for all: Paradoxes and prospects. In D. P. Baker & A. W. Wiseman (Eds.), *Education for all: Global promises, national challenges* (Vol. 8, pp. 1–31). Oxford: Elsevier.

Mundy, K. (2009). International and transnational policy actors in education: A review of the research. In D. Plank, G. Sykes, & B. Schneider (Eds.), *American Educational Research Association: Handbook on education policy research* (pp. 717–734). New York: Routledge.
Mundy, K., & Murphy, L. (2001). Transnational advocacy, global civil society: Emerging evidence from the field of education. *Comparative Education Review, 45*(1), 85–126.
Mundy, K., Cherry, S., Haggerty, M., Maclure, R., & Sivasubramaniam, M. (2008). *Basic education, civil society participation and the new aid architecture: Lessons from Burkina Faso, Kenya, Mali, and Tanzania* (pp. 1–59). Toronto: OISE.
Organization for Economic Cooperation and Development (OECD). (2005/2008). The Paris declaration on aid effectiveness and the Accra agenda for action. http://www.oecd.org/dataoecd/30/63/43911948.pdf. Accessed 15 Apr 2013.
Organization for Economic Cooperation and Development (OECD). (2008a). *The Accra agenda for action, 3rd High Level Forum on Aid Effectiveness*. Paris: OECD.
Organization for Economic Cooperation and Development (OECD). (2008b). Summary of written report: Roundtable 1 "Whose ownership? Whose leadership?" *Accra high-level forum on aid effectiveness*. Paris: OECD.
Pender, J. (2001). From 'structural adjustment' to 'comprehensive development framework': Conditionality transformed? *Third World Quarterly, 22*(3), 397–411.
Pender, J. (2007). Country ownership: The evasion of donor accountability. In C. Bickerton, P. Cuncliffe, & A. Gourevitch (Eds.), *Politics without sovereignty: A critique of contemporary international relations*. London: University College London Press.
Pieterse, J. (1995). Globalization and hybridization. In M. Featherstone, S. Lash, & R. Robertson (Eds.), *Global modernities* (pp. 45–68). Thousand Oaks: Sage.
Republic of The Gambia. (n.d.). *Gambia round table conference: The Gambia priority employment programme (GAMJOBS) 2007–2011*. Retrieved from http://www.gm.undp.org/rtable/gamjobs_summary.pdf
Republic of The Gambia. (1996). *The Gambia Inc. Vision 2020*. Banjul: Government of The Gambia.
Republic of The Gambia. (1997 [revised 2001]). *Constitution of the second Republic of The Gambia*. Banjul: Government of The Gambia.
Republic of The Gambia. (2002). *Strategy for poverty alleviation (SPA II) 2002–2007*. Banjul: Department of State for Finance and Economic Affairs.
Republic of The Gambia. (2006). *Poverty reduction strategy: 2007–2011*. Banjul: Department of State for Finance and Economic Affairs.
Republic of The Gambia/Department of State for Basic and Secondary Education. (2008). *Education sector medium term plan: 2008–2011* (pp. 1–86). Banjul: Department of State for Basic and Secondary Education.
Republic of The Gambia/Department of State for Education. (2006). *Education sector strategic plan 2006–2015* (pp. 1–106). Banjul: Department of State for Education.
Republic of The Gambia/Department of State for Basic and Secondary Education. (2007). *Technical proposal for support under the Education for All/Fast Track Initiative* (pp. 1–17). Banjul: Author.
Republic of The Gambia/Department of State for Education. (2003). *EFA proposal for the Fast Track Initiative* (pp. 1–39). Banjul: Republic of The Gambia/Department of State for Education.
Republic of The Gambia/Department of State for Education. (2004). *Education for all national action plan 2004–2015* (pp. 1–50). Banjul: Republic of The Gambia/Department of State for Education.
Robertson, S., & Dale, R. (2006). Changing geographies of power in education: The politics of rescaling and its contradictions. In D. Kassem, E. Mufti, & J. Robinson (Eds.), *Education studies: Issues and critical perspectives*. Buckinghamshire: Open University Press.
Schweisfurth, M. (2008). Education and democracy in The Gambia: Reflections on the position of development projects in a small African state. In D. Johnson (Ed.), *The changing landscape of education in Africa: Quality, equality and democracy* (pp. 63–75). Oxford: Symposium Books.
Sifuna, D. N. (2000). Partnerships in educational assistance to African countries: Rhetoric or reality? *Journal of International Cooperation in Education, 3*(2), 3–21.

Smith, H. (2005). Ownership and capacity: Do current donor approaches help or hinder the achievement of international and national targets for education? *International Journal of Educational Development, 25*, 445–455.

Steiner-Khamsi, G. (2004). *The global politics of educational borrowing and lending*. New York: Teachers College Press.

Steiner-Khamsi, G. (2006). The development turn in comparative education. *European Education, 38*(3), 19–47.

Steiner-Khamsi, G., & Stolpe, I. (2006). *Educational import: Local encounters with global forces in Mongolia*. New York: Palgrave Macmillan.

The Gambia Bureau of Statistics. (2003). *National census*. Serekunda: Author.

The Gambia Country Delegation Team One. (2012). *Strategies to address early grade reading in The Gambia*. Paper presented at the global partnership for education all children reading, workshop, Kigali, Rwanda.

The Gambia Ministry of Basic and Secondary Education. (2011). *Education: Country status report*. Banjul: World Bank, UNESCO, Pole Dakar, EFA-FTI.

UNDP. (2011). *Human development report 2011: Sustainability and equity: A better future for all*. New York: Palgrave Macmillan.

UNESCO. (1990). World declaration on education for all. Retrieved August 20, 2013, http://www.unesco.org/education/wef/en-conf/Jomtien%20Declaration%20eng.shtm

UNESCO. (2000). The Dakar framework for action: Education for all: Meeting our collective commitments *Adopted by the World Education Forum Dakar, Senegal, 26–28 April 2000* (pp. 1–78). Paris: UNESCO.

UNESCO. (2010). *EFA global monitoring report 2010: Reaching the marginalised*. Paris: UNESCO.

Vidovich, L. (2004). Global-national-local dynamics in policy processes: A case of 'quality' policy in higher education. *British Journal of Sociology of Education, 25*(3), 341–354.

Wood, B., Kabell, D., Muwanga, N., & Sagasti, F. (2008). Evaluation of the implementation of the Paris Declaration, phase one, synthesis report. http://www.oecd.org/dataoecd/19/9/40888983.pdf. Accessed 10 May 2013.

World Bank. (2009a). *Project appraisal document for a proposed Catalytic Fund grant in the amount of US$28.0 million to the Republic of The Gambia for a Education for All-Fast Track Initiative program*. Washington, DC: Author.

World Bank. (2009b). *Project information document for a proposed Catalytic Fund grant in the amount of US$28.0 million to the Republic of The Gambia for a Education for All-Fast Track Initiative program*. Washington, DC: Author.

World Bank. (2011). The Gambia: EFA-FTI Catalytic Fund 2009–2011 *Implementation status and results*. Washington, DC: Author.

World Bank. (2012a). World Bank dataBank: The Gambia. World Bank. http://search.worldbank.org/data?language=EN&format=html&qterm=The+Gambia. Accessed 1 June 2012.

World Bank. (2012b). *Global partnership for Education Catalytic Fund annual progress report for 2011*. Washington, DC: World Bank.

World Bank. (2012c). *Implementation status and results: The Gambia EFA-FTI Catalytic Fund 2009–2011 (P115427)*. Washington, DC: World Bank.

World Bank. (2012d). *The Gambia education sector medium term plan 2008–2011: Local donor appraisal report*. Washington, DC: World Bank.

Chapter 6
Nordic Aid and the Education Sector in Africa: The Case of Tanzania

Zehlia Babaci-Wilhite, Macleans A. Geo-JaJa, and Mwajuma Vuzo

Abstract The chapter studies the contribution of Nordic Aid to quality education in Africa with a focus on Tanzania. It reviews and draws heavily on existing evidence on the contributions to education and self-determination. The chapter asserts that traditional aid in general has not supported rights in education, but that Nordic aid supports the multiplicity of indigenous education that has retained an important place in human rights and self-sustaining development. The chapter argues that in Tanzania marketing English as a language of instruction is a roadblock to consciousness-raising for social reconstruction and participation of Tanzanians in their own educational development to enrich the development process. The chapter concludes by calling for a rethink of aid conditionalities that market colonial knowledge systems and replacing them with schooling that emphasize culture and voice in diversity, promote freedom with significant economic and social impact that broadens valuable capabilities.

Still, for most low-income countries official development assistance (ODA) remains a major source … Even with stronger efforts to mobilize more domestic resources and attract more private capital inflows, providing more and better aid are an important part of efforts to make worst times more futuristically humanizing (IMF 2005, p. 23).

This chapter explores political conditionalities and their role in promoting right-capability based education and development in Africa with a focus on

Z. Babaci-Wilhite (✉)
Department of Education, Faculty of Educational Sciences, University of Oslo, Postboks 1161, Blindern, 0318 Oslo, Norway
e-mail: z.b.wilhite@ped.uio.no

M.A. Geo-JaJa
McKay School of Education, Brigham Young University, Provo, UT 84602, USA
e-mail: Geo-JaJa@byu.edu

M. Vuzo
Department of Educational Psychology and Curriculum Studies, School of Education, University of Dar es Salaam, Mlimani, P.O. Box 35048, Dar es Salaam, Tanzania
e-mail: mvuzo@yahoo.co.uk

C.A. Brown (ed.), *Globalization, International Education Policy and Local Policy Formation*, Policy Implications of Research in Education 5,
DOI 10.1007/978-94-007-4165-2_6

Tanzania. When viewed and assessed in terms of its contribution to human rights and sovereignty, development aid in the twenty-first century is nontransparent (OECD 2010). The literature shows that donor aid has not promoted economic growth or poverty reduction (Easterly 2008; Stiglitz 2002). Donor's self-interest and the strategy of tying aid could be blamed for the unbalanced contribution of aid to sustainable human development in receiving countries. A significant part of the traditional aid comes in the form of "tied" aid, which is the subjugation of recipients to purchase goods and services from the donor country or from a specified group of countries. Tying arrangements may prevent a recipient from misappropriating or mismanaging aid receipts, but it may also reduce the value of aid.

The main problem with aid conditionalities is that, even if the donors' concept of beneficial reforms is fundamentally correct, the recipient government may not accept these reforms as their own priority. Conditionalities imposed on developing countries can weaken their governments' "ownership" of development and make the implementation of reforms formal, superficial, and unsustainable. Untying of aid is all about transferring ownership of development and education reforms from donor control to recipient control. Offering local businesses an opportunity to compete for contracts engenders more genuine partnerships relevant for education aid, which truly aims for social development. The debate on conditionalities has been contentious and has led to a questioning of what are the true intentions or objectives of aid. Is it truly aimed at reducing poverty and promoting rights and values consistent with those of receiving countries? Others have argued with supportive evidence that development aid fosters aid fatigue and ineffectiveness (Tandon 2008). Intentions and efficacy of development aid on self-sustaining development might be adduced from the aid allocation and sectoral distribution as agreed in the UN General Assembly Resolution in 1970 and also affirmed in many international agreements over the years, including many World Summits on Sustainable Development. At the first summit, governments reached a new consensus on the need to put people at the center of development. Leaders pledged to make the conquest of poverty the goal of full employment and the fostering of social integration as an overriding objective of development. Almost 30 years after the General Assembly Resolution, only a few countries have achieved the 0.7 % target of GNP to aid commitment. Clearly, most high-income donor countries have decreased the share of their gross domestic product (GDP) spent for ODA from the average of 0.5 % in the early 1960s to 0.3 % in 1990 and 0.2 % at the turn of the century. Figure 6.1 shows that the 22nd Development Assistance Committee (DAC) member states' average ODA: GNI ratio in 2005 was 0.47 %, still substantially short of the 0.7 % UN objective. Countries with the highest ODA: GNI ratios in 2005 were Sweden (0.94 %), Norway (0.94 %), the Netherlands (0.82 %), Luxembourg (0.82 %), and Denmark (0.81 %), according to Organisation for Economic Co-operation and Development (OECD) data. The ODA: GNI ratios of all these countries, therefore, exceeded the UN's 'Monterrey Consensus' ratio of 0.7 % and were also considerably above the DAC average of 0.33 %.

Based on Fig. 6.1, we can infer that donor aid continues to be used as a foreign policy enabler. In addition, it has also served as an important policy tool for

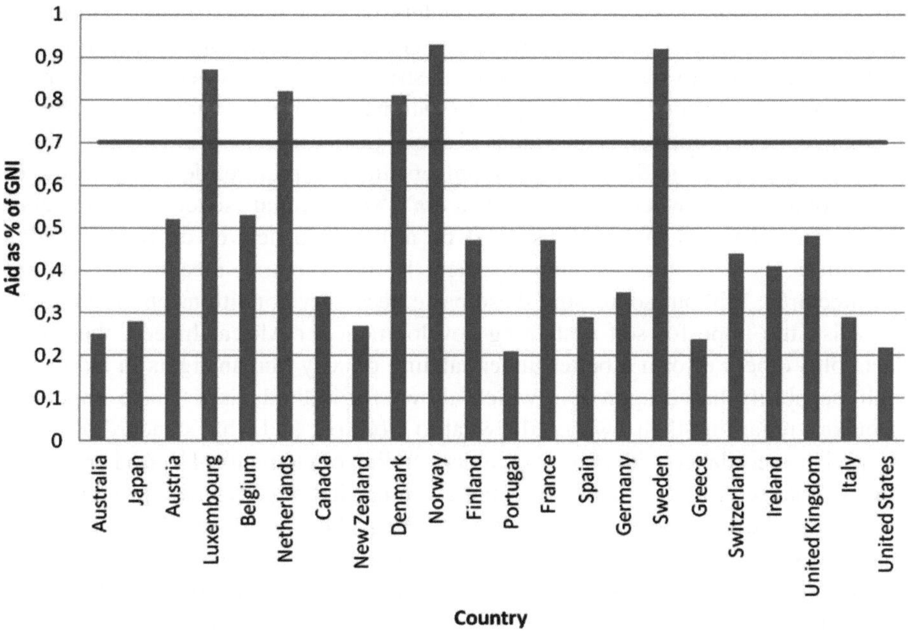

Fig. 6.1 Official development assistance in 2005 (Source: Data from OECD/DAC 2005)

expanding donors' influence upon international affairs and maintaining local and international economic stability. In this respect, foreign aid is no different from diplomatic or military policy or propaganda, as they are all weapons in the political armory of donor nations in post-Cold War era. More worrying is that donors have attached a long list of conditions to their aid such as privatization and liberalization policies, in the form of structural adjustment programs which are presumed to be the salvation of the developing world. As noted by Lancaster (2007), donor's economic influence, position in the international economy, extent of economic expansion and whether or not it used to be a colonizer country all influenced the extent of foreign aid used to support ideology or ideological partners. If aid that is crucial for sustainable development is to remain a truism, aid support touted as an agent for promoting rights in education will depend on donor's political institutions as well as on the modalities for providing and supporting the capacity to deal with issues critical for incorporating targets for mitigating sources of human deprivation. The concern of aid to education is in agreement that aid to education is not just an investment, but also rather an investment that promotes understanding of the roots of societies' challenges and protects sustainable development. Indeed, better understanding of the prevailing aid conditions that support their sustainability will enable formulating strategies for building schooling that meets the needs and interests of society.

Africa has for too long been a battleground for outside interests, as for decades aid 'systems' have developed without systematic intent. The system has just been muddling through, even as local stakeholders have demanded major reforms in quality and a big push on quantity from bilateral and multilateral donors. From this lack of adherence to that which citizens desire and recipients need, an important question is why neither the sovereignty of nations nor of individual human rights is recognized. This contradicts the values of social justice and the promotion of "own" development as well as the principle of universality that requires development aid to be operationalized in terms of 'duty-bearers', 'rights', and 'sovereignty holders'. What this means is that nations must be allowed to deliver on human rights commitments with citizens' empowerment by participating meaningfully in aid architectures. Without addressing these basic necessary conditions and roadblocks there is little hope for self-sustaining development for Africa. Indeed, the above facts plus others inform a better understanding of why human rights in aid or the right-capability based approach, which allows for individuals to make important decisions regarding their own needs, what to work on, and what standard of life is desired in accordance with their own understanding of elements of a good or worthy life is either relegated or denied or is not given needed priority in aid programs.

Katarina Tomasevski's 5A's – Acceptability, Adaptability, Affordability, Accessibility, and Accessibility that convey education effectiveness could reflect aid fatigue. In the sense, it is packaged in a weak rhetoric of sovereignty and a series of actions that isolate education from localities, social relations, and from its role as an equalizing instrument. Education rights are enshrined in countless human rights treaties, but there has been wholesale delegitimization process in which privatization under various nomenclatures has continued to routinely violate rights and to dominate aid recipients' policies. In order to make an inroad into the destabilization of rights in education under market fundamentalism Nordic countries' allocate quite systematically a high proportion of their aid resources to support basic education. This is based on a modified traditional aid mechanism – aid without strings attached but for human rights. With no conditionalities and no support for "international face of neoliberalism" (a world strategy of social discipline that doubles as an imperialistic penetration), it is presumed to facilitate language and curriculum indigenization. And, perhaps most importantly such aid framework is "normalizing" and "controlling". We may all differ on the identification and analysis of the problems, but no one can deny that it facilitates indigenizing curriculum and perhaps the most potent instrument for ensuring human rights – quality education. Such a process of sovereign right involves a redefinition of knowledge such that the local and diverse are both valued as legitimate forms (Babaci-Wilhite 2012a).

National governments should be in the driver's seat in aid design and have jurisdiction over education policies so as not to promote the "corporatization" of schooling. This suggests that anything contrary questions local ways of being, knowing, and thinking and might be a mechanism for social injustice. But unfortunately OECD aid to education, which comes with political conditionalities, in following this path that delegitimizes the sovereignty and resistance of recipients. An example of such an obvious development is donors demanding aid recipients to buy goods and services from the donor government. In a nutshell, aid ends up paying for high-paid consultants or for materials that are more cost-effective when purchased locally. Indeed, unpacking aid conditionalities or tied aid is consistent with the Paris Declaration on Aid Effectiveness with its action-oriented framework to improve the quality of aid and accelerate development ownership and country led education (OECD 2005). Conditional aid will have implications for the whole spectrum of substantive development partnership programs, including human rights (Killick 2008). Notwithstanding rhetoric around respect for country ownership and priorities, composition of aid to basic education is still determined by the suppliers (OECD 2011; Action Aid 2011). The only apprehension emerging out of this tendency is that education loses its critical intrinsic edge as it becomes nothing more than a mechanistic process. Perhaps most devastatingly, such aid framework has continued to keep traditional societies steeped in ignorance and extreme forms of exploitative socio-political aid constructs.

6.1 A Mantra of Aid Issues

Many critical issues must be addressed in Africa for aid to make any contribution to education or to sustainable development. These range from human rights considerations in aid, to the equity and sovereignty effects of clinging to tying aid and aid conditionality. How to adapt and respond and manage this complexity remains a roadblock. The 2011 survey on implementing the principles of the Paris Declaration of Aid Effectiveness, which by committing themselves to these principles, OECD meeting agreed not only to a set of principles, but also to meeting a set of normative and measurable targets. After the target year of 2010, the results make for sobering reading, as at the global level, only one out of the 13 targets established for 2010 were met (OECD 2011).

6.2 Aid and School Commodification

[A]t present our pupils learn to despise even their own parents because they are old-fashioned and ignorant; there is nothing in our existing educational system which suggests to the pupil that he [she] can learn important things about farming from his [her] elders. The result is that he [she] absorbs beliefs about witchcraft before he [she] goes to school, but does not learn the properties of local grasses; he [she] absorbs the taboos from his [her] family but does not learn the methods of making nutritious traditional foods. And from school he [she] acquires knowledge unrelated to agricultural life. He [she] gets the worst of both systems! (Nyerere 1968, p. 278).

Education quality ought to be the focus and foundation of any aid architecture. In order to build sustainable local capacity and respond to local conditions, aid programs ought to invest in quality education. To understand the dynamics of the current reform in education (expansion without quality or more markets and less government) means that one need only look at the political interests that determine the allocation and composition of aid in Africa (Stiglitz 2002). In the early years, cold war competition was manifest, as the Soviets and the West sought influence in Africa. Aid mechanisms in Africa have been underpinned by market fundamentalism and the Washington Consensus ideology that contrast with the above quote by President Julius Nyerere of Tanzania. Such aid framework is riddled with imperfections, inertia, and roadblocks that neutralize the Paris Declaration of Aid Effectiveness (2005) and result in devaluing or erasing of indigenous African knowledge. The core roadmap is that aid-receiving countries must set their own poverty reduction strategies, build their institutions, and systematically develop indigenous schooling to replace the current Global North education system associated with market orientation. But these have been caught up in the conflict dynamics of globalization and the Washington and post-Washington Consensus mix of World Bank reforms. This conventional package of reforms that seems to be obsessed with deadweight-loss according to Rodrik (2006) did not pay attention to stimulating the dynamic forces that lie behind the growth process nor was it focused towards enlarging rights in education.

The challenge of achieving Tomasevski's 5A's in basic education has been a daunting task for neoliberal privatization-decentralization reforms. However, while the expected results have not been forthcoming, a substantial number of children, particularly girls, remain out of school. According to the UNESCO Institute for Statistics (UIS), the world is not on track to achieve Education for All goals by 2015, despite progress on enrollment, as the pace of change appears to be slowing. With greater pressure on funding for education and education aid misallocation, millions of school-age youths leave the education system without having harnessed skills needed to build the knowledge societies of the twenty-first century. As we stand at this crossroad, education is at risk as slower economic growth and aid commitment to education has stagnated, even when available, as it does not reach those who need it the most. This has resulted in a human development crisis. Donors and governments should strengthen efforts to adhere to the principles of The Paris Declaration on Aid Effectiveness that lie behind dynamic growth processes, which support a balanced education (OECD 2005).

While in the past decades, there has been repaid progress towards basic education as some countries have achieved extraordinary advances, there are still 72 million primary school-age children out of school in 2010, while 67 million children were out of school in 2009. Disproportionate numbers of these out-of-school children live in Africa (43 %) and another 27 % in South and West Asia (UNESCO 2010). Globally, 51 % of all primary out-of-school children are expected to never enter school. Nigeria alone was home to almost 11 million out-of-school children or 37 % of its primary school-age population in 2009. According to new data from UNESCO, many other sub-Saharan African countries have managed to significantly reduce their numbers of out-of-school children during the last decade. Between 1999 and 2009, the share of out-of school children declined by more than 30 percentage points in Burundi, Mali, Mozambique, Niger, and Tanzania. Effective progress has been the result of removing the roadblocks of commodification of education, jurisdiction over education reform, and political conditionalities meeting human dimensions. Much of this knowledge informs us that it is no longer acceptable that the Washington Consensus with small state intervention is the only sure way to education development.

Getting girls and boys to attend school is only part of the challenge. Education quality still remains a pressing concern. The poor quality of basic education affects students by reducing their capacity to succeed in further education and the transition to skilled work. The economic transformation and political conditionalities of aid have left a profound mark on the system of education in African countries. Education was both transformed by the complex recommended World Bank reforms, which were meant to foster positive changes in the wider society. In line with the neoliberal orthodoxy, tied aid or aid conditionalities have both dismantled the old humanistic principles and helped create a market-oriented system. However, in most states, impoverished educational budgets stand in the way of implementing the new agenda and thus the power of aid to instrumentalize education.

Actually, despite the increase in aid to basic education, it has not brought children into quality school systems, nor has it impacted localization of curriculum, localizing of teaching pedagogy, or appropriately prioritizing and making commitments to local knowledge. For example, the 2005 Education for All (EFA) Global Monitoring Report pointed out that in 2001, 22 of the 30 sub-Saharan African countries were "far" from reaching the EFA goals. In addition to not achieving EFA goals, 25 of 48 countries were "seriously off-track" to meet basic education by 2015 (Fredriksen 2005; Carceles et al. 2001). These facts suggest that investment in human capital or human development seems not to be the driving force for aid allocation in education.

Indeed, development aid has not only been a roadblock for social and economic rights; it has made possible the marketization of education and its commodification in terms of focusing on instrumental factors. Further investigation reveals aid's irrelevance as far as the needs of society's rural/urban masses are concerned. In recognizing aid conditionalities and contribution to unbalanced education equity Geo-JaJa and Azaiki (2010) note that if there is to be anything like equality of opportunity, it is impossible to justify providing facilities for some and not for others or in relegating human rights in education reform. Furthermore, if education is to be universal and compulsory, equity requires that it should be free and common sense demands that it should last long enough for individuals to secure human rights.

Obviously there is no single model of "best practice in aid giving" as there is no single model of development, but without losing sight of this, we note that aid's links to economic growth depend on shifting from allocative efficiency to technical efficiency and from project aid to program support. These conditions satisfy the need to promote cultural, social, and economic rights in sustainable development. These are important points if the intention is to make education and aid programs capable of responding effectively both to the growing demand for knowledge and skilled labor in an increasingly knowledge-based economy. The problem is the desire for neoliberal mechanisms to be omnipresent and control everything in aid. It is certainly true that the adaptation of neoliberal education reform in many aid receiving countries with the promise of stimulating growth, promoting and protecting human rights, or comparably encouraging capacity-building for nation-building still has not materialized in Africa (see Geo-JaJa 2006; Geo-JaJa and Azaiki 2010; for Latin America see Ocampo 2004; and for a broader view see Kuczynski and Williamson 2003).

These lists of critical issues preoccupy this article in the context of how Nordic aid helps to address rights in education for sustainable development. In closing this section, aid in education is blamed for creating conditions ripe for brain drain and overqualified but unskilled applicants for jobs (Geo-JaJa 2004; Akyeampong 2000). Such views are largely set aside by orthodox aid architecture that justify the basis of producing greater efficiency as now the 'customers' (the parents) can vote with their feet and are not bound to a state monopoly. The continued crisis in Africa and the malfunctioning of the market mechanism calls for a paradigm shift (Stiglitz 2002; Kuczynski and Williamson 2003). Indeed, the evidence is that despite significant development aid, as well as market mechanisms (aid conditionalities), successes are few, and many developing countries have still not realized their 1990 social and economic standards. 'Aid has not inculcated inherent human rights – well being, freedom, or social recognition – emanating from liberating education' (Goulet 1971, pp. 464–466). Finally, in a context where the aid is conditional (restrictive) and where the education quality is questionable, development aid efforts at the bare minimum need to be selective and focus on the binding constraints rather than take a laundry-list of conditionalities (Rodrik 2006). Investment in poverty reduction education will offset the market forces that disadvantage the marginalized.

6.3 Human Rights in Aid and Quality Economic Growth: What Is the Relationship?

The role of human rights in aid for development should be considered both as an objective in its own right and a factor for improving well being. Human rights (individual) and sovereign rights (nations) codified in international treaties ought to be increasingly important in aid discourses to encourage social and economic progress. The absence of human rights in aid is seen as constitutive of the multi-dimensional definition of capability deprivation (Sen 1989; Nussbaum 2000, 2011). Sen (1999, p. 108), noted "The novel focus of the capability approach goes beyond legal rights and into the significance of moral rights". Educational policies based on this approach will contribute to individuals achieving the kind of lives they have reason to value or the set of valuable 'beings and doings' desired. This approach becomes crucial in understanding the realities of educational poverty. These components of the same reality are seen to be relevant for the moral evaluation of social arrangements beyond the development context. For example, its comprehensiveness makes it an effective tool for implementing the paradigm of equal educational opportunities of comparable quality for every child – a right in education. Such a broader functional and meaningful definition of inherent rights challenges the narrow focus on economic processes at the expense of duty-bearers and should be associated to human development. This is a reaction against the predominance of concern for market fundamentalism and more specifically against the policies of imperialist penetration. It provides a tool for understanding and addressing the multidimensional root causes of poverty, powerlessness, lack of political participation, and lack of access to basic capabilities, such as health care and education. Moreover, it can be said that a right-capability based approach is linked to the realization of quality growth that empowers and enhances the functionality of duty-bearers and right-holders to promote and ensure that every child gets education of comparable quality (OECD 2006, 2008; UN 2003). At the heart of the rights-capability approach is the recognition that unequal power relations and social exclusion deny people their human rights and keep them in poverty. A human rights focus helps to explain why women and specific groups, such as ethnic or religious minorities, are highly over-represented among the poor and why very often poverty is passed on from generation to generation.

A number of United Nations Declarations and Conventions provide the legal foundation for these rights. For example, rights in education is a powerful concept as it is intimately connected to the social, political, cultural, and artistic life of the people (Babaci-Wilhite et al. 2012). Rights in education in our context means local ideology; local knowledge and local language which constitute a substantive position in school curriculum. The obligations of aid donors exposed in the Universal Declaration of Human Rights, 1948 and the 1966 Covenant on Economic, Social and Cultural Right maintains that education is a fundamental right. Delivering quality education for all is an obligation of governments everywhere. We do note that even if the economic rates of return to education were poor, this should not negate the promotion and protection of education rights embedded in constitutions and international conventions. However, these rights that go beyond guaranteeing access to basic schooling, such as rights to adequate infrastructure, to relevant education, to transparent and accountable schools, and to quality learning made possible by donors aid effectiveness or with obligations to provide development aid mutual benefits with stakeholders committed to protecting and promoting rights in schools. The basic point is that development aid does not violate human rights – this do-no-harm principle is well known from the European reconstruction Marshall Plan aid. For instance, the marketization of aid or education must not result in exclusion of the poor or marginalized or vulnerable groups from access to public services, education in particular. Rather aid interventions must work towards empowerment of right-holders to claim and realize their rights by supporting the transplantation of right-capability principles back into the education policies.

The goodness of aid requires the engagement of both the donor and recipient to play the important catalytic role for sustainable communities by not throwing education open to the market. By focusing on supporting country-led education development, embracing a results-based orientation, and considering education a State responsibility in turn, education aid will support resisting the neoliberal assault. According to the report produced by European Network on Debt and Development (EURODAD 2008) based on several case studies in recipient countries and aimed at "bringing people back into the discussion" on aid quality, it was concluded that continued conditionalities are roadblocks to the principle of aid effectiveness and the concept of national ownership. Grudgingly, OECD donors and even the World Bank have come to stress aid conditionality with its dubious dependency on non-development intentions. Another well-placed commentator, OECD DAC (2011), notes how aid programs are often designed to serve donor strategic and economic interests. The goodness of aid requires the engagement of both donor and recipient to play the important catalytic role for sustainable development in communities and countries. By focusing on supporting country-led education development and embracing a results-based orientation, in turn, development aid will support better development outcomes. These assertions are also supported by the 2011 report to the UN General Assembly by the UN Special Rapporteur on the Right to Education entitled, The Promotion of Equality of Opportunity in Education (UN General Assembly 2011). This report, which captures the centrality of education in human development, stipulates that rights in education are all the more important because it is essential for the exercise of other rights. Here again, therefore, other rights entail the promotion and protection of civil, political, economic, social, and cultural rights. Countries that give aid prefer to mask their damage rather than to promote and protect self-deterministic development (see UNRISD 2000). This is the reason why the utilitarian approach has been so dominant and is still too economistic rather than humanistic. For instance, while the international community is committed to achieving the right to education for all, the gap between commitment and reality remains significant, and, since concrete and sustainable steps are not taken, devastatingly social exclusion and educational poverty have widened. For example, the dictate that basic curriculum prioritizes the learning of reading, writing, and counting in the alien language at the cost of the local knowledge and local language is said to be a major roadblock to knowledge acquisition or the idea of human development (Brock-Utne 2000; Babaci-Wilhite 2012b).

Understanding and removing these roadblocks that impede the enjoyment of all to the rights in education are urgent challenges for the entire international community. This has made aid inconsistent with the tenets of right-based approaches. Like minded-donors such as these Nordic donors – Denmark, Norway, and Sweden – are exceptions in that aid giving reflects socio-political welfare values. On the other hand, even though global North donors acknowledge equality of opportunity in education as an overarching principle that is reflected in core human rights treaties, OECD donors have not adopted measures to eradicate educational poverty and ensure offering more opportunities to quality education in applying indigenous knowledge in education. In our opinion, the continuing separation of human rights from aid allocation will surely have significant adverse consequences both from the viewpoint of the human rights regime and that of the evolving social development approach. The above critical issues espouse – that Africa remain stagnantly trapped in the viciousness of their educational deprivation and the serious problem of hunger starving the poor people call for a more harmonized front for aid channeled through recipients' own institutions and more control over policies by recipients rather than imposed political conditionalities. In this context, the rights-capability based framework that has the capability to identify common priorities for donors and partner nations, as a complete and holistic framework essential for ensuring effective use of aid to impact capacity development or sustainable social development, should be at the core of development aid.

6.4 The Facts of Development Aid Systems

In many ways, development aid has splintered many societies economically and socially. Market metaphors and supply-demand concepts, within this larger understanding, have not offered counter resistance to the tendencies of objectification of knowledge and shrinking State role in neoliberalism and have not improved aid, as patterns of aid allocation are further riddled with imperfections and bureaucratic 'entrepreneurship'. These aid frameworks whose intentions are assumed to be altruistic, noble, and neutral have come to neutralize aid effectiveness (Rodrik 2006).

Examples abound to support the above identification and analysis. In the era of scaled up aid and all types of conventions on human rights, development aid has not made a difference to education quality that could contribute to economic growth in recipient countries, particularly in the African region. Rather, aid has driven most well-resourced school aged children away from dysfunctional public schools and into private schools. This has led to the contention that aid without a state (assumed responsibility to ensure all citizens of rights to signed conventions), which is a sin qua non for distributive development has rendered educational development in Tanzania, Malawi, and Nigeria bankrupt (Geo-JaJa and Mangum 2003). For example the above countries' experiences are in strong congruence with a quote In Larger Freedom: Towards Development, Security and Human Rights for All Report. To quote the UN Secretary General (2005):

We will not enjoy development without security, we will not enjoy security without development, and we will not enjoy either without respect for human rights. Unless all these causes are advanced, none will succeed. (…) It would be a mistake to treat human rights as though there were a trade-off to be made between human rights and such goals as security or development.

The goals of social sustainability and a more explicit focus on a range of capabilities is largely ignored, as donors are not making aid effectiveness a high priority, nor are they reaffirming a commitment to the integration of human rights principles – such as participation, inclusion, and accountability – into policies and programs. This will often require altering the pattern of aid preferences or the relevant conditionalities required for aid decisions. In this light, to enable citizens to unlock the full range of their human capabilities depends on aid patterns and on human rights standards as reflected in human rights conventions (Geo-JaJa and Azaiki 2010; Alston and Robinson 2005). A development compact along the line of realizing basic indicators of the right to development and rights in education without simultaneously lowering any other rights avoids the difficulties with sovereignty and people's empowerment. According to Arjun Sengupta (as cited in Uvin 2004,

p. 200), the independent expert on the right to development, such a compact reaffirms our joint "citizenness and humanity … and that for all of us the certain unquestionable rights-so fundamental and inherent that nothing can abrogate them-rights that the entire world community guarantees" (p. 200). This is affirmed within the domain of economic, social, and cultural rights recognized in general terms in the Universal Declaration of Human Rights, The Declaration and Program of Action of the Vienna World Conference on Human Rights, The Copenhagen Declaration on Social Development and the Action Program of the World Summit for Social Development, and a range of other recent international policy statements (including the Declaration on the Right to Development) that serve to underline the importance of integrating human rights and development objectives. These also lay the problem of choice out best. This is against the backdrop in which the suppliers of aid have determined their allocation and composition despite rhetoric around respect for country ownership and support for human rights that ought to have evolved towards strategic approaches enabling opportunities to be exploited more systematically within a framework of longer term objectives. In closing, rights-capability based approaches to poverty reduction are increasingly in focus, linking empowerment of the marginalized and the rights of children to the framework of norms, standards and principles of the international agreements on human rights. They address the causes of educational poverty by identifying rights-holders and duty-bearers for the realization of all human rights.

6.5 Fallacies and the Evolving Efficacy of Education Aid: What Can Be Done?

Throughout history, economic liberalization and integration has challenged cultural identity and undermined local and national politics, even as it creates markets and wealth. In causing widespread poverty and social injustices, foreign aid came to be seen as a catalyst for social justice and poverty reduction. Rights in education or own development has continued to elude aid recipients over the past decades. Overall, while there seems to be an aid architecture that is determined by political negotiation between and within states on specific interventions they support in the aid allocation, the development path of aid receiving countries is left to a range of external factors. Reaching the marginalized or the neediest with aid has been problematic, as donors in controlling education have ignored education's contribution to human development or human capital formation or to the creation of a "softly structured society". There is recognition that education, which is supposed to be a catalyst for Africa's regeneration is no longer a factor that Africa can rely on due to the casualty of aid fallacies (Geo-JaJa and Mangum 2001; World Bank 2008). How can aid to education, particularly aid to basic education, best be restructured to enable schooling to unlock creativity and entrepreneurship on the continent as prerequisites for sustainable development?

6.6 Who Gives Aid and Why?

Undoubtedly aid is given with humanitarian motives in mind; however, most aid is given for a variety of political, strategic, and economic reasons that benefit aid donors. Both Nordic aid and China aid are said to center on improving the quality of life of people and in maintaining equity, sovereignty, and human rights. These principles that are cornerstones in national achievements and self-satisfaction are consistent with the Paris Declaration on Aid Effectiveness, which is predicated on the idea that culturally sensitive institutions convert aid support into quality growth and poverty reduction. Even more problematic is that Global North aid across groups is largely strategic or selfish in nature (Killick 2004). The causes of these distortions in aid allocation are:

Aid agencies decision-making in an uncoordinated way; and

Disagreement – even among donors for whom human rights are the sole or primary objective – about how to balance needs (focusing on income poverty, or a broader definition of poverty including inequality and security).

In contrast, Nordic aid allocation is oriented to promoting social development, humanitarian aid, economic development, democracy, human rights, women's rights, and equality. Among the Nordic countries democracy and the indivisibility of human rights stand out in aid giving. That which also appears to be a consistent norm is those civil and political rights, economic and cultural rights, and the right to own development is mutually supportive and should be implemented in parallel. None of the countries, however, specify what is meant by these expressions.

The Economist (1994, May 7) articulated that recipient needs minimally impacted the majority of OECD country aid allocation, as motives are clearly weighted towards the advancement of strategic economic interests or political concerns, or both. On the contrary, Berthémlemy (2006) shows that Norway, Austria, Ireland, the Netherlands, and Switzerland make aid decisions independent of relationships that exist between them and the different recipients. In comparison, we suggest that there is a set of "egotistical" countries whose primary need in aid support has been mainly concerned with containing the influence of China or for self-interest (to promote strategic, political, commercial, or other interests). There is also the question of promoting international public good – regional peace, health, stemming the flow of migrants, and international commitments under the Millennium Development Goals. The question is why do governments give aid? The answer seems much clearer as we examine Nordic aid to Tanzania that is presumed to be given "to make poverty history". To the Nordic countries, the "Marshall Plan for Africa" implies that aid exists as a means of helping the world's poorest people escape the ravages of poverty. We will return to this point later in the paper, as we discuss the Nordic region development aid to Tanzania.

Several other studies have unambiguously demonstrated that a good deal of Global North aid is to promote markets and goods dumping (McKinley and Little 1979; Baldwin 1985; Geo-JaJa and Mangum 2001). Depending on whom you listen to, aid is either a conspiracy of the Global North to offer solutions to socio-economic problems and altering basic social structures or to promote social justice and basic human rights for self-sustaining development. Our assessment is that there is a systematic difference between the like-minded countries commonly regarded as committed to universal human rights and social development that bind governments (Canada, Denmark, the Netherlands, Norway, and Sweden) and the other donors (US, Japan, France, Britain, etc.). To help understand this connection better, Lancaster (2007) explained that the history of aid is far more complex than today's rhetoric suggests since aid serves a multitude of often-conflicting purposes. There is, in fact, no single clear-cut answer to why governments provided aid in the past or why they continue to do so today.

6.7 Aid a Foreign Policy Compliment or Donor Imperialist Penetration Mechanism?

This section looks into the economic justifications for aid – filling 'gaps' in capital, technology and skills – after the Cold War. There appears to be a new trend questioning the adequacy of the motives of aid after the Cold War. Nowadays it looks like despite a multiplicity of issues pushing and pulling foreign policy, the flow of development to sub-Saharan Africa has recurrent patterns underpinned by geopolitical interests that diminished during the Cold War and the new realities of global international relations. New empirical evidence underscores the importance of geopolitical context in conditioning the causal impact of development aid and the evidence confirms that the end of the Cold War marked a watershed in the politics of aid in Africa (Lancaster 2007). He further provided one plausible thesis: "In traditional aid many vested interests are involved in their aid system, which is one reason why such systems have proven hard to change in fundamental ways or in effectiveness" (p. 7). Thus, many African governments have come to characterize such aid as inappropriate and misdirected in its mission. Therefore, the alleged stated self-interest rationale of aid giving is more clearly pronounced in OECD DAC than in Nordic aid policy. This is why aid support is full of paradoxes. Some of these paradoxes are outcomes of well-intentioned mistakes or calculated need to use aid as a foreign policy compliment. Evens Osborne of the Cato Institute questions the efficacy/integrity of aid, noting that; "If aid is not particularly given with the intention to foster economic growth, it is perhaps not surprising that it does not achieve its desired outcome" (Osborne 2002, p. 302). Further, the paradox of aid giving can be adduced from the quote attributed to Anthony Lake, National Security Adviser to President Clinton "Aid to Africa is not charity, it's an investment" (Geo-JaJa and Mangum 2000, p. 102). In the twenty-first century after the Cold War, aid has come to be dwarfed by foreign policy interests, as donors oblige recipients to import uncompetitive political interests. All this amounts to the transfer of economic and political control from poor countries to the Global North through trade liberalization.

The empirical record is unclear as to whether development aid has in fact improved the lot of the African poor; it may not contribute to economic growth, and may even undermine governance and the rule of law (Boone 1996; Alesina and Dollar 2000; Dalgard and Hansen 2000; Knack 2001; Svensson 2003). Other studies have also found that aid is heavily influenced by the geopolitical interests and foreign policy preferences of the donors (Boone 1996; Cashel-Cordo and Craig 1997; Alesina and Dollar 2000; Alesina and Weder 2002). The main problem with political conditionalities is that, even if the donors' concepts of beneficial reforms are fundamentally correct, the recipient government may not accept these reforms as its own priority. Other possible shortcomings of conditionalities is weakening governments' "ownership" of reforms and making these reforms' implementation formal, superficial, and unsustainable. Consequently, these and other reasons such as the credibility of the donor and the interactive strategic externalities are important reasons for the different outcomes of aid in different societies.

The Reality of Aid report (2008) stated that aid rooted in trade liberalization can only be effective when human rights and ownership are respected and prioritized. In 2002, regrettably but interesting to note, was that developing countries transferred almost $200 billion to the Global North. Net transfer of resources from the continent averaged 3.9 % of GDP per annum. These are both human and financial resources that should be promoting investment for growth or investment for building schools and hospitals. The established paradox from the above facts is that indeed it is aid recipients that give aid to donors. This situation also demonstrates that with unbalanced trade or conditionalities, development aid is another foreign policy tool and a market penetrating mechanism for dumping surplus domestic products or for vote getting at the United Nations (Andersen et al. 2006), rather than a restrictor of human capability in the sense used by Sen (2000).

6.8 Nordic Education Aid Initiatives in Tanzania

We, Ministers of developed and developing countries responsible for promoting development and Heads of multilateral and bilateral development institutions… resolve to take far-reaching and monitorable actions to reform the ways we deliver and manage aid…we recognize that while the volumes of aid and other development resources must increase to achieve these goals, aid effectiveness must increase significantly as well to support partner country efforts to strengthen governance and improve development performance" (Paris Declaration on Aid Effectiveness 2005, p. 1).

Nordic aid policy seeks to promote and protect fundamental human rights, equity, and social inclusion. In integrating the Paris Declaration on Aid Effectiveness principles in aid policies and programming, Nordic aid plays an important role in supporting recipient governments' efforts to respect, protect and fulfill human rights, without imposing conditionalities, and to integrate the Paris Declaration principles into their development strategies. Indeed, these Nordic aid policies that is right-capacity based, illustrate governments' strong commitment to the promotion of human rights, national sovereignty and respect of social justice norms (Ministry of Foreign Affairs 2003, 2004, 2007). Furthermore, Nordic countries express their commitment to provide aid in accordance with the overarching goal of the Millennium Development Goals (MDGs) – that is, halving the number of people living in extreme poverty by 2015, and adhere, as such, to people-oriented multilateral strategy of development. For instance, their respective and even joint aid policy documents illustrate that poverty reduction and sustainable development are core objectives of development aid cooperation. The choice is clear, it is the widespread poverty and social injustices in the world that drive the rational of Nordic development as illustrated in Norway's policy document (2004): "More than one billion people lack the most fundamental opportunities to protect themselves and their families from hunger and disease that can be prevented and cured by simple means. This is the greatest challenge of our time. (…). The fight against poverty is a fight for justice" (p. 5). It is important to recognize that human-wellbeing and reaching the marginalized, improving access to a portfolio of assets (human assets, knowledge assets, social assets, etc.) and opening international markets (Sweden 2003, p. 38) is the focus as they create aid policies and programs based on human rights approaches to development in which equality and non-discrimination and promotion of basic education figure prominently. This underscores Norway's policy document (2004) that states: "it is a matter of providing operating parameters that do not undermine the development opportunities of poor countries but expand them whether by cancelling debt or by providing fairer terms of trade so that developing countries' products have genuine access to markets in the North" (p. 5).

Nordic aid focuses on rights in education, strengthened educational experiences associated with genuine self-change, as it brought positive manifestation of culture and knowledge base of recipients. Indeed, it can be argued that it also allowed integration of culture and voice in diversity that promoted freedom, thus allowing nations to develop a desire education path. Indeed, these qualitative factors considered valuable inputs to improving learning outcomes and educational attainments have significant economic and social impact that broadened learning capabilities for over 80,000 secondary students. The project has also trained over 3,000 skilled tradesmen and positively impacted academic performance and the quality of education. The major challenge of the education project was sustainability, as it had no local counter-funding; hence it was not financially sustainable. Some might disagree with describing aid as a failure and instrumentalist, others have argued that aid should be intrinsic as well as instrumentalist (UNRISD 2000). Too much confidence in the "invisible hand" of unregulated markets in education aid has been matched by too little understanding of the necessary relation between education reform and development. The human capital paradigm commodification of education has failed to understand requirements of a well-educated and well-informed population on human right and social stability that grows out of an acceptable level of quality education.

This calls into question the need to reassert the value of equity and intrinsic norms into aid in an increasingly individualistic world, as markets in themselves have no capacity to imagine or create a decent society for all. Only the "visible hands" of governments and public-spirited people can bring both instrumental and intrinsic factors into education. Regardless of this contrast, what we do know is for aid to promote inter alia access to balanced quality education for quality growth, the empowerment of the poor, and expand opportunities and rights for the vulnerable. These are desired objectives of Nordic countries recent aid policy document. They have emerged as the voice of peace and as instruments and mechanisms for dialogue and co-operation between the continent and the world. Lessons from the past teach us that education is the first to be impacted by Nordic aid (Selbervik 2006a, b). This rethinking in donor aid has harnessed the right to education to build the knowledge and skill societies in aid receiving countries. This chosen aid path has enabled countries to develop more inclusive approaches linked to overcoming poverty and inequality.

The above understandings and analysis show that Nordic development aid is less driven by selfish interests, thus more effective today than during the Cold War era, when political conditionalities prevailed. In fact, there is a strong link between Nordic aid and avowed objectives. Nordic aid emphasizing human rights issues in the political dialogue with recipient countries is a well-established practice that can be pursued independently from the approaches to human rights mentioned above. Today, mutual benefit dialogue is used strategically to inform program design and to facilitate the gradual introduction of human rights projects in countries. The crucial reason for success was that they combined the practical and policy-relevant to match recipient's needs and international human rights. But on the contrary, what has made OECD aid, particularly French aid invaluable is that it promotes the preservation, spread, and maintenance of its self-interests, culture, and language through aid. The same is applicable to that of some other OECD countries. As pointed out by many authors, aid beneficiaries have a vote and purchase decisions by which they could communicate dissatisfaction to aid agencies. This is a useful practice of not following market frameworks of development, political reasoning, or colonial relationship ties. The purpose here is not to indict OECD aid but rather to indicate the need to focus aid in terms of indicators of socio-economic rights and sustainable development (OECD 2010). In this spirit, donor's self-interest and tied aid strategy should not drive aid allocation (as it can be blamed for the uneven and unbalanced development in the world), rather a determined effort must be made to improve the quality and targets of aid and design of a more innovative framework to fit the uniqueness and realities of a locality (aimed at poverty reduction and human insecurity inequality or for promoting rights and values). However, identified aid roadblocks and challenges mitigating the efforts of OECD development aid to provide quality education, or to scale up learning outcomes, or to support livelihood opportunities is avoided by Nordic aid distribution. Quality not quantity aid is often the roadblock that limits aid in promoting sustainable development and quality education for socioeconomic well being. In summary, Nordic aid may have been approaching, on some accounts, OECD DAC characteristics, but the overall impression remains that Nordic aid is poles apart from the OECD valued norm. Most importantly, Nordic aid has evolved without the influence of inter-governmental bodies that coordinate aid from OECD DAC countries. Indeed, if not uncoordinated, Nordic aid appears somewhat strategically focused to strengthening participation and creating space for critical investment. This is essential to addressing issues of powerlessness, and voicelessness. It is also positioned as a mechanism for ensuring the systematic involvement of civil society.

Currently, education in Tanzania is highly valued as a human resource and as a means for upward social mobility. Primary schooling is the major educational experience for citizens, though the number of students admitted to the secondary level has been increasing yearly. Nyerere's (1968) program of schooling, which he named famously "Education for Self-Reliance" [ESR], still remains central to formal education in Tanzania today–decades after the conceptualization of folk and classroom knowledge together receive considerable aid support from Nordic countries. Both primary and secondary schools stress the need to develop functional skills and knowledge and the right attitude for community building. The following sections examine and analyze the sustainability of Nordic aid to localization of education. To sum up, it is recognized that Nordic partnerships in programs of development cooperation and policies further the realization of human rights as laid down in the Universal Declaration of Human Rights, just as other international human rights instruments guide their development partnership, policies, and programming. The most tangible transformation in the modalities of aid in recent times has been the shift from individual projects ('owned' by individual donors) towards sector development programs (e.g. in education, health, roads, agriculture, etc. sectors), based on recipient needs and supported by a coordinated consortia of Nordic donors.

6.8.1 Denmark Aid – DANIDA

Danish aid plays an important role in supporting recipient governments' actions to implement United Nations Human Development Report (UNHDR) goals in practice. It seeks to identify the priority areas and resources needed for partner governments to better respect, protect, and fulfill human rights; at the same time it encourages aid partners, without imposing conditionalities, to integrate the Paris Declaration principles into their development strategies. In supporting many projects in Tanzania, Danish International Development Agency (DANIDA), has sought to mainstream human rights as a crosscutting issue in development projects beyond the direct support to human rights programs and stand-alone projects that support civil society organizations. Such aid support usually features the integration of a rights-capability approach, which empowers and gives voice and also enables enlarging opportunities and inclusion into policies and programs.

Not all donor programs are constructed in aid effectiveness terms, as boundaries between mission and frameworks are not watertight. However, DANIDA programs contextualized in specific human rights standards help define development partnership and focus programmatic objective actions, which link civil and political rights, economic, social and cultural rights. These effective development influences on human rights and social justice that also characterize Norway and Sweden aid architecture underpin the functionability of aid. This functional importance of human rights in DANIDA aid is demonstrated in The School Maintenance Project, which empowered citizens to claim their rights to basic education, nutrition, and health services.

Indeed, the School Maintenance Project is an exemplification of the relationships between different kind of rights and between human rights and development issues. This multitasked project facilitated the rehabilitation of staff housing, school feeding kitchens, and the reconstruction of facilities and physical plants in 142 secondary and post-secondary schools. In improving access to schooling and affordability as well as accessibility to many who might not have otherwise been able to attend school, the School Maintenance Project impacts educational poverty while accelerating achievement of the MDGs (DANIDA 1992).

6.8.2 Norway Aid – NORAD

The Paris Declaration of Aid Effectiveness has a people-oriented framework and its key principles – ownership, alignment, and mutual accountability – change the ways in which Norwegian aid is delivered and managed. The implication is that human rights underpin Norwegian aid programs. Human rights are used strategically to inform the design of aid programs and its global foreign policy. Aid processes support human rights analysis and assessment and help protect sovereignty and promote culturally sensitive aid approaches – towards enabling governments and national and local service providers to increase peoples' access to services and self-actualization. Contrary to the common understanding of aid driven by self-interest or imperialist hegemonic penetration, Norwegian Agency for Development (NORAD) aid to Tanzania is shaped by mutual benefit and focused on protecting and promoting human rights and integrating key inherent human rights principles into aid processes. As a major donor to a wide-range of education initiatives and programs and types – such as higher education development and Technical Vocational and Education and Training (TVET), – the main objective is to get the macro-economic imbalances corrected and to build capacities and accountability within the different layers of government (NORAD 2010). This localized participatory approach is informed by believing that decision-making and local jurisdiction in the use of aid resources present opportunities for addressing human rights and changing the international aid context.

In 2008, to integrate key human rights principles in aid, basic education received 87 % of aid disbursement to support quality improvement and access to basic education. Furthermore, to protect indigenous knowledge and to avoid jeopardizing the quality of education, aid support was targeted to mitigating imbalance in teacher demand-supply in local language skills and to ameliorating a shortage of basic learning materials and infrastructure. Norwegian aid also seeks to improve cooperation and local ownership of programs through empowerment and participatory decision-making. This approach to aid is in line with capacity building and conditioned on indigenous values and the buildup of stocks of highly educated populations. However, lately political conditionalities have to obtain broader legitimacy as did democratization, as human rights and good governance were now more explicitly tied to aid distribution (Selbervik 2006a, b). Contrary to the popular understanding of OECD DAC aid and without glorifying its shortcomings, it is significant to appreciate the fact that Norway's "participatory and combined approaches and methods" in aid continuity or intervention seems not to be true for other OECD DAC members. This is an interesting observation, as both OECD DAC and the Nordic countries stand steadfast in their own aid architecture.

From that which has been presented, it appears that Norway's aid integrating human rights principles, which is deeply rooted in equality in dignity and mutual rights in development, tends to link appropriately to Tanzania's development and education needs. For example, the Program for Institutional Transformation and Research Outreach (PITRO), a science and technology education program, contributed to capacity-building at the University of Dar es Salaam (UDSM), as well as ensuring long-term equitable access to high-quality education, knowledge, and research capabilities for sustainable self-development. The Language of Instruction in Tanzania and South Africa (LOITASA) with its right-capability ideological bent provides evidence of contribution to localized learning materials in promoting indigenous knowledge and achievement, as well as local language in education as an inherent right (Brock-Utne et al. 2010; Vuzo 2009; Babaci-Wilhite et al. 2012).

6.8.3 Swedish Aid – SIDA

This section overviews and evaluates the effects of Swedish International Development Cooperation Agency (SIDA) aid to the education sector in Tanzania. Swedish aid in Tanzania has been operated by SIDA for decades. In common with other Nordic donors, and in line with the Paris Declaration of Aid Effectiveness principles, SIDA aid programs assume an explicit link between right-capability strategies, aid effectiveness, and high levels of country participation in the development agenda. Ownership is thus recognized as a key issue in Swedish development aid. Swedish aid to education in Africa often involves the minimization of imposition of cultural conditionalities that create dependency and undermine indigenous educational patterns. This compatibility is the outcome of explicit discussion and consultation to foster partner country ownership and inclusion of locals through participation in the development process. Therefore, the significance of Swedish aid in some ways goes beyond simply its quantity: this involves precisely SIDA's role in initiatives such as the Nordic Partnership and in contributing to the work on closer donor harmonization and encouraging greater national ownership of development strategies.

Accessibility and adaptability to education and learning for children and adults as cornerstones in building a functioning democracy drives SIDA aid. Through budget support, project aid, and program support to the education sector, Sweden has participated in restructuring the education system. Aid to education reflects a prioritization of access to primary school, teacher skill development, TVETs, and language retention projects. According to Ishumi (1992), Tanzania has benefited from this partnership relationship in adult education, primary education, and vocational and technical training. He noted further that Swedish aid with Tanzania has successfully avoided neo-imperialist attitudes and has initiated the checks and balances necessary to prevent elite distortion of programs that are intended to benefit the poor. For example aid provided for distance teacher education and training served a total of 6,856 teachers, improved the academic and professional competence of primary, secondary, and TVET teachers throughout the regions (MoEC 2002). This example supports the fact that improved quality of teaching and creating an efficient and inclusive education are necessary conditions needed to ensure education as a crucial factor for learning and for strengthening human development and human rights.

Another project is the Languages of Tanzania project that is funded by SIDA/SAREC (The Swedish Research Cooperation). The project has focused on producing a language atlas showing the geographical location of the languages of Tanzania, number of speakers for each language, and the genetic classification. In addition the project has focused on producing a series of descriptive studies that document the grammar and vocabulary of the languages spoken in Tanzania, excluding Kiswahili. The Swedish government supports partners so that they better plan, produce, and use research for development and economic growth. The intention is that Tanzania should be able to conduct their own research of international standards in areas that they have prioritized.

In order to further understand the issues related to sustainability of traditional systems, as it has been argued, language policy and Global North education in colonized countries lead to the valorization and consequent dominance of English and the marginalization of ethnic languages in public space by pushing them away from the knowledge sphere. This kind of strategy had far reaching consequences. Aid recipients lose the will to sustain their own indigenous schooling systems, as indigenous knowledge and language are perceived to be inferior. This alien system gets people trapped in a vicious circle. This false perception of the viability of local learning processes is an alien concept of schooling in Tanzania. The false notion of uniformity of English over Kiswahili in Tanzania has had negative consequences for learning (Brock-Utne et al. 2010; Vuzo 2009; Babaci-Wilhite 2012a). The human rights focus of Nordic aid, particularly in education has been to mitigate linguistic genocide and local knowledge poverty practice of OECD aid. As we can see this is strong contrast to market fundamentalism, which has led to the decay in education and social arrangements as well as inhibiting the development of Kiswahili and stifling creative learning, and knowledge. The same seems to hold true for innovation that decreases the value and rights of local knowledge bases through defining ethnic languages as uncivilized. This has undone the socio-cultural, political, and economic gains of the 'Ujamaa' period. The purpose here is not to indict political conditional aid or un-ownership of aid programs, but rather to state that efforts, such as that by Nordic countries, must be made to improve the quality and targets of aid. If we put all these together, only the "visible hands" of Nordic aid have tried to bring to bear the contributory power of education to the promotion of human rights, national sovereignty, and quality growth (Rodrik 2006; Robeyns 2006).

To sum up, long-term relationships characterize the Nordic countries' aid efforts in Tanzania. More importantly Nordic aid is driven by developmentalist' than market concerns. It is still clear that Nordic aid is considerably more poverty oriented and human rights focused than most OECD donors. This is reflected in the fact that Nordic donors disbursed a higher share of aid around 50 % to developing countries, compared to DAC average of 26 %. As we have pointed out, more aid is allocated to social infrastructure and social services', which include education.

6.9 Conclusions

Aid to Africa has been touted as an instrument for socioeconomic transformation, to meet the internationally agreed Millennium Development Goals, and halve poverty by 2015. Africa is worse off today than 40 years ago despite several UN Millennium Project calls for investing in development as a practical plan to achieve African development goals and the enormous amount of aid resources expended. This chapter is intended to initiate serious reflection and debate on aid from the Global North on efficacy and distributive efficiency. Also reflected are type and conditions of aid architecture and the outcome of different types of aid support to Africa and possible future directions in education aid.

The conclusion reached is that despite decades of aid giving, no systematic attention seems to have been paid to closely understanding and drawing lessons relating to aid architectures, or to the consequences of aid mismatch on the continent. Thus we question aid as advocated by multilateral and bilateral institutions on human rights, social awareness, and public responsibilities. More so, it is asserted that aid support must be contextualized in the broader context of Africa's social, economic, and political rights and before integration into the global economy now and in the future.

In reviewing aid practices in Africa, we have observed that some OECD country's aid is predominantly instrumentalistic, while that of Nordic countries is more developmentalistic. This suggests a rethinking of the construction and reconceptualization of OECD DAC development aid if Africa is to take the path towards quality growth and sustainable development. Furthermore, we have argued that aid programs should include human rights and systemic participation in its design. This serves as a precondition for sustainable and equitable growth. Towards this end, only the "visible hands" of Nordic aid giving have tried to bring both instrumental and intrinsic factors into education for the promotion of human rights, national sovereignty, and quality growth.

For education, the objectives ought to be to allow local control of reforms, indigenize goals, provide quality aid, and suggest policy directions for joint considerations by education stakeholders. Aid failure in education is attributed to an underestimation of the complex political economy of education and tying of political conditionalities to foreign aid. And while perhaps not the first to do so, the authors insist that education, as a basic right, should receive a special priority in aid support.

A significant lesson from such practice is that a strong political commitment to a rights-capability approach is a pre-requisite for implementing politically difficult aid support. Not much can be gained from delivering more aid inefficiently if the aid is not sufficiently used for high impact tasks.

While education alone cannot help Africa addresses its challenges, if African countries had managed to achieve aid effectiveness, they would have been better equipped to handle quality of life challenges and to raise standards of living. Obviously, the need for African countries to adjust, rethink, and localize aid content will move their education systems to heights necessary and sufficient for poverty reduction and sustainable development. The authors note that current aid construction – focused on donor economic and political interests – cannot promote social equity or social justice. These must be given priority if development aid is to play the transformative role expected of it. Prioritizing human and social development drawn from the Nordic aid model will mark a significant change from post-WWII development, which has been characterized by the promotion of economic and political self-interest of donor countries, to the detriment of educational development in Africa.

References

Action Aid, Promoting Rights in Schools. (2011). South Africa action aid, real aid 3 report, 2011, UK.

Action Aid, Real Aid: Making Technical Assistance Work, July 5, 2006, p. 14; OECD Figures for 2004.

Akyeampong, E. (2000). Africans in the Diaspora: The Diaspora in Africa. *African Affairs, 99*, 183–215.

Alesina, A., & Dollar, D. (2000). Who gives foreign aid to whom and why? *Journal of Economic Growth, 5*(1), 33–63.

Alesina, A., & Weder, B. (2002). Do corrupt governments receive less foreign aid? *American Economic Review, 92*(4), 1126–1137.

Alston, P., & Robinson, M. (2005). Introduction: The challenges of ensuring the mutuality of human rights and development endeavors. In P. Alston & M. Robinson (Eds.), *Human rights and development: Towards mutual reinforcement* (pp. 1–18). Oxford: Oxford University Press.

Andersen, T. B., Harr, T., & Tarp, F. (2006). On US politics and IMF lending. *European Economic Review, 50*(7), 1843–1862.

Babaci-Wilhite, Z. (2012a). Local language of instruction for quality learning and social equity in Tanzania. In A. S. Yeung, E. L. Brown, & C. Lee (Eds.), *Communication and language: Barriers to cross-cultural understanding* (Vol. 7, pp. 3–23). Charlotte: Information Age Publishing.

Babaci-Wilhite, Z. (2012b). An analysis of debates on the use of a global or local language in education: Tanzania and Malaysia. In D. Brook Napier & S. Majhanovich (Eds.), *Education, dominance and identity* (Vol. 3, pp. 121–133). Rotterdam: Sense Publishers. Accessible at: http://link.springer.com/chapter/10.1007%2F978-94-6209-125-2_8#page-1.

Babaci-Wilhite, Z., Geo-JaJa, M. A., & Lou, S. (2012). Education and language: A human right for sustainable development in Africa. *International Review of Education, 58*(5), 619–647. doi:10.1007/s11159-012-9311-7. Accessible at: http://link.springer.com/content/pdf/10.1007%2Fs11159-012-9311-7.pdf.

Baldwin, D. (1985). *Economic state craft*. Princeton: Princeton University Press.

Berthémlemy, J. C. (2006). Bilateral donors' interest vs. recipients' development motives in aid allocation: Do all donors behave the same? *Review of Development Economics, 10*(2), 179–194.

Boone, P. (1996). Politics and the effectiveness of foreign aid. *European Economic Review, 40*(2), 289–329.

Brock-Utne, B. (2000). *Whose education for all? The recolonization of the African mind.* New York: Falmer Press.

Brock-Utne, B., Desai, Z., & Qorro, M. (Eds.). (2010). *Educational challenges in multilingual societies.* Cape Town: African Minds.

Carceles, G., Fredriksen, B., & Watt, P. (2001). *Can Sub-Saharan Africa reach the international targets for human development? Africa region human development* (Working Paper Series No 9). Washington, DC: The World Bank.

Cashel-Cordo, P., & Craig, S. (1997). Donor preferences and recipient fiscal behavior: A simultaneous analysis of foreign aid. *Economic Inquiry, 35*, 653–671.

Dalgard, C.-J., & Hansen, H. (2000). On aid, growth, and good policies. *The Journal of Development Studies, 37*(6), 17–42.

Denmark Develoment Agency (DANIDA). (1992). *Evaluation report: The school maintenance project Tanzania.* Denmark: Nordic Consulting Group A/S of Greve Denmark.

Easterly, W. (2008). Can the West save Africa? *Journal of Economic Literature, 47*(2), 373–447.

European Network on Debt and Development (EURODAD). (2008). Turning the tables: Aid and accountability under the Paris Framework: A civil society report. Brussels, Belgium.

Fredriksen, B. (2005). *Keeping the promise: What is holding up achieving primary education for all African children? Finance & Development.* Washington, DC: International Monetary Fund.

Geo-JaJa, M. A. (2004). Decentralization and privatization of education in Africa: Which option for Nigeria? *Special Issue of International Review of Education, 50*(3–4), 309–326.

Geo-JaJa, M. A. (2006). Educational decentralization, public spending, and social justice in Nigeria. *International Review of Education, 52*(1–2), 129–153.

Geo-JaJa, M. A., & Azaiki, S. (2010). Development and education challenges in the Niger Delta in Nigeria. In M. A. Geo-JaJa & S. Majhanovich (Eds.), *Education, language, and economics: Growing national and global dilemmas.* Rotterdam: Sense Publishers.

Geo-JaJa, M. A., & Mangum, G. (2000). Donor aid and human capital formation: A neglected priority in development. In P. Koehn & O. J. B. Ojo (Eds.), *Making aid work: Strategies and priorities for Africa at the turn of the twenty-first century.* Lanham: University Press of America.

Geo-JaJa, M. A., & Mangum, G. (2001). Structural adjustment as an inadvertent enemy of human development in Africa. *Journal of Black Studies, 32*(1), 30–50.

Geo-JaJa, M. A., & Mangum, G. (2003). Economic adjustment, education and human resource development in Africa: The case of Nigeria. *International Review of Education, 49*(3–4), 293–318.

Goulet, D. I. (1971). *The cruel choice a new concept in the theory of development.* New York: Atheneum.

Ishumi, A. (1992). Colonial forces and ethnic resistance in African education. In K. Schleicher & T. Kozma (Eds.), *Ethnocentrism in education.* Frankfurt am Main: Peter Lang.

Killick, T. (2004). Politics, evidence and the new aid agenda. *Development Policy Review, 22*(1), 29–53.

Killick, T. (2008). Taking control: Aid management policies in least developed countries (Background paper for the United Nations Conference on Trade and Development UNCTAD). The Least Developed Countries Report Growth, Poverty and Terms of Development Partnership 2008. www.unctad.org/sections/ldc_dir/docs/ldcr2008_Killick_en.pdf. Accessed 2012.

Knack, S. (2001). Aid dependence and the quality of governance: A cross-country empirical analysis (World Bank Working Paper). Washington, DC.

Kuczynski, P., & Williamson, J. (2003). *After the Washington Consensus: Restarting growth and reform in Latin America.* Washington, DC: Institute for International Economics.

Lancaster, C. (2007). The Chinese aid system. Center for Global Development. www.cgdev.org/files/13953_file_Chinese_aid.pdf. Accessed 21 Feb 2008.

McKinley, R., & Little, R. (1979). The U.S. aid relationship: A test of the recipient need and the donor interest models. *Political Studies, 27*(2), 236–250.
Ministry of Education and Culture (MoEC). (2002). *Education projects and programs*. Dar es Salaam: Ministry of Education and Culture.
Ministry of Foreign Affairs. (2003). Human rights in Swedish foreign policy. Government Communication 2003/4: 20, 118, Sweden.
Ministry of Foreign Affairs. (2004). Fighting poverty together. A comprehensive development policy. Report no. 3 (2003–2004) to the Storting. Oslo, Norway.
Norwegian Agency for Development (NORAD). (2010). Publications on Norwegian development aid. http://www.norad.no/en/tools-and-publications/publications. Accessed 2012.
Nussbaum, M. C. (2000). *Women and human development: The capabilities approach*. Cambridge: Cambridge University Press.
Nussbaum, M. C. (2011). *Creating capabilities: The human development approach*. Cambridge, MA: Harvard University Press.
Nyerere, J. K. (1968). Education for self-reliance. In N. Ujamaa (Ed.), *Essays on socialism* (pp. 44–76). Dar es Salaam: Oxford University Press.
Ocampo, J. (2004). Latin America's growth and equity frustration during structural reforms. *Journal of Economic Perspective, 18*(2), 67–88.
Organisation for Economic Development and Cooperation (OECD). (2005). Paris declaration on aid effectiveness. Retrieved from http://www.oecd.org/dataoecd/11/41/34428351.pdf. (2012).
Organization for Economic Cooperation and Development (OECD). (2006). *Integrating human rights into development: Donor approaches, experiences and challenges*. Paris: OECD The Development Dimension Series.
Organization for Economic Cooperation and Development (OECD). (2008). Human rights and aid effectiveness: Key actions to improve inter-linkages. Paris. http://www.oecd.org/dataoecd/13/63/43495904.pdf. Accessed 2012.
Organization for Economic Cooperation and Development (OECD). (2010). Donors' mixed aid performance for 2010 sparks concern, Development Assistance Committee. http://www.oecd.org/document/20/0,3343,en_2649_34447_44617556_1_1_1_37413,00.html. Accessed 2012.
Organization for Economic Cooperation and Development (OECD). (2011). *Paris declaration of aid effectiveness 2005–10: Progress in implementing the Paris declaration*. Paris: OECD Publishing.
Osborne, E. (2002). Rethinking foreign aid. *Cato Journal, 22*(2), 297–316.
Robeyns, I. (2006). Three models of education rights: Rights, capabilities and human capital. *Theory and Research in Education, 4*(1), 69–84.
Rodrik, D. (2006). Goodbye Washington consensus, Hello Washington confusion? A review of the World Bank's economic growth in the 1990s: Learning from a decade of reform. *Journal of Economic Literature, 44*, 973–987.
Selbervik, H. (2006a). *Donor dilemmas and economic conditionality in the 1990s: When Tanzania is as good as it gets*. Paper presented at XIV International Economic History Congress, Helsinki 2006 Session 86.
Selbervik, H. (2006b). *Nordic exceptionalism in development assistance? Aid policies and the major donors: The Nordic countries* (CMI Report 2006: 8). Oslo: CHR.
Sen, A. (1989). Development as capability expansion. *Journal of Development Planning, 19*, 41–58.
Sen, A. (1999). *Development as freedom*. Oxford: Oxford University Press.
Sen, A. (2000). *Development as freedom*. New York: Anchor Books.
Stiglitz, J. (2002). *Globalization and its discontent*. New York/London: Norton Press.
Svensson, J. (2003). Why conditional aid does not work and what can be done about it? *Journal of Development Economics, 70*(2), 381–402.
Sweden. (2003). *Human rights in Swedish foreign policy*. Government communication 2003/4: 20 Ministry of Foreign Affairs 118.
Tandon, Y. (2008). *Ending aid dependence*. Geneva: Fahuma Books.
The Economist. (1994, May 7). The kindness of strangers. Reprinted in J. T. Rouke (Ed.), *Taking sides*. Guilford: Dushkin/McGraw-Hill, 1998.

The Paris Declaration on Aid Effectiveness (2005) and the Accra Agenda for Action (2008). Paris: OECD.

The Reality of Aid. (2008). *Aid effectiveness: "Democratic ownership and human rights"*. Quezon City: IBON Books.

United Nations. (2003). The human rights-based approach to development cooperation: Towards a common understanding among the UN agencies. http://www.undg.org/?P=221. Accessed 2012.

United Nations. (2005). *In larger freedom: Towards development, security, and human rights for all*; Report of the Secretary-General, U.N. Doc. A/59/2005 (2005).

United Nations Educational, Scientific and Cultural Organization (UNESCO). (2010). EFA global monitoring report. (2010). *Education for all: Reaching the marginalized.* Paris: Oxford University Press.

United Nations General Assembly. (2011). Interim report of the Special Rapporteur on the right to education to the 66th session of the UN General Assembly, 2011. New York: UN General Assembly document A/66/269.

United Nations Research Institute for Social Development (UNRISD). (2000). Visible hands: Taking responsibility for social development project Title: Geneva 2000: The Next Step in Social Development Geneva: Switzerland.

Uvin, P. (2004). *Human rights and development.* Bloomsfield: Kumarian Press.

Vuzo, M. (2009). Revisiting the language policy in Tanzania: A comparative study of geography classes taught in Kiswahili and English. In B. Brock-Utne, M. Qorro, & Z. Desai (Eds.), *LOITASA: Reflecting on Phase I and entering Phase II* (pp. 102–123). Dar es Salaam: E & D Publications.

World Bank. (2008). *The evolving allocative efficiency of education aid: A reflection on changes in aid priorities to enhance aid effectiveness.* Paper prepared for the World Bank High-level Group Meeting on EFA, 16–18 December 2008 in Oslo, Norway. Washington, DC: World Bank.

Chapter 7
Quality with Equity in Primary Education: Implications of High Stakes Assessments on Teacher Practice in Bangladesh

Jaddon Park and Manzoor Ahmed

Abstract The purpose of this study is to investigate the teacher change process and understand how the variability of primary school teachers' in Bangladesh implementation of innovative pedagogies, such as active learning, reflects attitudes, behaviors, and concerns about the new education policy promoting high stakes exams. Qualitative data was collected from a sample of 10 teachers in 10 rural primary schools. Interviews were also conducted with staff responsible for the teachers' professional development. Four main findings emerged. First, teachers suggested that the exams influenced their behavior and led them to question the pedagogic appropriateness of active learning. Second, the increasing focus on exam results seemed indicative of a larger trend towards placing greater value on high stakes exams. Third, exams were to serve as a common standard of outcomes for all students, yet deficiencies in technical preparation, development of concepts and methods of competency-based assessment, and clarity about purposes and use of the assessment have become obstacles to sound teacher practice and undermine the purposes of assessment. Fourth, donor support for assessment and high stakes examination at the primary level has provided legitimacy to problematic assessment policy and practices.

A key component of quality education is ensuring positive cognitive and affective learning outcomes for students. According to Stephens (2005),

> [p]olicy makers, education officials, and teachers need to have empirical evidence about students' acquisition of knowledge, competencies, and skills, as well as factors that contribute to or detract from their acquisition, in order to incorporate this information into improved planning, management, and teaching (p. 1).

J. Park
Ullens Education Network, Lalitpur, Kathmandu, Nepal
e-mail: jaddon.park@utoronto.ca

M. Ahmed (✉)
Institute of Educational Development, BRAC University (BRACU-IED), Dhaka, Bangladesh
e-mail: manzoor.ahmed@bracu.ac.bd

C.A. Brown (ed.), *Globalization, International Education Policy and Local Policy Formation*, Policy Implications of Research in Education 5,
DOI 10.1007/978-94-007-4165-2_7

Among the earliest international policy documents advocating an increased emphasis on accountability and evaluation in low-income country contexts was the document adopted by the "World Conference on Education for All (EFA): Meeting Basic Learning Needs" in Jomtien, Thailand in 1990 (Inter-Agency Commission 1990). A decade later, at the World Education Forum in Dakar, Senegal, most governments and EFA partners reaffirmed their commitment to achieving education for all (EFA). Increasingly, across Africa and Asia, the diffusion of large-scale assessments and evaluation practices by international aid agencies is becoming a key tool for meeting this demand. Specifically, in Bangladesh there is a move within the education system to outcomes-based and standards-based education in school reform.

The requirements by government agencies for student performance coupled with mandatory testing and public reporting of results has experienced unprecedented expansion in low-income countries since the 1990s (Anderson 2008; Kamens and Benavot 2011). A critical dimension of the standards-based education movement is that schools as organizational units are held accountable for the quality of student learning, that consequences are linked to this accountability, and that schools are expected to improve where student results are below par (Anderson 2008). In 2009, the national primary education system in Bangladesh began the first stages of an attempt to assess overall levels of learning and identify differences in achievement across groups of students by introducing the primary school completion examination. Also known as the *shomaponi* exams (pronounced: shoma-ponee), the new public exams were the result of a major policy concern and commitment to bringing qualitative changes to the primary education system, while reducing gaps in the quality of education and increasing equity between urban and rural areas.

Across Bangladesh, primary school teachers' concerns about the new education policy promoting high-stakes exams have been strong. This chapter focuses on the attitudes, behaviors, and concerns of a small group of primary school teachers working within a non-governmental organization (NGO) and struggling to deal with the consequences of the new public exam policy. Efforts of the well-established NGO, which runs several hundred primary schools applying the official curriculum and standards, to adopt and respond to the demands of the *shomaponi* exam can be regarded as typical of the problems and prospects faced by schools and teachers in Bangladesh.

This chapter is organized into four sections. In the first section, relevant literature pertaining to student assessment and evaluation in low-income country contexts is reviewed. In the second section, the national context of the study is presented including a brief overview of the land and people of Bangladesh, followed by a summary of the current state of primary education in Bangladesh. The second section ends with a description of the NGO and its primary education program, which was the research site for this study. In section three, the research design and methodology are outlined and research methodologies are justified as suitable groundings from which to collect and analyze the data. This is followed by an overview of the findings from the study with specific reference to the teachers' ability to manage conflicting pedagogical and policy-related pressures like national assessments. Section four discusses implications of donor policy on teacher change and ongoing professional development in Bangladesh.

7.1 Student Assessment and Evaluation in Low-Income Country Contexts

National assessments similar to those being used in Bangladesh's primary education system can be advantageous at different levels within the education system. At the student level, national assessments can be used to provide better details about student learning as well as to diagnose common learning problems. At the system level, large-scale assessments are a public good in that they provide transparency regarding the outputs of educational systems (Wagner 2012). This form of assessment is typically designed to evaluate the quality of the education system as a whole and curriculum delivery by schools and teachers at a particular grade level (Lockheed and Verspoor 1990). Other purposes for large-scale student assessments include support for teacher professional development and continuous improvement of instructional designs. This type of evaluation can provide useful information to education policymakers within the government and among international agencies, external donors, as well as national and international NGOs. According to Kamens and Benavot (2011), national assessments tend to be more contextually appropriate and are designed for a particular country's intended curricular policies and educational structure.

Numerous studies point out that attempts by countries around the world to impose high-stakes examinations often lead to undesirable side effects in educational systems. National examinations place pressure on schools, administrators, teachers, and students (Keeves 1994). According to Torrance (2009) "testing does impact on the curriculum but that it narrows the curriculum to that which is tested and, in so doing, probably lowers rather than raises educational standards" (p. 84). The adverse impact on teachers entails a tendency towards preparing students for examinations and an emphasis on factual information delivered in a didactic fashion (see Goldstein 2004; Howie 2012; Tabulawa 1997). High-stakes examinations such as the *shomaponi* examination in Bangladesh are based on standardizing or "normalizing" students (Peters and Oliver 2009). These policies fail to recognize individual differences, talents, and achievements of students — especially those from minority groups and those with disabilities and special education needs. In addition, high-stakes assessments promote standardization of education for all students while encouraging a school climate that stigmatizes and excludes students (as well as their teachers), reinforcing an education system with the potential to increase segregation and ability tracking, as well as school drop-out rates (Peters and Oliver 2009, p. 273).

Two main reasons for assessing students are: (1) to help their learning – assessment for learning, and (2) to find out and report on what they have learned – assessment of learning. The purposes and the methods used may be different, but they are not opposed to one other. They are united by the aim of making a positive contribution to student learning. "Decisions that are involved in assessment, about the evidence to gather, how it is judged and by whom, how the results are used and by whom, follow from the reasons for the assessment" (Harlen 2007, p. 3). There is often confusion or at least lack of clarity about the reasons for assessment, and consequently, the methods used and the uses made of the assessment results. As noted above, the intended uses range from making judgements about individual pupils to monitoring accountability of the components of the education system, such as teachers and the curricular content, to evaluating effectiveness of schools or educational services in a geographical area. The use of a single assessment result for multiple purposes without adequate attention to clear definition of the objectives and matching of purposes and methods is at the root of deficiencies and abuse of student assessment in educational systems.

The term 'high stakes' refers to the use of student assessment results to make important decisions for the student, the teacher, the school, or for all of them (Harlen 2007). In the case of primary school students, it is indeed high stakes, when the assessment results determine whether they go to a secondary school or which one. It is worse when the child is branded as successful or a failure on the basis of the assessment, affecting a child's self-esteem and self-confidence. The problem is compounded when the validity and reliability of the assessment is suspect.

In the more developed education systems, such as those in the United Kingdom, where public assessment of student learning has been in use and has been in development for several decades, the use of assessments and their consequences remain a continuing concern.

> The consequences of pupils not achieving at certain levels can be severe, including the school being described as having 'serious weaknesses', being placed in 'special measures' or even closed. To avoid these consequences, inevitably teachers place emphasis on making sure that pupils' test results are maximised, with all that this implies for teaching to the test and giving practice tests (Assessment Reform Group 2002, cited in Harlen 2007 p. 3).

The new primary school terminal examination in Bangladesh strives to provide a standardized and more transparent test for primary school leavers across the country. Unfortunately, a major policy concern facing educational planners and policymakers in Bangladesh is that the intended outcomes of the *shomaponi* exam are not being met, which is jeopardizing efforts to improve quality and equity issues across the primary education system. The national examination results are not being used to identify weaknesses in the system such as the overwhelming use of didactic pedagogical approaches. Furthermore, the focus on examinations is narrowing teaching content and undermining teacher professionalism and the capacity for creative innovation.

A review of Bangla test question papers for the last 3 years in the primary school completion examination shows that there is little scope to assess some of the basic linguistic abilities of students such as listening, speaking, and reading skills through the test. The tests do not test at least 11 terminal competencies specified in the primary curriculum within the three broad skill areas. The analysis of test questions indicates that they do not quite match the intended terminal competencies. The tests require responses based on memorized answers from the textbook, instead of demonstration of students' linguistic abilities. A majority of the test items are taken from exercise sections of the textbook, and learners are encouraged to memorize selected items for the test. The assessment items lead to a backwash effect on primary classroom instruction encouraging memorization and focus on low level cognitive skills rather than building the linguistic and communications foundation of students for further education and learning (Dey and Siddiqee 2012).

The national examination process appears to be having a deleterious effect on students' educational experiences. It is commonly understood among educators in Bangladesh that the *shomaponi* examinations are frequently used to grade and label students and declare a large proportion of 11 and 12 year olds as "failures". There is clearly an excessive emphasis on memorization and the creation of incentives for schools not to re-admit students who fail the examination (Swedish International Development Cooperation Agency 2011). These practices by schools have a negative effect on students' future prospects not to mention their self-esteem. In the next section, an overview of the education policy context followed by a description of the primary education system in Bangladesh.

7.2 Educational Development in Bangladesh

7.2.1 Bangladesh: Land and People

Bangladesh, which means "Country of Bengal," is located in the Bay of Bengal in South Asia and shares a border with India and Burma (Myanmar). The country itself is a massive delta flood plain formed by the deposit of silt from the Ganges, Brahmaputra, and Meghna rivers that pass through Bangladesh. Despite being recognized as being extremely vulnerable to climate change, Bangladesh's population is approximately 158,570,535 making it the seventh most populous nation and one of the most densely populated counties in the world (Central Intelligence Agency 2011). Over the past two decades, amidst many odds, Bangladesh's socioeconomic achievements have been impressive despite poor initial conditions at the time of independence and frequent exposures to severe floods and other natural disasters. Rapid economic growth and public expenditures toward social services for the poor have contributed to progress in poverty reduction. Despite such progress, Bangladesh is still one of the world's poorest countries with 81 % of the population living below $2.00 per day (Population Reference Bureau 2011). The United Nations Development Program's measure of poverty, the Human Development Index (HDI), has gained currency in recent years as a reliable benchmark for country comparisons based on human progress. Based on an examination of three aspects: (1) a healthy life (infant mortality, life expectancy), (2) education (adult literacy, gross enrolment ratios), and (3) standard of living (purchasing power parity, income), Bangladesh's measure in 2011 was 0.500 placing it 146 out of 187 countries with available data (UNDP 2011).

The country has an agrarian-based economy with 76 % of the population living in rural or village settings (Population Reference Bureau 2011). Gender inequities permeate society and there is generally very low status for girls and women. Bangladesh is also characterized by linguistic, ethnic, and cultural homogeneity. The main religion practiced in Bangladesh is Islam (89.6 %), but there is a significant percentage of the population that adheres to Hinduism (9.3 %) (BANBEIS 2012). The near universality (98 %) of Bangla – the lingua franca of the country – and its use as the language of instruction in all government-run public schools is particularly advantageous for the spread of literacy and basic education (Central Intelligence Agency 2009).

7.2.2 Education Policy Context in Bangladesh

Modern education first developed in Bangladesh during British colonial rule in the latter half of the nineteenth century CE. This period is most notable for the widespread expansion of education among the masses. In 1854, an enquiry by the British about the state of education in the region led to the Wood's Educational Dispatch, which recommended the promotion and provision of modern education across what is present-day Bangladesh. Some of the earliest official education policies in the form of education acts attempted to establish uniformity within the primary education system. The Primary Education Act of 1919, mandated that school management and responsibility for primary school provision was with provincial governments and the Bengal (Rural) Primary Education Act of 1930 sought to introduce universal primary education across the Bengal region (Sabur and Ahmed 2011).

During the period of Pakistani rule (1947–1971), the pace of educational development was slow and formal education remained the preserve of a select few. A 1961 population census reported that 82 % of the people of East Pakistan (present-day Bangladesh) were illiterate (Schendel 2009). Across the country, primary education suffered as the East Pakistan government was largely indifferent to providing basic education to the whole of the country. In 1971, the year of Bangladesh's independence, evidence of the lack of headway in developing the primary education system was best illustrated by primary school participation rates reaching only 40 % (Nath and Mahbub 2008). Initiatives to increase access to primary education were generally either small-scale and local, or administratively driven from central ministries in Dhaka, with little local infrastructure in place (Unterhalter et al. 2003). In post-liberation Bangladesh, nationalization of education was the goal. The government enacted the Primary School (Taking Over) Act in 1974 that nationalized primary schools and made teachers government civil servants. Under this law, the government centralized school management thus removing the role of the district, local government bodies, and community participation in school management. According to Ahmed et al. (2007), this law failed to recognize the important role of the local community in supporting basic education:

> A century's old culture of community involvement running primary schools was effectively curbed. By implication, the law discouraged non-government providers, such as institutions run by non-government organizations (NGOs) or private providers (cited in Sabur and Ahmed 2011, p. 169).

Despite high expectations for improvements in social welfare in the post-liberation era, the first decade of independence saw limited growth or improvement in education. Although education constantly appeared on the government 5-year plans for education policy, there was little change until the mid 1980s when the government finally started to allow NGOs to provide basic primary schools in an attempt to meet the demand for places and to cover up the chronic shortfall of government provision, especially in the poorest areas.

A later attempt by the government to re-establish a modicum of decentralization into the management of primary education involved the Primary Education Act of 1981, which advocated for greater efficiency and organization in the system through provisions for the establishment of local education authorities (LEA) at the district level. This administrative reform aimed to enable the LEAs to appoint and manage teachers and supervise the functioning of primary schools, manage budgets, and conduct examinations (Sabur and Ahmed 2011). However, change of regimes hampered policy continuity and implementation. Other than a few school construction programs, primary and mass education objectives were never fully implemented in part due to President Zia's assassination and General Ershad's assumption of power and military rule in 1982 (Asian Development Bank 1986; Muhith 1999).

The period of greatest educational expansion coincided with the country's first period of democratic multiparty politics. In 1990, Bangladesh adopted the Primary Education (Compulsory) Act, which entitled all children to free primary education and books. This education act was in line with the government's commitment to the Education for All (EFA) goals adopted at the World Conference on Education for All in Jomtien, Thailand. Additional pressure on the government to improve on its primary education commitment may have come from successes of NGO interventions and increasing influence of donor support and financing in primary education provision. By the early 1990s, the largest NGO education provider alone had over one million students enrolled in over 35,000 non-formal primary schools across the country (BRAC 1996). According to Hossain et al. (2002), there were quite possibly more local NGO schools in villages scattered across rural Bangladesh than there were state schools.

The period from 1998 to 2010 has been associated with continuing government and NGO concern about access, particularly for 'hard to reach' children and increasingly for children that have historically been excluded from primary education including children with special needs, over-aged children, working children, street children, children from ethnic/language minority populations, and children living in remote and inaccessible areas. This period has also seen government policies that focused on issues of quality—with regard to curriculum, pedagogy, and management (Unterhalter et al. 2003). While a lack of continuity in government policy and practice has had a somewhat deleterious effect on quality education provision in Bangladesh, progress in the form of large-scale sector-wide approaches to education development have had modest successes to date.

Recently, the Government of Bangladesh formulated a New Education Policy (2010). According to the Minister of Education, "There has to be qualitative increase in both government and non-government investment and cooperation for education" (Government of Bangladesh 2010). By acknowledging the need for diversity and multiplicity in the provision of primary education, the Honorable Nurul Islam Nahid, Minister of Education, appears to provide a modicum of endorsement and recognition of NGO programs, as well as madrasas (private Islamic schools), and a variety of private and semi-private schools so long as they register and are in compliance with set rules. Other key strategies of the New Education Policy specifically addressing primary education issues include: (1) extending free and compulsory primary education from grade five to grade eight, (2) instituting a uniform curriculum and syllabus for government, non-government, private and *ebtedayee*[1] madrasas (excluding *quomi* madrasas), (3) reducing drop-out rates among girls, children from ethnic groups, physically challenged students, and other ultra-deprived children, (4) employing interactive teaching methods, and (5) ensuring greater community participation in school development and activities. The new education policy's emphasis on expanding access to children will likely require the government to look to alternative education providers including NGOs. The question remains to what extent the government is willing to cooperate with existing education programs beyond tacit tolerance of their existence. To achieve the goals of the latest education policy, it is recommended that the government explore alternative approaches for meaningful collaboration with non-state education providers in order to increase both access and the overall quality of primary education.

7.2.3 Primary Education System in Bangladesh

In Bangladesh, expansion in the variety of education providers is the result of a combination of complicated factors including: (1) the government's inability to address the needs of population groups that are marginalized or disadvantaged for different reasons, (2) generally low-quality learning opportunities for children attending many of the government schools leading parents to look for alternatives

[1] Bangladesh has two kinds of madrasas: *Alia* madrasas, which are privately owned but supervised by the Bangladesh Madrasa Education Board and *Quomi* madrasas, which are unregistered madrasas which constitute a "nonformal" stream of religious education that remain outside the scope of government regulations and do not receive government support. The *ebtedayee* madrasas are the institutions providing primary education within the *Alia* madrasa system. Today, the majority of graduates of *Alia* madrasas are considered to be "modernists" and they typically merge into the general stream of higher education by continuing their academic studies in public and private colleges and universities (Asadullah and Chaudhury 2006).

(Rose 2002), and (3) resource and capacity constraints compelling the government to harness the support and supplementation of resources by non-state institutions (Sabur and Ahmed 2011).

The diversity of non-state primary education provision is significant. The primary education system currently comprises grades one through five, although once the new National Education Policy 2010 is implemented, the primary education program will be extended up to and including grade eight. There remain huge gaps in the government provision, however, which have led to the development within the country of different types of primary schools. Presently, the delivery of primary education occurs through a complicated system of 10 types of secular and non-secular, formal and non-formal, semi-private, private Bangla and/or English medium, and NGO-funded schools. However, the main providers are the government primary schools, registered non-government primary schools, madrasas, and NGO-operated schools (see Table 7.1). Recognizing Bangladesh is the seventh most populated country in the world, the education system must cope with extremely large numbers of students. For example, by 2010, there were over 82,000 primary schools, over 380,000 teachers, and approximately 17 million students (BANBEIS 2012). These numbers do not include thousands of private education institutions and some 40,000 non-formal primary schools operated by various NGOs, serving over 1.5 million children and poor families across the country (Ahmed 2011). These schools are generally one-room, one-teacher classes that usually offer an accelerated 4-year primary education program with learning objectives in-line with those in the national curriculum. As well, the *quomi* madrasa numbers are also not reported although it is estimated that the number of such institutions around the country is 15,000 and enroll more than two million students, an overwhelming majority coming from poor families in rural areas (Park and Niyozov 2008; Sikand 2004).

According to the Education For All (EFA) Global Monitoring Report 2009, Bangladesh is one of the few countries in the world to have met the Dakar and Millennium Development Goal (MDG) targets of achieving gender parity in primary and secondary education by 2005—and it did so ahead of schedule (UNESCO

Table 7.1 Percentage distributions of primary school students by school type (2008)

Type of school	Enrolment (percentage)	Number of institutions (rounded numbers)
Government Primary School (GPS)	56.9	37,700
Registered Non-Government Primary School (RNGPS)	18.7	20,100
Non-Formal Primary School	9.6	>30,000
Madrasas	7.0	16,000
Kindergartens	4.7	2,700
Primary school attached to high schools	1.3	1,000
Others (Community schools, unregistered, etc.)	1.8	3,900
Total	100.0	81,400 + >30,000 NFPE

Source: BANBEIS (2012), Nath and Chowdhury (2009), p. 63

2010). Despite these accomplishments in education provision, Bangladesh still faces obstacles towards the long-term success of its education system.

For example:

- The rate of completion of the 5-year primary cycle varies between 50 % (Ahmed et al. 2007) and 65 % (UNESCO 2009).
- Government expenditure on education as a percentage of Gross Domestic Product (GDP) was 2.4 % in 2009, which was the lowest in South Asia (UNESCO 2011).
- At least 11 % (estimated to be 1.835 million) of children between 6 and 10 years of age are out of school and have never enrolled in any type of primary level institution (UNESCO 2009).
- The recent ratio of students to teachers in government primary schools remains high (46:1), reflecting low quality of the teaching and learning environment (UNESCO 2009).
- For the school year ending in 2004, only 56 % of primary school teachers had any formal teacher training (UNESCO 2009).

Additional statistics concerning the quantity as well as the quality of primary education in Bangladesh, as well as India, Nepal, and Pakistan can be found in Table 7.2.

Even though a steady increase in enrolment rates, gender parity, and the rapid construction of new schools across the country has accelerated progress in basic education provision, formidable challenges remain for the Government of Bangladesh to overcome deficiencies in the quality of primary education.

Table 7.2 Primary education indicators for Bangladesh and selected countries

Indicators	Bangladesh	India	Nepal	Pakistan
GER (Male)	88	114	123	101
GER (Female)	95	109	125	83
NER (Male)	83	90	81	73
NER (Female)	90	87	78	57
GPI in NER	1.08	.96	.96	.78
% Trained Teachers	56	–	66	85
Student- Teacher Ratio	45	–	38	40
% Repeaters (all grades)	10.9	3	16.8	5
SRG 5 (Male)	52	66	60	68
SRG 5 (Female)	58	65	64	72
PCCR (Male)	63	73	50.9	68
PCCR (Female)	67	73	65.2	72
% Female Teachers	40	–	56	46
EDI Index & Rank	.718 (112)	.775 (105)	.704 (115)	.651 (117)

Sources: UNESCO (2009, 2010)

Notes: *GER* gross enrolment rate, *NER* net enrolment rate, *GPI* gender parity index, *SRG* survival rate to grade 5, *PCCR* primary cohort completion rate, *EDI* education for all development index

7.2.4 National Assessment System

Regarding student evaluation and assessment, the New Education Policy 2010 dictates that in grades one and two there will be continuous assessments; while from grade three onwards, quarterly, half-yearly, and annual examinations will take place. Students from all types of schools across Bangladesh completing grade five will be required to take a "terminal examination" with an identical set of questions (GoB 2010). Known as the *shomaponi* examinations, they comprise six subjects (Bangla, English, mathematics, social studies, general science, and religion) and consist of three examinations of 2 h each, scheduled each day over a period of 3 days. Students hoping to continue their studies into secondary school (grade six) are required to pass these new high-stakes accountability examinations at the end of grade five. In an effort to address inequity in the national assessment system, since 2009 every grade five student required to write the terminal examinations also had the opportunity to earn a scholarship. Prior to the introduction of the *shomaponi* examination, only a select group of higher achieving students were permitted to write a separately arranged and relatively exclusive scholarship examination. Despite efforts by the government to improve the quality and increase equity within the student assessment system, the existing competency-based curriculum has some inherent limitations. For example, the New Education Policy 2010 mentions that existing evaluations and assessments of students address only the acquisition of specific knowledge and factual information. The objectives of the new examination system include: (1) a greater focus on identifying more creative evaluation methods that do not emphasize rote learning, and (2) initiatives that promote evaluations reflecting the continual growth of students' emotional and intellectual development (GoB 2010).

7.3 The Study: National Assessments and Education Reform at One NGO in Northeast Bangladesh

7.3.1 The NGO

The study was carried out with a local NGO in the Sylhet division of northeastern Bangladesh. The NGO operates a primary education program, and at the time of the study the program consisted of 112 primary schools for children in underserved rural communities. The primary education program aims to develop and demonstrate a high-quality education model in an inclusive non-threatening classroom environment. According to one senior program officer with the NGO, "the primary education program works on a small scale but without it many children would simply not be able to get an education" (23/08/10). The NGO's primary education program offers a pre-school program (age five) through to grade five (approximately age 10). There is a class size limit of 30 students. The primary education program conforms to the government primary curriculum from class one to class five. The schools use the government textbooks alongside supplementary materials designed by the NGO to make curriculum and lessons more child-centered and user-friendly.

The NGO aims to provide quality education in all of its schools through the use of activity-based learning materials and methods. The executive director of the NGO defines active learning as using "many varied teaching techniques, all of which follow the principle that the key to successful learning is being fully engaged and being an active partner in discovery, rather than a passive receiver of knowledge". According to a program document on the NGO's curriculum and methodology, "the teacher who implements active learning methodologies in the classroom must have a solid understanding of active learning principles and goals. He or she needs to be a skilled practitioner and an active partner in delivering the curriculum".

7.3.2 Study Design and Research Methods

The study aimed to better understand the extent that contextual factors like national assessments exert influence on teacher concerns, mastery, and patterns of classroom innovation use. According to Datnow et al. (2002), government policies may occupy an influential place in the context of education reform, causing schools to attempt to balance multiple, and at times, conflicting demands. In the case of Bangladesh, in 2009, the Ministry for Primary and Mass Education (MoPME) implemented a new national education policy requiring all students attending government, non-government, and semi-private schools to write the *shomaponi* or national primary education terminal examination at the end of grade five.

For this study, qualitative data was collected from semi-structured interviews with NGO staff working for the primary education program and 10 teachers in 10 different rural primary schools operated by an NGO in northeastern Bangladesh. The focus of each interview addressed contextual conditions including the impact of assessment policies on teachers' professional practice. The development of interview questions was generated based on a grounded theory approach to data collection and data analysis. Grounded theory can work particularly well when using semi-structured interviews as a data collection method because the flexibility of the grounded theory approach allows the researcher to develop questions and pursue areas of interest as they arise in the interview process (Kosnik et al. 2009). Both confidentiality and anonymity of participants was ensured. Participants' real names were changed to pseudonyms and identifying geographical and or school locations were also altered.

Regarding the issue of generalizability, in qualitative studies it is normally not the goal, and therefore is not paramount (Kirby et al. 2010). This study is well positioned to discuss matters relating to a teacher's concerns and perception of national assessments. It is important to note that the analysis and synthesis of findings is not based on data obtained from a wider population of teachers in Bangladesh, and the study is not attempting to make empirical generalizations. Nevertheless, there is no reason to assume that the sample of Bangladeshi teachers chosen and the subsequent analysis is atypical. Within the context of the NGO, teachers all come from the same region of the country, every teacher has received the same pre-service and in-service professional development and support, and the majority of teachers have grown up having experienced similar social and economic hardships.

7.3.3 Key Findings

For the NGO's primary education program, the first time their students were required to sit and write the end-of-primary examinations was in 2009. Unfortunately, Bangladesh's primary curriculum is overburdened and the end-of-cycle examinations are comprehensive, factually oriented, and not particularly child-centered. This may explain why a high proportion of the NGO's grade five students' terminal examination results were discouraging. The Executive Director of the NGO commented that the increasing attention and importance directed towards test scores was "a global issue" (17/08/2010). According to the Executive Director, the importance given to test scores was not an inherent objective of the NGO.

> We would like to see that children are able to learn and achieve. One the one hand, students should be able to be fluent readers, able to express his or her views, able to write, able to do the basic mathematic operations well. Critical thinking, abstract reasoning skills, and being able to learn to learn. Morally, we'd like to build a kind of pluralistic, diverse, tolerant, society with different children from different ethnic communities working and living together (17/08/2010).

Having promoted a school culture of activity-based teaching and learning in which competition was carefully controlled, the Executive Director acknowledged,

> [o]ur students have not done that well in this kind of competitive exam. So one of the things that we have to do is help students do better on these exams. There needs to be a balance (17/08/2010).

While acknowledging the importance of examination results, a senior leader of the NGO also described the goal of the primary education program as helping to empower and guide students in their personal and social development.

> Our larger goal is to basically empower people, to empower women, men, and children. Primary education helps build that foundation of human potential. Education helps build certain human qualities and skills and an attitude and knowledge that helps in building and developing a human being to his or her full potential (17/08/2010).

Similarly, a high degree of consensus occurred among central office staff and teachers participating in the study regarding the mission or educational goals of the NGO schools. For example, while interviewing Muna who was the youngest participant in the study and also quite new to teaching with less than 2 years of experience, she stated:

> [t]he main objective of this school is to educate the underprivileged children of this area, also to make them independent in the society and to prosper in future (27/07/2010).

Various teachers also mentioned that personal and social benefits were an important objective of education. Both Afzal, who has been teaching grades two and three for less than 2 years and Ritu, who has the dual role of teacher and school principal and had been with the NGO for more than 5 years, seemed to prize certain learning objectives or values related to the morality of students and the inculcation of certain life skills. For example, Afzal spoke of the importance of educating students "properly" and teaching moral values,

> I mean education and being literate is not same thing. However, if they [students] are not educated properly they can't be morally developed. Our main objective is to develop them as moral and good citizens of the country. It is our duty to present the good things to them and prevent them from the bad things (26/07/2010).

While teachers appeared to have tried to instill students with the knowledge and appreciation for being respectful and contributing members of the community, their secondary focus remained largely academic. For example, Wasifa who has been a teacher with the NGO's education program for 7 years commented that after completing elementary school, "A student should achieve basic literacy skills as well as increased confidence" (25/07/2010). Some other experienced teachers like Hana, who has been a teacher at the NGO for 8 years, warned against encouraging students to memorize their lessons.

> The government schools promote memorization. It is better to teach using a method that actively engages students. We use several materials and games to help them learn and they can easily remember the lesson (20/07/2010).

Interestingly, none of the participants in the study mentioned the importance of examination results when asked about their school's mission or goals. One possible interpretation of these findings was that teachers did not directly associate the active learning approach with adequately preparing students to write examinations such as the *shomaponi* examination.

Defining and implementing a clear policy that supported a balance between outputs and a child-centered pedagogical approach appeared to be a challenge for teachers, trainers, and program officers. Parvin, a senior program officer with the primary education program, described how she was trying to decide what message she would convey to her teachers about the increasing focus on test scores.

> I am looking for the answer. I think next year, maybe this time it would be more appropriate to answer. But my initial impression is that methodology is not the whole thing but the objective or goal of the organization or program is also important. Earlier we focused more on the process, not the output. If I compare with BRAC,[2] as I heard from people and as I know BRAC, they are more focused on output. It is the attitude of an organization, it is what they want to see. Do they want to increase the glamour of the process or are they focused on the output? I don't care which methodology we follow but at the end of the day I want results. But I think we are implementing a very modern and very effective methodology but we need to focus on the outputs. We need to balance actually the methodology and the output (23/08/2010).

---

[2] BRAC is the largest national non-government development organization in Bangladesh. Founded in 1972, it currently operates the largest private, secular education program in the world, with 15,000 pre-primary schools and over 30,000 non-formal primary schools.

Achieving some consensus among trainers and senior program officers as to how to address the demands of the terminal examinations while simultaneously remaining faithful to the active learning approach was clearly a challenge. In particular, it seemed that the suitability of implementing an active learning methodology from preschool through to grade five was being questioned. Shafiqah, a senior teacher trainer, highlighted the challenge facing teachers and trainers.

> I think that active learning should only be continued until grade three and after that we should switch to the national curriculum for students to have a shot at doing well at the grade five terminal exams (19/08/2010).

Although the new grade five terminal examinations had only been around for one academic year, it appeared that teachers were already being asked to adapt their lessons and teaching strategies, at least in grade five classes, in an effort to better prepare students. According to Azom, a senior teacher trainer with the NGO,

> [t]his year, management decided 'anyhow, anyway you will get better exam results'. In this year maybe, we are not following the teacher resource guides. This is only for grade five, next year we hope that all teacher resource guides and active learning methods and materials will be used (21/08/2010).

While interviewing the teachers sampled in the study, some suggested that the terminal examination exerted a powerful influence on their behavior and forced them to question the pedagogic appropriateness of the active learning methodology. When teachers were asked to describe in more detail the kinds of pressures they were experiencing, many commented on feeling responsible for primarily preparing students for syllabus-based national examinations. For example, Bushra, who has been teaching with the NGO for the past 7 years, spoke of her experience over the past year preparing her students for the terminal examination and pointed out her concern about test scores.

> We always need to make sure that our students do better and the head office constantly checks up on us. We are always worried about how to help our students do better in the exams (19/07/2010).

The pressure felt by Bushra to increasingly focus on examination results seemed to be indicative of a larger trend among the study participants towards placing more and more value on high-stakes examinations. Muna also spoke about her desire to see her students do well on examinations and the pressure that was having on her.

> At the time of students' assessment, I want all the children to understand what I taught in my lesson. I feel pressure to teach better. At examination time, I feel pressure because I want my students to do better than students from other schools. I worry that teaching until 3:00 PM is not sufficient so I have arranged to extend classes after regular school hours (27/07/2010).

It appeared that teachers were also receiving mixed messages from their superiors. Despite some teachers being instructed during monthly meetings and other professional development workshops to focus more on adequately preparing students for their examinations, there remained an expectation that teachers would continue to faithfully follow the NGO's mandated lesson plan guides. Parvin provided an explanation regarding the complexity of trying to accommodate the multiple demands facing the NGO's teachers.

> My senior colleagues and maybe my team members, [maybe they] are confused. I understand their confusion. Maybe they are thinking that the primary education program is going to ignore the active learning methodology in the future. Because of the *shomaponi* exam pressure, maybe we need to think about a more traditional approach. My idea is that the methodology was not responsible for the results. To me the challenge is to instruct them that this is a good methodology. So I am thinking about establishing more active learning methods in our program (23/08/2010).

Although Parvin, along with many of the teachers, was a strong believer in the efficacy of the NGO's active learning pedagogy; the ongoing dialogue between teachers, supervisors, and trainers about the need to improve examination results appeared to be having an impact on teachers' attitudes and use of active learning approaches.

During the complex process of data analysis, a number of themes or factors emerged supporting a focus on adequately preparing students for the national primary level examinations and themes or factors supporting teachers' implementation fidelity of the NGO's indigenous active learning model. Table 7.3 notes some of the key qualities, attitudes, and behaviors that appear to limit or support changes in teachers' practice.

Table 7.3 Factors limiting and supporting examination preparation

Factors supporting student preparation for national primary level terminal examination	Factors supporting implementation fidelity of active learning program
Teachers' attitudes, beliefs in active learning are less critical, more complacent	Teachers' attitudes, beliefs in more constructivist-oriented learning strategies like active learning are positive
Teachers try to closely follow the NGO's expectations	Teachers try to closely follow the NGO's expectations but are willing to exert more individual freedom
Supervisors' expectations and support geared towards closely following lesson plan guidelines and preparing students for examinations	Supervisors quietly support adaptations to lessons to better address individual student needs
NGO and International Donor pressure to produce strong examination results	Teacher's priority is to ensure a quality learning experience possibly at the expense of strong examination results
Teachers lack confidence, experience, competency	Teachers are confident, experienced, competent
Teachers have limited teaching experience, skills, or subject-matter knowledge	Teachers have adequate/strong pedagogical content knowledge, subject-matter knowledge, skills and experience
Priority is to complete daily lesson plans as prescribed in the teacher resource guides	Priority is total student engagement in meaningful learning
Teachers are less willing or able to adapt lessons to meet individual learners' needs	Teachers willing and able to adapt lessons to meet individual learner's needs

7.4 Implications of Findings

According to Hurst and Rust (1990), efforts to improve the quality of education around the world are frequently undermined by poor working conditions for teachers including low salaries, excessive workloads, limited availability of resources, low parental involvement, and difficult environmental conditions. This is a description that fits the Bangladesh situation. The findings from this study highlight the additional challenges facing Bangladeshi educators as a result of the policy decision requiring all students completing grade five to write high-stakes national examinations.

The findings show that the study of one NGO's struggle to deal with the consequences of high-stakes examinations was useful in exploring the policy concerns. This NGO is well known and highly regarded for its professional and technical capacity and integrity. It's primary education program is considered by both the government and donors to be an innovative and effective model for NGO contribution to achieving national quality and equity goals in primary education. Despite the extensive experience and educational success of this NGO, it is struggling to adapt to the change introduced by education authorities in student assessment with the avowed purpose of improving quality.

The conflicting demands being placed on the teachers confirms Datnow et al. (2002) assertion that government policies force schools, and in this case the NGO and its teachers, to try and find a workable balance between policy and practice. This tension is evident in the call for change in student evaluation and examinations in the new educational policy of Bangladesh and the implementation of public examinations at the primary level.

The policy calling for changes in student evaluations and the push for more comprehensive primary school terminal examinations is embodied in the most recent National Education Policy (2010). The Minister of Education in Bangladesh promises "to ensure the rights and the opportunities for education for all..." and looks upon student evaluation as one means to achieve this goal (NEP 2010, p. 5).

In terms of international donor support for education reform in Bangladesh, the last sector-wide primary education reform called the Second Primary Education Development Program (PEDP II) was launched in 2004 and financed by a consortium of 11 donors, led by the Asian Development Bank. One key objective of PEDP II was strengthening institutional capacity within the education system including curriculum and examination reform. The Swedish International Development Cooperation Agency (SIDA), one of the international donors of PEDP II, viewed the introduction of the grade five terminal examinations across Bangladesh as a positive change. According to a SIDA (2011) the new public examination "offers a more objective means for both government, private, and non-government organization schools to prepare and assess pupils prior to moving onto secondary education. The examination also provides better protection from inconsistent or corrupt activities practiced in the past" (p. 10). The approval of high-stakes testing by the consortium of donors for PEDP II provided legitimacy to the new examination and the form it took and muted the questions and criticism about such an approach and its negative consequences noted above. The challenges facing the teachers working for the NGO highlighted in this study are indicative of the problems encountered in the education system as a whole in Bangladesh.

Among the challenges facing the NGO, it appeared that the credibility of its primary education program was becoming increasingly dependent on demonstrating that students perform well in the public examinations. The reputation of quality earned by the schools run by the NGO now depended on the majority of their students obtaining high scores in the public examinations. Yet, this new focus on examination performance appeared to involve a significant conceptual shift in the NGO's original norms and values about quality of education. In the case of the teachers in this study, they coped with the conflicting pressures with varying degrees of success. The added challenges facing teachers were the mixed messages they were receiving from various supervisory personnel within the NGO. The apparent lack of consistency or clarity about the NGO's expectations required teachers to try and adapt their teaching approach by trying to decide what should be continued and what is to be abandoned from familiar and well-established pedagogical practices and cultures they have acquired in the NGO.

The process by which innovations in education get adapted to varied contexts of change in which they are implemented has long been studied (Berman and McLaughlin 1976). In the case of the NGO, the process of preparing students for the *shomaponi* examination involved active and dynamic interactions between supervisory staff and the local educators working together within the social, organizational, and political life of the school (Datnow et al. 2002). Regardless of whether the emphasis on examination results were driven by government mandate, pressure from the international donor community, or a combination of the two, it affected the messages delivered from senior staff at the NGO about what teachers were expected to accomplish in their classrooms.

The lack of consistency about what pedagogic practices and student learning were most important meant that teachers needed to be "adaptive learning experts" (Bransford et al. 2000; Darling-Hammond 2006). Teachers had not only to use many of the child-centered teaching and learning strategies they had been trained to use but also had to exercise a relatively high level of flexibility to adapt their teaching when the existing routines did not appear to be sufficient. For example, many of the teachers interviewed commented on the difficulties they faced trying to reconcile their commitment and belief in the NGO's child-centered instructional strategies with the growing pressure to ensure that students were adequately prepared for the national primary completion examinations. As Hattie (2009) noted, "adopting any innovation means discontinuing the use of familiar practice" (p. 252). The challenge facing teachers supports Datnow's (2002) argument that "even when policies are seemingly straightforward, they are implemented very differently across localities, schools, and classrooms" (p. 219).

How realistic is the expectation that teachers in Bangladesh primary schools would be the "adaptive learning experts" and work out the balance between development of basic competencies through an active learning approach and the new clamor for scoring high marks in competitive public tests based on the textbook content? For a long time, the teachers in the present study appeared to measure their effectiveness in the classroom more in terms of the satisfaction and praise they received from the supervisors, trainers, principals, and parents for "doing it right" in terms of implementing active learning. As Hopkins' (2002) observed over a decade ago, "one of the threats to child-centered learning is the narrowing of the definition of effective student learning to … test scores…" (p. 281). The school culture of the NGO has been deliberately against narrowing the definition of learning to test scores. Now they are hearing that examination scores are of paramount importance. The challenge now facing teachers, trainers, and senior education officers is to figure out alternative ways of teaching by adapting the active learning approach that they have known and used.

In terms of other more subtle factors related to the challenges facing teachers in the study is the question of teachers' working conditions and more specifically, whether teachers are viewed and developed as "professionals". The professional status of teachers and the drive toward greater professionalization of teachers has been the focus of extensive study (see Hurst and Rust 1990; Louis and Smith 1990; Rosenholtz 1989). Defining teachers as "professionals" in the sense of having deep curriculum and pedagogical content knowledge, a wide-ranging repertoire of instructional skills and teaching strategies, classroom management skills, the capability to accurately assess student learning and use their autonomy in the classroom to adapt their teaching and student support relative to their individual needs does not always fit with the realities of the increasingly bureaucratic and regulated conditions of most schools around the world (Louis and Smith 1990). The professional image and role of the teacher is generally regarded as too idealistic in the context of Bangladesh, but this vision has been harbored in the NGO schools at least as a longer term aspiration. The premium on test scores and the high stakes for students, teachers, and schools make it that much more difficult to nurture the professional role and image of the teacher.

Balancing an idealistic view of teaching-learning, the concept and definition of learning outcomes, and how these are measured and assessed, on the one hand, and what is pragmatically possible and achievable, on the other hand, keeping high on the agenda the principle of equity in opportunities, are challenges in all educational systems.

Among the teachers participating in this study, the majority perceived themselves to be working within a relatively restrictive structure in which they are stymied by the government's curricular expectations and organizational constraints. The new public examination appears to have tied the teachers down further to set routines geared to test scores. So what should be and can be done? Can something positive be salvaged from the student assessment method introduced with the intention of improving the quality of student learning?

According to Spencer (2001), "the work of teachers has become deskilled through relegating teaching into a set of highly specified tasks within prescribed units of curriculum and instruction" (p. 819). This is meant to be a negative comment about common pedagogic practices. Can this structuring and creating a pattern of pedagogic behavior, in the context of numerous teaching learning constraints, including general educational qualifications and background of teachers, contribute to improved student learning and performance? The NGO's professional development opportunities and support for teachers should be re-examined. How does this support, through a collective, coordinated, and adaptive process of change, with the aim of balancing the educational objectives of students, contribute toward achieving core competencies and performing well in test scores? The two sets of objectives can, in fact, be realized provided that the tests are designed appropriately, and used in the right way, while recognizing their limitations.

According to Hopkins (2002), an adaptive approach is more sensitive to the context of the individual school and is concerned with developing a capacity for change within the school rather than adopting a specific approach. "What is clear is that conditions need to be created within the school that ensure that individuals are supported through the inevitably difficult and challenging process of altering their ways of thinking and doing" (Hopkins 2002, p. 276). Overall, it seems that the new national examination policy for primary education had forced the NGO to reassess its existing program and consider new pedagogical reform models. It is important that the national examination model itself be critically examined, taking into consideration the generic limitations of public examinations, the specific problems of test design and construction at the primary level in Bangladesh as noted above, and the uses made of the test results for the benefit of children and improving the performance of schools, teachers, and the education system.

Some administrators appeared to support foregoing existing components of their child-centered program (at least for grade five students) while others seemed steadfast in their commitment to providing a child-centered, active learning program that supported a wide range of student learning competencies across grade levels.

7.5 Conclusion: Some Policy Challenges

In Bangladesh, as in many low-income countries, teachers are struggling under numerous constraints to implement new education policies advocating progressive educational reforms – one of which is the well-intentioned learning assessment approach with high-stakes public examinations at the primary level. The examinations have been introduced to serve as a common standard of outcomes for all students that could signal levels of performance of students, teachers, schools, and the system. But deficiencies in the necessary technical preparation, development of concepts, and methods of competency-based assessment at the primary level, and clarity about purposes and use of the assessment results in improving learning performance have become serious obstacles. As a result, teachers are faced with challenges that they are not equipped to tackle and can rely on little professional support and resources. Overcoming these deficiencies poses policy challenges in a number of areas described below:

- The consequences and implications of learning assessment based on summative public examinations at the primary education level have to be critically examined. The extension to the primary level of the well-recognized use of public examinations at the higher secondary level for selecting students and allocating opportunities for further education raises serious policy issues. These relate to policy and strategy concerns regarding how the tenets of universal primary education and right to education are best fulfilled. What is applicable at the secondary level are not necessarily appropriate in the same way at the primary level, both from the point of view of pedagogy for young children as well as with regard to the rights of children and obligation of state regarding basic education.

- Serious and systematic work needs to be done to make the tests valid and reliable tools for assessing basic competencies regarded as critical at the primary level. Contrary to practices in most countries where large-scale public assessments at the primary level are used, Bangladesh's examinations are administered for all the subjects at the primary level included in the primary curriculum (and based on textbook content), rather than on core competencies, such as language and mathematical skills.
- The efficacy of any learning assessment must be judged by it consequences for students. A method that ends up declaring a large proportion of the children as failures or low performers, especially at the primary level with all the negative consequences for children's self-esteem and motivation cannot be educationally or morally defensible. This is precisely the consequence of the Bangladeshi primary school examination in which letter grades are assigned to students and public lauding of individual students and institutions generates a highly competitive atmosphere.
- Technical and professional capacities have to be developed for continuously analyzing test domains, items, scores, and variability factors to improve validity and reliability of the tests. A major task is to move the tests away from textbook content and material and turn them into genuine measures of key competencies. Standardized expected performance levels for different grades for different competencies have to be established. How the summative assessment is linked to formative assessment in the classroom is another concern. The signals from the analysis of the test results for policy in respect of curriculum, textbooks, teaching-learning practices, teacher training, and tackling equity concerns need to be discerned through a research and analysis program. A permanent and well-resourced institutional base for technical and professional capacity building for these tasks should be established in partnership with appropriate academic institutions, rather than as a unit within the educational bureaucracy.

Examinations and tests send strong signals to the education sector, the teacher development system, and the skills required of teachers. When the examinations are of low validity, measuring rote learning rather than actual competencies, and of low reliability across time, space and socio-economic groups of examinees, and at the same time high stakes for students and the system, the overarching goal of quality with equity is liable to be seriously compromised.

References

Ahmed, M. (Ed.). (2011). *Education in Bangladesh: Overcoming hurdles to equity with quality*. Dhaka: BRAC University Press.

Ahmed, M., Ahmed, K. S., Khan, N. I., & Ahmed, R. (2007). *Bangladesh country analytical review on primary and secondary education*. Dhaka: BRAC University Institute of Educational Development.

Anderson, S. E. (2008). *Moving change: Evolutionary perspectives on educational change*. Ontario: Ontario Institute for Studies in Education, University of Toronto.

Asadullah, M. N., & Chaudhury, N. (2006). Religious schools, social values and economic attitudes: Evidence from Bangladesh. From http://www3.qeh.ox.ac.uk/RePEc/qeh/qehwps/qehwps139.pdf. Accessed on 12 Oct 2012.

Asian Development Bank (ADB). (1986). *Bangladesh: Sector study on education*. Manila: Education Division, Infrastructure Development.

Assessment Reform Group. (2002). Testing, motivation and learning. Retrieved from http://www.assessment-reform-group.org

Bangladesh Bureau of Educational Information and Statistics (BANBEIS). (2012). Basic education statistics. From http://www.banbeis.gov.bd. Accessed on 9 Aug 2012.

Berman, P., & McLaughlin, M. W. (1976). Implementation of educational innovation. *The Educational Forum, 40*(3), 345–370.

BRAC. (1996). *Annual Report*. Dhaka: BRAC Prokashona.

Bransford, J., Brown, A. L., Cocking, R. R., National Research Council (U.S.), Committee on Developments in the Science of Learning, and National Research Council (U.S.), Committee on Learning Research and Educational Practice. (2000). *How people learn: Brain, mind, experience, and school* (Expanded Ed.). Washington, DC: National Academy Press.

Central Intelligence Agency. (2009). *World Factbook*. From https://www.cia.gov/library/publications/the-world-factbook/index.html. Accessed on 15 June 2010.

Central Intelligence Agency. (2011). *World Factbook*. From https://www.cia.gov/library/publications/the-world-factbook/index.html. Accessed on 30 Sept 2012.

Darling-Hammond, L. (2006). Constructing 21st-century teacher education. *Journal of Teacher Education, 57*(3), 300–314.

Datnow, A. (2002). Can we transplant educational reform, and does it last? *Journal of Educational Change, 3*(3–4), 215–239.

Datnow, A., Hubbard, L., & Mehan, H. (2002). *Extending educational reform: From one school to many*. New York: RoutledgeFalmer.

Dey, J., & Siddiqee, M. N. (2012). Assessing curriculum competencies: Review of Bangla test questions in primary education terminal examination. *Bangladesh Education Journal, 11*(2).

Goldstein, H. (2004). Education for all: The globalization of learning targets. *Comparative Education, 40*(1), 7–14.

Government of Bangladesh. (2010). *National education policy 2010*. From http://www.moedu.gov.bd/index.php?option=com_content&task=view&id=602&Itemid=416. Accessed on 2 Oct 2012.

Harlen, W. (2007). *The quality of learning: Assessment alternatives for primary education*. Cambridge: University of Cambridge, Faculty of Education.

Hattie, J. (2009). *Visible learning: A synthesis of over 800 meta-analyses relating to achievement*. New York: Routledge.

Hopkins, D. (2002). The Aga Khan Foundation school improvement initiative: An international change perspective. In S. E. Anderson (Ed.), *Improving schools through teacher development: Case studies of the Aga Khan Foundation projects in East Africa*. Lisse: Swets & Zeitlinger.

Hossain, N., Subrahmanian, R., & Kabeer, N. (2002). *The politics of educational expansion in Bangladesh*. Brighton: Institute of Development Studies.

Howie, S. (2012). High-stakes testing in South Africa: Friend or foe? *Assessment in education: Principles Policy and Practice, 19*(1), 81–98.

Hurst, P., & Rust, V. D. (1990). The quality of education and the working conditions of teachers. In V. D. Rust & P. Dalin (Eds.), *Teachers and teaching in the developing world*. New York: Garland Publishing.

Inter-Agency Commission. (1990). *World Declaration on Education for All*. (Document adopted by the World Conference on Education for All: Meeting Basic Learning Needs, Jomtien, Thailand, 5–9 March, 1990). New York: Inter-Agency Commission.

Kamens, D. H., & Benavot, A. (2011). National, regional and international learning assessments: Trends among developing countries, 1960–2009. *Globalisation, Societies and Education, 9*(2), 285–300.

Keeves, J. P. (1994). *National examinations: Design, procedures and reporting*. Paris: UNESCO: International Institute for Educational Planning.

Kirby, S. L., Greaves, L., & Reid, C. (2010). *Experience research social change: Methods beyond the mainstream* (2nd ed.). Toronto: University of Toronto Press.

Kosnik, C., Cleovoulou, Y., & Fletcher, T. (2009). The use of interviews in self-study research. In C. C. Lassonde, S. Galman, & C. Kosnik (Eds.), *Self-study research methodologies for teacher educators* (pp. 53–69). Rotterdam: Sense Publishers.

Lockheed, M., & Verspoor, A. (1990). *Improving primary education in developing countries*. Washington, DC: World Bank.

Louis, K. S., & Smith, B. (1990). Teacher working conditions. In P. Reyes (Ed.), *Teachers and their workplace: Commitment, performance, and productivity* (pp. 23–47). Newbury Park: Sage.

Muhith, A. M. A. (1999). *Bangladesh in the twenty-first century: Towards an industrial society*. Dhaka: University Press Limited.

Nath, S. R., & Mahbub, A. (2008). *Inside schools*. Dhaka: Academic Press and Publishers Library.

Nath, S. R., & Chowdhury, A. M. R. (2009). *The state of primary education in Bangladesh: Progress made, challenges remained*. Dhaka: Campaign for Popular Education.

Park, J., & Niyozov, S. (2008). Madrasa education in South Asia and Southeast Asia: Current issues and debates. *Asia Pacific Journal of Education, 28*(4), 323–351.

Peters, S., & Oliver, L. A. (2009). Achieving quality and equity through inclusive education in an era of high-stakes testing. *Prospects, 39*(3), 265–279.

Population Reference Bureau. (2011). Bangladesh. From http://www.prb.org/DataFinder/Geography/Data.aspx?loc=378. Accessed on 15 Oct 2012.

Rose, P. (2002). *Is the non-state education sector serving the needs of the poor? Evidence from east and southern Africa*. Paper presented at the making services work for poor people: World development report 2003/04 Workshop.

Rosenholtz, S. (1989). Teacher commitment: District-level influences. In S. Rosenholtz (Ed.), *Teachers' workplace: The social organization of schools* (pp. 167–204). White Plains/New York: Longman Inc.. Ch. 7.

Sabur, Z., & Ahmed, M. (2011). Diversity in primary education provisions: Serving access with quality and equity. In M. Ahmed (Ed.), *Education in Bangladesh: Overcoming hurdles to equity and quality*. Dhaka: BRAC University Press.

Schendel, W. V. (2009). *A history of Bangladesh*. Cambridge, UK: Cambridge University Press.

Sikand, Y. (2004). Reforming the Indian madrassas: Contemporary Muslim voices. In S. P. Limaye, M. Malik, & R. G. Wirsing (Eds.), *Religious radicalism and security in South Asia* (pp. 117–143). Honolulu: Asia-Pacific Center for Security Studies.

Spencer, D. A. (2001). Teachers' work in historical and social context. In V. Richardson (Ed.), *Handbook of research on teaching* (4th ed., pp. 803–825). Washington, DC: American Educational Research Association.

Stephens, M. (2005). Activities to measure learning outcomes in developing countries: Results of an exploratorysurvey.Retrievedfromhttp://www.equip123.net/docs/e2-MeasuringLearningOutcome_IssuesBrief.pdf

Swedish International Development Cooperation Agency (SIDA). (2011). Reality check Bangladesh 2010: Listening to poor people's realities about primary healthcare and primary education, year 4. From http://www.swedenabroad.com/SelectImageX/193243/Realitycheck2010.pdf.pdf. Accessed on 9 Sept 2012.

Tabulawa, R. (1997). Pedagogical classroom practice and the social context: The case of Botswana. *International Journal of Educational Development, 17*(2), 189–204.

Torrance, H. (2009). Pursuing the wrong indicators. In K. E. Ryan & J. B. Cousins (Eds.), *The Sage international handbook of educational evaluation* (pp. 483–498). Los Angeles: Sage.

UNESCO. (2009). *EFA global monitoring report 2009: Overcoming inequity: Why governance matters*. Paris: UNESCO.

UNESCO. (2010). *EFA global monitoring report 2010: Reaching the marginalized.* Paris: UNESCO.

UNESCO. (2011). Global education digest 2011. From http://www.uis.unesco.org/Library/Documents/global_education_digest_2011_en.pdf. Accessed on 2 Dec 2011.

United Nations Development Program (UNDP). (2011). Human development report 2011: Sustainability and equity: A better future for all. From http://hdr.undp.org/en/reports/global/hdr2011/. Accessed on 7 Nov 2011.

Unterhalter, E., Ross, J., & Alam, M. (2003). A fragile dialogue? Research and primary education policy formation in Bangladesh, 1971–2001. *Compare, 33*(1), 85–99.

Wagner, D. A. (2012). Compare forum: Debate on learning assessments in developing countries. *Compare, 42*(3), 509–512.

Chapter 8
No Nation Is an Island: Navigating the Troubled Waters Between Indigenous Values and Donor Desire in the Republic of the Marshall Islands

Paul Robert Sauer

Abstract Donor nation funding can have a significant impact on the educational priorities of the recipient nation. In the case of the Republic of the Marshall Islands (RMI) that impact is further complicated by a complex colonial heritage that includes the dramatic specter of nuclear testing and the ongoing relationship of the RMI to the United States through a Compact of Free Association. Issues of donor funding impact educational prioritization of non-native instructional language, foreign curricular content, and Western-values based teacher training programs. While not always explicitly tied to donor funding, the values and expected educational outcomes of the donor nation are often enforced through Western accreditation standards upon which much of the donor funding is dependent. This essay attempts to highlight areas where educational values and priorities in the RMI may have been impacted by the donor nations and highlights recent attempts by Marshallese educators to assert greater control over their own educational destiny.

The current educational system in the Republic of the Marshall Islands is largely a product of the country's colonial history (Hezel 1975). Even with the removal of formalized colonial relationships at its constituting as an independent nation state in 1986, colonial relationships and influence continue, through significant foreign donor-nation support (Hezel 2001). Targeted funding, particularly in the areas of education and health care, are also provided to the government of the Marshall Islands through benefits established bilaterally with the United States in a Compact of Free Association first begun in 1986 and renewed in 2003 (Compact of Free Association Amendments Act 2003).

The 2000 *Education for All* report by the United Nations Educational, Scientific, and Cultural Organization (UNESCO) documents the level of Marshallese dependence

P.R. Sauer (✉)
Assistant Professor of Religion, Concordia College-New York, Bronxville, New York, NY, USA
e-mail: paul.sauer@concordia-ny.edu

C.A. Brown (ed.), *Globalization, International Education Policy and Local Policy Formation*, Policy Implications of Research in Education 5,
DOI 10.1007/978-94-007-4165-2_8

on donor support for their educational program, "Funds from local sources are not sufficient even to cover personnel salaries, 20 % of which is met for (sic) through United States grants" (Langmoir 2000, p. 1). In addition to U.S. aid, the report also highlights the broad range of educational donor support to the Marshall Islands including UNESCO; the Asian Development Bank; Japanese Grants; Australian Government Overseas Aid Program (AUSAID) from Australia; Secretariat of the Pacific Board for Educational Assessment, University of the South Pacific, which is itself largely funded by donor nations; New Zealand Aid; and The British Government.

Given the critical nature of donor support, discussions about educational reform in the Marshall Islands, as was contemplated by the 2008 *Ej Ju Bwe'n Lonjat* conference report (Ministry of Education 2008), are not easily disentangled from donor policy. This chapter will describe how colonial history in the Marshall Islands has contributed to the challenges facing its current educational system and created a structural dependency where donor support is both needed and accepted. It will then explore areas where donor funding has created challenges for a Marshallese educational reform that seeks to embrace the educational values of Marshallese culture and meet the needs of Marshallese society. Finally, it will highlight recent donor partnerships that have advanced the aims of the *Ej Ju El Bwe'n Lonjat* report.

8.1 A Colonial Legacy

8.1.1 A Brief History

It wasn't until 1526 that the first Europeans came into contact with the Marshall Islands. Its remote location and its resource poverty compared to other Pacific Islands, as well as its reputation for hostility toward outsiders, limited Marshallese contact with European ships in the years following (Hezel 1983). Spanish sovereignty over the Marshall Islands was finally declared in 1874, but their territorial claim was quickly sold to Germany in 1884. With the German post-WWI renunciation of their territorial claims in the Pacific, the Marshall Islands fell under the colonial control of Japan in 1920 by mandate of the League of Nations. Following the victory of the United States over Japan in WWII, the U.S. was given Trusteeship of the Marshall Islands by United Nations mandate. Under U.S. administration of the Trusteeship, the United States tested 67 nuclear weapons on the northern Marshall Islands of Bikini and Enewetak. In 1986, the Marshall Islands achieved independence and as a free nation entered into a Compact of Free Association with the United States, which provides military and economic support to the Marshall Islands in return for the granting of United States strategic interest in the area (Hezel 1995). While it may seem strange that the Marshall Islands has freely entered into association with its former colonizer, given their strategic geopolitical importance, many leaders felt that they had no choice:

> In an effort to make the best of the geopolitical realities and the battle between superpowers for dominance in the Pacific, they have maintained strong ties with the U.S. in their new

political statuses. To the newly independent countries of the south Pacific, this may have seemed like an unacceptable compromise. To Micronesian decision-makers, however, it appeared the only realistic course (Hezel 1991, [n.p]).

As it seeks to chart its course forward as an independent nation, the Marshall Islands finds itself balancing its independence with ongoing relationships with former colonial powers both in the East and the West.

8.1.2 Societal Impact of Colonialism

In addition to the direct impact of its colonial history on the educational system, which will be discussed in the next section, the colonial period fundamentally impacted Marshallese society in ways that would also impact education. The first was the creation of a culture of dependency during the Trust Territory years, where total aid money flowing into the Marshall Islands increased from $1 million in 1947 to $119.9 million in 1982 (Hanlon 1998). The aid dependence continues under the Compact of Free Association, where U.S. aid per capita alone is large enough to classify the Marshall Islands as a middle-income country by World Bank standards (Aiyar 2008).

Culturally, this created a tension between the *iroj* or tribal chiefs, who were historically responsible for the welfare of the community, and the aid programs funded by foreign donors and administrated by the Marshallese government (Hezel 2001). With this increased societal role, the government was forced to seek additional donor revenue sources to meet their programmatic needs that were once met by traditional leadership (Pikcunas 1991). The result was a constant awareness of donor aid that continues to the present. This awareness is evidenced by reading the nation's only newspaper *The Marshall Islands Journal*, which provides a monthly listing of foreign donor support and frequently notes criticism when donor funds are not utilized and must be returned to the donor nation.

A second impact was in the development of the Marshall Islands from a sustenance-based economy to a cash-based economy and the corresponding movement toward participation in the global economy (Hezel 1984). This economic shift resulted in an educational shift, which has sought to prepare students for this changed economic reality (Hezel 1975). As a result, the emphasis in education has shifted from *knowing* to *schooling*, as once informal means of passing on knowledge and tradition became centralized and standardized in formalized educational structures (Kupferman 2004).

The new cash economy, in addition to displacement caused by nuclear contamination, also resulted in a growing urbanization of the population and has led to a division within the Marshall Islands between the large cash-based urban centers of Majuro and Ebeye, and the outer islands that are still largely dependent on copra farming and fishing (Conklin 1984; Belau 1971). It has led to the additional problem of a brain drain in outer island communities as outer islanders who are educated in the urban centers are often reluctant to return to outer islands where their opportunities to utilize their education will be limited by the sustenance-based economy (Belau 1971).

8.1.3 A Brief History of Education in the Marshall Islands

Formalized education in the Marshall Islands does not have a long history. In pre-colonial times, education consisted primarily of *bwij,* or family clans, passing on traditional knowledge of fishing, shipbuilding, and atoll farming from parent to child (Hezel 1983). Even traditional medicine was taught on an informal basis and such exclusive knowledge was to be protected rather than shared (Taafiki et al. 2006). This educational approach was in keeping with what was traditionally an oral society:

> The written word is only a recent introduction. The wealth of knowledge the Marshallese possessed before the coming of the foreigners was embodied in the form of stories and chants: the knowledge that was environmental, technical or spiritual, about the social and inter-personal codes of ethics, and geographical determinants; all vital for the survival of the people in an atoll environment. (Spenneman 1992, p. xiii)

With the arrival of the colonial powers, first as trading partners, later as missionaries, and then finally as colonizers, formalized systems of education began to develop, as did a formalized written language (Hezel 1995). Protestant missionaries founded the first formalized school in the Marshall Islands on Ebon Atoll in the 1850s, an endeavor that met with mixed success as the school was opened and closed repeatedly until it finally stabilized in the 1860s under the leadership of Hawaiian missionaries (Hezel 1985). With the colonial acquisition of the Marshall Islands, first by Spain and then by Germany, the Missionaries of the Sacred Heart and Jesuits arrived and established their own schools as a part of the mission effort. Under the Germans, such schools often came with a mandate from the colonial government to assist in the Germanization process of the islands (Hezel 1985). With the Japanese takeover of the Marshall Islands in 1914, the German schools were closed and the Catholics expelled. In its place a Japanese school was implemented, which was controlled by the Japanese Bureau of Education and followed a Japanese language and culture curriculum that sought to increase the loyalty of the Marshallese to the Japanese emperor through a process of Japanization (Hezel 1985).

In the first few years of the United States Trusteeship following WWII, a decentralized school system was developed that sought local community control with U.S. financial assistance (Conklin 1984). In the late 1950s, the U.S. began to face international pressure at the United Nations to improve the standard of education in the Trust Territory (Belau 1971). Given that the U.S. interest in Micronesia was predominantly strategic and military, development goals, including education, that did not have a direct military impact often did not receive funding priority (Dorrance 1992). In 1962, U.S. President Kennedy commissioned a task force to study what might be done to facilitate "the movement of Micronesia into a permanent relationship with the U.S. within our political framework" (Belau 1971, p. 2). The result was the confidential 1964 *Solomon Report*, which included among its educational goals an "introduction in the school system of U.S. oriented curriculum changes and patriotic rituals" (Belau 1971, p. 11). With that goal in mind, "School curricula for the [Trust Territory of the Pacific Island] and Guam were adopted primarily from the California state system without any adaptation for the Micronesian setting. The program was academic, not vocational" (Conklin 1984, p. 10). U.S. governmental programs, like the Peace Corps, were enlisted in the implementation of this new Americanizing approach to education, and the foundations for a centralized school system to serve students through grade six were laid (Conklin 1984).

With independence the Marshallese attained greater administrative flexibility to manage their own schools. This flexibility, however, is still dependent upon U.S. development aid, "For both the Ministries of Education and Health, a large part of their budgets come from the U.S. government. Dependence on U.S. funding is particularly extreme for the Ministry of Education, which is receiving $20,038,137 – 90 % – of its total from U.S. sources" (Johnson 2011). The significance of that U.S. development aid, along with that of other countries and non-governmental organizations, brings with it assumptions about the type of educational programs and infrastructure that should be supported. As Kupferman (2004) notes, "An American system of education has been imposed upon the [Marshall Islands] and on a culture that does not readily adopt U.S. ideas of education as its own, yet is forced to by dint of economic-political realities" (p. 42).

The result of an imposed system is that there is little community involvement or ownership of the school, since many stakeholders are unclear about what the purpose of education should be for Marshall Islanders. Donahue (1998) describes the disconnect:

> Historically, support for education in the United States has been based on the beliefs that education furthers democratic participation and that it provides individuals with economic opportunities. Neither of these notions is well developed in the pacific, where democracy sometimes uncomfortably coexists with traditional leadership and where economic advancement through education is limited to a very small minority. (p. 2)

8.2 When Cultures Collide: Educational Challenges and Donor Funding

The recognition that education in the Marshall Islands has its own unique non-western cultural context has been frequently articulated (Conklin 1984; Heck 1996; Hezel 2002; Kupferman 2004; Low et al. 2005). What is not as clear is what a uniquely Marshallese educational context would look like. Given the rapid change that Marshallese society has experienced over the past decades, Marshallese themselves do not always speak with one voice. Hezel (2002) outlines three different approaches to education: manpower training, which involves vocational training for employment; cultural preservation, which involves inculcation of *manit* or

Marshallese customary practice; and academic skills, which involves teaching children how to read, write, and think (p. 1). The Ministry of Education's *Ej Ju El Bwe'n Lonjat* report (2008) likewise struggles to find a balance between the competing interest of an education system that "prepares our children for a competitive and sustainable future… that teach them skills and knowledge needed to be globally competitive in the 21st century" and one "that promotes and preserves our Marshallese identity by incorporating our values, culture and traditions into our teaching and our learning endeavors" (p. 2). Given, the already delicate educational balancing act, the influence of outside donor spending and priorities has the potential to provide undue influence or drown out Marshallese voices.

8.2.1 Federal Funding, Mandates, and Assessment

Along with the significant foreign donor aid that the Marshall Islands receives comes a desire by those donors to ensure that the donor funds are properly spent. In the case of the Ministry of Education of the Marshall Islands, the bulk of their educational funding comes through Compact funding administered through the U.S. Department of the Interior. In return for funding, they are "held accountable for 20 indicators of educational progress" (Heine and Emesiochi 2007). Although neither mandated nor tied to the funding, the Ministry of Education is encouraged to align with other U.S. educational policies. This meant that in 2002 they were encouraged "to adopt provisions from the *No Child Left Behind Act of 2001*, such as standards and benchmarks, aligned curricula and instruction, and assessment systems that measure standards and benchmarks" (Heine and Emesiochi 2007, p. 1).

The desire to integrate centralized Marshallese educational standards with those from the United States may be seen as a continuation of 1964 *Solomon Report*, albeit now managed by the Marshallese government itself (Kupferman 2004). This centralization process had as its result to remove the schools from local community control and privileged academic content over the values of the local community. As such "in time, schools became strange places to many community members. They were not only strange places, but teaching values and beliefs contradictory to island lifestyles as well" (Hezel 2002, p. 7).

8.2.2 Teacher Training

One area where the *No Child Left Behind* Act of 2001 standards is not currently being met is in the area of teacher training and certification (Heine and Emesiochi 2007). As of 2007, only 47 % of teachers in the Marshall Islands are certified despite the Ministry of Education introducing significantly lower certification standards than those mandated by the *No Child Left Behind Act* (Heine and Emesiochi 2007), and 40 % of teachers have only a high school education (Kupferman 2004). The failure to meet what may be an unreasonable Western standard has led the Ministry of Education to develop a hybrid solution to the problem that involves the importation of foreign teachers while working to build local teacher training capacity (Kupferman 2004). Volunteer teacher programs from both the United States and Japan, as well as teacher recruitment efforts in Fiji and the Philippines, have attempted to address teacher shortages. While this has increased the number of teachers with post-secondary education, it has failed to address issues related to teacher training capacity, and given that the program is paid for by the Ministry of Education through funding from the Compact of Free Association, it may in fact be contributing to capacity related issues by directing limited resources away from current teacher training programs (Kupferman 2004).

While there are few U.S. Federal grants available for teacher development programs, money has been allocated out of the general education budget funded in large part by Compact of Free Association Funds (Heine and Emesiochi 2007). In recent years, a program has been established with these allocated funds to provide in-service summer training towards an associate's degree through the College of the Marshall Islands. While participation levels have been high, the program has met a number of logistical challenges, particularly in meeting the needs of outer island teachers who often must deal with unreliable transportation to attend the courses. As a result outer islands teachers have lagged behind their urban center counterparts, with nearly 70 % of them having only a high-school diploma compared to 39 % of urban teachers. As Heine and Emesiochi (2007) note,

> Teacher preparation programs across the Pacific Region are modeled on continental U.S. programs where students are generally close to the program sites. For the Pacific islands . . . the logistics of housing, transportation, and family support can discourage teachers from attending. (p. 18)

Perhaps more problematic is the implicit assumption that Western academic standards are the main educational goal, and as such a college-educated Westerner is in a better position to teach Marshallese children than a Marshallese teacher with only a high-school diploma. Such decisions privilege an educational emphasis on academics over cultural values in a way that does not reflect the careful balance that the Ministry of Education seeks in *Ej Ju El Bwe'n Lonjat*.

8.2.3 English

One of the consistent educational approaches throughout the various colonial periods was that each colonizing power set up schools to teach the Marshallese the colonizing language (Hezel 1975). Prior to formal colonization by Europeans and the Japanese, English-speaking missionaries from Hawaii began schools that used English for instruction while the missionaries learned the local languages and began training Marshallese pastors and teachers to take over the mission (Hezel 1985).

While these schools largely outlasted the successive colonial powers, in part because by that time, they were operated primarily by native Marshallese. The use of English in education received its greatest expansion through implementation of the *Solomon Report* (Heine and Emesiochi 2007). Under a new emphasis on Americanization, English became the official medium of instruction in schools (Hezel 1975). Continued fiscal reliance on the United States in the Compact of Free Association has helped to ensure a continued educational emphasis on English in the curriculum (Heine and Emesiochi 2007).

Current educational practice is a transitional bilingual program that emphasizes Marshallese in the early grades with a gradual increase in the amount of English instruction. Heine and Emesiochi (2007) note "In grades 1–3 the MOI [means of instruction] is two-thirds Marshallese and one-third English. By grade four, the MOI is two-thirds English and one-third Marshallese. By grade five, English is the MOI with Marshallese used only in Marshallese and physical education classes" (p. 6).

As Heine and Emesiochi (2007) observe the emphasis on English instruction at the expense of Marshallese in the upper grades has potentially deleterious effects on Marshallese culture itself. "Limiting the teaching of Marshallese in the upper grades to 45 minutes per day curtails student's exposure to higher-level concepts that are central to the culture" (p. 6). English language test scores have not benefited as a result of the English instructional emphasis, in part because of the large numbers of Marshallese teachers who are themselves uncomfortable with teaching in English. This privileging of English language usage disenfranchises native Marshallese teachers who lack English language proficiency. A 2004 Marshall Islands English Language Test for Teachers found that only 33 % could read and write English at an 8th grade level (*Marshall Islands Journal* 2004). As a result large numbers of non-native Marshallese instructors are brought in to teach, which has the effect of further devaluing native Marshallese language and cultural instruction, while reinforcing out of necessity based on available qualified personnel, the use of English only in the classroom.

The solution proposed by the head of the Western Association of Schools and Colleges (WASC) accreditation team conducting accreditation at the College of the Marshall Islands was to recommend that the Ministry of Education begin teaching English from age three (Heine and Emesiochi 2007). The *Ej Ju El Bwe'n Lonjat* report (2008), took a different approach with its third recommendation, "Integrate Marshallese values, culture, language, customs and traditions into formal and non-formal education systems" (p. 9), placing it at odds with WASC's advocacy for the privileging of an English Language academic focus over Marshallese cultural values.[1]

[1] The East West Center just released a news report that starting in 2015 the US will no longer provide funding for Marshallese teachers that are not certified (have at least an AS degree). This will impact, roughly 40 % of the native Marshallese teachers.

8.2.4 Accreditation

Perhaps nowhere has donor policy impacted education in the Marshall Islands more than in issues of accreditation. The College of the Marshall Islands (CMI) is accredited by WASC, which in turn allows it access to U.S. federal educational aid programs. Over half of CMI's budget in 2012 came from tuition fees paid by Pell grants (*Marshall Islands Journal* 2012). Given the extent of CMI's dependence on U.S. federal aid, lack of access to this aid would result in the closing of the college (Woodard 1998). Kupferman (2004) describes the dilemma:

> Without accreditation, CMI loses all rights to US federal funds, including financial assistance for students (primarily in the form of Pell grants from the US department of Education)...Since 95 % of the student body – 580 out of 611 students enrolled in the Spring of 2005 – depends on such aid, CMI would in essence lose its student population, along with the $2.3 million in Pell grants awarded to CMI students annually, and be forced to cease operations. (p. 47)

Because most teacher training in the Marshall Islands is done through CMI, the loss of accreditation would have a ripple effect on education that would be felt in the primary and secondary grades as well (Kupferman 2004). Kupferman (2008) observes, "The driving force behind the College of the Marshall Islands (CMI) is accreditation" (p. 71). So important is U.S. Pell grant funding that the Fiji-based University of the South Pacific is also seeking accreditation for its Marshall Islands campus in large part to obtain access to U.S. aid through the Compact of Free Association for students at that campus (Kupferman 2008).

With access to funds provided by accreditation, however, comes a responsibility to non-Marshallese standards and agencies. The demands of accreditation have led the way in establishing priorities for the college in a number of important areas but have done so with the "use of external consultants to advise and build capacity – a literal 'importing' of technical expertise into our isolated region of the Pacific which has a dearth of such expertise" (Office of the President 2007, p. 1). As a result of the accreditation process, all teaching faculty must now have at a minimum a master's degree (WASC 2007). While provisions are made for the support of current teachers who lack degrees to obtain them, the overall effect of this policy severely limits the ability of CMI to hire Marshallese teachers, who often lack both the degree and the teaching experience being sought.

An additional financial burden created by the accreditation standards was the need to implement a $27 million facilities upgrade plan. The WASC (2007) report notes, "The college has made dramatic changes to its previously woefully inadequate and dangerous campus. A well-managed physical master plan is guiding the changes, and when completed in 2011 will result in a campus that is unrecognizable from what it was in 2006" (p. 12). While facility improvements are important, the prioritization of a significant amount of spending by a cash poor institution to meet standards set by non-Marshallese consultants is problematic. Kupferman (2008) highlights the central issue, "U.S. accreditation, it seems, is the means through which the institution is being reified, for reasons of both funding and a call to implement WASC standards" (p. 71).

8.2.5 *U.S. Standards*

Accrediting agencies are not the only outside influence on CMI. As a part of their receipt of U.S. Compact funds, the college must provide a yearly performance-based budget (PBB). In examining the funding priorities in the 2007 report, Kupferman (2008) notes that the push is toward western standards of excellence, including western business models of organization and structure. The *Progress Report* on accreditation relies heavily on these models and explicitly recognizes the consultation provided by The Association of Governing Boards, a Washington, DC consulting organization, in implementing them (Office of the President 2007). The educational disconnect described by Hezel (1975) is further perpetuated by academic and organizational standards created by non-Marshallese and implemented by non-Marshallese administrators.

8.3 Positive Developments

8.3.1 *Finding a Place for Marshallese*

There are, however, hopeful signs. As a part of its 2012 *Strategic Plan,* CMI continued its four major vision components from 2007:

1. Be a source of national pride and hope;
2. Provide tailored, quality educational opportunities;
3. Provide a window on the global community; and
4. Serve as a center for research and inquiry for national advancement (College of the Marshall Islands 2012, p. 2).

Included in the strategic plan for the implementation of this vision for the first time, however, was Supporting Institutional Goal 4.3: "The College of the Marshall Islands considers Marshallese knowledge as legitimate, and encourages its transmission, development, and application both within and outside the classroom, throughout and beyond the curriculum, and in alternative spaces that do not yet exist within the college structure" (College of the Marshall Islands 2012, p. 7). This institutional goal, though listed after the goals on facility improvement and ecological responsiveness, recognizes the important place of Marshallese learning within the college community, even as it recognizes that such learning has not to date not been emphasized as much as it should have been.

8.3.2 *Vocational Programs*

In recent years there has also been a greater emphasis on vocational programs, as recommended by the 2008 *Ej Ju El Bwe'n Lonjat* report. A vocational training program was begun in 2010 with the support of the Republic of China to provide certifications in plumbing and electronics (Rowa and Laukon 2011). U.S. Compact funding has also supported the *Waan Aelon in Majel*, traditional canoe building and navigation program that is involved in the teaching of life skills (Marty 2013). In September of 2012, a Life Skills Academy (LSA) was opened by the Ministry of Education to replace the National Vocational Training Institute. The LSA is a mix of academics and life skills training that is designed to get participants a general educational development (GED) tests equivalency degree coupled with vocational training that will lead to employment (Hosia 2013).

8.4 Conclusion

Donor funding of education in the Marshall Islands has been used to support an educational structure that is in many ways an alien imposition. The changing nature of Marshallese society has, however, made a high-quality, academic education indispensible for the future prosperity of both the nation and its citizens. The 2008 *Ej Ju El Bwe'n Lonjat* report seeks to strike a delicate balance between Marshallese knowledge and culture and academic excellence. Recent developments in Marshallese education offer hopeful signs that the long-neglected Marshallese component of education is finding a space in the educational program. What is important for its continued growth is a recognition of the role that donor funding can play in either supporting or upending that delicate balance.

References

Aiyar, S. (2008). Small states: Not handicapped and under-aided, but advantaged and over-aided. *Cato Journal, 28*(3), 449–478.

Belau, T. (1971). *The Solomon report: America's ruthless blueprint for the assimilation of Micronesia*. Berkley: Friends of Micronesia.

College of the Marshall Islands. (2012). *Strategic Plan 2012–2017*. http://cmi.edu/images/stories/strategic-planning/cmistrategicplandraft03-19-12.pdf. Accessed on 18 Aug 2013.

Compact of Free Association Amendments Act of 2003. Pub. L. No. 108–188. http://rmiembassyus.org/Compact/Compact%20Public%20Law%20108-188.pdf. Accessed on 18 Aug 2013.

Conklin, N. (1984). *Culture and education in Micronesia*. Portland: Northwest Regional Educational Lab.

CMI needs to cut costs in a timely manner. (2012, December 28). *Marshall Islands Journal*, p. 4.

Donahue, T. (1998). *Achieving educational excellence in Majuro, RMI*. Honolulu: Pacific Regional Education Laboratory.

Dorrance, J. (1992). *The United States and the Pacific Islands*. Westport: Praeger.

Hanlon, D. (1998). *Remaking Micronesia: Discourses over development in a Pacific territory 1944–1982*. Honolulu: University of Hawaii Press.

Heck, R. (1996). Leadership and culture: Conceptual and methodological issues in comparing models across cultural settings. *Journal of Educational Administration, 34*(5), 74–97.

Heine, H., & Emesiochi, M. (2007). *Preparing and licensing high quality teachers in Pacific region jurisdictions*. Honolulu: Pacific Regional Education Laboratory.

Hezel, F. (1975). In search of a home: Colonial education in Micronesia. In *Topics of culture and learning* (pp. 125–131). Honolulu: East-West Center. http://micsem.org/pubs/articles/education/frames/insearchfr.htm. Accessed on 18 Aug 2013.

Hezel, F. (1983). *The first taint of civilization: A history of the Caroline and Marshall islands in pre-colonial days, 1521–1885*. Honolulu: University of Hawaii Press.
Hezel, F. (1984). A brief economic history of Micronesia. In *Past achievements and future possibilities* (pp. 11–62). Majuro: Micronesian Seminar.
Hezel, F. (1985). *Schools in Micronesia prior to American administration*. Micronesian Seminar. http://www.micsem.org/pubs/articles/education/frames/schlmicfr.htm. Accessed on 18 Aug 2013.
Hezel, F. (1991). Recolonizing islands and decolonizing history. *Journal of the Pacific Society, 13*(4), 1–6. http://micsem.org/pubs/articles/historical/frames/recoldecolfr.htm. Accessed on 18 Aug 2013.
Hezel, F. (1995). *Strangers in their own land: A century of colonial rule in the Caroline and Marshall Islands*. Honolulu: University of Hawaii Press.
Hezel, F. (2001). *The new shape of old island cultures: A half century of social change in Micronesia*. Honolulu: University of Hawaii Press.
Hezel, F. (2002). *Taking responsibility for our schools: A series of four articles on education in Micronesia*. Honolulu: Pacific Regional Education Laboratory.
Hosia, H. (2013). LSA gives new look to MOE. *Marshall Islands Journal, 44*(7), 24.
Johnson, G. (2011). Marshalls relies heavily on US funding in new budget. *Marinas Variety*. http://www.mvariety.com/component/content/article?id=39631. Accessed on 18 Aug 2013.
Kupferman, D. (2004). *Jelalokjen* in flux: Pitfalls and prospects of contextualizing teacher training programs in the Marshall Islands. *Journal of Educational Studies, I*(1), 42–54.
Kupferman, D. (2008). No Western agenda left behind: A comparative analysis of higher education institutions in the Republic of the Marshall Islands. *The International Journal of Learning, I*(2), 69–77.
Langmoir, P. (2000). *EFA assessment country report: Marshall Islands*. UNESCO. http://www.unesco.org/education/wef/countryreports/marshalls/rapport_1.html. Accessed on 18 Aug 2013.
Low, M., Penland, D., & Heine, H. (2005). *The language question in Pacific education: The case of the Republic of the Marshall Islands*. Honolulu: Pacific Regional Education Laboratory.
Marty, I. (2013, February 15). Three cheers for WAM grads. *Marshall Islands Journal, 44*(7), 4.
Ministry of Education. (2008). *Ej Ju El Bwe'n Lonjat: Rethinking Education in the Marshall Islands Conference, Summary Report of Conference Activities & Action Plan*. http://www.yokwe.net/ydownloads/Reports08/RethinkingReport08.pdf. Accessed on 18 Aug 2013.
Office of the President. (2007). *Progress report prepared for the accrediting commission for community and junior colleges*. http://www.cmi.edu/images/stories/accreditation/accjc/Progress_Report_15Oct2007.pdf. Accessed on 18 Aug 2013.
Only one third of teachers pass test. (2004, October 8). *Marshall Islands Journal*, p. 3.
Pikcunas, D. D. (1991). Is the US perpetuating the welfare state in Micronesia? *Conservative Review, 2*, 7–11.
Rowa, A., & Laukon, A. (2011). *Marshall Islands men get vocational job training*. http://yokwe.net/index.php?module=News&func=display&sid=2770. Accessed on 18 Aug 2013.
Spenneman, D. R. (1992). *Bwebwenatoon etto: A collection of Marshallese legends and traditions*. Majuro Atoll: Republic of the Marshall Islands, Minsitry [sic] of Internal Affairs, Historic Preservation Office.
Taafiki, I., Kabua-Fowler, M., & Thaman, R. (2006). *Traditional medicine of the Marshall Islands: The women, the plants, the treatment*. Suva: University of the South Pacific, IPS Publications.
WASC. (2007). *Progress report: College of the Marshall Islands evaluation team visit, December 4–7, 2007*. http://www.cmi.edu/images/stories/accreditation/accjc/Progress_Repprt_4_7Dec2007.pdf. Accessed on 18 Aug 2013.
Woodard, C. (1998, July 24). 3 small Pacific nations fear loss of Pell grants could wipe out their colleges. *The Chronicle of Higher Education*, p. A33.

Chapter 9
Education and Gender Rights in Latin America

Ezequiel Gomez Caride

Abstract The study explores the development of gender rights in Latin America's legal and educational fields from the 1980s –when the previous legal frameworks were first implemented– to the late 2000s, when Argentina, Chile, and Uruguay reformed their educational laws. In a relatively small number of years, Argentina (2006), Chile (2009) and Uruguay (2008) changed their national education legislation, including gender as a relevant element of the law for the first time. The investigation analyzes, from a poststructuralist perspective, the situation that "suddenly" brought gender to the forefront as a major issue for educational policy in the southern part of Latin America. The chapter describes how gender was able to emerge as a category only when three elements – a set of powerful institutions represented by international organizations, a vast corpus of knowledge attached with a salvific rhetoric, and a set of local experts represented by women's non-governmental organizations – were able to construct a language about gender that compelled national stakeholders to include gender rights in their educational national laws.

For 20 years the educational legislation in the South Cone (Argentina, Chile and Uruguay) did not take into account gender rights. Surprisingly, in the past few years the three countries changed their educational laws including a vast array of gender rights. In a relatively short amount of years, Argentina (2006), Chile (2009) and Uruguay (2008) changed their national education legislation. Through a discourse analysis this study analyzes the development of gender rights in Latin America's legal educational scenario from the 1980s when the previous laws were first implemented to the 2000s when the countries changed their educational laws. Following Popkewitz (1997), this "linguistic turn refers to a focus on language as a constitutive element in the construction of social life and 'identity'" (p. 136). The study aspires to explore gender feminism in Latin America rather than women. I focus exclusively

E. Gomez Caride (✉)
School of Education, University of Wisconsin Madison, Madison, WI, USA
e-mail: ezequielgomezcaride@gmail.com

C.A. Brown (ed.), *Globalization, International Education Policy and Local Policy Formation*, Policy Implications of Research in Education 5,
DOI 10.1007/978-94-007-4165-2_9

on the national laws of education of Argentina, Chile, and Uruguay since they illustrate how politics played out in the educational sphere. My questions are oriented to explain the situation that "suddenly" brought gender to the forefront as a major issue of educational policy. Hence, my research studies what conditions allowed legislators to enact gender rights in the last few years? To what extent international organizations and non-governmental organizations (NGOs) were crucial institutions in this emergence of gender rights?

In order to analyze gender emergence in Latin America I organized the study with six sections. First, I explain the understanding of gender deployed throughout the study. Second, I described the methodological approach. Third, I briefly described the genesis of women's struggle for education in Latin America. Forth, I turned to the political context of each country and tracked gender development through an analysis of educational laws. Later, my project aspired to study how international organizations and local NGOs influenced educational national laws in relation to gender rights. My project then analyzed the role of specific international organizations regarding gender and looked at the Latin American women's international meeting of NGOs called *Encounters*. I did not establish a dichotomy between international actors versus local stakeholders. On the contrary, recent literature regarding the role of non-state actors promoting public policies "serves to break down the oft-used analytical dichotomy between what goes on in states (the domestic realm) and what goes on outside them (the international realm). In this new literature, the borders of states are treated as potentially extremely porous" (True and Mintrom 2001, p. 50). Studying this range of discourses in the implementation of educational policy allowed me to consider the development of gender in the Latin American scenario as a category to be seen and acted upon. In the development of educational legislation, I also came to see the very development of gender itself as a category that suddenly was legislated in Latin America.

Joan Scott in *Gender and the Politics of History* (1988) provides a useful definition of gender as a "constitutive element of social relationships based on perceived differences between the sexes, and gender is a primary way of signifying relationships of power" (p. 42). Additionally, she goes further with four interrelated elements: culturally available symbols that evoke multiple representations; normative concepts that set forth interpretations of the meaning of symbols; a reference to social institutions and organizations that goes beyond kinship; a subjective identity that includes a historical point of view. This theoretical standpoint is the basis of current gender studies.

Since my study analyzes the development of educational national legislations, I focus on "the normative concepts that set forth interpretations" (Scott 1988, p. 42), that is, I look at how the legislation depicts gender or not as a category. Following Scott, these concepts are "expressed in religious, educational, scientific, legal and political doctrines and typically take form of fixed binary opposition" (Scott 1988, p. 43). Hence, the analysis of educational laws is a suitable space to explore the normative concepts about gender that set forth interpretations in Argentina, Chile and Uruguay. Finally, my findings do not have the aspiration of being full and closed answers; on the contrary, their role is more like the unveiling of new viewpoints that help to start to see the landscape from a broader perspective to foster a deeper understanding of how social changes occurred in Latin America.

9.1 Methodology

The particular situation in which my object of study is situated includes a vast array of entities, levels and relationships. Therefore, I examined laws, international organizations, and NGOs using a methodology that considered the overlapping relation between the set of practices and the regime of truth. The normative influence of the educational laws is not disentangled from the everyday life of schools, and subjects and vice versa. In fact, borders are blurred and distinctions such as local experts/international experts or international organizations/local organizations are not clear. All these complexities are relevant in the selection of my theoretical framework. I deployed poststructuralist authors such as Ian Hacking and Michel Foucault to study how, after decades of silence, in the last few years gender was forged as a category that refers to a specific kind of people in the educational laws. Applying Hacking's (2006) five ideas of dynamic nominalism to gender, I explored the notion of gender in Latin America as the "making up" of a specific kind of subject. I explored only three features of Hacking's framework: (a) the institutions, mainly international organizations, (b) the knowledge produced or available regarding gender, and (c) the experts, represented by women's NGOs.

In order to frame the emergence of gender rights in Latin America first I focused on the political conditions that at a certain time and place make gender rights possible in the young democracies of South America. Following Foucault,

> It was not a question of showing how these objects were for a long time hidden before finally being discovered [in this study gender]....It was a matter of showing by what conjunctions a whole set of practices – from the moment they become coordinated with a regime of truth- was able to make what does not exist (madness, disease, delinquency, sexuality, etcetera), nonetheless become something (...) It is not an illusion since it is precisely a set of practices, real practices, which established it and thus imperiously marks it out in reality (2008, p. 19).

As I demonstrate, in the first cluster of educational laws gender was completely ignored. The goal was to show how, suddenly in the last few years gender became a reality in the Latin American educational scenario.

In order to track the whole picture of gender in Latin America, social policy should have a broader perspective of analysis as opposed to an analysis of single institutions or actors (Sabatier 1991, p. 148). Certainly, studying gender evolution in Latin America, isolated from international organizations and its role, would undermine the complex process of gender emergence. However, the fact that international organizations or NGOs do have a role in creating the category of gender does not imply a linear causality. In the same way, gender appeared in Latin America neither as a mere repetition of international actors or as a unique and totally isolated Latin American concept. Finally, historicizing the cultural practices that produce patterns of thought about gender also provided a way of interpreting the relation of the global and the local, as well as the universal to the particular (Popkewitz 2005, p. 32).

9.2 Looking to the Past, Gender and Education in Latin America

Women's education in Latin America evolved in three stages: (1) the initial or colonial period, (2) the debate around the content of women's education, and finally (3) the establishment of educational institutions that admitted females (Miller 1991, p. 36). In the colonial epoch, the education of the daughters of the elite usually was done by private tutors and the vocational training for poorer women was usually organized by female Catholic charitable societies (Miller 1991, p. 39). The debate about the education for women changed drastically from a *marianism* perspective (*from Medieval cult of Mary*) in the sixteenth century with ideals of purity and chastity to a broader curriculum in the eighteenth century that included religious instruction, literacy, music, French and embroidery (Miller 1991). It was with the emergence of the national states around the mid-1800s that through Societies of Beneficence government reformers such as the Argentinean Bernardino Rivadavia established the first public elementary school for girls. However, only at the end of the nineteenth century with the introduction of government supported schools that admitted women from the emergent middle class and trained them to become teachers, did women finally acquire a path to social advancement education.

The process of greater access of women to secondary education and universities started between 1910 and 1940. This tendency was reinforced after 1945 when "female education in Latin America became a particular focus of international agencies such as: the *Comision Interamericana de Mujeres (CIM)* and UNESCO" (Miller 1991, p. 60). The fact that since the mid-twentieth century international organizations have a relevant role fostering educational opportunities for women cannot be underestimated in the history of women's search for education in Latin America.

9.3 Recent Political Context and Educational Legislation

The first set of analyzed documents for this study were the educational laws that appeared after the military regimes in Argentina, Uruguay and Chile. However, in the case of Chile, the educational law was promulgated during the last days of the military regime before the transition to democracy. The second set of laws could be considered as the product of settled democracies because these laws were promulgated in the three countries after several decades of democratic regimes. Certainly, my study did not consider these educational laws as the unique set of normative concepts that completely explain gender in Latin America. Neither did I try to circumscribe the variety or diversity of possible manifestations of gender rights only with the analysis of the educational legislation. In the next section, I divided the analysis of each country in three sections. First, I depicted a brief political context, next I described the first national educational laws with respect to gender, and finally I examined the current educational law as related to gender rights.

9.4 Uruguay

9.4.1 Description of Political Context

In Uruguay at the beginning of the 1980s, the politics started a slow process of political openness after the military strike in June of 1973. In March of 1985, Uruguay returned to a democracy with the assumption of Julio Maria Sanguinetti, from the Red Party. The institutional environment at the time was tumultuous, but Uruguay has a long tradition of civil rights and respect to the laws. The Law for the Emergency of the Education (15,739) passed in 1985 in this political context. Finally, Tabare Vazquez, an oncologist trained in Paris, former Major of Montevideo, with the leftist political coalition assumed the presidency in 2005 defeating the traditional Red and White parties. After a complex arrangement, difficulties and criticism from the right and the extreme left, the majority of the government coalition with the exception of the Communist Party passed the educational law in December of 2008.

9.4.1.1 Gender in the Law of Emergency for Teaching (LET) 15,739 (1985)

Gender is the main concept absent in the first Uruguayan Law of education. However, I found a broad enunciation against discrimination: "The National Administration of Public Education (ANEP) will: promote the respect of convictions and beliefs of others; foment in the students skills related to its social and civic responsibility and; eliminate all forms of intolerance" (LET, Ch. 2, art. 6, 1985).[1] After analyzing the law, I found several general enumerations of rights but gender does not appear specifically in any enumeration of rights nor in guidelines or in principles.

[1] Translations of the Laws are mine.

9.4.1.2 Gender in the Law of General Education of Uruguay (LGE) 18,437 (2008)

A very different picture appeared in the new educational legislation. The law described the principles of Public Education affirming, "[the State] will promote the transformation of discriminatory stereotypes related to age, gender, race, ethnic or sexual orientation." (LGE, Ch. 4, art. 18) Additionally, the Law established nine principles that permeate all the different levels and curriculum of the National System of Education. Some examples of these principles are: human rights education, environmental education, artistic education and sexual education. Later, the Law stated: "Sexual education will have as a goal to provide adequate tools to promote in teachers and students critical reflection regarding gender relations and sexuality for a responsible enjoyment of the latter" (LGE, Ch. 7, art. 40).

Then, when the document enumerates the rights and obligations of students, mothers, or fathers, the article says "pregnant students will have right to continue with their studies, especially to access and stay in the educational institutions, to receive supplementary support and to have absences before and after the birth without risking their regular attendance requirement" (LGE, Ch. 9, art. 74). Another interesting remark appeared when the document referred to the parents. The law expresses an original enumeration of the actors. The law referred to "the rights of mothers, fathers or responsible" (LGE, Ch. 9, art. 75).

Undoubtedly, gender now had a drastic manifestation in the educational arena of Uruguay. In the first law of education, gender was absent; however, the new law has a detailed description and statements regarding the goal of sexual education to promote critical reflection of gender relations in teachers and students. In addition, the State appeared as an active actor that had to eliminate gender or sexual stereotypes that might imply discrimination.

9.5 Argentina

9.5.1 Description of Political Context

In 1983, democracy returned to Argentina after 7 years of military rule. Raul Alfonsin of the Radical Party was elected president on the 1983 elections and started to reorganize the State. However, democracy was still weak and Alfonsin suffered several military strike attempts and was compelled to pass an amnesty law to finish the trials to military authorities. In a huge economic crisis, Carlos Saul Menem of the Peronista Party won the elections and assumed the presidency in 1989. The government of Carlos Saul Menem implemented a comprehensive liberal program. In the educational area his government approved three different laws: the Decentralization Law (1992), the Higher Education Law (1995) and the Federal Law of Education-LFE- (1993), which was the most comprehensive one. Those laws promoted a vast transformation of the educational system.

Within this neoliberal ideology the country ended in a huge political crisis in 2001 with unemployment rising to 25 %, street riots, six presidents in 2 weeks, and an international economic default. Nestor Kirchner assumed the presidency in 2003 with a leftist political program. In December of 2006, Nestor Kirchner promulgated a new law of Education. After an extended debate between different actors of society, including teachers unions and media, the new legislation promoted a change from the previous neo-liberal educational law.

9.5.1.1 Gender in the Federal Law of Education of Argentina (LFE) 24,195 (1995)

The LFE depicted a broad enunciation against discrimination. The law aimed for "the concretion of equal opportunities and possibilities for all the citizens and, the rejection of every form of discrimination" (LFE, Ch. 1, art. 5). The same article stated "the triumph over all the discriminatory stereotypes in pedagogical materials" (LFE, Ch. 1, art. 5). However, the actors involved or the subjects of such efforts were not defined. A point to remark is that in several sections the Law referred to both the masculine and feminine, for example (boys and girls) (LFE, Ch. 7, art. 40). However, the educational law did not refer specifically to gender. Additionally, the text did not tackle any specific mention of sexuality or sexual education. Furthermore, since the law does not mention any specific type of discrimination, the goal of fighting discrimination seemed blurred and utopian. Therefore, after analyzing the Law, I can state that in spite of the sexual identification of students (boys and girls) gender did not emerge as a relevant issue tackled by the law, at least in an explicit way.

9.5.1.2 Gender in the National Law of Education, Argentina (LNA) 26,206 (2006)

A different portrait emerged in the National Law of Education. One of the new goals of education is "to ensure the same educational conditions respecting the differences between persons, without accepting gender discrimination or other forms of discrimination" (LNA, Ch. 2, art. 11). Additionally, article 11 "promotes…the elimination of all the forms of discrimination in all the educational levels".

Regarding gender and cultural diversity, in the section of Continual Education of Adults and Youth, the Law affirmed that the curriculum and the institutional approach of schools should have as a goal "the incorporation of gender equality and cultural diversity" (LNA, Ch. 9, art. 48). Furthermore, regarding Rural Education, the Law affirmed that one of its goals is "to promote equal opportunities and possibilities for all ensuring gender equality" (LNA, Ch. 10, art. 50). In the same section, the document states that "the [Secretary of Education] will organize non-formal educational services that enhance job training and cultural promotion of rural population, focusing on the conditions of women" (LNA, Ch. 10, art. 51). Moreover, the Law established that the Secretary of Education will promote policies oriented to "battle situations…of gender discrimination" (LNA, Ch. 2, art. 79).

In addition, the Law established that "the State will guarantee all the material and cultural conditions necessary for students success independently of their social background, geographic location, gender or cultural identity" (LNA, Ch. 1, art. 84). Furthermore, the Law stated that all the different jurisdictions of the State "should include materials and strategies that promote relationships grounded in equality, solidarity, and respect between every sex in agreement with the *Convention on the Elimination of All forms of Discrimination against Women* and other Laws related to women's rights" (LNA, Ch. 2, art. 92).

In sum, the National Law of Education took a strong stance for gender rights. This effort can be tracked in the active role that the Law provided to the State and jurisdictions to combat gender discrimination, the inclusion of strategies and curriculum related to gender issues, and finally the incorporation of others Laws (24,632; 26,171) related to women's rights.

9.6 Chile

9.6.1 Description of Political Context

The last day of the military regime in Chile (1990) the Organic Constitutional Law of Education (LOCE) was promulgated by Pinochet's administration. However, the LOCE continued in force until April 2009 during the presidency of Michelle Bachelet, probably because of the difficulties of gaining political majority support in such a heated area.

The new Law of Education (2009) is the result of a special commission formed after the "Penguins Revolution", named for the high school student riots during 2006. Those riots ended with the resignation of the Minister of Education, Martin Zilic. The students' goals were basically to win more support from the State for public education and reduce the marketization of public education. Since the Chilean political system makes very difficult any drastic change, the current law was the result of a complex arrangement reached by Bachelet's government with the right leaning parties.

9.6.1.1 Gender in the Organic Constitutional Law of Education (LOCE) 18,962 (1990)

The LOCE can be described as an educational law that potentially could produce spaces in favor of gender discrimination. In the LOCE there were no references to gender or sexual education. The only right that referred to gender established that "pregnancy and maternity will not be impediment to access and permanence in educational institutions whatever the level and educational institutions should accommodate for these cases" (LOCE, Ch.1, art. 2). Later, the Law affirmed that "the teaching provided by educational institutions do not have limitations other that those imposed by moral, good practices, the public order and the national security" (LOCE, Ch.1, art. 6). Consequently, gender was not considered in the legislation and in fact, the emergence of gender rights could be obstructed by the diffuse and equivocal enunciation of terms such as "good practices" or "moral".

9.6.1.2 Gender in the Chilean General Law of Education (LCGE) 20,370 (2009)

In contrast, the new National Law of Education affirmed that the State should "guarantee the equality of opportunities and inclusive education ensuring specifically the reduction of inequalities resulted of economic, social, ethnic, gender or geographical location" (LCGE, Ch.1, art. 4). In addition, the Law affirmed that teachers and other school staff should have moral sufficiency, and one of the requirements regarding moral competence is that teachers had not been convicted because of domestic violence (LCGE, Ch.3, art. 46). Besides, the Law established as a goal of elementary education the recognition of equal rights for men and women (LCGE, Ch.3, art. 46). In sum, the recent law introduced gender issues with a very different scope. This inclusion goes beyond the enunciation of pregnant students' rights of the LOCE, reaching issues of gender discrimination and domestic violence.

9.7 Gender Eruption in Latin American Legislation

Throughout the three national laws I described, a crescendo of gender crystalized in the new educational legislation. This process goes from a complete absence in Uruguay or the weak appearance of women's pregnancy rights in Chile and Argentina prior to 2000, to a much wider and potent scope of gender rights beginning in the mid 2000s. After almost two decades of democracy in the three countries, only in the last few years did gender become *legislated* as a topic in the educational national laws. Consequently, the expected questions are: Why suddenly in the last few years do I find an eruption of gender rights in the educational legislations? Is this a sudden appearance in the laws or is this a progressive process of accumulation? Is this process determined by the international organizations or is it more influenced by horizontal pressures from NGOs? Or, are both international organizations and NGOs acting simultaneously? If so, to what extent does each one influence social policy regarding gender?

9.8 International Organizations

In Latin America, international organizations were key players in the emergence of gender rights. In a globalized world seemingly most of the research accepts the relevance of international organizations. However, it is not clear how this influence is absorbed by national States. Throughout the last decades a significant corpus of knowledge regarding gender was created in developed countries and in international agencies. As I mentioned earlier, already during the 1950s gender had become a target for international organizations. In order to track the influence of international organizations, I focused on the work of UNESCO, the World Bank and the Organization for Education and Cooperation (OECD) because the undeniable impact of these institutions with their vast resources reflects the role of such international organizations.

Regarding gender, the scope and diffusion of activities and documents issued by international organizations is almost overwhelming, ranging from gender e-conferences to the UNESCO World Atlas of Gender Equality in Education. In fact, UNESCO has a special Division for Gender Equality that "carries out capacity-building and coordinates cutting edge research in order to provide informed policy advice to Member States" (UNESCO n/a). The website of the Division for Gender Equality includes resources such as publications, multimedia, useful links, conventions, declarations, and events. Currently, one of the main policies of UNESCO is *The Education for All Goals*. These goals have a clear stance in favor of reducing gender disparities by 2015. For example, the fifth goal aspires to "eliminate gender disparities in primary and secondary education by 2005, and achieve gender equality in education by 2015, with a focus on ensuring girls' full and equal access to and achievement in basic education of good quality" (UNESCO n/a). Moreover, UNESCO promotes worldwide events like the International Day for the Elimination of Violence against Women.

In a similar vein, since the 1980s' gender has become a pressing topic at the World Bank. The World Bank has a division called Gender and Development. According to the World Bank website the strategy of the World Bank to foster gender equality is through:

> lending and grants, and knowledge and analysis. Only in the last five years (2006–2010) more than USD 65 billion, or 37 percent of the World Bank's lending and grants, were allocated to gender-informed operations in education, health, access to land, financial and agricultural services, jobs, and infrastructure" (Implications of World Development Report 2012).

The amount of money is significant and more so if it is oriented to developing countries. As an example, during the period of 1999–2005 the World Bank lent more than $5.5 billon only to girls' educational programs ("IDA and Gender" 2009). Additionally, the World Bank has specific policies in almost 90 countries oriented to achieve *Education for All* goals.

Finally, the OECD has a Division called Gender equality and Women's empowerment that provides articles, statistics, events, reports, policy briefs, etc. In order to foster gender equality OECD has launched an interdisciplinary project called "Gender Initiative" oriented to "strengthen gender equality in education, employment and entrepreneurship" (OECD 2012). This initiative is a comprehensive project, and some of its goals are to produce knowledge about gender equality and it barriers, establish standard indicators to measure progress in gender areas, and to draw conclusions for policymakers.

All these discourses and resources construct a travelling corpus of knowledge and influence countries and their policies. As a remarkable note, gender issues are present as a key factor to foster development in most of the documents issued by international organizations. Yet, at the same time, this knowledge from international organizations is commonly presented in Latin American countries within a salvation narrative. In a way this international corpus of knowledge acts as a religious Decalogue that aims to show the right paths countries have to follow to achieve "salvation" or "development". Certainly,

> The social and educational sciences have embodied a redemptive culture; that is, science is to save and rescue the child and society….The roles of science and the scientist are sanctioned in a way that was previously reserved for religious cosmologies of social and personal change. (Popkewitz 1998, p. 2)

This salvific rhetoric related to international organizations and its policies enhance the impact of this corpus of knowledge produced by international organizations. At the same moment, this salvific rhetoric makes difficult the critical analysis of such knowledge produced by international organizations.

9.9 Non-governmental Organizations

Throughout the last few decades the wide scope and variety of NGOs related to gender in the three analyzed countries created a corpus of information beyond the scope of this chapter. Therefore, in order to analyze the role of NGOs I focused on an international gathering called *Encounters* that acted as a buffer of dozens of NGOs related to gender organizations from Latin America. Since the first meeting in 1981 in Colombia, this gathering has taken place on a biennial or triennial basis in different countries of Latin America. One interesting feature of these *Encounters* is the criteria of self-financing "to deflect any suggestion that the *Encounter* was being manipulated by outside interests" (Miller 1991, p. 218). The aim of the Encounters is to participate in shaping a real Latin American perspective regarding gender. These spaces are highly relevant because they "have served as critical transnational sites in which local activist have refashioned and renegotiated identities, discourses, and practices distinctive of the region's feminism" (Alvarez et al. 2003, p. 537). Because the flux of information (experiences and strategies) has flowed from different Latin American countries, these international gatherings also reoriented movement practices, cultural discourses, and State policies (Alvarez et al. 2003, 540). The relevance of transnational networking has been described as "the primary force driving the diffusion of gender-mainstreaming bureaucracies" (True and Mintrom 2001, p. 50). The case of Latin America's recent history confirms the importance of transnational networking.

However, this aim of autonomy of NGOs is balanced many times since funding usually comes from international organizations. Just as an example, one of the most prestigious Chilean NGOs that works on topics about gender (*Humanas*), points in its web page to seven main donors. All the seven are international organizations such as UNESCO or the European Community.

Furthermore, they are more combative than international organizations in their attitude towards government. NGOs are often closer to local situations and serve as watch dogs and policy advocates shaming national and local governments that do not achieve international standards regarding human rights (Suárez et al. 2009, p. 209). This closer relationship with local stakeholders makes NGOs able to produce specific interventions in relevant political moments. For example, in Argentina, the *Argentinean Network of Gender Science and Technology* (RAGCyT) organized conferences during the legislative debate (2006) with the explicit goal of including gender perspectives in the new Argentinean educational law. Finally, "feminists not only increasingly entered the State apparatus and mainstream parties but also began providing the civil society–based component of feminist policy advocacy and research by founding NGOs" (Lebon 1993, 1998; Alvarez 1999; Alvarez et al. 2003, p. 548).

Following these insights, gender NGOs were able to construct grounded strategies and to impact effectively in the Latin America political scenario providing experts and pressing legislators and stakeholders. In this regard, the fact that women's groups were perceived by politicians as appealing to groups of voters certainly influenced their receptivity and desire to comply with them (Nelson 1996).

9.10 Conclusion

The political conditions during the studied period of each country were very different; however, I find a shared revision process of educational legislation in recent years in Argentina (2006), Uruguay (2008), and Chile (2009). In the three countries, I uncovered a crescendo of gender rights during the last few years. This process goes from a complete absence in Uruguay or the discrete appearance of women's pregnancy "rights" in Chile and Argentina to a much wider and potent spectrum of gender rights in the current legislation. However, this progress was recently crystallized after several years and different democratic governments. After more than two decades of democracy in the three countries, only in the last few years does gender become a legislative topic. I discovered that the enunciation of gender rights in Latin America was the result of decades of struggles that went beyond the educational scenario. The educational laws help to show this complex historical process of gender rights.

The key outcome of these educational laws is the recognition of women as subjects beyond pregnancy. In her last chapter of *Ser Política en Chile* (1990), Kirkwood states that "the feminist movement in Latin America has almost a decade,…but everywhere it is starting the conversion of women into subjects" (p. 235). The analysis of the educational laws showed that only in the recent educational laws did women become a recognized as subject by the States. Previously, only pregnant women were considered. Thus, in the case of pregnant woman, a specific situation was being considered, the pregnancy and not a complete subject. This subject status gained was a previous condition to receive any right. Without a subject of rights any formulation of rights or obligations at the legislative level was impossible. Therefore, the appearance in the scenario of woman as an individual subject is a crucial result since it produces as an outcome gender right's recognition from the State. This recognition of the woman as a subject of rights presented in the current laws through different abovementioned examples is of utmost importance in the development of gender rights in the three countries.

In sum, following Hacking's (2006) framework, gender was able to emerge as a category only when these three elements – a set of powerful institutions represented by international organizations, a vast corpus of knowledge attached with a salvific rhetoric, and local experts represented by women's NGOs – were able to produce a language about gender that compelled national stakeholders to include gender rights in their educational national laws. In doing so, a process of slow accumulation better explains the making up of gender and the role of international organizations and NGOs in the educational laws of Latin America.

References

Alvarez, S. E. (1999). Advocating feminism: The Latin American Feminist NGO 'Boom'. *International Feminist Journal of Politics, 2*(1), 181–209.

Alvarez, S. E., Friedman, E. J., Beckman, E., Blackwell, M., Chinchilla, N. S., Lebon, N., Navarro, M., & Tobar, M. R. (2003, January 1). Encountering Latin American and Caribbean feminisms. *Signs, 28*(2), 537–579.

Foucault, M., & Collège de France. (2008). *The birth of biopolitics: Lectures at the Collège De France, 1978–79*. Basingstoke: Palgrave Macmillan.

Hacking, I. (2006, August 17). Making up people. *London Review of Books*. p. 23–26.

IDA and Gender: Working Toward Greater Equality. (2009). Retrieved from http://siteresources.worldbank.org/IDA/Resources/IDA-Gender.pdf

Implications of World Development Report. (2012). *Gender equality and development for the World Bank group* (2011). Retrieved from http://siteresources.worldbank.org/DEVCOMMINT/Documentation/23004019/DC2011-0011%28E%29WDR2012_Gender.pdf

Kirkwood, J. (1990). *Ser Política En Chile: Los Nudos De La Sabiduría Feminista* (2nd ed.). Santiago: Editorial Cuarto Propio.

Lebon, N. (1993). The Brazilian Feminist movement in the post-constitutional era: Assessing the impact of the rise of Feminist non-governmental organizations. *Florida Journal of Anthropology, 18*, 17–26.

Lebon, N. (1998). *The labor of love and bread: Volunteer and professionalized activism in the São Paulo women's health movement*. Ph.D. dissertation, University of Florida.

Miller, F. (1991). *Latin American women and the search for social justice*. Hanover: University Press of New England.

Nelson, S. (1996, January 1). Constructing and negotiating gender in women's police stations in Brazil. *Latin American Perspectives, 23*(1), 131–148.

OECD. (2012). *Final report MCM, gender equality in education, employment and entrepreneurship* (2012). Retrieved from http://www.oecd.org/els/family/50423364.pdf

Popkewitz, T. S. (1997, March). The production of reason and power: Curriculum history and intellectual traditions. *Journal of Curriculum Studies, 29*(2), 131–164. doi:10.1080/002202797184107.

Popkewitz, T. S. (1998). The culture of redemption and the administration of freedom as research. *Review of Educational Research, 68*(1), 1–34. doi:10.2307/1170688.
Popkewitz, T. S. (2005). *Inventing the modern self and John Dewey: Modernities and the travelling of pragmatism in education*. New York: Palgrave Macmillan.
Sabatier, P. (1991). Towards a better theory of policy process. *PS: Political Science and Politics, 24*(2), 147–156.
Scott, J. W. (1988). *Gender and the politics of history* (Gender and culture). New York: Columbia University Press.
Suárez, D. F., Ramirez, F. O., & Koo, J.-W. (2009, July 1). UNESCO and the associated schools project: Symbolic affirmation of world community, international understanding, and human rights. *Sociology of Education, 82*(3), 197–216.
The National Chilean General Law of Education 20,370 (2009).
The National Federal Law of Education of Argentina 24,195 (1995).
The National Law of Education, Argentina 26,206 (2006).
The National Law of Emergency for Teaching 15,739 (1985).
The National Law of General Education of Uruguay 18,437 (2008).
The National Organic Constitutional Law of Education 18,962 (1990).
True, J., & Mintrom, M. (2001, March 1). Transnational networks and policy diffusion: The case of gender mainstreaming. *International Studies Quarterly, 45*(1), 27–57.
UNESCO. (n/a). *Gender equality division*. Retrieved from website http://www.unesco.org/new/en/unesco/themes/gender-equality/about-us/

Chapter 10
Where to From Here? Analysis of Cambodia's 2009–2013 Information Communication Technologies in Education Plan

Jayson W. Richardson, John B. Nash, Lyda Chea, and Chivoin Peou

Abstract In 2009, the Cambodian Ministry of Education, Youth and Sport released the *Master Plan for Information and Communication Technology in Education.* This Master Plan was intended to inform policy and projects at the national level and will ideally improve technology use across the education system. This chapter gives an insiders' perspective on this policy and how it has impacted local schools. Two authors are Cambodian researchers who were working at the Royal University of Phnom Penh while the other two have worked on various technology initiatives in the country. In late 2011, the researchers conducted a technology infrastructure readiness assessment in a sample of three upper secondary schools around the country to determine the actual state of technology. They also conducted focus group interviews with students and teachers in these schools. These data, along with current economic, educational, and technological data, will be used to frame our analysis of this plan. The chapter concludes with suggestions to the Cambodian Ministry of Education, Youth and Sport on moving forward.

There is increasing interest in the field of international educational policy that centers on effectively adopting and implementing digital technologies into the education system. In less developed countries, designing, promulgating, and implementing national policies on information communication technologies (ICT) is often predicated on strong relationships with, and funding from, non-governmental agencies and other benefactors. Such is the case in a country like Cambodia where education is a focus of many of its development efforts. For example, in 2009 the Cambodia Ministry of Education Youth and Sport (MoEYS) released the *Master Plan for*

J.W. Richardson (✉) • J.B. Nash
University of Kentucky, Lexington, KY, USA
e-mail: jayson.richardson@uky.edu; john.nash@uky.edu

L. Chea • C. Peou
Royal University of Phnom Penh, Phnom Penh, Cambodia
e-mail: lyda.dmc.ifl@gmail.com; peouchivoin@gmail.com

C.A. Brown (ed.), *Globalization, International Education Policy and Local Policy Formation*, Policy Implications of Research in Education 5,
DOI 10.1007/978-94-007-4165-2_10

Information and Communication Technology in Education. This plan was informed by over a decade of ICT in education efforts in the country that were aimed at building infrastructure, allocating ICTs, improving teacher preparation, and changing classroom pedagogy. One such effort was UNESCO's (2004) *Establishing the Effective Use of ICT in Education* project. The current ICT in education plan for Cambodia is also informed by and built on the successes and lessons learned from its legacy policy: *Policy and Strategies on Information and Communication Technology in Education in Cambodia* (MoEYS 2004).

As is common in less developed countries, these policies and plans are inextricably linked with the goals and motivations of leaders within international funding agencies who tend to be the chief authors of the policy or plan. For example, the updated Cambodian ICT in education plan was developed through a partnership with the MoEYS, UNESCO, and the Open Institute. Thus the plan builds on strengths, missions, and goals of UNESCO and of the Open Institute within the context of the perceived and expressed needs of the MoEYS. When the missions and goals of such organizations match those of the government, there is a positive step forward. However, if the missions and goals clash with that of the government or with competing priorities within the country, then policies, plans, and programs tend not to be successful (see Richardson 2005). Well-intentioned plans thus must match the environment in which they exist. In this chapter we explore if Cambodia is ready in terms of capacity and infrastructure to fully embrace the promise of this new *Master Plan for Information and Communication Technology in Education* (MoEYS 2009). Additionally we offer guidance as to what might be done now that the plan is nearing its end. Our aim is to inform future ICT in education policies, plans, and projects in the country of Cambodia.

We employed a country social analysis to frame our work. The World Bank (2007) defines a country social analysis as one that "integrates social, economic, political, and institutional analysis to understand the influence of country context on policy reform and development outcomes" (p. 107). Such an analysis can be used to gain a robust understanding of the context of a given reform in an effort to determine "likely risks to the predicted impact of the policy reform" (p. 107). The World Bank country social analysis framework was used in this chapter to understand the current economic, educational, and technological situations, investigate the current state of ICTs in three upper secondary schools, and juxtapose those realities with the goals and objectives of the 2009–2013 Cambodian ICT in education plan.

10.1 Cambodia's ICT in Education Plan for 2009–2013

The *Master Plan for Information and Communication Technology in Education* for 2009–2013 sets forth four main objectives (MoEYS 2009). The first objective focused on increasing access to formal and non-formal education through the use of ICTs. The second objective focused on improving relevance and effectiveness of education through using ICTs in teaching and learning. The third objective focused on increasing ICT skills of Cambodian students so that they can compete in the ever-increasing technology-suffused and interconnected job environment. The forth objective focused on increasing efficiency of school management as well as efficiency within the MoEYS itself.

The MoEYS (2009) noted how success of *Master Plan for Information and Communication Technology in Education* hinges on monitoring the outputs and impacts of the plan:

> Any society is marked by disparities that cannot be solved entirely by the education system but this Master Plan and all other plans of the Ministry attempt to ensure that all their actions will help reduce these disparities and in no case increase them. Monitoring and correcting are the main tools that this Plan will use to detect and correct any negative effects of the work that will take place under it. (p. 27)

The analysis that follows serves to offer the MoEYS a single snapshot, albeit small, of the current progress of ICT in education efforts especially with regards to the upper secondary school level.

10.2 Review of the Literature

The term ICT for development (ICT4D) refers to the broad set of opportunities in which information technology, including but not limited to radio, television, mobile phones, computers, and network hardware, software, and satellite systems, are employed as an agent of development (Kleine and Unwin 2009; Lund and Sutinen 2010). ICT4D has grown from a niche area of interest into a full-fledged field of study with a broad and long-standing set of theories regarding how innovations and industrial advances can play a role in shaping the economic pathways of less developed countries.

Some scholars have noted that ICT diffusion has had a significant positive impact, albeit to varying degrees, on outcomes such as GDP growth (Baliamoune-Lutz 2003; Jalava and Pohjola 2002; Oliner and Sichel 2000; Pohjola 2001). However, drawing firm conclusions about impact of ICT on development has been a challenge, particularly in the time-period referred to by Heeks (1998) as ICT4D 1.0. On the heels of a 1998 World Development Report from the World Bank and the creation by G8 countries of the Digital Opportunities Task Force in 2000, ICT4D became an agenda item for international development agencies and non-governmental organizations (NGOs) seeking to improve the lives of millions of people residing in less developed countries (Heeks 1998). Solutions sought during this period were marked by many quickly installed one-off interventions that delivered some form of ICT to a limited subpopulation within less developed countries. Although profits from ICT companies increased, broader outcomes in terms of improved living standards generally did not occur.

There are many lessons to be learned from ICT4D 1.0, however one point seems clear: Physical access to ICTs is far from sufficient for critical access. As Mansell and When (1998) noted, "plans for investment in ICTs bring the best results when they are embedded in, or informed by, a vision of the future that is consistent with the local or national environment" (p. 100). Thus there is a growing sense among policy makers within less developed countries that policy plays an increasingly important function in putting ICT focused development goals in context. Additionally there is a need to set a baseline for where a country's capacity resides at the time the policy is made. There is also a need to provide benchmarks against which progress can be measured. Thus localizing of ICT4D efforts has many benefits. In short, it helps ensure that efforts of well-intentioned international development agencies and NGOs are aligned to the existing needs of a country and thus provides a buffer against failure (and colonizing effects) that may evolve.

Without ICT access, many less developed countries face isolation and lost economic opportunities. Nevertheless, that very access can create new forms of marginalization, particularly when these countries accept technological solutions that have succeeded in industrial countries but remain untested, and are potentially unsuitable, in developing ones. As Baliamoune-Lutz (2003) noted "the transfer of ICT to developing countries may not contribute to economic development the same way it did in industrial countries, and that it may be best to localize technology and focus on its use in education" (p. 152).

In this light, Richardson (2008) analyzed the *Policy and strategies on information and communication technology in education in Cambodia* (MoEYS 2004) by focusing on three streams: Policies, problems, and politics. Richardson found that the first Cambodian ICT in education policy stalled due to a failure to address and merge these three streams, noting that the following issues greatly impacted the policy's success:

1. The policy was implemented as a top-down effort with minimal stakeholder input.
2. In an effort to maintain cultural norms, the government was grappling with how technology was being used and if and how the government should limit certain innovations.
3. Scarce resources, competing interests, and corruption were major issues impacting the financial viability of implementing the policy and supporting projects.
4. The 2004 ICT in education policy was not aligned with the needs and resources of other policies and programs such as the Education Strategic Plan.

Richardson concluded that the "streams of politics, problems, and policies united to create the potential of an ICT in education reform in Cambodia. However, the failure to forge the political stream with the streams of problems and policies continues to hinder the mass adoption of this reform" (p. 77).

From this analysis, Richardson (2008) offered five main suggestions. First, the MoEYS should proactively develop an action plan detailing what efforts are funded and by whom and which efforts need resources so funders can better initiate projects that meet agreed upon needs. Second, the government of Cambodia needs to focus on anti-corruption laws in a good faith effort so that progress is not halted. Third, building ICT infrastructure in all schools should be a main goal of the MoEYS. Fourth, Cambodia should embrace modern and emerging technologies rather than relying on old technologies (e.g., adopt mobile Internet versus fixed line subscriptions). Finally, Richardson noted how the MoEYS needs to partner with local level, grassroots providers to "increase quality, sustainability, and scalability of ICT in education projects" (p. 78).

The literature on ICT4D is clear in noting that policies, plans, and programs must be aligned with local needs. To best meet local needs, projects should include the input of local stakeholders for its entire duration. Further, to increase sustainability, spread, and scope ICT4D policies and plans must take into account politics, problems, and policies and ensure that all three work together synergistically.

10.3 Review of Cambodian Social Development Indicators

In this section, we analyze various social development indicators to frame the research problem. A country social analysis uses social development indicators as a way to contextualize the problem, assess the country's performance, identify trends, and note potential gaps in the data (World Bank 2007). We used this analysis framework to better understand the localized context in which the current Cambodian ICT in education plan exists. The social development indicators include Cambodia's economic situation, education system, and technology infrastructure. Aspects of the ICT in education plan are then discussed in light of these realities.

10.3.1 Economy

Based on 2011 data, the CIA World Fact Book (2012) reported that Cambodia's gross domestic product (GDP) is $13.2 billion. Its per capita income is $2,300 with a national real growth rate of 6.7 %. Cambodia's main agricultural products include rice, rubber, corn, vegetables, cashews, tapioca, and silk.

As of 2011, Cambodia's population was 14.9 million with a labor force consisting of 30.9 % agricultural, 22 % industrial, and 40 % services (CIA 2012). In 2007, the latest year for which data were available, the unemployment rate was 3.5 %. The country has 32 % of its population in the 0–14 age range whereas 64.1 % of the population is between 15 and 64 years old. As of 2007 the Cambodian population had a 1.69 % growth rate. Educational expenditures were 2.1 % of the GDP. The budget has revenues of $1.69 billion and expenditures of $2.54 billion. This represents a −6.4 % budget surplus.

It is interesting to note that the Cambodian labor force is rapidly shifting. Cambodia is experiencing a steady decrease in the industrial and agricultural sectors and a substantial increase in the service sector. In the 1990s, it was estimated that 80 % of the population was categorized as agricultural workers. The Cambodian economy shifted to favor the industrial sector in the late 1990s and early 2000s with a boom in the garment industry. After 2005 a greater shift occurred in the service industry as industrial sector jobs were being relocated to lower developed countries such as those in sub-Saharan Africa. These shifts have been, in some part, a result of urbanization, foreign investment, and the global economic slowdown in the latter part of the first decade of the century.

Florida (2002) refers to this type of a shift in his book, *Rise of the Creative Class.* In it he noted that as economies shift towards a service-oriented economy, there becomes a greater need for educated, creative thinkers. This shift requires technologically advanced workers who can adjust to the changing climate and meet the demands of a global workforce. These types of workers are referred to as knowledge workers (OECD 1996). If Cambodia follows the same trajectory as other parts of the world (and there is no reason to think this is not the case) then the use and mastery of modern digital technologies will play an increasingly pivotal role in this shift. Given that 32 % of its population is between 0 and 14 years old (formative schooling age), it is imperative that these students obtain the skills and dispositions required to meet the needs of the changing economy within the country.

Currently, the Cambodian government is running at an $8.47 million annual deficit. ICT in education initiatives are expensive and wrought with challenges. Unless the government plans to prioritize the ICT in education plan and other ICT in education initiatives, the reality is that Cambodia will rely on the assistance of outside agencies to bridge this financial gap. Looking at the 2009 ICT in education plan, we determined that this is indeed the case. The summary of the *Master Plan for Information and Communication Technology in Education* (MoEYS 2009) concludes as follows:

> Funding is secured for all short-term and most probably for some longer-term items, it is hoped that this Master Plan will help the Ministry's development partners understand its commitment to use ICT to improve its management and the quality of education it provides and therefore support the rest of this Plan. The Plan is therefore open to all possible partners, in terms of both participation and resources (financial, technical and human). (p. 3)

Admittedly, as noted by the MoEYS (2009) itself, the *Master Plan for Information and Communication Technology in Education* falls short in committing to the needed resources to achieve each of the objectives set forth but rater expresses hopes for the best.

10.3.2 Education System

The formal education system in Cambodia includes 3 years of pre-school, 6 years of primary school (1–6), 3 years of lower secondary school (7–9), and 3 years of upper secondary school (10–12). Upper secondary schooling can follow either an academic or a vocational track. The local authors note that the vocational track is, in practice, almost non-existent. Vocational training, as it exists now, is generally provided as remedial or skill-support programs outside of the formal educational system.

The World Bank (2012) reported that the adult literacy rate (for those greater than 15 years old) as of 2008 was 78 %. This indicator has been steadily increasing from 67 % in 1988 and 74 % in 2004. Further, Cambodia's primary gross enrollment is 127 % as of 2010 (The World Bank 2012).

Article 67 of the Cambodian Constitution notes that "the State shall adopt an educational program according to the principles of modern technology and foreign languages" (UNESCO 2011, p. 3). As such, with respect to ICTs, UNESCO (2011) describes that at the primary level, students receive one lesson per week in technology in Grades 1, 2, and 3. This increases to two lessons per week in grades 4, 5, and 6. At the lower secondary level (grades 7, 8, and 9), this increases to three lessons per week. Grade 10 has no ICT lesson requirement. In grades 11 and 12, ICT and technology classes are presently offered only as electives. These data may be in a state of flux since the *Master Plan for Information and Communication Technology in Education* (MoEYS 2009) mandates ICT courses for students in the upper secondary schools.

With regards to the formal education system, the Cambodian *Master Plan for Information and Communication Technology in Education* (MoEYS 2009) focuses primarily on secondary education. To a much lesser degree, the *Master Plan for Information and Communication Technology in Education* also includes a focus on higher education institutions, teacher training colleges, and the MoEYS itself. This original data collected for this study (see below) however is limited to only upper secondary schools. In this regard, UNESCO (2011) and the MoEYS (2010) noted that in 2009/2010 there were 383 upper secondary schools with 323,583 students with a net enrollment of 19.4 %. The MoEYS (2010) further noted that the average student to teacher ratio in upper secondary schools in Cambodia was 32.2–1. Students in Cambodian upper secondary schools have a 26.1 % completion rate.

Nonetheless, the *Master Plan for Information and Communication Technology in Education* (MoEYS 2009) primarily focuses on the needs of teachers and all but neglects the needs of students. The plan does note that Grade 10 students will engage in an ICT-based professional skills curriculum and students in Grades 11 and 12 will have the opportunity to follow an elective vocational education program. The MoEYS (2009) noted "students will learn from these courses how to use computer applications that are fully translated to Khmer and adapted to Cambodian culture" (p. 12). Thus, although there is a mention of students, the actual outcomes of course content are vague and somewhat arbitrary.

In our analysis, the Cambodian *Master Plan for Information and Communication Technology in Education* (MoEYS 2009) is narrowly focused on a small subset of technical skills and not on the critical skills needed to compete in a knowledge economy. This is despite the fact that the ICT in education plan notes that the MoEYS has a "long-term vision (10 years) in which all students graduating from secondary education will have acquired the necessary ICT technical skills and the critical knowledge and thinking skills" (p. 11) that will allow them to shift quickly into the workplace or into higher education. The overt focus on learning productivity software means that students may not develop the twenty-first Century literacies demanded of a global workforce. The National Council for Teachers of English (2008) details how these skills include not only proficiency in applications and tools but also cross-cultural collaboration; designing and sharing information to global communities; managing multiple streams of information; creating and critiquing multi-media texts; and gaining an ethical responsibility required in technologically-suffused environments. In short, the Cambodian Cambodian

Master Plan for Information and Communication Technology in Education (MoEYS 2009) stresses the need to build skills in certain desktop application (i.e., productivity software) but fails to support the education system in developing twenty-first Century competencies.

10.3.3 Technology Infrastructure

The Cambodian Ministry of Posts and Telecommunications (2011) is the policy maker and regulator of everything related to the Internet and mobile communications within Cambodia. It reported that as of 2010, only 1.4 % of the population had an Internet subscription. However, 54.6 % of the Cambodian population had a mobile phone subscription compared to 2.6 % of the population having a fixed landline subscription. It should be noted that other sources have reported mobile phone penetration rates as high as 87 % in late 2011 (BuddeComm 2012). These numbers fail to capture the true picture due to the fact that, according to the in-country authors, many Cambodians have more than one phone number by using multiple SIM cards. This reality is coupled with the fact that high penetration rates are a way for mobile providers to flout the success of their company. The subscription rates, therefore, are not an accurate proxy of actual connectedness or of use.

Data on Internet subscriptions in Cambodia are also misleading. Given Cambodia's mobile phone penetration rates and the fact that mobile phones are becoming increasingly smart with Internet accessibility, data on fixed line Internet subscriptions does not offer an accurate portrayal of how many Cambodian are actually online. Additionally, many initiatives and efforts are currently in place to provide wireless Internet services either over Wi-Max or through mobile providers via Internet connecting wireless dongles. As late as spring 2012, advertisers claimed the speed of mobile Internet connections can surpass that of most fixed line subscriptions.

To understand the growth of the mobile market, it is important to look at cellular providers in Cambodia. There were three cellular companies in 2002 (International Telecommunications Union 2002) and no less than nine in 2011 (Ministry of Posts and Telecommunications 2011). The co-authors of this chapter, who live and work in Cambodia, note that as of summer 2012 this number will reduce to seven due to pending mergers. No statistics were found related to the penetration rates of smart phones in Cambodia.

Although the *Master Plan for Information and Communication Technology in Education* (MoEYS 2009) focuses narrowly on computer skills and exposure to productivity software, it misses how students and teachers can use technologies to collaborate, to share, to access information, and to create. The data show that students sitting at a desktop computer using the school's landline Internet access may not be the solution for Cambodia. The promise may be in the nation's burgeoning wireless systems and students' own wireless devices.

For the balance of the chapter we turned to survey and focus group data collected for the present study. We then describe the findings and discuss them in light of the analysis. We conclude this chapter with policy and planning recommendations.

10.4 School Readiness and Technology Use

The data presented in this study were collected between November 2011 and February 2012 from three public upper secondary schools in Cambodian provincial cities of Phnom Penh, Pursat, and Siem Reap. The three upper secondary schools, Upper Secondary School #1 (Phnom Penh), Upper Secondary School #2 (Pursat Province), and Upper Secondary School #3 (Siem Reap) represent typical public upper secondary schools in various regions in terms of number of teaching staff, number of students, and resources. The researchers believe that these schools accurately represent the best-case scenario for upper secondary schools in the country. From our experiences, if technology and ICT resources are not available in these schools, they are likely not available in smaller, more rural locations throughout the country.

Data collection was divided into two phases. The first phase included a readiness assessment to determine the current status of ICT infrastructure and technical capacity at each upper secondary schools. In the second phase, focus group discussions were held to better understand use and skills of and attitudes toward computers and the Internet.

10.4.1 Instruments

The readiness assessment was conducted with a member of each of the schools' management teams by the researchers using a structured questionnaire. The assessment aimed to document each upper secondary school's current ICT readiness and its ability to implement the Cambodian *Master Plan for Information and Communication Technology in Education* (MoEYS 2009) by investigating four issues:

1. Physical and technological infrastructure and access level at each upper secondary school,
2. ICT-based professional skills training for teachers,
3. ICT-based professional skills training for students, and
4. Level of awareness of the plan and the types of school support mechanisms for the provision of computers and the Internet access.

Other aspects of this assessment included electricity access, inventory of ICTs, access to ICTs, ICT training for teachers, ICT training for students, and *Master Plan for Information and Communication Technology in Education* (MoEYS 2009) knowledge and support.

Table 10.1 Focus group demographics

Group	Participants	School	Male	Female
1	Students (Grades 10–12)	School #1	4	6
2	Teachers of Khmer Literature, English, Civic Education, Biology, Computers	School #1	4	7
3	Students (Grades 10–12)	School #2	4	5
4	Teachers of Khmer Literature, Computer, Civic Education, Mathematics, Physics, Chemistry	School #2	7	3

The student and teacher focus groups were conducted following an in-house protocol developed to understand experiences and perceptions around ICTs. The focus groups interviews focused on types of training received, experiences using computers and the Internet, and attitudes about computers and the Internet. Four focus group discussions were conducted with students and teachers at School #1 and School #2. The first focus group discussion comprised of 10 students in grades 10–12 from School #1, six of whom were female. The second group was comprised of 10 teachers from School #2, three of whom were female. The third group had nine students from grades 10–12 at School #2, five of whom were female. The last group consisted of 11 teachers from School #1, seven of whom were female (Table 10.1). The participating students were purposely selected to represent a variety of grade levels, computer competencies, and Internet competencies. Additionally, teachers from different subjects and a variety of ICT competencies were chosen to participate in the focus group discussions. The data from the focus group discussions were used to contextualize realities in the field. These data were not reported in totality, but rather judiciously to inform and supplement findings from the readiness assessment.

10.5 Results of Readiness Assessment

The readiness assessment was used to understand ICT training and infrastructure issues at each of the three schools. Again, the readiness assessment focused on ICT resources, ICT training, ICT availability, and school leaders' understanding of the *Master Plan for Information and Communication Technology in Education* (MoEYS 2009). Below is a summary of the results by each school.

10.5.1 Upper Secondary School #1

Phnom Penh is the nation's capital and largest city with 1.3 million people. Upper Secondary School #1 is one of 29 schools in the capital city of Phnom Penh. For the 2011–2012 academic year, School #1 had 79 upper secondary teachers

Table 10.2 Staffing information for upper secondary school #1 (2011–2012)

Total management staff	5
Total administration staff	9
Total teaching staff	79
Total students	1,292 (32 classes)
Grade 10	397 (10 classes)
Grade 11	350 (10 classes)
Grade 12	545 (12 classes)

where 31 were female. School #1 was the smallest of the upper secondary schools in the study with a 2011–2012 enrollment of 1,292 students. Table 10.2 above details the academic information for this upper secondary school.

10.5.1.1 Physical and Technological Infrastructure and Access Level

10.5.1.1.1 Electricity

Upper Secondary School #1 is connected to the public electrical grid that cost about 1.5 million riel per month. With a limited budget, the school restricts the use of electricity to only computers used for administrative tasks as well as those used to teach computer courses.

10.5.1.1.2 Computer Labs and Computers

Upper Secondary School #1 had two computer labs. One lab was no longer used because all of the computers were reportedly broken. These computers were second-hand units donated by Korea in 2001 under a memorandum of understanding between the MoYES and Korea. The other lab had 26 new computers, donated by Room to Read in 2006, an nonprofit education organization. In total, School #1 had 26 working computers, five of which were used for administrators and 21 of which were used for computer classes.

10.5.1.1.3 ICT Equipment

Upper Secondary School #1 received five printers and one photocopier from the MoEYS. Out of its annual bought, the school bought one additional photocopier. For use in the English remedial class, the school received one television, one CD player, and 50 sets of earphones from Room to Read. It had one telephone that was sponsored by Metfone Viettel, a private Vietnamese telecommunication company.

10.5.1.1.4 Computer Access

Students could only access computers in the computer lab during their allocated computer class. Teachers could access the computer lab when classes were not in session. However, teachers rarely accessed the lab because of their demanding teaching schedules.

10.5.1.1.5 Internet access

The school principal was the only person who had access to the Internet. The principal was using a dial-up connection with limited speed. This service was donated by Metfone Viettel.

10.5.1.2 ICT-Based Professional Skills Training for Teachers

Upper Secondary School #1 had two specialized computer teachers, one of whom taught computer skills for 10 h a week. The second teacher's sole responsibility was teaching computers. There were four additional teachers of computers as a second subject.

The school sent its administrative staff to attend basic computer training on Microsoft Word and Excel at a local training institution. When training becomes available from the MoEYS, the school planned to send the computer teachers on an as-needed basis.

10.5.1.3 ICT-Based Professional Skills Training for Students

ICT training for students was primarily focused on increasing technical computer skills. The computer training was reserved for students in Grades 10 and 11 for 1 h a week using the Khmer language ICT textbook. The content of these courses was focused only on teaching computer applications using Khmer Open Office software (Khmer OS). Students in Grade 10 were trained using Open Office Calc and students in Grade 11 were trained using Open Office Impress.

10.5.1.4 Awareness of the *Master Plan* and Level of School Support Mechanisms

School #1 did not receive a copy of the *Master Plan for Information and Communication Technology in Education* (MoEYS 2009) but the principal reported that he had heard about its dissemination. He and one specialized computer teacher were invited to join the ICT in education training hosted in Korea in 2006. The principal claimed that the school was implementing the plan given that the school had computer teachers and provided computer trainings to students based on the IT curriculum from other private schools.

Following the request from the MoEYS, the school sent names of other teachers and administrators who lacked basic computer skills in hopes they might receive future training. To date however, there had been no response from the MoEYS as to when training will be available. The principal noted that in order to take advantage of being integrated into the Association of South East Asian Nations (ASEAN) in 2015, it was important that Cambodia's upper secondary school teachers and students gained relevant ICT skills.

10.5.2 Upper Secondary School #2

Pursat province has 14 upper secondary schools. For the 2011–2012 academic year, School #2 had 2,676 students of which 852 were in tenth grade, 932 were in grade 11, and 892 were in grade 12. The school had a teaching staff of 104 where 37 were female (Table 10.3).

10.5.2.1 Physical and Technological Infrastructure and Access Level

10.5.2.1.1 Electricity

Upper Secondary School #2 was connected to the public electrical grid that costs the school approximately two million riel per month. Given a constrained budget, the electricity was only used for administrative purposes and for computer courses.

10.5.2.1.2 Computer Labs and Computers

Upper Secondary School #2 had one library and three computer labs. The library and one computer lab were built by Room to Read while the other two computer labs were housed in an area known as a resource school. This was a building built by the MoEYS under the ESDP-II ADB loan (Second Education Sector Development Project) in 2009. There were 58 working desktop computers in Upper Secondary School #2. Four were used for administration purposes and 54 were used for teaching computer courses. These 54 computers were located in the two labs.

Table 10.3 Staff information for upper secondary school #2 (2011–2012)

Total management staff	4
Total administration staff	5
Total teaching staff	104
Total students	2,362 (54 classes)
Grade 10	708 (17 classes)
Grade 11	700 (17 classes)
Grade 12	954 (20 classes)

10.5.2.1.3 ICT Equipment

The school received eight printers, one LCD projector, and two pairs of loudspeakers from the MoEYS under the ESPD-II ADB loan. Upper Secondary School #2 purchased one digital camera from their own funds to photograph 12th grade students for the upper secondary school certificate upon their completion of 12th grade.

10.5.2.1.4 Computer Access

Students could only access computers in the computer labs during computer classes. Computers were not available for academic or personal use before or after class. In principle, teachers could also access computers in the computer labs when the labs were not in use. However, the lab was often too busy, therefore access was extremely limited.

10.5.2.1.5 Internet Access

Only one computer teacher had access to the Internet using a Metfone mobile broadband dongle modem (10 Kbps). No other computer had Internet accessibility.

10.5.2.2 ICT-Based Professional Skills Training for Teachers

Upper Secondary School #2 had six specialized computer teachers who taught computers for about 8 h a week and two teachers of computers as a second subject. Of the six specialized computer teachers, one was responsible for computer maintenance for 18 h a week in addition to teaching computers and Khmer literature.

For 3 years starting in 2007, two computer teachers were trained on basic maintenance and computer networking by Room to Read. The teachers were also trained on how to teach computers using a train-the-trainer textbook produced by Intel.

10.5.2.3 ICT-Based Professional Skills Training for Students

ICT training for students was provided to only Grade 11 students at Upper Secondary School #2. This was offered as a life skills course focused on software applications. It was provided for 1 h per week using the Khmer language ICT textbook that was jointly produced by the MoEYS and the Open Institute. The training was on Open Office Writer and Open Office Calc.

10.5.2.4 Awareness of the *Master Plan* and Level of School Support Mechanisms

Upper Secondary School #2 did not receive the *Master Plan for Information and Communication Technology in Education* (MoEYS 2009) nor were its leaders made aware of such a plan. Nevertheless, by hosting computer training for students, the school was implementing aspects of the Master Plan. In addition, the school placed priority on computer maintenance training for computer teachers but not for non-computer teachers.

10.5.3 Upper Secondary School #3

Siem Reap is the third largest city and is commonly known as the cultural capital of Cambodia. It is the home of the famous Angkor Wat temple complex. Siem Reap has 148,000 habitants. In Siem Reap province, there are 19 upper secondary schools, one of which was Upper Secondary School #3. The school had 50 upper secondary teachers in total with 3,219 students. It had 888 students in tenth grade, 1,060 students in Grade 11, and 1,271 students in Grade 12 (Table 10.4).

10.5.3.1 Physical and Technological Infrastructure and Access Level

10.5.3.1.1 Electricity

Upper Secondary School #3 was connected to the public electrical grid at a cost of approximately two million riel per month. Electricity was used only for administrative and computer training purpose.

10.5.3.1.2 Computers Labs and Computers

Upper Secondary School #3 had three computer labs. One lab had 20 computers that were donated by Room to Read. This lab however was no longer used because all of the computers were broken. The school also had a second lab that was built

Table 10.4 Staff information for upper secondary school #3 (2011–2012)

Total management staff	5
Total administration staff	12
Total teaching staff	50
Total students	3,219 (44 classes)
Grade 10	888 (13 classes)
Grade 11	1,060 (15 classes)
Grade 12	1,271 (16 classes)

by the MoEYS under efforts by the ESDP-II ADB loan. A third lab was located in the girls' dormitory. This lab was sponsored by Bamboo Shoot, a local organization affiliated with the Girl Scholarship Program. This lab was not part of the school and was not used for school purposes.

The school had 38 working computers. The administrative staff used six computers while the other 32 were used for teaching. This number excluded computers in the dormitory. The 32 computers were located in the second lab housed in the resource room that was built using funds from the ESDP-II ADB loan.

10.5.3.1.3 ICT Equipment

Upper Secondary School #3 received two printers, one LCD projector, one television, and one photocopier from the MoEYS under the ESDP-II ADB loan.

10.5.3.1.4 Computer Access

Access to computers by teachers and students was only available during regular computer classes. Students could not access computers before or after class. Teachers could access these labs. However, to conserve electricity the teachers normally did not access the lab.

10.5.3.1.5 Internet Access

The school was currently not connected to the Internet. No computer had an Internet connection.

10.5.3.2 ICT-Based Professional Skills Training for Teachers

Upper Secondary School #3 had two specialized computer teachers, one of whom was a computer teacher in Phnom Penh but came to Siem Reap to teach every Saturday. The school also had two teachers of computers as a second subject. These two teachers taught computers for about 14 h per week.

Two computer teachers had Bachelor's degrees in computer science and were trained at the National Institute for Education (NIE) for 1 year on how to use the Khmer operating system. The computer teachers received training on computer maintenance by the Asian Development Bank for 1 week in 2010. No other teachers had formal ICT training.

10.5.3.3 ICT-Based Professional Skills Training for Students

ICT training was only for students in Grades 10 and 11 for 1 h a week as a life skills course using the Khmer language ICT textbook. The training focused on the use of Open Office Writer for Grade 10 students and Open Office Calc for Grade 11 students.

10.5.3.4 Awareness of the *Master Plan* and Level of School Support Mechanisms

The management at Upper Secondary School #3 did not receive the *Master Plan for Information and Communication Technology in Education* (MoEYS 2009) nor were they made aware of its existence. The leadership believed, however, that the computer training currently offered was contributing to the implementation of the MoEYS's plan for ICT in education.

10.6 Policy and Planning Implications

In this section we compared data from the readiness assessment and focus groups with key aspects of the ICT in education plan. We will pull out sections of the *Master Plan for Information and Communication Technology in Education* (MoEYS 2009) and compare those with the data from our research.

Objective 5.5: ICT is used to facilitate administration of schools and teacher training centers that have access to electricity. This study confirmed that all three schools were connected to the electrical grid. Thus access to electricity was not an issue for these schools. We found that the cost of electricity, however, was an impediment to using computers for purposes other than administration and teaching computer classes. With regard to teachers and students, this meant that leaders often requested or mandated that computers not be used outside of computer classes. This limited the ability of learners to extend practice, expand their skills, and even develop new techniques of using the ICTs. This also limited the teachers' ability to integrate technology into teaching and learning. In short, the cost of electricity was a major impediment to extending the use of these ICTs. This issue, however, should be moot. The *Master Plan for Information and Communication Technology in Education* (MoEYS 2009) notes that:

> One of the major barriers to the use of ICT in Education – the cost of connectivity for education administration as well as for educational purposes – was overcome in 2009 by a private sector donation from Viettel which agreed, at no cost, to permanently connect all administrative offices of the Ministry as well as all public schools, universities, and Teacher Training Centers with access to electricity. (p. 9)

In this study, we found that this was not the case. The full costs of electricity were a noted burden on schools.

Objective 5.8: Investment costs and recurrent expense in implementing ICT in education are shared with stakeholders (MoEYS 2009). Aside from electricity, recurrent expenses related to ICTs included Internet access, computer maintenance, and computer repairs. All three of these schools were in a dire situation when trying to address each of these issues. Data from the three schools indicated that Internet access was not an expense being covered or shared by stakeholders. In Upper Secondary School #2, one computer teacher was using a mobile dongle donated by Metfone Viettel. Thus to have better access, this teacher had to spend his own money. At Upper Secondary School #1 and Upper Secondary School #3 Internet access was not available at all.

Computer maintenance and repair were costs not covered by any of the three schools, the MoEYS, or any other stakeholders. Two of the schools reported having an array of broken machines that could not be used. It was uncertain if these computers needed major repairs or simply needed minor maintenance. However, it was noted that some of these machines were over a decade old, thus repairing the machines may be futile. Nevertheless, these schools had no funding mechanism to cover these recurrent costs. As an example, one computer teacher from Upper Secondary School #2 reported during the focus group discussion that the school had no budget allocated for anti-virus software thus leaving computers vulnerable.

Essential Element – 6.2.1 – Equipment for schools and teacher training centers. The *Master Plan for Information and Communication Technology in Education* (MoEYS 2009) notes that each school will have a computer lab with 26 computers to serve 40–60 students. Each of the three schools did indeed meet the minimum number of working computers for student use. Upper Secondary School #2 and Upper Secondary School #1 had acceptable student to computer ratios with 12:1 (limited to Grade 11) and 35:1 (limited to Grades 10 and 11) respectfully. Upper Secondary School #3 had a student to computer ratio of 60:1 (limited to Grades 10 and 11).

Under Sect. 6.2.1 the *Master Plan for Information and Communication Technology in Education* (MoEYS 2009) noted that the computer to teacher ratio should be 1:5 to 1:10. Upper Secondary School #3 had a computer to teacher ratio of 1:1.5 while Upper Secondary School #2 had a computer to teacher ratio of 1:1.9 and Upper Secondary School #1 had a computer to teacher ratio of 1:3. However although the ratio set forth by the master plan was achieved, physical availability was not indicative of accessibility of these ICTs. In all three schools, it was clear that access to computers was not available to teachers before, during, or after school outside of the allocated computer course time. Thus the only teachers who had access to computers were in fact only the computer teachers.

With regard to Internet accessibility, the *Master Plan for Information and Communication Technology in Education* (MoEYS 2009) provides a minimal level of guidance. It noted:

> The main offices of the Ministry in Phnom Penh will be connected through a local network or a VPN over the Internet as soon as possible and will be able to share information. Over the long run this network must cover all the Ministry offices and all public higher education institutions. As much as possible the network will have to be owned by the Ministry or by the government to avoid recurrent connectivity costs that will otherwise grow significantly when large numbers of centers are connected. The network will also grow to cover as many upper secondary schools and Teacher Training Centers as possible on the long run. (p. 25)

The three upper secondary schools in the current study represented what we believed to be the best-case scenario of ICT saturation across the country. Given that none of these schools were connected to the Internet via broadband and given the fact that at best one to two computers were connected to the Internet via a wireless prepaid dongle, it may be safe to assume that Internet connectivity is nearly nonexistent in Cambodian upper secondary schools.

To reiterate, the number of computers does not provide an accurate portrayal of computer access for students at the three schools. For example, students in the focus groups were asked if they had ever received an assignment or homework requiring them to use a computer. None of them had such experience at their public school. Only students who enrolled in private computer or after school English classes were given tasks requiring computer use.

Objective 5.5: ICT is used to facilitate administration of schools and teacher training centers that have access to electricity. In the three schools in this study, each allocated a set of computers to be used for administrative purposes. In fact, each school described commitments to continue financing electricity required to run these particular computers. With regard to computers reserved for administrative uses, Upper Secondary School #3 had six, Upper Secondary School #2 had four, and Upper Secondary School #1 had five. Thus each school appeared to be prioritizing and meeting this need.

Objective 1.2: Improvement of in-service teachers' pedagogical skills and effectiveness in providing better education. The *Master Plan for Information and Communication Technology in Education* (MoEYS 2009) is forthright in noting that "not all teachers can be trained in the first 5 years of the Master Plan, however, so priority will be given to teachers from schools with an adequate and regular supply of electricity" (p. 12). In this study we found that the computer teachers and the teachers who teach computers as a second subject tended to be trained on computer applications. However a limited number of administrative staff were trained on basic computer skills. The *Master Plan for Information and Communication Technology in Education* described what it might look like to achieve this objective. The plan described that "all schools which have computers for education have trained 90 % of their upper-secondary school teachers on ICT based professional skills by 2013" (p. 12). However, in these three schools where electricity was available, no general education teacher had been trained on how to use computers or how to link ICT and pedagogy.

Many focus group teachers from Upper Secondary School #2 reported they spent their own money to use computers and the Internet. Teachers at all three schools reported not receiving any formal training on technology use. These teachers noted how cost was a huge impediment to them seeking training at private computer schools. Most teachers reported learning to use a computer through self-study or at a friend's residence.

Objective 3.2: Upper secondary schools have qualified ICT teachers to deliver the ICT curricula. The plan noted that an indicator of success for this objective is that "by 2013, the new ICT curricula is delivered at all upper secondary schools that have computers by qualified teachers who have been specifically trained by NIE to deliver these curricula" (p. 18). In this regard for these three schools, this goal did seem to have been met. These three schools each had a number of full-time trained computer teachers and/or a number of teachers who taught computers as a second subject although we were uncertain if training was provided to these teachers.

The plan also stated that, "starting in 2009–2010, the National Institute of Education will train all Math, Physics, English, Economics and Agriculture teachers also as ICT teachers as a second subject." As the result, "40 % of all new teachers will be prepared to teach ICT in their schools" (p. 23). In the three schools surveyed, this aspect of the plan had not been achieved. However, one school indicated that the MoEYS did request estimates of teachers needing training, but as of fall 2011 ICT training for these teachers had yet to be completed.

Objective 1.1: The equipping of secondary education graduates with the ICT-based professional skills needed either by the labor market or for success in higher education – and to be able to continuously benefit from life-long learning. Section 6.2.1 of the plan stated that only software for approved textbooks can be used. This is to "ensure that students acquire professional competencies and not only technical skills" (p. 24). The plan stated that "by 2013, students of all schools, which will have computers for education, will have received some ICT-based professional skills at school, either as a life-skill in grade 10 or as an optional course in grades 11 and 12" (p. 12). However, ICT-based professional skills training for students at the three schools took the form of technical software training, focusing on the Open Office productivity software. Upper Secondary School #1 and Upper Secondary School #3 provided this course to 10th and 11th graders for 1 h per week. Upper Secondary School #2 provided this course to 11th graders for 1 h per week. The mandate to use a single software suite as stated in the plan was most likely the result of the partnership between the MoEYS and the Open Institute. As noted, each of the three schools was using Open Office based on the national ICT in education textbook.

In the focus groups, students were asked about the benefits of learning computer skills. Students noted how computers were the norm thus learning how to use them was vital. One student at Upper Secondary School #1 said, "employers seek those with computer literacy. Having no computer skills makes it hard to find employment." As this student indicated, there is a need to have a broad base of computer skills to be competitive in the job market.

Access to the Internet was non-existent in the schools. However, in the focus groups we asked if students ever used the Internet outside of school. Students typically said their Internet use was rare and limited. However, for those who did have Internet access, it tended to be on a smart phone. Students tended to use the Internet for communicating with friends, downloading music, and social networking.

10.7 Policy and Planning Recommendations

The current Cambodian *Master Plan for Information and Communication Technology in Education* (MoEYS 2009) expired in 2013. The nation has made great strides in the past decade thinking about, planning, and initiating various educational technology initiatives. Given that an updated ICT in education plan may soon be released, the MoEYS will hopefully prepare this plan based upon lessons learned in implementing the soon-ending plan. From the social policy analysis above, we are able to make a few recommendations to move the Cambodian *Master Plan for Information and Communication Technology in Education* into its next phase.

10.7.1 Need for Technology Leadership

As evidenced in these three upper secondary schools, there is a need to get the leadership at all levels committed to achieving the goals of a national ICT in education plan. It is the leader who can support initiatives and policies. It is the leader who can ensure ICT in education professional development is offered internally or externally. It is the leader who ensures that the budget will support these ICT in education initiatives. In fact, the plan notes that, "school directors will also be a focus of the Ministry and taught how to support the teaching of ICT in their schools" (p. 25). This is a forward thinking statement by the MoEYS and should be aggressively pursued in the coming years.

10.7.2 Need for Continued Professional Development of Teachers

The researchers found that professional development was perhaps the greatest need in these schools. This was also a finding of a previous study that looked at teacher trainers in Cambodia (Richardson 2011). There is no reason to believe that other grade levels or other schools in the Cambodian education system are better situated with regards to professional development than those in this study. In fact, it is believed that these three schools may represent the best-case scenario in Cambodia.

10.7.3 Focus on Quality Infrastructure Rather than Quantity

Each of these three schools benefited from past efforts to improve infrastructure. These efforts were appropriate and even progressive for the time and place. Cambodian schools however are now in an era when the important factor is not just the number of computers and the amount of ICT equipment, but it is about the quality of these ICTs. Students and teachers are gaining access to the Internet at home and via mobile technologies. To increase user adoption and improve user experiences, it is vital that tools meet the needs of the end user.

10.7.4 Investigate Mobile Options

Cambodia was one of the first countries to have more mobile phones than landlines. It currently has an impressive wireless network in the major cities. Perhaps the solution for Cambodia is wireless, and not wired. Thus mobile devices will most likely play a major, transformative role in Cambodia's formal, non-formal, and informal education systems.

10.7.5 Knowledge-Based Skills Require Access to the Internet

The Cambodian ICT in education plan notes the need for students to develop skills to make them competitive in a knowledge economy. However, participation in this economy requires the Internet. Students who are not participating in this community are simply not developing these needed skills. Again, mobile technologies and wireless access offer promising solutions in the Cambodian context.

10.7.6 Supplement Costs of Electricity and Internet

The cost of electricity proved to be a major impediment to ICT use in Cambodian upper secondary schools. The researchers believe this reality is mirrored in schools across Cambodia. Each of the three schools in this study reported being committed to funding the electricity to run computers for administrative purposes and for the required courses, but leaders of each school also indicated that outside of these uses, access was limited or nonexistent. In an effort to extend use of those resources currently available, the MoEYS should work to remove, or in the very least, lessen this burden.

Schools can also extend use of the computer labs before and after school by initiating a small user fee that will offset electricity consumption costs. NGOs might also partner with schools and offer afterschool programs where these costs are paid for by funders rather than the end users.

10.8 Concluding Thoughts

The 2009–2013 *Master Plan for Information and Communication Technology in Education* (MoEYS 2009) had four objectives. Our analysis revealed that ICTs are minimally being used to increase access to formal education; yet we are uncertain if efforts for this first objective are underway in the non-formal sector. Increasing the effectiveness of education, the second objective, does not seem to be achieved since ICTs are currently restricted to computer classes that focus only on using productivity software. The third objective is focused on skills. To this end the plan is increasing student skills on how to use a given set of software, albeit with a narrow, tool-orientation. Finally, the forth objective focuses on increasing the efficiency of school management. The analysis herein revealed that ICTs were being used for administrative purposes, however measuring their efficient and effective use was out of the purview of this study.

The 2009–2013 Cambodian *Master Plan for Information and Communication Technology in Education* (MoEYS 2009) contains many hopeful elements. It falls sort in action, but it makes up for it in vision. With an added focus on training, continued professional development, leadership, and quality infrastructure, the next ICT in education plan can build on the impacts and lessons from the current ICT in education plan. We sincerely look forward to the third generation of the Cambodian ICT in Education Plan. Cambodia is poised to make great strides with regards to ICT in education, however it must do so in its own way.

10.9 Reflections from the Cambodian Authors: A Local Perspective

The Cambodian government's recognition of the importance of infusing ICTs into its transitional educational system are commendable. At the same time, the financial and technical support from donors and non-governmental partners has been critical to the development of ICT in education in the country over the last decade. Whether this development has been satisfactory, however, is subject to the political and social context of Cambodia. From a local point of view, the *Master Plan for Information and Communication Technology in Education* (MoEYS 2009) is judicious; for it is both visionary and sensitive to the realities of Cambodian educational system. On one hand, it shows an awareness that ICTs are crucial to keeping the country on track for development and regional competition through their utilization in the educational sector. On the other hand, it makes no illusion that the objectives and goals can be achieved by initiating projects that do not take into account the deprived situation of the educational sector. Nevertheless, that success of the soon-to-expire plan has been only partial. The situation and future prospect are still, and will remain, hampered by financial and cultural factors that need to be addressed not only within ICT in education planning and policy setting but also through action in the wider political and social arenas.

The weak financial capacity of the Cambodian government to implement large-scale ICT in education programs is common knowledge. Thus, policy and plans have become well-intentioned tools that are visionary yet at times indifferent to results. The funding of ICTs, such as computer and Internet access, remains dependent on good will from donors or one-off programs from the government and/or its development partners. This reality drastically impacts the sustainability of initiatives (e.g., ICT maintenance and replacement). The need to save on electricity also points to the government's lack of financial strength to fulfill ICT ambitions. There may be localized solutions such as establishing a user fee system or partnership initiatives, but this will require not only management capacity in individual schools but also the political will of the MoEYS to permit such decentralized autonomy in an administrative system that remains strong in centralized control. Thus the possibility to develop such localized solutions is not likely.

This context of financial shortages also means that minimal efforts to infuse ICT in education may exacerbate current educational inequalities. Financing for ICT in education is not only about shouldering the costs of infrastructure and trainings for teachers, leaders, and students. It is also about improving educational governance and provisions, which are also hampered by the government's financial capacity and transparency. The school level data in this chapter presents a best-case scenario in upper secondary schools in Cambodia. If harnessing of ICTs for school administration, teaching, and learning is only partial present in these three schools, this means inferior schools, especially the rural ones, have not presently been empowered in any way by the development of ICT in education.

Additionally, the *Master Plan for Information and Communication Technology in Education* (MoEYS 2009) rests on the assumption that teachers will do their job; while the reality is that they often must supplement their meager government salaries by moonlighting or teaching extra-school classes. It is then possible (as has been the case with the introduction of compulsory English learning into the state curriculum) that the quality of the teaching and learning of ICT skills rests on the financial resources of the students and their willingness to attend extra classes or go to better schools. The growing gap between those with quality access and knowledge of ICTs and those with less quality access or no access at all can only exacerbate current educational inequalities. A better level of ICT in education achievement can, in our view, be attained through the political capacity of the government to put into perspective the interdependence of ICT in education with its financial management and political agenda.

The cultural context remains yet to be substantially dealt with through Cambodia's ICT in education policy and planning efforts. Foremost is that of the pedagogical legacy of Cambodian education, particularly teaching and learning habits, which have been shaped by not just Cambodia's ravaged past, but also, more importantly, its cultural tradition toward learning and knowledge. The highly unequal relationship between a teacher and a learner is among the most persistent hierarchies in Cambodian society (Chandra 1996). This has established the unquestionable authority and wisdom of the teacher, while the learner is subdued to a position of absorbing information without much opportunity and habit to question and take the initiative for self-learning. As a result, teaching in Cambodia today remains teacher-centered across all levels and subject areas (Nith et al. 2010).

This cultural reality has limited the potential of harnessing ICTs for educational quality. To date, the achievement of ICT in education in Cambodia appears to be at the level of quantity, in terms of figures of teachers trained, number of trainings, software skills provided, coverage of programs, and so forth. The inherent value of ICTs for education is that it provides an independent, self-paced, and goal-oriented learning experience (Knight et al. 2006). Unfortunately, there has not been evidence of Cambodian teachers utilizing ICTs to fulfill this potential. As far as we are aware, no teachers have made use of ICTs to provide a student-centered learning experience, while the most common ICT innovation is distributing typed, instead of previously hand-written, lesson notes and other study materials. The provision of ICT education, particularly in computer courses, is most often delivered through a teacher-centered approach. The hope rests in a new generation of educators. However for such hope to materialize there needs to be interventions that pay close attention to this cultural legacy.

Acknowledgements This work was conducted under a grant from Freedom House, funded under USAID. The authors extend humble gratitude for their support, professionalism, and commitment to human rights issues.

References

Baliamoune-Lutz, M. (2003). An analysis of the determinants and effects of ICT diffusion in developing countries. *Information Technology for Development, 10*, 151–169.

BuddeComm. (2012). Cambodia – telecoms, mobile, internet and forecasts. From http://www.budde.com.au/Research/Cambodia-Telecoms-Mobile-Internet-and-Forecasts.html. Accessed on 6 July 2012.

Central Intelligence Agency (CIA). (2012). The world factbook: Cambodia. From https://www.cia.gov/library/publications/the-world-factbook/geos/countrytemplate_cb.html. Accessed on 1 July 2012.

Chandra, D. (1996). *Facing the Cambodian past. Selected essays 1971–1994*. St. Leonards: Allen & Unwin, Syndney.

Florida, R. (2002). *Rise of the creative class: And how it's transforming work, leisure, community, and everyday life*. Cambridge, MA: Basic Books.

Heeks, R. (1998). *Information technology and public sector corruption*. Manchester: Institute for Development Policy and Management.

International Telecommunications Union. (2002). Khmer Internet: Cambodia case study. Retrieved from http://www.itu.int/asean2001/reports/material/KHM%20CS.pdf

Jalava, J., & Pohjola, M. (2002). Economic growth in the new economy: evidence from advanced economies. *Information Economics and Policy, 14*, 189–210.

Kleine, D., & Unwin, T. (2009). Technological revolution, evolution and new dependencies: What's new about ICT4D? *Third World Quarterly, 30*(5), 1045–1067.

Knight, C., Knight, B. A., & Teghe, D. (2006). Releasing the pedagogical power of information and communication technology for learns: A case study. *International Journal of Education and Development Using Information and Communication Technology, 2*(2), 27–34.

Lund, H., & Sutinen, E. (2010). *Contextualised ICT4D: A bottom-up approach*. Paper presented at the 10th WSEAS international conference on applied computer science. Hamido, Fuji.

Mansell, R., & When, U. (Eds.). (1998). *Knowledge societies: Information technologies for sustainable development, report prepared for the United Nations Commission on Science and Technology for Development*. Oxford: Oxford University Press.

Ministry of Education Youth and Sport. (2004). *Policy and strategies on information and communication technology in education in Cambodia*. From http://planipolis.iiep.unesco.org/upload/Cambodia/Cambodia_Policies_strategies_ICT.pdf. Accessed on 15 May 2012.

Ministry of Education Youth and Sport (MoEYS). (2009). *Master plan for information and communication technology in education*. Phnom Penh: Ministry of Education, Youth and Sport.

Ministry of Education Youth and Sport (MoEYS). (2010). *Education strategic plan 2009–2013*. Phnom Penh.

Ministry of Posts and Telecommunications. (2011). *Telecom infrastructure in Cambodia*. Phnom Penh.

National Council for Teachers of English. (2008). The NCTE definition of 21st century literacies. Retrieved 17 Mar 2012. From http://www.ncte.org/positions/statements/21stcentdefinition. Accessed on 14 Feb 2012.

Nith, B., Wright, W. E., Ear, S., Bredenburg, K., Singh, M. (2010). *Active-learning pedagogies as a reform initiative: The case of Cambodia* (research report). American Institutes for Research.

Oliner, S., & Sichel, D. (2000). The resurgence of growth in the late 1990s: is information technology the story? *Journal of Economic Perspectives, 14*, 3–22.

Organisation for Economic Cooperation and Development (OECD). (1996). The knowledge based economy. From http://www.oecd.org/dataoecd/51/8/1913021.pdf. Accessed on 1 June 2012.
Pohjola, M. (2001). Information technology and economic growth: A cross-country analysis. In M. Pohjola (Ed.), *Information technology, productivity, and economic growth: international evidence and implications for economic development*. Oxford: Oxford University Press.
Richardson, J. W. (2005). Towards democracy: A critique of a World Bank loan to the United Mexican States. *Review of Policy Research, 22*(4), 473–482.
Richardson, J. W. (2008). ICT in education reforms in Cambodia: Problems, politics, and policies impacting implementation. *Information Technologies and International Development, 4*(4), 67–82.
Richardson, J. W. (2011). Challenges of adopting technology for education in less developed countries: The case of Cambodia. *Comparative Education Review, 55*(1), 8–29.
The World Bank. (2012). Cambodia. From http://data.worldbank.org/country/cambodia. Accessed on 17 Mar 2012.
UNESCO. (2004). Establishing the effective use of ICT in Education in Cambodia. From http://www.unescobkk.org/education/ict/ict-in-education-projects/training-of-teachers/establishing-effective-use-of-ict-in-efa-in-cambodia/. Accessed on 17 Mar 2012.
UNESCO. (2011). World data on Education: Cambodia. From http://unesdoc.unesco.org/images/0019/001931/193177e.pdf. Accessed on 20 May 2012.
World Bank. (2007). Tools for institutional, political, and social analysis of policy reform. From http://siteresources.worldbank.org/EXTTOPPSISOU/Resources/1424002-1185304794278/TIPs_Sourcebook_English.pdf. Accessed on 3 June 2012.

Chapter 11
International Aid Influences on South African Policy Development in Education and Training

Peliwe Lolwana

Abstract Theoretically, the purpose of international aid to developing countries is to accelerate economic development for sustainable growth. However, research shows that international aid rarely affects poverty of a country. Political factors dominate the act of giving, influencing decisions about who gives what to whom and why. There has been a growing tendency by international donor countries to influence policy of recipient countries.

During the transition from an apartheid state to democracy, South Africa received international aid from high income countries. This chapter serves to interrogate the influence of this aid in education. Education is a terrain in the South African governance and political area in which contestations were fought during the struggle years. It is also where many far-reaching policies were introduced. This chapter concludes that, while foreign countries wanted to encourage South Africa toward democracy, regarding specific education policies, the education transformation discourse was shaped more by internal forces than external influences.

Studies in donor funding have largely concentrated on asking questions about the donor country as well as the donor recipient country. The theory behind this kind of scrutiny is that there is a pattern of giving that can be understood by analyzing both the donor and recipient countries' conditions (Alesina and Dollar 2000). In fact there is hardly any study that shows that there are no conditions that are attached to the act of donor funding. Some studies factor in the external conditions that affect both the donor and receiving countries at a given time, such as the Cold war politics (Dunning 2004); whilst others look at rent-seeking activities that tend to be induced by foreign aid (Svensson 2000); and some look at the conditions that accompany foreign aid in different countries (Harrison 2001). Some countries are said to have given money to encourage certain styles of governance described as being democratic and open (Alesina and Dollar 2000; Manji 1997). However, there seem to be

P. Lolwana (✉)
Researching Education and Labour Centre, University of Witwatersrand,
Johannesburg, South Africa
e-mail: peliwe.lolwana@wits.ac.za

C.A. Brown (ed.), *Globalization, International Education Policy and Local Policy Formation,* Policy Implications of Research in Education 5,
DOI 10.1007/978-94-007-4165-2_11

very few instances where donor money is given because of the country's poverty levels, confirming the hypothesis that donor money is given for ulterior motives other than to aid the alleviation of poverty. The effect of donor funding in Africa tends to dominate the literature, as this continent has been the destination of more foreign donor funds than anywhere else in the world.

This chapter is an attempt to expand on this literature by looking at the case of South Africa as a donor recipient in education and training. South Africa presents an interesting case in the area of foreign aid. Firstly, there is not much written about this country as a foreign aid recipient. Partly this is because South Africa can be regarded as a newcomer in donor funding since there was an interruption in international relations due to the apartheid policies the country pursued. In other words, there was no country with sensibilities who would give money to South Africa for a long time. The coming back to the international fold of South Africa in the early 1990s marked a momentous occasion for the country that warrants closer scrutiny. We need to know who gave money and for what? Secondly, as many studies have shown that there is no free lunch in the foreign aid world, we want to find out about the nature of the payment that South Africa had to give in receiving foreign aid. All this will be done specifically in the education and training sector. Thirdly, if no conditions could be found, we want to know how international influences got into the South African education and training system.

As South Africans ponder the seemingly intractable problems we encounter in our education and training system today, this reflection is important as it provides an historical account of how we came to this point. If we are to improve our education and training system, we have to reflect on what we are doing, what we are achieving against what we set out to achieve, and why deviations or unexpected results are occurring. We cannot advance without making mistakes on the way, but we must evaluate and learn from our successes and mistakes. Without this we cannot improve. The lessons here are not only meant for South Africa but for other countries as well who might find themselves in the midst of similar circumstances. This paper tries to make a contribution from an academic platform, a distance away from the policy making arena and therefore provide other scholars with something to think about on the topic discussed here.

This chapter will present information that could be gathered with regard to the nature of aid in South African education. This information is collected from interviews with government officials who have been working in this area and those who have been involved in the administration of donor funds. However, these reports tend to be anecdotal rather than evidence-based or empirical. We will look at the major policy shifts that have occurred since the new democratic government took over. Then an interrogation of the nature of engagement of international donors during this phase when the education was being reconstructed in the country will be made. This analysis will be done in order to see whether or not the international donors did influence these policy developments. The period under analysis here are the last 20 years (1991–2011) during which the South African government has changed the policies of education and training. But first let us take a quick tour and chronicle the history of donor funding in the country during the period under review.

11.1 The Complex Act of Giving Money to a Country in Transition

Research shows that the pattern of giving is dictated by political and strategic considerations (Alesina and Dollar 2000; Svensson 2000; Manji 1997; Dunning 2004). There is evidence that many formerly colonised countries receive more money from their colonisers than the rest. There is evidence that in some instances political alliances matter for most donors. For example whereas United Nations voting is something that matters a lot for countries like France, for the United States of America, its interest in the Middle East tends to influence who they give money to and how much (Dunning 2004). According to Dunning, in all instances, the Cold War seemed to dominate the interests of the West in buying allegiances in Africa. South Africa has also been caught up in similar global dynamics. But in the case of South Africa, it is my opinion that the act of foreign aid giving has been propelled by double guilt. It was the colonisation guilt that comes from the British and the Dutch and on top of that apartheid that subjugated the indigenous people to poverty and slavery and denied them complete citizenship in the country of their birth. Whilst many former colonies in the continent continued to recover from the brutality of colonisation, South Africa continued with the internal conflict caused by the apartheid system well into the 1990s.

During the apartheid years, the country was in serious conflict with itself. But the greatest galvanisation against apartheid was happening outside the country by those who were in exile together with the countries and groups in the anti-apartheid movement. When the exiles or returnees came back, they brought back the greatest potential for foreign aid to be used in building the country that was ravished by the apartheid wars. Foreign aid did not come only after the 1994 independence. There were many countries who had decided to work with non-governmental organizations (NGOs) during the apartheid years. As Habib and Taylor (1999) note, the position adopted by foreign donor countries and multinationals who worked with NGOs in South Africa was atypical. This set out a different trend for the relationship that foreign aid was to have with the country. Giving money to education was logical as political struggles in education dominated the news with the Soweto uprising of 1976 being the apex of all that symbolised youth revolution against apartheid education. Therefore, donor funding in South African education can be chronicled in three phases spanning the period that precedes the new democratic government (1991–1994); the establishment phase (1994–2004); and the consolidation phase (2005–2011).

Interviews with key individuals who managed large sums of funds donated to the ruling party, as a government in waiting, during the early 1990s are instructive about the patterns of funding before and after the democratic government came into power. Pre-1994, the anti-apartheid movement abroad was galvanised as friends of the oppressed in South Africa. Through this movement, different countries gave funding to NGOs that were intervening in the education of the oppressed inside the country. The volume of foreign aid that flowed into these NGOs was huge and in some instances created formidable entities inside the country. One example would be the Kagiso Trust that managed huge sums of money and funded various education projects. The South African Council of Churches (SACC); the South African Bishop's Conference (SABC); and the Trade Unions were some of the notable conduits for donor funding. Adult education, early childhood education, and basic skills training programmes were the main beneficiaries of donor funding. This in many ways encouraged the neglect of these sectors by government later on.

During the period between the release of former President Mandela and the onset of the new government there was a heavy traffic of funds from the 'friends' of South Africa. This was the period when the African National Congress (ANC) as a 'government in waiting' was busy preparing for its policies in government. A National Education Policy Initiative (NEPI) was a huge policy development that endeavoured to cover all aspects of education with which the new government would deal. Between 1991 and 1993, the best progressive intellectuals in the country gathered to discuss and establish policies that would replace the apartheid system of education. The group of policy makers was a mix of academics who had been in the country writing about the system and those who had just returned from exile. These policies became the bedrock of the new democratic government's education policies when it took over.

From 1994, the establishment phase of the new government was characterised by great expectations in education. New policies were introduced to replace the abhorrent apartheid education system. In schools, a policy of outcomes-based education was introduced. In 1995, the South African Qualifications Authority (SAQA) Act was promulgated, which brought about the National Qualifications Framework. In 1996, a Higher Education Commission was set up to look into the establishment of a new higher education system. In 1998, a Committee for Further Education and Training was set up to look into the technical college system. There were many other investigations that followed, such as inclusive education, adult education, etc. In 1998, the Department of Labour introduced the Skills Development Act. The whole education and training system was in flux. This was not an easy period for donor funding as the set up in the country was quite complex. By 1994, a package of alternative educational needs was on the table and influenced the type of relationships the government was to have with donors.[1] For example, adult education was a favourite for the Swedes, and yet this was not an area that was high up in the government's agenda at the time. The Japanese only wanted to build schools and were less interested in policy development. The European Union had a history of funding adult education, early childhood development, and skills development.[2] The question that was being asked was how the previous initiatives with NGOs were to be channelled to the new areas that the new government was focusing on and how to migrate from NGO funding to government funding.

[1] This is based on an interview with the longest serving government official on international donor funding in education – Mr Jeppie Galiep.

[2] This is based on an interview with Mr. Gareth Rossiter, who was involved in managing the largest fund that the European Union gave to the country.

The contestation about whether or not donor funding should continue coming through NGOs started early in the first years of the new government. The government needed budget support as government needs were extensive. Treasury stepped in to coordinate the process and convened the donor sector, resulting in all funding coming through the then Reconstruction and Development Office. In the first 10 years of the new government, there was still a huge donor presence, some giving large sums and some giving smaller sums of money. This was the Mandela Presidency era, and many countries wanted to be seen to be on the right side of South African politics as well as establish a presence that was considered to be strategic and moral. As Jansen (2004a) aptly puts this sentiment:

> In this context, a large number of international donor agencies lined up at the door of South African government and its department of Education, offering assistance. The dramatic termination of apartheid, accompanied by the powerful media images that marked the transition (Mandela's 'walk to freedom' through his prison gates, the crowds of first-time voters, the wrenching public confessions of 'truths' – if not reconciliation) combined to make South Africa – at least for the moment –the first choice destination of foreign aid. (p.215).

However, the coordination of donor funding would not run smoothly until later, as donors continued to have their preferred projects or provinces. During the early years, the donors were dealing with a 'young' civil service that did not understand the donor funding procedures well. The added disadvantage was that there was not a lot of information about the national education system. Apartheid education was a fragmented system that did not produce a detailed and complete picture and was thus extremely weak on information systems. In 1996, the Swedes funded the School Register of Needs survey, which documented in great deal the national picture of the school education system.

It was only during the next 5 years of government that the coordination of donor funding was streamlined. The Tirisano project of the second minister in the new government defined niche areas for donor funding and even a consideration of channelling some of the funding to the NGOs to speed up delivery was on the table. In the middle of this period, an event far away from South Africa occurred. The U.S. invaded Iraq, and the West was called upon to give support to the U.S.'s activities in war. When the rumors surfaced that the United Kingdom was going to cut short funding it gave to South Africa through the Department for International Development (DfID) in order to divert the money to support the American war in Iraq, the Minister of Education was beyond being angry. This was the first time that the Ministry had to engage DfId as a funding agency in a more confrontational way about the aid, demanding a fulfilment of earlier commitment to the country by the United Kingdom and would not back down when told the funds were being diverted to other international causes. This in some ways showed that aid was not necessarily dispensable and South Africa needed this funding. On the other hand, South Africa remained focused on what the country will take money for and what it will not. For example, there is a view that one of the reasons why the World Bank has never been big in funding education in the country is because of the Bank's insistence on funding primary education whereas South Africa did not consider this to be a priority.[3] Donor funding levels remained constant during this period.

When the country entered its third cycle of elections in 2005 and the education system got its third minister, different shifts were beginning to unfold. First, the country was being recognised as a middle income country and donors began to look at South Africa differently. For example, the requirement for reciprocity in funding began to be an issue during this period. In other words, the country had to indicate how much it was bringing to the table for most donors to fund a project. Secondly, the donor discourse was changing around the world as donor countries were beginning to assess the benefit to them. Thirdly, many countries that had been strong donors initially, like the Scandinavian countries, had pulled out or were in the process of pulling out of funding South African education. Fourthly, South Africa also started to get requests from other countries for support as well, especially from the Southern African Development Economic Community (SADEC).

At the time of writing this chapter, the country is in its fourth cycle of political elections and has two ministers of education as the portfolio has been split into basic and higher education ministries. The country is no longer a favourite as a donor funding destination. The country competes for external aid as a middle income country. Countries that give funds have dramatically shrunk to a handful. Basic education, which is composed of 12 grades of school education, is still receiving the bulk of funding. Further education and training is beginning to receive attention, but it is a sector that is not as high priority as higher education and basic education. The new Higher Education and Training Department has been constructed from the University and Further Education and Training section of the previous Department of Education as well as the Skills Development section of the Department of Labour. It is for this reason that we touch on the donor funding of the latter section in this narrative. The Skills Development section of the Department of Labour has been a benefactor of huge funds for labour market and skills development from many countries.

11.2 Major Education and Training Policy Shifts in Post-apartheid South Africa

There is no governmental function that has received as much attention for change as the education system in South Africa. Whilst in some government departments change meant introducing black people to govern or replacing whites, in some changes in administration and in some instances starting new services; in education there was an urgency to change the whole policy system of apartheid education as it was at the core of apartheid. In changing apartheid education, not only was the administration involved, but the whole society as education tends to attract the attention of the whole public, since everybody has a stake in education. The policies that will be

[3] Based on interviews with Mr. Gareth Rossiter and Ms Jennifer Biscard who handled European Union and USAID funding streams respectively.

selected below for discussion do not represent the totality of changes in education and training, but a few that can be considered to represent a big part of the transformation of the education and training system in the country. Further, these policies are very useful for interrogating the issue of international aid in education policy making in South Africa. The selected policies are: (1) the National Qualifications Framework (NQF); (2) the Outcomes based Education (OBE); and (3) Skills Development. This also represents the sequence in which new policies were introduced in the South African education and training system by the new government. Although these policies were targeting different educational issues, they speak to the same mantra of reform in education and training.

11.2.1 The National Qualifications Framework

The National Qualifications Framework (NQF) was the first Act to be introduced by the Department of Education in 1995 (SAQA 1995). The first publication on the NQF in South Africa was published by the Human Science Research Council in September 1995. In this document, the proponents and developers of the NQF advance the position that this new policy was to help South Africa find a whole new way of thinking about its education and training system:

> Although not yet a commonplace in thinking of a majority of South Africans, a major initiative called the National Qualifications Framework has been proposed to address some of the urgent reforms needed in South African education and training. The thinking which has been done about the National Qualifications Framework, or NQF as it is more commonly known, has been done in the hope of finding a holistic view of the personal, social, and economic needs of our rapidly developing society, and then propose ways forward to address all these concerns on a broad and integrated front (HSRC 1995, p.5).

The document goes on to argue that it is difficult to imagine that there is anyone in South African education who cannot understand the difficulties experienced quite acutely by people as they try to grapple with working through a multitude of educational bodies inherited from the apartheid state. Here, the policy makers hit a raw nerve as apartheid was characterized by many educational bodies that were racially based. The NQF was introduced as a body that would put everyone and all kinds of learning in one system, something South Africans were eager for.

The NQF in South Africa was introduced as part of the revolutionary shift of introducing an integrated and equal education system in South Africa, moving away from the separate and unequal education and training authorities systems of the apartheid government. Young (2004) points out that NQFs are top down initiatives led by governments or government agencies and based on a set of general principles about how qualifications should be designed and what they should achieve. This was the case with the introduction of the South African NQF. The introduction of the NQF in South Africa was a result of a seemingly unlikely alliance between business and trade unions, which were incidentally solving different problems, of an integrated system in which skills development was an important element. There was at the time a raging international debate on integration and lifelong education with strong attempts to bring both adult and vocational education to the main stream of education (Jansen 2004a, b). This will be further elaborated on in the section on skills development.

The introduction of a National Qualifications Framework was an important symbolic shift for a government put under pressure to move away from the apartheid system of education (Jansen 2004a, b). This shift was important because it was sending a message that the South African state, in entering the realm of global politics and economics, was going to pick on the most modern features in its policy-making. The concept of the National Qualifications Frameworks was new as it was just a handful of countries that had introduced the concept at the time. Although South Africa can be regarded as one of the early introducers of the NQF, many countries have since followed and many more countries are introducing the NQFs (Allais 2010). What makes this policy spectacularly popular? Are there positive results to show the usefulness of this policy in making the education system better? I will draw from Allais' (2010) work in looking at the usefulness of this policy choice for South Africa. Although Allais has written widely on NQFs, this particular piece used here is a research done in 16 countries to show that South Africa is not in a unique situation on the failures and these failures are not just about weaknesses in the implementation of the NQF.

Allais (2010) first gives the following common reasons why countries introduce NQFs:

- Improving the communication of qualification systems;
- Improving the transparency of individual qualifications through learning outcomes;
- Reducing the 'mismatch between education and the labour market';
- Implementing a system for credit accumulation and transfer;
- Recognizing prior learning' access;
- Establishing quality assurance systems and new regulatory, assessment, and certification mechanisms;
- Reforming delivery of education and training;
- Improving parity of esteem for TVET and skills qualifications;
- Increasing private sector financial contribution, especially for TVET and skills training;
- Gaining international recognition and labour mobility; and
- Establishing broader goals, e.g. social cohesion; access to education by marginalised groups; international competitiveness; and generally transforming the education labour market, economy and society in general.

In the case of South Africa, Allais (2010) found that none of the goals that the NQF had set out to achieve were achieved through the NQF as a chosen policy. Instead, the formal education system had sidestepped the NQF system and continued as before. Jansen (2004a, b) is of the opinion that the school education policy development process was already behind when the NQF, led by the training sector, was established.

> It came down to education inserting singular lines about schooling into an already elaborate policy on training. This is partly explained by the fact that, unlike education, 'framework thinking' and competency-based thinking were rooted in long-developed constituency deliberations of the powerful trade union, COSATU (p.206).

It was the rest of the system, mainly training, that had valiantly tried to implement the NQF. Where attempts to implement the system were small, this part was weak and new. As a result, very few of the thousands of qualifications and unit standards in the South African Qualifications Authority (SAQA) base were actually being taken up by learners, fewer were finding currency in other learning institutions and industry, and generally there was no visible and positive impact of such an expensive policy. During the implementation of the NQF policy, it was soon becoming clear that the policy was failing to address the issues it faced after years of apartheid education. The policy also failed because of its optimism in using weak and marginal institutions to transform education and society. In addition, if one looks closely at the reasons for introducing this policy, one finds that it was regarded as a panacea for all that is wrong in education and society. For example the assumption that this policy could have power to influence job creation and a just and cohesive society cannot be correct. This policy has been reviewed twice, but the government of the day has not had the courage to abandon and move away from it.

11.2.2 The Outcomes-Based Education System

The outcomes-based education (OBE) system was one of the first suites of policies to be introduced by the new government in South Africa. Underpinned by Dr. William Spady's, a renowned North American academic, philosophy of OBE, South Africa developed its own OBE model. Fundamental to this model is the so-called Critical Cross-field Outcomes. These outcomes, which are generic in nature, were subdivided into seven critical and five developmental outcomes. An analysis of these outcomes reveals that cultivation of cognitive capacity has prominence. The Critical Outcomes have their origins in the NQF discourse, and that makes South African OBE uniquely South African and complex. This relationship between OBE and NQF can also be seen as an important attempt of the school education system to relate to what was assumed to be 'representative' of the whole education and training system, the NQF. To ensure that these Critical Outcomes did not remain mere visionary benchmarks, attempts were made to operationalize them within the South African school system by means of an outcomes-based curriculum. As a result, an OBE curriculum was introduced in schools from 1998—initially by means of Curriculum 2005 (C2005), which was followed by the Revised National Curriculum Statement (RNCS) and by the National Curriculum Statement (NCS). OBE has received wide criticism from academics and the public at large in the country.

Chisholm (2010) argues that it is wrong that the ruling party's (African National Congress) vision on education has become identified with OBE. She argues that there is no basis for this mistaken identity. But OBE has become the face of what is wrong with the school system in South Africa. OBE was introduced at the early stages of the new government. Literature shows that OBE was not borrowed from one specific country or one person's ideas. For example Spreen (2001) shows that OBE was not only introduced in South Africa but that the South African version was actually an amalgam of the early debates about competency-based education in Australia, Canada, New Zealand, and some of Spady's work. OBE represented a dramatic shift from the previous education system calling for a paradigm shift from a content-based teaching and learning system to one that is outcomes based. However, Spreen (2001) is of the opinion that the South African version of OBE was different from other OBEs in the world and was specifically adapted to local responses. Jansen (2004a, b) disputes this and explains it as denialism on policy borrowing that resulted in the South African version of OBE. One of the key differences was the attempt to tie the school curriculum to the National Qualifications Framework by introducing Critical Outcomes, an NQF language. This made South African OBE a very indigenous and localized policy, but also very unwieldy.

The first graders of 1998 were the first cohort to be introduced to OBE in the classroom and although they were supposed to continue with this curriculum through the 12 grades of their schooling years; this never was, as the department of education had to call for the policy's review in 2001. There are two questions that we have to ponder in this chapter about this policy: (i) why did this policy that later elicited so much criticism in education circles resonate so much with the transformation agenda in the country? and (ii) was there any donor influence in the adoption of such a widely criticised policy?

According to Chisholm (2010), the concept of an outcomes-based education first appeared in the South African Qualifications Authority Act (SAQA) (1995) before it was taken over in the basic education, which is composed of 12 years of schooling. The initial reference to outcomes-based education before this was only in reference to adult basic and further education, not in school education. What brought this shift about seems to have been subtle and pervasive moves through which policy ideas travel. Chisholm and Leyendecker (2008) give us an analytical account of how OBE appeared and was regarded as a fitting replacement for the unjust and undemocratic apartheid education. They argue that the OBE concept was strengthened at the same time that concepts like learner-centered education were. Both concepts are seen as being closely linked with democracy, social justice, and economic and political goals. Much has been written about how unfounded these assumptions have been (Jansen 1997, 1999, 2004a, b; Jansen and Christie 1999; Muller and Taylor 1995). After the promulgation of the SAQA Act, OBE was developed in the Department of Education as a policy in 1997 and implemented in 1998. The new policy of OBE incorporated most of the features of the learner-centred ideas, in spite of the latter not having been successful in countries in which it was introduced, like Namibia (Chisholm and Leyendecker 2008).

In South Africa the finger is always pointed to Dr. William Spady[4] as the main transporter of OBE. However, Spady has defended himself in spite of him often

[4] A North American academic.

being introduced as the 'Father of OBE' during his first trip in South Africa, in 1997, when he conducted a nationwide lecture on OBE (Spady 2007). In fact Spady reports that he was horrified when he saw what evolved as Curriculum 2005 and was eventually taken to be OBE. Spady's version of his role in the development of the South African OBE is further corroborated by Jansen (2004a, b) who assigns a foreign consultant role to Spady's role in the process. According to Jansen, Spady was brought in the middle of the process by a government that was insecure about the OBE policy and facing a deluge of public criticism. Dr. Spady, as an international expert, was the perfect intervention the government needed to help change the public's perception on OBE. For reasons not explained to Spady, what was later going to be known as OBE, was greatly influenced by the National Qualifications thinking and development. What Spady also could not read is the complexity of the bureaucracy of the new government that was made up of old bureaucrats who wanted to pursue their own policy agendas and the new bureaucrats who were keen to transform the education system but were very inexperienced in government administration. In the process, Spady's script on OBE was lost, and he has come to distance himself from the South African OBE.

11.2.3 The Skills Development

The skills revolution has been part of South Africa's reconstruction agenda with intentions to move away from an apartheid state characterised by 'master-slave' skills polarization. To this end then the skills development policy was one of the key policy initiatives launched by the post-apartheid government in South Africa. The assumption that was being made was that there would be a single education and training system in the same lines as was the case in many OECD countries. The integration of education and training did not happen until 2009. Prior to this date, training was the responsibility of the Department of Labour. The entry of donors in support of the training function has been quite different from that experienced in education and this is worth taking a closer look at.

Carton and King (2004) stitch for us a rich tapestry of the role of international agencies in the evolution of the skills development policies in the country. This tapestry has been further confirmed by two of the key architects of the skills development policy in South Africa, Bird and Jansen (2004a, b). Accordingly, the start of international support was located within the union movement in the country before it moved to the government space. The Swedish funder, Swedish International Development (SIDA), was in the forefront of supporting nongovernmental organizations (NGOs) under 'solidarity' funding to individuals and organizations that were seen to be advancing a just cause. The German Chambers of Commerce followed this trend in the mid-1980s, supporting the workers' advancement through special training schemes. It was in the late 1980s that a large union, the National Union of Metal Workers, in South Africa (NUMSA), began to take a lead in shaping the skills development agenda in the country. NUMSA was greatly aided by the support it received from the Australian union movement. This was the time when it was becoming clear that there would be a political change in the government of South Africa. By the time the new government took over, the technical assistance given to the South African unions had grown beyond the Australian source and included the United Kingdom's Department for International Development (DfID), the Germans (GTZ), the Danish funding agency (Danida), the Irish, the Scandinavians, the Koreans, the Japanese, and the European Union(EU).

The GTZ and EU contributions to the skills development agenda of South Africa present us with particular cases that are worth closer examination here. There is no single funder in this whole process that had the length, breadth, and intensity of support as GTZ in the skills development agenda of South Africa. GTZ had moved from supporting individual projects to having an integrated approach to skills development agenda in a period of more than a decade in the country. GTZ also had one country director for 13 years in the country, who in the words of Carton and King (2004) became a 'trusted advisor' to the government. GTZ facilitated some pilots in the unfolding skills development agenda in South Africa. The sectorial program support given by the Germans built a lot of confidence for the developing system. Then the European Union came with the largest donor funding for one single project South Africa had ever experienced (approximately €254 million). Unlike the German support, which was mainly facilitative and back-stopping, the EU came with an army of technical experts to help South Africa implement its ambitious skills development program. This program was, according to the GTZ director: "Possibly the one of the most advanced skills development plans developed by any nation in the world" (Carton and King 2004, p. 28). The teams of international technical assistance brought by the EU were located within the Department of Labour and reported to the South African officials. We shall return later to the dynamics of this arrangement. We must first look at what was happening in the country as this money was flowing in.

11.2.4 Internal Shifts in the Skills Development Arena

What started as a union-to-union cooperation in skills development matters soon became a coalescing of a creative alliance of trade union educators, progressive employers, academics, and even individuals from government. This coalescing was gearing up to mount oppositional policies to the National Training Board (NTB), which was the custodian of training policies for the apartheid government. In 1991 the NTB had presented its new National Training Strategy as a reform of the apartheid policies. However, the NTB lacked legitimacy as an apartheid created organization. By 1993, the Congress of South African Trade Unions (COSATU) and the now ruling political party, the African National Congress (ANC), were working closely together in developing policies that would replace the National Training Strategy of the NTB. The major criticisms of the National Training Strategy were lack of representation and transparency. The incorporation of the ANC as a government in waiting was inevitable, and COSATU's muscle was not only through its alliance with the ruling party, but its knowledge of the skills development issues it had accumulated over the period in which it had worked closely with other international trade unions, which made it a valuable partner. The National Training Strategy Initiative (NTSI) was then borne, comprised of the apartheid government, the government in waiting, trade unions, and employers. This is the period that McGrath and Badroodien (2006) term "shifting from resistance to policy thinking," (p. 7) and it was clear that the National Union for Metal workers of South Africa (NUMSA) as a union was leading.

The NTSI was made up of eight working groups, and the work of the Working Group 2, on "integration of education and training, competencies and career paths and Certification" (McGrath and Badroodien 2006, p. 9), is of particular interest in this discussion. According to McGrath and Badroodien (2006), both the business representatives and COSATU were finding a degree of common ground at the NTSI and were keen to adopt policy debates that were taking place internationally.

> In September 1993, the leading business representative on this committee, Bryan Phillips, from the mining firm, GENCOR, responded to the emergent COSATU thinking about a National Qualifications Framework (NQF) with an explicit drawing on New Zealand model, as well as English and Scottish practice. The document seemed largely oriented towards showing the wider business community that the COSATU position could be reworked in ways that were advantageous to employers (McGrath and Badroodien 2006, pp.9).

The lobbying that took place between business and trade unions was clearly targeting the resistance coming from the old state, but it was strongly informed by international debates and policy trends.

11.2.5 International Influence on Policy Making in South Africa

If you ask anyone in South Africa who has knowledge of donor funding, past and present, if international aid had an influence on policy making in the country's education, the answer is always unequivocally "no". This response is also collaborated by research done on South Africa and the donor community (Carton and King 2004; McGrath and Badroodien 2006; Jansen 2004a, b). There are three reasons always given about why donor money was never used to promote specific policies in South Africa. One reason is that international donor funds were always used as budget support and not for policy development. The second reason given is that South African education and training budget is too large and international funds are too small to carry out governmental budgets. The most important reason given for the absence of direct influence of donor funding into South African policy making is a combination of factors in the country that ensured that the policy making process and outcomes were going to be homemade, namely the overwhelming determination to innovate and change; the availability of intellectuals who have thought and written on the matters that needed attention and change; the very principles on which the new order was being built on, such as participation and transparency; and the financial muscle the country had in accepting and rejecting aide. South Africans embraced the reform with much enthusiasm and in the process brought in a whole range of new policies in the education system, which were to change the education discourse. These new policies were not uniquely South African but borrowed from all over. The next question then is about the nature of this borrowing if it did not come as a condition for international aide.

In spite of the absence of directives from donors regarding international aid given to South Africa for education and training, there was a complex interaction that happened between South Africans and the international community that resulted in borrowing of policies from all over the world. First, the need to move dramatically away from the apartheid legacy was a strong driving force for almost all South Africans. Policy makers, academics, workers, and NGOs raided the world looking for answers. In the early 1990s, South Africa produced a number of experts of different calibers who were advocating for one or another policy. Some South Africans had already had close working relationships with different countries even before international aid could come formally into the country, and all they had to do was to grow and intensify those relationships. The case in point is the relationships that were formed by the South African Trade Unions and Australian Trade Unions and the anti-apartheid movement abroad. Even though this aide came in the form of solidarity initially, as the political system was quickly getting overturned, this aid also soon changed to policy transfer (Carton and King 2004). The first policy to be put on the table was that of the National Qualifications Framework and the subsequent policies of outcomes-based education and skills development were based firmly on the National Qualifications framework. In the initial policy of the NQF, the trade unions were leading the debates and so was it with the skills development. It is still not clear why school educationists felt obliged to take on these policies. Perhaps it was a matter of being 'progressive,' and these were the only concepts that were on the table.

The timing of this borrowing is also illuminating. Carton and King (2004) trace the steps that were travelled by the policies that became global policies. For example, they are of the opinion that the reason Australia was to become a fertile source of ideas for South African ideas in skills development and qualifications frameworks was because they themselves had recently undergone major restructuring of their industry and economy due to a massive loss of jobs that preceded their establishment of their bible of Australia's industrial skills revolution. The Australians themselves had travelled to Sweden, Germany, the United Kingdom, Denmark, Belgium, and Luxembourg to borrow the best policies. The message was clear:

> That high skills and high wages would be critical to Australia's global competitiveness, and that this would mean massive changes to its own version of 'apartheid' in which there was an extremely rigid skills system, with little or no flexibility or mobility of workers within its own different provinces (p. 22).

This reconstruction was to be followed by New Zealand. When South Africa came along looking for ideas, there was a lot of resonance with the new look policies as they were seemingly addressing similar concerns as those of South Africa. It was therefore not surprising that when the ideas of a new training strategy emerged in the discussions prior to the onset of the new government both the trade unions and business participants who were familiar with the New Zealand and Australian policies immediately found each other and led the course of development.

The events about the OBE were slightly different, though. The question that we must return to is whether or not South Africans were sold a policy in OBE that has come to haunt them, directly or indirectly. This is a difficult question to answer as the dynamics at play are quite complex. There are various OBE policies all over the world and South Africa was not the first country to adopt such a policy. Was there money given through aid to help the country to travel this path? The answer to this question is "no". However, South Africa started its new democracy with an urgent need to transform the apartheid education. So, the country was searching for new and cutting edge ideas. There is no doubt that the country was susceptible to external influence in its attempt to modernize its education system.

South Africa at the beginning of the new democratic government was intent on democratizing and modernizing all parts of its society and government. In education OBE was the modern democratic trend. In the early days of the new government, there was money for education trips to go and examine emerging ideas deeper. These policy excursions were always going to be dangerous because it seemed like the new government was bent on getting new ideas for no apparent reason other than to replace the much hated apartheid education. In other words it was political rather than educational expediency. But the ideas always germinated from inside the country, and this has even been confirmed by academics that were critical of OBE (Soudien 1997; Chisholm and Leyendecker 2008; Chisholm 2010). Therefore, there was no justification for the exorbitant funds that were spent on the expensive trips for policy 'lessons'. To add to this complexity, donor support often came with technical advisory that was brought in to enhance the ideas being contemplated if the countries giving support did not have technical advisory inside the country. New officials in the department who had no experience in government were often vulnerable to these seemingly big ideas that have been tried in seemingly successful education systems. They had no idea what it would take to implement the new ideas and the risk they were putting the country into as they pushed ahead for change at all cost. So, in the case of OBE, it was a major and modern policy shift for the country that was introduced. It was a global idea that was operating in many countries around the world. Donors knew about it, the new officials who had been living outside the country had heard about it, and some academics had studied it and were supportive of it. OBE did not work in the majority of South African schools, as it is a policy that requires well resourced schools with expert teachers who could handle a curriculum that is not dependent on a single textbook. The failures of this policy led the government to review it in 2000, only 2 years since its implementation, simplifying and strengthening its character. In 2009 there was a further review of its implementation in order to remove further constraints. In spite of all the efforts put into improving the efficacy of this policy, there remain many lingering criticisms on the ground, and all that is not working in education is blamed on OBE as a foreign policy to South Africa that should not have been introduced in the first place.

Having stated earlier that there was no direct donor agency influence in the policy development of the South African education, let me end by contradicting myself on the possibility that this could have played a role, even small, in the decisions made about giving money. The role of donor agencies in supporting the policy development, even though it was indirect, is something that cannot be completely overlooked. Donor support provided financial ability to travel and learn about the latest ideas in education. There is also a subtle connection that can be made regarding common ideals and values between the giving and receiving country. This connection is not direct nor is it overt but takes some sophisticated analysis and knowledge of the countries involved in giving and receiving. For example, Carton and King (2004) outline for us this pattern:

- The Danish concerns with democratizing South Africa leading to the support it gave to the education system that would equalize opportunities for all in the country in the form of skills development;
- The EU's decision to intervene in poverty alleviation and thus put aid in skills development;
- DfID's concerns with the promotion of better education and health and thus assisting in changing school education to OBE.

This mapping can be extended to other donor countries as the general concern was that of aiding South Africa in its transition to a better, equal, and just society. Where it becomes complicated is when we start looking at the role of the international officials positioned at the international aid offices in the country. Carton and King (2004) suggest that the dynamics, which shaped the policy discourse of borrowing were at play were not straightforward.

> The aid agencies *were* thus faced in South Africa with the same type of issues as some which have been discussed for more than a decade in their home countries. Their policy concerning South Africa *would* then depend on their own national political context as well as on the way they *were* managing the new aid trends (poverty, coherence, aid versus trade, etc. (p.13).

But the South Africans, by and large, managed technical support in government. For example, technical experts reported to government officials not to donor agencies.

Then the timing itself of international aid flowing to South Africa coincided with a particular stage in donor history. According to Carton and King (2004) this was the time when there was emphasis on basic education after the 1990 World Conference on Education for All. This conference shifted policies for many countries including those that were to give donor funding to South Africa. The consequence of this was that most countries had reduced capacity of expertise in the areas in which South Africa was introducing innovations. With the exception of Germany, the donor staff that came to South Africa was not strong in the areas to which they were giving money. The South Africans borrowed a lot of policy from the international arena, but they made sure that this was 'South Africanized' and that they led the process of borrowing.

11.3 Conclusion

South Africa did not get aid for its policy development from its colonizers only, but the nature of resistance against apartheid had galvanized a lot of countries over the years. When democracy was imminent, these countries were at the country's doorstep to give aid – small and big. There do not seem to be any conditions that were attached to the aid given, but it was definitely clear that aid was an encouragement for democracy, human rights, and a just society. Any policy changes that fitted broadly in this realm were to be encouraged and supported. Also, South Africa was seen as a gateway to African trade and therefore a useful economic partner later on.

The National Qualifications Framework became the launching pad for introducing new policies in education and training in the country. It became the root policy for both the outcomes-based education and skills development policies. This policy was sold to the public under the guise of integrating education from the disparate education authorities of the apartheid government and integration of different types of education and outcomes into one system. These policies were appealing to policy makers as they also spoke to modern international debates in education and training at the time.

Although there is no evidence of donor agencies selling any specific policies, the role of international officials who worked in international aid offices was complex, indirect, and sometimes inept. From the beginning of this process, there was already a lot of policy borrowing that had been done by the different policy makers in the country. International aid helped the borrowing by financing a range of exchanges and policy making travel. Because the policy debates in South Africa engaged in during the time of donor giving were current, it was easy for the aid workers to identify with the issues as these were also germane back home. They sounded like the right things to support.

What makes South Africa different from its African counterparts is the fact that the country has been relatively wealthy and the government has been able to afford most of the country's provisioning needs. According to Carton and King (2004), South Africa at the time of rapid change needed knowledge more than infrastructure. When donor funds came into South Africa, there was already a level of policy development sophistication in the country that sometimes was more advanced than in donor countries. The opportunity to change government made South Africa bold and ambitious. The changes that came to be were a result of an extensive search by South Africans to reform but met with an army of donors who were eager to help South Africa make the transition to democracy. South Africans have nobody to blame for the policy mistakes they have made but themselves.

References

Alesina, A., & Dollar, D. (2000). Who gives foreign aid to whom and why? *Journal of Economic Growth, 5*, 33–63.

Allais, S. (2010). *The implementation and impact of National qualifications frameworks: Report of a study in 16 countries*. Geneva: International Labour Office.

Carton, M., & King, K. (2004). Transforming the labour skills arena in South Africa: the international dimension. http://www.iued.unige.ch – publications@iued.unige.ch. Accessed on 1 June 2013.

Chisholm, L. (2010). A Discussion paper on outcomes-based education: demystifying and de-demonising our national curriculum. Unpublished paper.

Chisholm, L., & Leyendecker, R. (2008). Curriculum reform in sub-Saharan Africa: when local meets global. In R. Cowen & M. Kazamias (Eds.), *International handbook of comparative education* (pp. 675–692). New York: Springer Science + Business Media B.V.

Dunning, T. (2004). Conditioning the effects of aid: Cold war politics, donor credibility, and democracy in Africa. *International Organization, 58*, 409–423.

Habib, A., & Taylor, R. (1999). South Africa: Anti-apartheid NGOs in transition. *International Journal of Non-profit Organisations, 10*(1), 73–82.

Harrison, G. (2001). Post-conditionality politics and administrative reform: Reflections on cases of Uganda and Tanzania. *Development and Change, 32*, 657–679.

Human Science Research Council. (1995). *Ways of seeing the National Qualifications Framework*. Pretoria: HSRC Press.

Jansen, J. (1997). Essential alterations? A critical analysis of the state's syllabus revision process. *Perspectives in Education, 17*(2), 1–11.

Jansen, J. (1999). A very noisy OBE: The implementation of OBE in grade 1 classrooms. In J. Jansen & P. Christie (Eds.), *Changing curriculum: Studies on outcomes-based education in South Africa*. South Africa: Juta, Academic.

Jansen, J. (2004a). Importing outcomes –based education into South Africa: Policy borrowing in a post-communist world. In D. Philips & K. Ochs (Eds.), *Educational policy borrowing: International perspectives* (pp. 199–220). Oxford: Symposium.

Jansen, J. (2004b). Importing outcomes based education into South Africa; policy borrowing in a post-communist world. In D. Phillips & K. Ochs (Eds.), *Globalisation, standards and professionalism: Teacher education in times of change*. Dordrecht: Kluwer Press.

Jansen, J., & Christie, P. (1999). *Changing curriculum: Studies on outcomes-based education in South Africa*. Claremont: Juta, Academic.

Manji, F. (1997). Collaboration with the South: agents of aid or solidarity? http://www.jstor.org/stable/4028894. Accessed 26 Apr 2012.

McGrath, S., & Badroodien, A. (2006). International influences on the evolution of skills in South Africa. *International Journal of Educational Development, 26*(5), 483–494.

Muller, J., & Taylor, N. (1995). Schooling and everyday life: Knowledge sacred and profane. *Social Epistemology, 9*, 257–275.

Soudien, C. (1997). Transformation and outcomes-based education in South Africa: Opportunities and challenges. *The Journal of Negro Education, 66*(4), 449–459.

South African Qualifications Act. (1995). No. 58 of 1995: Government Gazette: Pretoria.

Spady, W. (2007). It's time to end the decade of confusion about OBE in South Africa. http://www.edulibpretoria.files.com/. Accessed 21 May 2012.

Spreen, C. A. M. (2001). Globalization and educational policy borrowing: Mapping outcomes-based education in South Africa. Unpublished dissertation. University of Columbia.

Svensson, J. (2000). Foreign aid and rent-seeking. *Journal of International Economics, 51*, 437–461.

Young, M. (2004). National qualifications frameworks: Their feasibility and effective implementation in developing countries. An unpublished report prepared for the International Labour Organisation.

Chapter 12
A View from Latin America: Two Generations of Reforms on Higher Education; Towards a New Decade of Collaboration

Jorge Uribe-Roldán

Abstract This chapter addresses the question of how international educational policy has influenced policy formation in Latin America and tries to determine to what extent two generations of reforms in higher education have served the needs of Latin America towards development and social inclusion. The chapter focuses on the political and institutional contexts in Latin America over the last 20 years and enquires as to how the international tertiary education agenda has been formulated, and to what extent the reforms implemented have achieved their objectives. It is argued that policy formation is determined by conflicting views about the role of higher education on development. Likewise, implementation processes face different approaches to legitimizing an international cooperation mandate that appears to ignore pressing local policy issues such as equity and inclusion, or quality and access. A new scenario of openness of higher education systems where all stakeholders involved take part in the policy formation debate, cooperation at intergovernmental level is the norm, and collaboration among higher education institutions is the course of action is suggested.

Latin America as a whole started the second decade of the new millennium with confronting "imaginaries and ideals" (Arocena 2005) about democracy, regional integration, political reform, and social and economic development. The political scenario is very diverse with new and very active stakeholders, and it has moved from neoliberal market oriented regimes to those of socialist neo-Bolivarian and indigenous types that certainly share conflicting views about the role of higher education.

Nevertheless, due to the lessons learned during the "lost decade of the eighties" (Ocampo and Martin 2003) and the painful recovery that followed in the 1990s, the

J. Uribe-Roldán (✉)
Ed.D. Candidate, Universidad Pedagógica Nacional, Bogotá, Colombia
e-mail: juriberoldan@gmail.com

C.A. Brown (ed.), *Globalization, International Education Policy and Local Policy Formation*, Policy Implications of Research in Education 5,
DOI 10.1007/978-94-007-4165-2_12

region seems to be moving towards a more complex scenario where "emerging" countries, such as Brazil, México, Chile, and Colombia still fail to tackle, on a comprehensive basis, tertiary education policy and integration as the main driver for social and economic change.

In relation to higher education reform, loud voices coming from British, French, and even Canadian university students are resonating in Latin America in what seems to be a new student movement demanding new answers and better opportunities in education and employment. These spreading voices of youth popular discontent together with high rates of unemployment cannot be ignored. They demand far more inclusive solutions and another national and international governance framework detached from globalized market oriented policies. They are also looking for solutions that will address local needs where the role of higher education and the use of knowledge in a post-capitalistic and post-European era is taken into account as a driver of change and development for the region and the world.

The recent students uprisings in Chile and Colombia against higher education reforms based along the lines of neoliberal private rationales are not the exception to this wide spread sentiment of despair among the world's youth. The "viral effect", highly contagious through the social networks, proved to be effective and somehow could make policy making of any kind more difficult to articulate. The question is whether national governments and international donors are prepared to accept those new realities and change the course of action, implementing more indigenous type policies, or decide to push forward unpopular reforms that will have social and political costs.

Latin America in that respect should be taken differently, not only for the large social inequalities and demographic shifts that have characterized the region for decades, but also because of its complex intercultural and political diversity. As such, Latin America should be understood as a special unit of analysis for the formulation of public international policy in tertiary education. Furthermore, the debate between private and public funding, development and aid, social inclusion and cohesion, and the educational ideals immersed in previous policy objectives deserve to be translated at national levels under new international collaboration paradigms. Latin American academia and researchers alike are beginning to suggest international comparative perspectives and studies on the subject, tackled from the emancipated South, (Santos 2009). Views from the social sciences perspective that contribute to an international debate could at the same time enlighten policy makers, politicians, and higher education stakeholders at large. Multi-stakeholder approaches that consider higher education as a global public good (Marginson 2011) and a source of horizontal cooperation and collaborations between the declining North and the emerging South, as the international tendencies tend to suggest, could become in the near future a much better paradigm for international policy cooperation and implementation.

12.1 Latin American Perspectives on International Education

In order to understand future implications of international policy on higher education reform in Latin America, and to determine its impact and contribution to social development, it is necessary to tackle the question from three distinctive analytic perspectives:

12.1.1 Development Perspective

This perspective comes from a widely accepted discourse on the relationship between education and development and has been adopted as a paradigm for reform by the international governmental and non-governmental bodies. A top down approach is carried out as an international mandate, and local politicians and bureaucrats in the recipient country take for granted the international consensus on development, its social and economic dimensions, and the policymaking models to follow. Under this perspective nobody is responsible for poor implementation, and any political tension that may arise is blamed on the failures and oversights of the international system as a whole, or as it was the case in Latin America during the 1990s, on the Washington Consensus Mandate and the series of reforms in all areas of development that followed.

Since 1990 when the United Nations Development Program (UNDP) launched the first Human Development Report, and with it the human development index (HDI) as a source of poverty and quality of life measurement (Desai 1991), mostly all policy formation regarding education has been adopted and formulated along the lines of the UNDP annual reports indications, without further debates at national level, and with a tacit understanding that one medicine is good for all. Recent analysis made by Sassen (2006) on the institutional assemblages and desassembagles that situations like this made not only at a territorial level but on policy formation and authority are worth nothing. Political discourses that took place in the 1980s in Latin America as part of a North-south relationship are beginning to change, shifting from the mandate of the North to a more open a collaborative approach. Even though, as Alkire (2010) has suggested in a critical revision of UNDP Human Development Reports, the approaches, definitions, and dimensions on the idea of development and its relation to education have varied, and today there is much more political tension and conflicting approaches regarding human development and poverty reduction.

However, most of the efforts and medicines coming from abroad by way of international cooperation and overseas development assistance and aid for education in general were, at least in Latin America, concentrated in policies aimed at primary and secondary education developments and reform; higher education was set aside as part of the early 1990s recommendations and misconceptions (Coraggio 1997) made mainly by the World Bank as the main donor. At that time the World Bank did not consider higher education a top priority nor an important driver for development.

12.1.2 Emancipation Perspective

This perspective departs from the Westernized Eurocentric approach that supports the international community policies for development and takes as a reference the ideas of alternative development put forward by the World Social Forum, Porto Alegre, Brazil in 2001, where there was not only a disenchantment with the international policy mandate imposed by the West, but also an urgent need to take distance from the capitalistic North. Critical analyses to formulate policies from within the countries local realities that answer the aspirations of the emancipated South were of the essence.

These ideas were put forward by the Portuguese scholar Boaventura de Sousa Santos (2002) and have echoed in Latin America where social dimensions and cultural realities of the subcontinent cannot be ignored by public policy at large and as Santos. B.d.S (2009) suggested “a contra-hegemonic use of a hegemonic instrument” has to be put in place to balance power relations. This confrontation of imaginaries and a bottom up emerging approach places popular political movements together with other actors and stakeholders, different than those of the political establishment and government officials, at the center of the policy making process, and at the same time makes possible to translate into new narratives and in the context of another globalization, as claimed by the Brazilian author Milton Santos (2004), the paradoxical encounters of the West with the rest under a new emancipating paradigm.

12.1.3 Marketization Perspective

This perspective accepts globalization as an unavoidable phenomena, and the resulting policies cross borders with high intensity due to parallel trade liberalization tendencies, making markets and territories more vulnerable, and institutional spaces more open. To deal with this geo-economic reality, economic perspectives prevail and market-oriented forces are supposed to align and correct the imbalances created not only by the trade-related policies implemented, but also by the assemblages and des-assemblages in the local territory, authority, and rights the globalization drive has created (Sassen 2006), as mention before.

Higher education as a study field, and as industry did not escape from this new scenario. Under the General Agreement of Trade in Services, GATS (1994), education in general but also higher education was included in the multilateral trade negotiations and considered since then as a commodity and a service that can be openly traded subject to privatization and market rationales. The role of governments becomes marginal, leaving to technocrats the administration of international aid and cooperation; to new providers of higher education services the regulation of education markets, and to higher education institutions public and private, the urge to search for funding in places where they were not used to, forcing universities to implement internationalization strategies for recognition and to adopt languages that do not necessarily respond to their traditional academic orientation or research capabilities. Recent tertiary education attempts to reform higher education systems, implemented in Chile and Colombia, as part of their efforts to integrate and to participate in an open world trading system seem to be the case.

Even though there has been a great deal of debate on the impact of globalization in general terms, and as an economic phenomena, the political declarations that deal with the subject on higher education, at UNESCO level (CRES 2009; WCHE 2009), or in the context of multilateral relations between Latin America and Europe (Rio Declaration 1999 to Madrid Action Plan 2010) are very much misunderstood by local politicians and seem to be implemented in Latin America by way of *standardization or imposition* (Dale 2000) by policymakers and bureaucrats without much participation of all stakeholders concerned.

It is worth noting that the idea of "stakeholders activism" in higher education, or even participation in decision making, was very rare in Latin America and not until recently did UNESCO (2005) acknowledge their functional power. The guidelines for quality provision of cross border higher education (Annex of Document 33C/42 issued in cooperation with the OECD, September 2005) besides defining for the first time cross border higher education, identified six categories of stakeholders: governments; higher education institutions/providers including academic staff; student bodies; quality assurance and accreditation bodies; academic recognition bodies; and professional bodies.

Paradoxically, the international governance debate on higher education is being originated from the policies set up by the World Bank, UNESCO, and now by the World Trade Organization, ignoring complex realities of Latin American subcontinent in favor of an agenda based on global development ideals that in the end are not properly understood by government officials of the countries concerned. Global drivers of change, such as the global economic crisis, the emerging power of non-western economies, rapid demographic and population shifts, and a vibrant open-flat-smart world, driven by mostly young populations, are demanding some sort of international collaboration approach based on openness and transparency that could override competition and marketization ideals, making possible a more realistic, more effective, and new narrative about human development.

This trend towards a collective construction of a new paradigm in the case of higher education should cause the international community, particularly the inter-governmental institutions, to re-think their approaches to the political emerging south and also their future cross-border international higher education relations with institutions and academic communities as actors in the same system.

12.2 Higher Education Systems Transformation and Reformist Approaches

World figures on higher education published by UNESCO (2009b) prior to the World Conference on Higher Education celebrated in Paris showed an unprecedented expansion in tertiary education, not only in Latin America but worldwide, indicating that over a period of 10 years big changes and transformations occurred in the size of tertiary education systems. Indeed, Latin American gross enrolment ratios (GER) increased five-fold from 6 to 34 % between 1970 and 2007. This very significant rise since 2000 when the ratio was 22 %, reached a student population on tertiary education of 17.8 million in 2007 that is growing at an annual rate of 6.8 %.

Latin America's estimated total population stands today at 595,648,000 according to the UN world population prospects. These figures confirm that over a period of 10 years that higher education systems in the region moved from elite to mass systems (Trow 1973), putting extra pressure on governments and policymakers.

Similar conditions and pressures are happening today in larger systems of education such as the Indian subcontinent where the Indian government should have to build about 1,000 new universities and 50,000 colleges by 2020 in order to accommodate expected demand of 370 million Indian school-age citizens (ages 6–23), representing a cohort larger than the entire population of the U.S. and three times the total population of Mexico (Marmolejo 2011).

Even though Latin America does not face demographic challenges and pressures of such proportions, growth and enrolment figures deserve a closer look to determine to what extent tertiary education systems would be able to respond to this explosive demand, and how the education reforms that took place in the 1980s and the 1990s, under the auspices and tutelage of the international donor community have been effective. Six main traits can be identified as common denominators or characteristics for policy formation and implementation for reform on higher education systems Latin America; Somehow they reflect the main dichotomies of the region and the main concerns of the international community.

- Policy formation and government intervention
- Access and equality
- Performance and quality of education
- Public-Private financing and management
- Graduation and production of human capital for labor markets
- Outputs in terms of science, research, innovation, and technology

In terms of national performance and results measured by the numerous performance indexes or rankings that proliferate in the international arena, it seems that Latin American higher education systems have not been able to address those common objectives, making the debate about effectiveness more necessary. Therefore, to gain a better insight as to how Latin America stands in relation to international policy formation on higher education, it is worth considering the different approaches that have been envisaged as a means of implementing international policy.

The first approach based mainly on ideology has been summarized by Brunner (2009) referring to a study made by Neave and Van Vught (1994) in the region, which paradoxically was titled "Dr. Prometheus visits Latin America", makes a metaphorical reference to the shifts in the relationship between the state and the universities, as Prometheus, chained by the state to a rock. The ideological debate on higher education between traditionalists and modernists is taken as a departing point to justify their arguments and reformist ideas.

For traditionalist "the chained Prometheus justifies the university status quo as it demonstrates the risk to university autonomy from neo-liberal policies." In this case the ideas of "self-evaluating, self-regulated" make sure that the state can control from afar, whereas for modernists, Prometheus "neither robbed the goods nor is chained" (Brunner 2007, p. 268), is forced to re-evaluate his contract with the state. Even though he is paid very little for not doing much, he, the universities, has to get a part-time job to finance part of his education.

As Brunner (2009) points out, during those 20 years, as the UNESCO figures demonstrate, "higher education systems have been transformed; 'massified' and have grown more differentiated and complex" (p. 268), making theory and analysis as well as values and sentiments part of a new common language. Indeed, the Neave and Van Vught (1994) notion of the "evaluating state" and the autonomous university became part of the ideological debate in which reforming culture evolved in Latin America.

In other words, the role of the state was changed, and it became some sort of an evaluation and coordination body with limited regulatory powers. The lack of long-term higher education policies, together with no continuity or little experience from national government officials, meant that Latin American openness to new realities made the idea of globalization and its discontent (Stiglitz 2002) part of the educational challenge. But as Brunner concludes, (2009) nations are absorbed first by ideologies before being neutralized by practice, showing the continued divide between words and deeds, which in the end made policy making and implementation during those years, even more complex, diverse and decentralized.

It is worth noting, as suggested by Krawczyk and Vieira (2007), that in the ideological divide on higher education policy and reform that took place in Latin America there was a tendency to preserve the international status quo to facilitate and guarantee the homogenization of international policy making in order to assure funding and international aid; Mexico went through a "conservative break", Chile trough a "conservative continuation," Brazil through a "conservative renovation," and Argentina through an "interrupted break."

The second approach was more political and was mainly based on the neoliberal ideas predominant in the late 1980s, which gained force at the end of the last century under what was known as the *Washington Consensus*. Liberalization, decentralization, the diminishing role of the state, and the free self-regulation of the markets were the driving forces of change and the inspirational tools for international policy and reform. The World Bank was the main agent of the *Washington Consensus* and with the blessing of neoliberal reformists, timidly recognized the role of tertiary education as driver for development and economic change but only if it was regulated under the basis of open free markets for its financing.

In 1994 the World Bank published a document called "Higher Education; the Lessons from Experience", that besides setting the "new knowledge for development agenda", recognized its shortsightedness on the role that higher education played as a key driver for development. This historical shift, justified by purely economic rationales, triggered a series of reforms in Latin America aimed at tackling the three main problems diagnosed by the World Bank: poor quality due to the growth and expansion of higher education systems, inefficiency in the use of public resources, and equity or inclusion problems in terms of access and distribution of income and opportunities among young population. The diagnosis came rather late, as said before, with a remedy applied homogenously to all countries in the region by the World Bank and followed religiously by the international donor community: increased institutional differentiation, strengthened financing base, and improved quality in education and research.

The third approach, which was the logical consequence of the previous one, was mainly thematic, and it based its developments on the socioeconomic and sociocultural environments in which the international policies envisaged in Washington were supposed to be implemented and executed. Therefore, the triad enrolment-quality-equity was embraced by policymakers, national governments, and education technocrats at large mainly as precondition for financing precarious systems of higher education. Good governance, accreditation models, public-privates financing, markets, cost-benefit, new providers, and internationalization of higher education became then the buzzwords for change at all institutional levels and circles in Latin America. However, very little is found about the questioning of those policies, their real impact on development, and the way funds attached to them were actually spent. Case studies, successful experiences, reports, and documents produced by the international organizations, governmental and intergovernmental bodies, and local recipients involved in the implementation of those international policies registered only the manner in which educational programs were carried out or made relevant justifications on the usefulness and applicability of the economic model set up since then by the World Bank (Krawczyk 2001).

Robertson (2008) makes similar claims about the market multilateralism that followed the World Bank's recipes and remedies for all and pointed out six forces that to some extent could be considered as a reminder of the mistakes made in the past when policies were formulated from outside, and also as a contribution for the academic and policymaking debate:

> 1. The historical collapse of the higher education sector in low-income countries because of WB conditionalities (no public subsidies to higher education), 2. The global division of labor tied to global production, 3. Recent transformations in both national (denationalization) and wider global economies arising from the globalization of neo-liberalism, 4. The emergence of a meta-narrative around knowledge as the engine of development and cross-border supply as a means for generating higher education capacity for low-income and developing countries, 5. The converging agenda of market multilateralism amongst the powerful international agencies as mechanism of global governance, and 6. The strategic use of governmental techniques, such as the construction of indexes and other methodologies,

to produce the conditions and social relations for a new long wave of accumulation (Robertson 2008, p. 2).

12.3 Policy Issues and Legitimacy

Another aspect that has to be considered in the context of the debate proposed by this book is the legitimacy and sustainability issues associated with the validation and implementation of international policy reform. Krawczyc (2002) did an interesting review of higher education reforms that took place over the last 20 year in Latin America, from the perspective of the international agencies and donors, mainly the World Bank, UNESCO, Comisión Económica para América Latina CEPAL, Programa de Promoción de la Reforma Educativa en América Latina y el Caribe PREAL, and Unesco's Oficina Regional de Educación para América Latina y el Caribe OREALC and pointed out the political, financial, and technical rationales that as a precondition justified these policy reforms:

From the political point of view, international policy reform should come out as part of an open, consensus-building exercise with the participation of all political actors and formulated as state policy under the umbrella of framework legislation, regardless of the government in turn. Following strategies and implementation actions supervised by central government agencies assures continuity. From the technical point of view, legitimacy is based on the autonomy given to regional actors and decentralized administrative bodies that share responsibilities and practices. From the financial point of view, the main rationale was cost-benefit and return on the investment. In that respect diversification of sources of financing to assure proper distribution of funds, regardless of the economic and social impact to the direct beneficiaries of the policies, was the prevalent model.

Furthermore, the Latin American Faculty on Social Sciences, FLACSO, made in 1998 (Tedesco 1998) a well informed and critical balance of the reforms on higher education, confirming that if the 1980s was the lost decade in terms of economic development for Latin American countries, the 1990s saw a backslash for higher education systems and the performance of public universities. Their main argument was that knowledge in all its manifestations—production, distribution, and use—was not a main objective of all educational reforms. The diagnosis made by FLACSO was later taken by the UNESCO (2005) report on knowledge societies stating that there are not one but many knowledge societies in the world and there is a huge and widening knowledge gap between the OECD countries and Latin America. The problems described could be summarized as follows:

- Homogenization of policies, based on the assumption that the economic and political problems faced by the region were similar.
- Wrong interpretation of international educational policies., not only international policy from the part of government bureaucrats and technocrats but also its translation into national strategies and implementation at the local level.

- Conditionality, educational reform at all levels was conditioned to the overall regional economic development programs and there was little maneuvering from national governments; besides, higher education's contribution to economic and social development was not yet a top political priority.
- Unfavorable social conditions, lack of knowledge of the cultural and social diversity of the region and an unclear identification of the actual recipients of the policies was evident.
- Political conflict in the region and displacement towards big cities were not considered as essential parts of educational policies. It was necessary unplanned adjustment and not much was known as it is today on the reconciliation of educational policies in areas of civil war or political turmoil.
- Decentralization, designed as organizational tools for institutionalization was executed with no regard for diverse geographical and socioeconomic conditions in many areas of Latin America.

The following chart summarizes what had been the rationale, justification, and objectives in which the last two decades of reform in Latin America have taken place and suggests some contrasting ideas as to what the future scenario could be (Fig. 12.1).

The 1990s can be considered the decade of evaluation in which policies were formulated from the top responding to forces and tendencies envisaged from outside by the indisputable consensus of the World Bank and the international donor community that followed its recommendations. The public alliance between national government and the international community was strong; bureaucrats were charged with implementing policy on the basis that higher education was a public service that had to be guaranteed in the form of quality, access, and equity in order to bring economic prosperity. In return, national governments should evaluate higher education and systems performances and to account for the imbalances or inefficiencies to the international community.

The new millennium decade can be described as the mercantilization decade; higher education becomes a private service and a commodity that can be offered by other providers different than the state or public higher education institutions. The debate includes delocalized moving from UNESCO to World Trade Organization trade negotiations, in the international arena and at national levels, financing, decentralization and institutional governance to guarantee proper use of resources. These became the norm. Public and private sector alliances for more efficient allocation of resources, whether economic or human to attend to an ever-increasing mass of population in search of education for employment, becomes the force that drives and integrates all policies and actions. Market forces are supposed to respond to national and international imbalances in development and poverty.

The first decade of the millennium that came with the apparent international enthusiasm for the controversial university rankings and the increased globalization of knowledge, which confirm the idea that international policy reforms and remedies that could be attempted in the future should be thought from different perspectives, taking into account multiple and conflicting dimensions that today characterized higher education in Latin America.

Years	Drivers of Change	Governance	Rationales	Actors	Higher Education	Development objectives	Consequences
1990 to 2000	Globalization and Neo-liberalism Knowledge for Development Demographic Changes, migrations Brain Drain TIC's revolution The west and the rest	Decade of Evaluation Top Down policies Lineal model	**1. Quality** Efficiency and Efficacy Accreditation **2. Access** Growth and enrollment **3. Equity** Social Cohesion	The State Bureaucrats International Organizations UNESCO World Bank	Public Service	Economic Development	Autonomy and Self-regulation Mass education
From 2000 to 2010	Anti-globalization Movements Knowledge societies and economies Demographic shift Brain Gain TIC's consolidation Internationalization & cross-border HE	Decade of Mercantilization Market forces and policies Integration Model	**1. Financing -** No subsidies, Private-Public, Use and distribution, Accountability/ Results **2. Institutional Governance -** Diversification **3. Decentralization**	Higher Education Institutions Technocrats Public-Private Sector WTO OECD	Private Good Trading Service	Economic Development Poverty reduction. MDG	Competition and competitiveness New Providers International Rankings Homologation
Future Scenario	New Globalization Knowledge sharing and distribution Brain Circulation and mobility Networked smart society. Social Urbanization and new skills Common Integrated Systems of HE	**Decade of Collaboration** Bottom-up policies Systemic and networked Model	**1. Collaboration-**Institutions and knowledge and communities of practice **2.Sustainability-**Economic-social and environmental **3. Equity-**Social Inclusion	HEInstitution Central and Local government Education 6 Stakeholders Academic and Research Networks	Global Public Good	Sustainable Development Human development Quality of Life	Respect for Identity and diversity Science and Humanities Ethnicity/Gender Vocational/Rural Recognition Innovation

Fig. 12.1 Two Decades of Latin America Higher Education Reform. Towards a new decade of collaboration

12.4 Towards a New Scenario

Today, new complex realities and lessons learned from the experiences of the past are suggesting a new decade of collaboration in higher education. An era that departs from those previous two wasted decades where evaluation and mercantilization were the rationales behind them. Even though expanding access, improved equity, increased quality, and relevance continue to be the "credo" of the reformist agenda, no new remedies and alternative approaches as to how tackle the failures of the past have been suggested.

As mentioned above, the student uprising from all continents demands new thinking and approaches to solve the deadlock and the conflicting ways in which international policy making on higher education is being implemented in Latin America. There seems to be a shift in the World Bank education strategy, and an admission that market forces failed to allocate resources for education. Also the social return of higher education probably exceeds the private returns, which makes it a key factor for economic prosperity, and is worth recognizing. But despite the wide consultation made by the World Bank to formulate new foresighted approaches to education, it persists in its "interventionist" tone to justify public spending and financing of higher education on the grounds of efficiency and equality of opportunity. Furthermore, no mention is made of the sociopolitical and socioeconomic differences of the region or the recent developments in the internationalization of higher education that are taking place as drivers of academic mobility, curricular integration, and research collaboration.

Though urbanization as a key demographic shift is considered, it has to be admitted that there are vast rural areas in Latin America that will never be part of the urbanization drive, so new approaches on rural higher education for a region rich in natural resources and biodiversity need to be addressed on a global scale. In addition climate change for sustainable development is absolutely necessary and has to be considered equally by the international donor communities. It is in this particular instance that the debate for global development takes place. Access and quality of life as sources of rural integration are needed. India and China face the same problems, and it has to be recognized that their needs are neither the same nor are their priorities.

From the international perspective, there are new stakeholders involved in higher education with conflicting views that somehow have to be reconciled from the political and conceptual perspectives. The World Bank is promoting investing in people's knowledge and skills for economic development and poverty reduction. The World Trade Organization is viewing education as a service that can be traded freely on a cross border basis with new providers of tertiary education as part of the solution, and UNESCO is demanding autonomy, self-regulation, and integration of systems, complicating the multilateral scenario and the possibility for across the board dialogue among them and with all actors concerned.

There is not consensus as to how to conceive the public dimension of higher education: whether a service or a good that regardless of its supply somehow benefits the individual and the society as a whole. In today's complex world, the public sphere boundary also becomes complex to define, as Marginson (2011) insists. However, those institutional views and multilateral discourse continue to disregard the academic contribution to the debate, increasing the risk of making the same mistakes of the past. García Guadilla (2005) who has been studying trends and developments of higher education in Latin America from the comparative point of view as well as the writings of Boaventura de Sousa Santos (2009) well known in the academic circles for their contribution to contra-hegemonic approaches towards the dominant west, suggest new scenarios for thinking about international policy making and educational reform in Latin America.

Latin America finishes the second decade of the new millennium with numerous conflicts in higher education; students in Chile and Colombia were going out to the streets demanding more education budget and free education for all; Brazilian public universities recovering after months of strikes without getting all they wanted; the Venezuelan system was on the verge of collapsing due to nationalization; Buenos Aires University was threatened due to an unexpected budget cut, and the Mexican National Autonomous University was under continuous strike and public demonstrations. These and many other similar situations show that the Latin American systems of higher education continue the struggle for new identities and are debating the traditional reformist background and survival under political regimes less interested in opening the public debate, investing in higher education; or either changing, strengthening, or integrating the systems willing to surrender to the forces of another globalization that after all disregard collaboration not only as a driver of change but also as the new force for international mutual understanding.

References

Alkire, S. (2010). *Human development: Definitions, critiques, and related concepts* (OPHI Working Papers No 36). Oxford: Oxford Poverty and Human Development Initiative.

Arocena, R., & Sutz, J. (2005). Latin American universities: From an original revolution to an uncertain transition. *Higher Education, 50*(4), 573–592.

Brunner, J. J. (2007). Dr. Prometheus visits Latin America. In *Towards a cartography of higher education policy change. A Festschrift in Honor of Guy Neave* (pp. 265–271). Enschede: Center for Higher Education Policy Studies. Twente University, Holland.

Coraggio, J. L. (1997). Las porpuestas de Banco Mundial para la educación: ¿sentido oculto o problemas de concepción? En J. L. Coraggio y R.M Torres, *La Educación según el Banco Mundial.* Buenos Aires: CEM.

Dale, R. (2000). Globalization and education: Demonstrating a common world educational culture or locating a globally structured educational agenda. *Educational Theory, 50*(4), 427–448.

Desai, M. (1991). Human development: Concepts and measurement. *European Economic Review, 35*(2–3), 350–357.

García Guadilla, C. (2005). *Tensiones y transiciones. Educación superior latinoamericana en los albores del tercer milenio.* Caracas: CENDES y Nueva Sociedad.

Krawczyk, N. R. (2001). La reforma educativa en america latina desde la perspectiva de los organismos multilaterales. *Revista Mexicana De Investigación Educativa, 7*(16), 627.

Krawczyk, N. R., & Vieira, V. L. (2007). Homogeneity and heterogeneity: A comparative study of educational reform in the decade of the 1990s in Argentina, Brazil, Chile and Mexico.

[Homogeneidad y heterogeneidad: Un estudio comparativo sobre la reforma educativa de la década del 90 en Argentina, Brasil, Chile y México]. *Estudios Pedagogicos, 33*(2), 59–80.
Marginson, S. (2011). Higher education and public good. *Higher Education Quarterly, 65*(4), 411–433.
Moreno, L. A. (2011). A regional economy on the move. In Inter-American Development Bank (Ed.), *The decade of Latin America and the Caribbean, a real opportunity*. Washington, DC: Inter American Development Bank..
Neave, G., & Van Vught, F. (1994). Government and higher education in developing nations: A conceptual framework. In *Government and higher education relationships across three continents: The winds of change* (Vol. 2, pp. 1–21).
Ocampo, J. A., & Martín, J. (2003). *A decade of light and shadow: Latin America and the Caribbean in the 1990s*. Tokyo: United Nations University.
Robertson, S. L. (2008). *Market multilateralism, the World Bank Group and the asymmetries of globalising higher education: Towards a critical political economy analysis*. Bristol: Centre for Globalisation, Education and Societies. Accessed on 1 Aug 2013, from http://www.bris.ac.uk/education/people/academicStaff/edslr/publications/27slr/
Santos, B. d. S. (2002). *Toward a new legal common sense: Law, globalization, and emancipation*. London: Butterworths Lexis Nexis.
Santos, M. (2004). *Por otra globalización: Del pensamiento único a la conciencia universal*. Bogotá: Convenio Andrés Bello, Bogotá Colombia.
Santos, B. d. S. (2009). *Una epistemología del sur. la reinvención del conocimiento y la emancipación social*. Ciudad De México: Siglo XXI.
Sassen, S. (2006). *Territory, authority, rights: From medieval to global assemblages*. Princeton: Princeton University Press.
Tedesco, J. C. (1998). Desafíos de las reformas educativas en américa latina. *FLACSO, Propuesta Educativa. 19–9* 19–23. Buenos Aires: Novedades educativas.
The World Bank. (1994). *Higher education: The lessons from experience* (Development in practice). The World Bank Publications, Washington D.C.
Trow, M. (1973). *Problems in the transition from elite to mass higher education*. Berkeley: Carnegie Commision on Higher Education, Berkeley.
United Nations Educational, Scientific and Cultural Organization (UNESCO). (2005). *Towards knowledge societies: UNESCO World report*, UNESCO reference works, Paris.
United Nations Educational, Scientific and Cultural Organization (UNESCO). (2009a). *Global education digest 2009: Comparing education statistics across the world*. Montreal: UNESCO Institute for Statistics.
United Nations Educational, Scientific and Cultural Organization (UNESCO). (2009b). *Las nuevas dinámicas de la Educación Superior y de la Investigación para el Cambio Social y el Desarrollo*. Paris, 8th July 2009. Draft, Final Comuniqué.

Chapter 13
Global and Local: Standardized Testing and Corruption in Admissions to Ukrainian Universities

Ararat L. Osipian

Abstract This chapter addresses public discourse at the intersection of standardized testing, the role of international organizations in it, and the problem of corruption in higher education. It is aimed to resolve by conducting a systematic research of the major Ukrainian media sources for the 5-year period from 2007 to 2011. The standardized test becomes a subject of national public discourse conveyed through the media outlets. The media does not mention virtually any international organizations in its reporting on standardized testing, despite a significant role that foreign agencies have played in the testing initiative in Ukraine since its very inception, nor do the media refer to Western experiences with testing.

Perceptions are in no way a perfect measure of corruption, but publicized perceptions are still important when it comes to shaping popular opinion and directing public discourse. The 2011 Corruption Perceptions Index (CPI) by Transparency International (2011), which measures the perceived levels of public sector corruption in 183 countries and territories around the world, assigned Ukraine a score of only 2.3 out of 10. Ukraine was placed in the 152nd position, so the country ranks with such former Soviet republics as Tajikistan, and such African nations as Congo, Kenya, and Zimbabwe.[1] Rampant corruption in Ukraine includes widespread corrupt practices in the country's higher education institutions (HEIs), once renowned for high quality education. This chapter considers corruption in higher education in Ukraine, focusing on such aspects as corruption in admissions to HEIs and in grading and assessment of academic and scholastic abilities with the help of standardized testing.

[1] The CPI ranks countries based on how corrupt their public sector is perceived to be, on a scale of 0–10, where 0 means that a country is perceived as highly corrupt and 10 means that a country is perceived as very clean.

A.L. Osipian (✉)
Peabody College of Education, Vanderbilt University, Nashville, TN, USA
e-mail: ararat.osipian@vanderbilt.edu

C.A. Brown (ed.), *Globalization, International Education Policy and Local Policy Formation*, Policy Implications of Research in Education 5,
DOI 10.1007/978-94-007-4165-2_13

Standardized testing has become a global tool for academic assessment. The knowledge assessment sector is a sprawling industry in numerous developed and developing nations; however, Ukraine stayed aside of this major trend in educational development until recently. For Ukraine, introducing standardized testing equates to globalizing, becoming more open, internationally minded, and oriented toward the European Union. Moreover, some role in developing this openness or this internationalization has been played by international organizations. The media has the potential to provide a local perspective on international donor policy in education, but even more so it offers information and insights on the test itself and the way it is perceived by different strata of the population. This chapter addresses public discourse in the intersection of standardized testing, the role of international organizations in it, and the problem of corruption in higher education that it aims to resolve by conducting systematic research of the major Ukrainian media sources for the 5-year period from 2007 to 2011.

13.1 Higher Education Corruption and Standardized Testing

Ukraine has a large and well developed higher education sector. There are around 900 HEIs in Ukraine, including universities, colleges, academies, and branches. Around two million students attend HEIs of third and fourth levels of accreditation, while another 400,000 students are enrolled in HEIs of first and second levels of accreditation. The Minister of Education suggests that Ukraine needs only around 90 HEIs, referring to universities and academies of third and fourth levels of accreditation. He thinks that some of the most successful HEIs may be enlarged through mergers, while less successful ones should be closed for low quality of educational services provided and the lack of student enrollment. Both the state through accreditation mechanisms and the market forces through competition will drive poor quality HEIs from the higher education sector. Data on the number of students enrolled in HEIs in Ukraine during the 5-year period from 2007/2008 to 2011/2012 academic year are presented in Table 13.1.

Table 13.1 Number of students enrolled in HEIs in Ukraine, 2007–2012

Type of HEI	2007/2008	2008/2009	2009/2010	2010/2011	2011/2012
HEIs of 1st and 2nd levels of accreditation	441,300	339,300	354,200	361,500	356,800
HEIs of 3rd and 4th levels of accreditation	2,372,500	2,364,500	2,245,200	2,129,800	1,954,800

Source: V Ukraine pyatyj god podryad snizhaetsya kolichestvo studentov [Number of students in Ukraine declines for 5 years in a row]. *Bagnet*, February 25, 2012. http://www.bagnet.org/news/society/175725

As follows from the data, Ukraine experiences a steady decline in the number of students enrolled in HEIs, primarily due to negative demographic trends. The state currently covers the tuition of about one half of all students. Competition for government funded scholarships among prospective students varies depending on a particular discipline, major, and HEI's reputation. When it comes to entering a prestigious HEI or a prestigious major, some prospective students and their parents resort to dishonest and corrupt means. These means include bribery, fraud, nepotism, and the use of good relations with faculty members and HEI administrators. During the Soviet era and later in the post-Soviet period, HEIs administered their own entry examinations. As a result, faculty members sitting on the admissions committees and the university administration members took chances in abusing their discretionary authority over who got enrolled. When the Soviet Union collapsed, corruption in admissions became rife. The idea of replacing corrupt entry examinations with standardized independent testing aimed at drastically reducing corruption in admissions. Moreover, it was thought that depending on the results obtained by prospective students on their tests would be tied with an educational voucher of a certain value, which would help them cover the cost of education. Standardized tests, even though administered at the completion of high school, are not exit examinations. They are designed specifically as university entry examinations.

There is a small bloc of scholarly literature that addresses the issue of educational corruption, including conceptualizing, defining, and categorizing higher education corruption (Heyneman 2004; Osipian 2007a, b; Rumyantseva 2005). Hallak and Poisson (2007) present a comprehensive account of education corruption around the world and offer some managerial and organizational solutions of corruption in higher education. Different forms of corruption in higher education in different countries, including the US, Russia, and the UK, are also presented in Osipian (2008b, 2013b). Some researchers focus on groups of countries, such as Russia and Azerbaijan (Petrov and Temple 2004), Georgia, Kazakhstan, and Kyrgyzstan (Heyneman 2007), and Azerbaijan and Central Asian countries (Silova et al. 2007), while others research particular countries, including Georgia (Orkodashvili 2010, 2011), Russia (Osipian 2012d, e), and the US (Johnson 2008; Osipian 2009c, 2012a). The negative impact of higher education corruption on economic growth, development, and household income in micro- and macro-economic perspectives is investigated by Heyneman et al. (2008) and Osipian (2012c). Corruption, coercion, and politicization of universities is addressed by Osipian (2008c), including in Central Eurasia (Osipian 2009a), Russia (Osipian 2012b), and Ukraine (Osipian 2010b), with rent derived not in the form of money, but in loyalty to the ruling political regime. Administrative hierarchies and university governance are linked to corruption in works of Osipian (2009d, 2010c, 2013a) and Waite and Allen (2003). In addition to college education, corruption in doctoral education is addressed in Osipian (2010a, d, 2012d). Of all these publications, only one focuses on the role of standardized testing in reducing corruption in higher education, addressing the question of whether educational vouchers, standardized tests, student loans, and privatization in higher education will help tackle corruption in the Russian higher education sector. The research concludes that:

> [T]he reform using vouchers has failed. Vouchers were a perfect vehicle for selling the reform to the public. The educators did not buy the reform, though, and the general public is apathetic, accepting the idea that free access to higher education has vanished. Educational vouchers were a part of the new system. The failure of one part of that system reveals problems and contradictions in the entire design. For example, the test was never solidly connected to the admissions policies. The introduction and nationwide implementation of the test reached far beyond the initially established goals of reducing inequalities in access to higher education and curbing corruption in admissions to HEIs. The expansion of higher education has reduced inequalities in access, while the increasing number of for-tuition programmes is restraining corruption in admissions, because access is open to all those able and willing to cover the full cost of education (Osipian 2009b, p. 57).

When it comes to corruption in higher education in Ukraine, this bloc of literature becomes even smaller and dwindles down to a handful of research done by Round and Rodgers (2009) and Osipian (2008a, 2009e, f, 2010b, in press). Corruption in higher education may have serious implications and negative influences, impeding economic growth and future development in Ukraine (Osipian 2009f). Despite the paramount importance that the problem of educational corruption has for the future development of Ukraine, the vivid scholarly discussion of this problem is simply not in sight. This study continues the string of earlier works on the burning issue of educational corruption in Ukraine.

A set of works on the new educational assessment regimes in Eurasia, including Ukraine, Georgia, and Kyrgyzstant, is presented by Drummond and DeYoung (2012), Drummond and Gabrscek (2012), Kovalchuk and Koroliuk (2012), Orkodashvili (2012), and Shamatov (2012). The authors describe higher education admissions reforms based on standardized testing, implemented in these former Soviet states. They also offer their view on the present and possible future impact that the testing initiative will have on access to higher education and the high level of corruption in admissions to publicly financed HEIs.

Testing as the anti-corruption measure came to Ukraine later than to Russia. As distinct from Russia, where the standardized test as a pilot project was introduced in several regions as early as 2001, in Ukraine the standardized test was introduced only in 2008. Initially, in 2006, the test was introduced in some of the largest cities, while other universities ran admissions based on the old system of oral and written examinations. Starting in 2008, the standardized test was introduced nationwide and became mandatory for admissions to HEIs. In April of 2008, prospective students took tests in 11 subjects, including Ukrainian Language and Literature, World Literature, Ukrainian History, World History, Mathematics, Biology, Physics, Chemistry, Geography, General Economics, and General Political Science. All tests were scored as computer-based, multiple-choice assessments. A certificate with the results of the test gave the exclusive right to apply to HEIs. This exclusivity meant that HEIs, both public and private, were only allowed to enroll students with certificates from the Center for the Independent Testing. Those who graduated from high schools in previous years also had the opportunity to take the test. Organizing the nationwide testing has been a logistical challenge. Over half a million Ukrainian high-school graduates took the standardized test in 34,758 classrooms. The authorities delivered 4,200 sealed containers with testing materials to the testing sites, where security and protection of the materials were the responsibility of 8,000 police officers. In addition, over 6,000 public observers monitored the event, including those from parents' groups and state educational organizations.

Standardized testing may be found in each of the former Soviet republics. Nevertheless, curbing corruption in admissions to reputable HEIs and majors with scholarships financed by the government remains a challenge. In Ukraine, standardized testing carries the name of the External Independent Knowledge Testing [Zovnishne nezalezhne otsinyuvannya (ZNO)]. Aims of the test are to provide a better mechanism for regulating access to higher education and also controlling for the level of knowledge of high school graduates. According to Pottroff (2009), "Ukrainian policymakers have identified three main reasons for ongoing educational reforms: (1) Improving the quality of Ukrainian education; (2) Seeking "harmonization" with educational systems currently existing; member states of the European Union, in anticipation of Ukraine's entry into the European Union; (3) Fighting corruption in higher education" (pp. 100–101). The data, collected by this author, indicates that most of the respondents think that the external testing was implemented to fight corruption (Pottroff 2009, p. 101). Thus, the emphasis is made, not on better quality or more involvement with the world, but precisely on educational corruption.

13.2 Role of International Organizations

The role of international organizations in the testing initiative in Ukraine is significant, including in its attempt to curb corruption in higher education. It appears that US agencies were major foreign actors in the testing initiative design and implementation. While Ukraine traditionally aimed at European Union membership or association and continuously declares its harmonization of educational process with those in the EU, the EU institutions do not play an active role in implementing the standardized testing in Ukraine. The only exception is the European Union Project Tempus, but even Tempus is not nearly as strong and developed in Ukraine now as it was in the 1990s. On the contrary, projects administered by the American Councils for International Education (ACTR/ACCELS) for the United States Agency for International Development (USAID) in the post-Soviet space included the Ukrainian Standardized External Testing Initiative (USETI) and Kyrgyz Independent Educational Testing Organization (ITO) and Test Development Initiative. The Ukrainian Standardized External Testing Initiative (ZNO) was initially conducted in Ukraine from April 2007 to April 2009, in partnership with the Ukrainian Center for Educational Quality Assessment (UCEQA)[2] and American Institutes for Research.

[2]The Ukrainian Center for Educational Quality Assessment (UCEQA) http://www.testportal.gov.ua/

The USETI complements the activities of the Government of Ukraine and international donors to build capacity in Ukraine for carrying out activities connected with test development, administration, and implementation and to institutionalize a testing system protected from corruption that will support non-corrupt admissions to higher education.[3] It is clear from this very definition of the task that the test was aimed at tackling corruption in admissions to HEIs. The World Bank's Equal Access to Quality Education Project, run from 2006 to 2009, shared the cost of the UCEQA operation and test administration with the Ukrainian government (Kovalchuk and Koroliuk 2012, p. 53). The Ukrainian government joined the Millennium Challenge Account Threshold Program, funded by the USAID, and received $48.1 million to implement this program aimed at reducing corruption in the public sector.[4] As stated by the Millennium Challenge Corporation (MCC),[5] combating corruption in higher education is one of the major components of the Threshold Program in Ukraine.[6] The level of influence that the US agencies may have on testing is significant. In December of 2011, a large and representative delegation of Ukrainian educators and education officials visited Washington, DC, and had a series of productive meetings in the US Department of State, US Department of Education, George Washington University and other organizations, sharing views and experiences on standardized testing and trying to build on mutual understanding. This is of no surprise since Ukrainian authorities strongly support the implementation of standardized testing and are eager to learn from other countries about their experiences and problems. On May 31, 2010 in the offices of the ACTR/ACCELS in Kyiv the first constituent meeting was held of a new international initiative. The initiative is aimed at implementing external independent testing in Ukraine and is called Alliance USETI. The Global

---

[3] It was anticipated that the initiative results in trained cadres of Ukrainian professionals needed to create independent examinations and to further sustain the institution of standardized testing. It will mobilize and energize public involvement in the creation and institutionalization of a knowledge assessment system that serves as a reliable tool for every citizen. It will deliver concrete products to be used in laying the legislative foundation for implementation of unified exams for all higher education institutions. See the program website at http://www.useti.org.ua/pages/6/about-useti.html

[4] Ukraine's 2-year, $48.1 million Threshold Program aims to reduce corruption in the public sector by strengthening civil society's monitoring and exposure of corruption, judicial reform, increased government monitoring and enforcement of ethical and administrative standards, streamlining and enforcing regulations, and combating corruption in higher education. USAID oversaw implementation of the Ukraine threshold program on behalf of MCC. USAID partnered with the US Department of Justice to implement several of the threshold program's activities. Retrieved July 1, 2012, from http://www.mcc.gov/pages/countries/program/ukraine-threshold-program

[5] The Millennium Challenge Corporation (MCC) is a bilateral foreign aid agency established by the US Congress in 2004, separate from the US State Department or USAID.

[6] Recognizing the importance of reducing corruption within the educational system, a national testing center, the Ukrainian Center of Evaluation of Education (UCEE), has been established. Assistance is required, however, to fully implement the external testing system as well as to ensure its integrity. The goal of this component is to reduce corruption in higher education by establishing a legal framework requiring a minimum test score for admission to universities; developing a functioning security system for test results; and ensuring that 100 % of students are tested and the test centers are fully operational. Retrieved July 1, 2012, from http://www.mcc.gov/pages/countries/program/ukraine-threshold-program

Development Alliance Ukrainian Standardized External Testing Initiative was ratified by the USAID on April 8, 2010 (ADUSTI 2012) The goals of USETI Alliance set for 2010–2012 under the patronage of the USAID are as follows: to strengthen the ability of the UCEQA to create valid and reliable tests and methods to administer them in accordance with international standards; to assist in developing a normative legislative basis on which to create test materials and ensure their confidentiality; to strengthen Ukrainian citizens' support of reforming the admission system to establishments of higher education (HEIs); to encourage the creation of private initiatives in the sphere of external independent testing (EIT) in Ukraine (ADUSTI, 2012). Some of Ukraine's leading universities, state and non-governmental organizations are members of the USETI Alliance.[7]

An overview of education corruption by Chapman (2002) commissioned by the USAID a decade ago, indicated USAID's longstanding interest in the issue of corruption in education throughout the world. Thus, it is of no surprise that this US based organization, funded by the US taxpayers' money, has a strong interest and practical involvement in the testing initiative in Ukraine. At the same time, a clear understanding of the nature and function of standardized testing in Ukraine is lacking (Bazhal. *Dzerkalo tyzhnya*, 31, August 23, 2008). Each year, the testing campaign has been accompanied by heated debates and corruption scandals (Vstupitel'naya kampaniya-2009. *Dzerkalo tyzhnya*, 33(761), September 5–11, 2009). Recent corruption scandals with the standardized testing in Russia and in the US, which include paid impersonators, bribes, and numerous violations in administering the test, add heat to such debates.

13.3 Theoretical Frame

With the disintegration of the Soviet Union, the media is much less controlled by the state. The information flow is no longer monopolized by the Communist ideology. The development of the Internet made access to information much easier, while the task of controlling the content and access became much more difficult. A relatively free and independent Ukrainian media reports on problems, which, during the Soviet era, were left largely unattended due to their negativity and a relatively small scale. One such problem is corruption in higher education, which has grown significantly

[7] The following organizations are members of USETI Alliance: United States Agency for International Development (USAID); American Institutes for Research (AIR); American Councils for International Education (ACTR/ACCELS)—coordinator; The Fakt Publishing House; the OPORA Civic network; the company Pro.Mova; the L'viv City Community Organization Center for Educational Policy (CEP); the Ivan Franko National University of L'viv (LNU); the Ministry of Education and Sciences of Ukraine (MoES); the International Renaissance Foundation (IRF); the National Academy of Management (NAM); the National University Of Kyiv-Mohyla Academy (NAUKMA); the European Union Project Tempus IV Educational Measurement Adapted to EU Standards (Mälardalen University); the Ukrainian Center for Educational Quality Assessment (UCEQA); the Petro Mohyla Black Sea State University (BSU).

since the end of the Soviet era. In general, there is an obvious link between mass media and politics (Street 2011). It is quite possible that the media shapes public opinion more than it reflects on it. By doing so, the media sets public discourse. Corruption in education as an explicit form of unethical and indeed illegal behavior normally attracts a lot of public attention. On one hand, those involved in educational corruption naturally prefer to stay in the shade; they do not like to see their shady dealings come to the light of day, to the attention of law enforcement and public scrutiny. On the other hand, the public wishes to know about someone else's shady dealings. A majority of young Ukrainians want to receive higher education and hence admission procedures are of high priority. When individuals' personal interests are at stake, media reports on corruption and standardized testing become a significant issue in public discourse. Media becomes not simply reflective, but proactive in shaping public opinion regarding given state policies and initiatives and the role of other agencies in these initiatives.

Standardized testing remains a highly controversial initiative. The standoff between those in support of the testing initiative and those in opposition may not be the only confrontation that develops in the education sector. There may be yet another major confrontation, either real or imaginary, with Ukrainian politicians fighting the windmills of international organizations, thus propelling their own political standing domestically. Explaining corruption in education is not enough, and yet it can turn out to be more rewarding than designing the anti-corruption strategy and implementing it. In Edelman's (1988) words:

> An explanation for a chronic social problem can never be generally supported. It is offered to be rejected as much as to be accepted. Its function is to intensify polarization and so maintain the support of advocates on both sides. The reasons offered are crucial to the self-esteem of concerned people and to the viability of interested groups, organizations, and causes. They all draw support from the evocation of a spectacle that shows their rivals as threats. An explanation for a troubling condition is typically more important to partisans than the possibility of eliminating the condition; the latter is a rhetorical evocation of a remote future time unlikely to arrive, while the explanation is vital to contemporary political maneuver (p. 18).

The media facilitates dissemination of information among the population, shaping public perceptions regarding particular processes and events. The media may be as good at shaping popular opinion and directing public discourse as it is at disguising or hiding certain issues, which may be even more important and more fundamental than those which the media is highlighting. Thus, the role of the media, including both official news sources and independent media, is not only to focus on urgent problems, such as educational corruption, but also can be to distract the attention of the public from the underlying processes and forces hidden behind the reforms. For instance, it can place an emphasis on the role of globally oriented international organizations and agencies in particular nations and locales; or equally so, it can hide the merits of such global and regional players on the local scene.

Standardized testing means globalization simply because it denotes the process of sharing world experience. This experience is being brought and seeded in the Ukrainian locale. As far as the Ukrainian higher education sector is concerned, corruption in admissions to HEIs and standardized testing are the focus of public discussion. Specifically, by presenting interviews, cases, scandals, difficulties, and some superficial data on higher education corruption, the media manipulates public opinion and diverts the discussion from other issues and hides the role of international organizations in advancing the standardized testing initiative, including both technical help and financial aid.

13.4 Research Methodology

Scholarly literature on standardized testing in Ukraine is not just lacking, but is virtually nonexistent. This study turns to media sources in order to construct a general picture of the discussion on standardized testing that takes place in Ukrainian society and presents a local perspective on the international donor policy in the education sector. Specifically, it aims at discovering the issue of media reporting on the role of international organizations in the standardized testing initiative. It searches and analyses both Ukrainian and Russian language national media coverage. Ukrainian is the official state language, while Russian is the second most popular language, used by some, but not all media outlets. This study uses a major national newspaper entitled *Newsru.ua*, available in electronic format. This electronic newspaper is, in essence, a large and well-structured thematic media portal, which assembles and reprints news from the leading Ukrainian media outlets.

Newsru.ua is perhaps one of the most popular daily news sources offered to the reader in both Russian and Ukrainian. As such, this study uses a range of major national newspapers available in electronic format, including *Golos Ukrainy, Uryadovy kur'er, Dzerkalo tyzhnya, Doba*, and many others. *Golos Ukrainy* is a daily newspaper available in both the Ukrainian and Russian languages and serves as one of the two official outlets for the Ukrainian government. *Uryadovy kur'er* is the official newspaper of the Ukrainian authorities, produced daily and only in the Ukrainian language. *Dzerkalo tyzhnya* is a weekly newspaper produced in both Ukrainian and Russian languages and is one of the most popular media outlets in Ukraine. *Doba* is a weekly newspaper that offers reports in the Ukrainian language only.

The aim of this media search is to identify reporting on the role of international agencies in the testing initiative and the role of testing in eliminating corruption in admissions to HEIs. We are looking for reports on standardized tests which also mention corruption in admissions, corruption in testing, problems with testing, the role of international organizations in the testing initiative, or Western experience with standardized testing. Accordingly, we formulate the following categories, based on whether each particular report mentions corruption in admissions, mentions corruption in testing, mentions problems with testing, underlines the role of international organizations, or refers to Western experience. In order to search these media sources for reports related to standardized testing, this study uses such terms as test, standardized test, standardized testing, independent testing, university, admissions to HEI, admissions campaign, corruption in admissions, bribery in admissions and other related terms. These search terms were used in both the Russian and Ukrainian languages. The media outlet was analyzed for the period of 2007–2011. This study does not double-count each report in the Russian and Ukrainian languages, instead counting each such report as one report.

13.5 Major Findings

There were a total of 166 media reports on standardized testing in Ukraine for the period of 2007–2011 found in *Newsru.ua*. The list of media sources, to which *Newsru.ua* refers in its reporting, includes *Delo, Doba, Dzerkalo tyzhnya, Ekho Moskvy, Gazeta po-kievski, Golos Ukrainy, Interfax-Ukraina, Kommersant' Ukraina, Komsomol'skaya pravda, Liga Biznes Inform, Podrobnosti, Segodnya, Svidomo, TSN, Ukraina moloda, Ukrainskaya pravda, Ukrainskie novosti, UNIAN,* and *Uryadovy kur'er.* Such a wide variety of leading media outlets helps to set up the base for this research. The reports contained some information on all the categories that we formulated in the methodology section. Data on media mentions of corruption in admissions, corruption in testing, problems with testing, references to Western experiences with testing, and the role of international organizations in relation to the testing campaign in Ukraine during the 5-year period are presented in Table 13.2.

As follows from the data presented in Table 13.2, the number of media reports in 2007 was only seven, and this is despite the fact that during 2007 standardized testing was administered as a pilot project in several cities. Some HEIs were running admissions based on the results of the test, and the nation was preparing for the country-wide introduction of the test in 2008. In 2008, the picture changed drastically. There were 59 reports, of which 13 mentioned corruption and 12 mentioned problems with testing. Clearly, the public started worrying about standardized testing only when it was introduced nationwide. In 2009, the number of reports declined

Table 13.2 Media mentions of corruption in admissions, testing, and the role of international organizations, 2007–2011

Category	2007	2008	2009	2010	2011	Total
Number of reports	7	59	46	34	18	166
Mentions corruption in admissions	1	13	14	10	3	41
Mentions corruption in testing	0	2	1	3	0	6
Mentions problems with testing	0	12	9	8	6	35
Underlines role of international organizations	0	1	1	1	2	5
Refers to Western experience	0	4	2	2	2	9

Source: Completed by the author

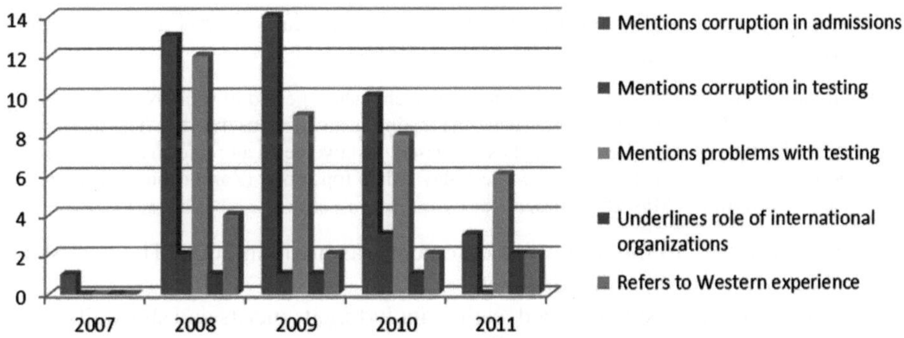

Fig. 13.1 Media mentions of corruption in admissions, testing, and the role of international organizations

to 46, with further declines to 34 reports in 2010 and 18 reports in 2011. One may speculate that once the test was introduced nationwide, the discussion of it started declining year after year as the public did not see any major problems with it. However, the share of reports which mention problems with testing does not decline over the years. Apparently, the media tries to downplay the significance of the testing campaign, but not so much the problems associated with it.

Corruption in admissions and problems with testing are mentioned frequently in the reports, while corruption in testing, the role of international organizations in the testing campaign, and references to Western experiences are very rare. Out of a total of 166 media reports in the 5-year period, corruption in admissions is mentioned in 41 reports, and problems with testing are mentioned in 35 reports. At the same time, only five reports underline the role of international organizations with Western experiences mentioned in nine reports. As the number of reports on testing declines, so does the number of reports which mention corruption in admissions and problems with testing. It is interesting to note that even though the struggle against corruption in admissions to HEIs has been declared one of the major goals and reasons for introducing standardized testing, if not the major one, in 2007, the year preceding the nationwide test introduction, out of seven media reports on testing only one mentioned corruption. The dynamics of media mentions of corruption in admissions to HEIs, corruption in testing and problems associated with the test, and the role of international organizations during 2007–2011 is presented in Fig. 13.1.

13.6 Interpretation of the Results

The results show the scarcity of reports, including those not even highlighting or discussing, but merely mentioning involvement of international organizations in the testing campaign. One report says that foreign experts are satisfied with the testing of Ukrainian graduates. The report refers to a USETI specialist from Latvia, Al'gidras Zabulionis, who says that

> traditions, of course, will not be able to form in such a short period of time. Nevertheless, society now understands much better what the testing is and how useful it is. The interest to the problems of independent testing has increased: just two years ago information on this issue was rarely seen in the media, while today it is a top topic. (Zarubezhnye eksperty dovol'ny. *Newsru.ua*, May 25, 2008).

One should keep in mind that this comment was made in 2008. The data show that in later years the reporting declined.

The discussion over standardized testing, including its merits and shortfalls, even though productive and useful, is still far short of the deep analysis needed to comprehend the magnitude and depth of the problem of corruption in education. In general, reports are repetitive, with parts of previous reports attached, and otherwise are very brief and abrupt. For instance, the phrase

> Let us remember that first independent testing took place on April 27. According to the opinion of its initiators, independent testing will make it possible to eliminate corrupt schemes and provide equal access to higher education independently from material conditions of pupils (Shkol'niki uzhe mogut registrirovat'sya. *Newsru.ua*, December 1, 2008).

Here is yet another catchy phrase on corruption:

> According to Timoshenko, the government will develop real mechanisms, 'which will put an end to corruption without the shock therapy'. (Timoshenko protiv "eksperimentov na detyakh". *Newsru.ua*, April 21, 2008)

These phrases are everywhere, and we had to count them as a mention of corruption in each report.

All mentions of corruption point to the potential for corruption in admissions rather than real facts of corruption. The reports carry no actual facts, and some of them are aimed at discrediting the testing initiative. Very few reports underline the role of international organizations in the testing initiative, even when we include everything into the meaning of an international organization: US Embassy, independent observers from an NGO sponsored by a foreign agency, etc. The media did not highlight international organizations taking part in testing. References to Western experiences are very scarce, and in most instances mention the Bologna Declaration and prospective mutual recognition of academic credentials rather than systems of standardized testing in foreign countries, the problems they face, and the solutions they find. Thus, the media featured more speculative reporting than informative reports that would be useful in terms of comparisons.

Media reports oftentimes mention corruption in admissions to HEIs, not because results of the standardized tests replaced corruption associated with the entry examinations, but because adding grade point averages from high school diplomas and transcripts and selective examinations conducted by the HEIs individually to the test de facto reinstates corruption in admissions. Such mentions are, again, speculations not based on any cases or data. The USETI specialist mentions the absence of traditions and experience of testing in Ukraine, referring to the short period of time for the preparation of the testing campaign and a few years during which some small scale pilot projects with testing took place (Zarubezhnye eksperty dovol'ny. *Newsru.ua*, May 25, 2008). It would be interesting to see what media reports say about the Western experience with standardized testing.

13.6.1 Western Experience

In light of Ukraine's orientation toward the European Union and adoption of the Bologna Declaration in its higher education sector, a good argument in support of the test would be positive Western experiences with standardized testing, including those in European countries. However, this does not seem to be the case with Ukrainian media. Instead, the media portrays the testing as "an experiment" with children, adding a negative connotation to the testing campaign (Ukraina stavit "eksperiment". *Newsru.ua*, April 22, 2008). In 2008, the Chairman of Ukraine's Parliament [Verkhovna Rada], Vladimir Litvin, offered a prognosis that in the future Ukraine will return back to examinations as the system of evaluating students' knowledge. According to Litvin, Ukraine should not repeat previous mistakes of human regress: "The whole world is starting to move away from testing, and we are just introducing it." Litvin reminded the public that external testing has been planned for introduction with the intention to struggle against corruption in HEIs, "even though everyone knows that corruption cannot be defeated, but it can only be led." The Chairman of Verkhovna Rada says that no one approach to evaluation of knowledge should be elevated to the level of absurdity. Litvin notes, "I am certain that we will boil in it for a while and then return to the old system" (Litvin prognoziruet. *Newsru.ua*, December 17, 2008). Such a prognosis, made by a top state official after the first wave of the nationwide testing campaign, clearly cannot be regarded as optimistic for the future of standardized tests. Litvin's pessimistic prognosis is based on world experiences that he claims show the impetus to go away from testing practices, but no details or specific examples are offered by the Chairman of Verkhovna Rada.

In one 2008 media report, Western experience with the test is referred to as follows:

> The majority of countries conduct state examinations by the way of external testing. In particular, results of exit and at the same time entrance examinations are accepted in Australia, England, Bulgaria, Italy, Slovenia, Hungary, and Finland. Germany and France can also be added to this list, as the results of graduation examinations are accepted for admissions to universities (Ukraina stavit "eksperiment". *Newsru.ua*, April 22, 2008).

Countries named in this list are those with free higher education, while the Ukrainian government covers the cost of education for about half of all students. Nevertheless, testing experiences in the US are also mentioned in one of the reports:

> It is very important for us to prepare an ability test. The renowned American SATdetermines the ability to study rather than a set of acquired knowledge. This is a very complex test and it takes 3 years for preparation. No one did anything like this in Ukraine. We have to form a group of people who have at least a basic idea about it. In the future, tests may be able to replace examination sessions in HEIs and exit examinations in ninth grade (Vmesto vstupitel'nykh ekzamenov. *Newsru.ua*, October 1, 2008).

Again, traditions and experiences are given a priority in this passage, which contradicts Litvin's earlier predictions regarding the prospects for the test.

The Minister of Education, Dmitry Tabachnik, also mentions foreign experiences with the test. Specifically, Tabachnik refers to both Russian and US standardized examinations:

> The Russian EGE is better than the Ukrainian test. This is unpatriotic, but this is true. It is better because the Russian EGE is closer to Oxford, Harvard, and Cambridge examinations (SSHA hotyat, chtoby Ukraina. *Newsru.ua*, May 31, 2011).

Indeed, the Ukrainian ZNO is not tied to any particular university, but that was the intent of the testing agencies. The test is independent of the schools and conducted by the state agency, but it also intended to make the enrollment decisions independent of universities. Moreover, this appears to be the line encouraged by international organizations and foreign agencies involved in the design and implementation of the standardized test in Ukraine.

13.6.2 International Organizations

A most surprising finding is that the media does not mention virtually any international organizations and US agencies in its reporting on standardized testing. This is despite a significant involvement of the USAID, ACTR/ACCELS, and American Institutes for Research in all aspects of technical aid and expertise related to the testing initiative. Perhaps the only exception is the note that foreign experts are satisfied with the testing of Ukrainian graduates mentioned in a previous section (Zarubezhnye eksperty dovol'ny. *Newsru.ua*, May 25, 2008). This absence appears even more surprising when considering a significant role that foreign agencies have played in the testing initiative in Ukraine since its very inception. The only mention is that of the Renaissance Foundation (Fond Vidrodzhennya), Ukraine National Initiatives to Enhance Reforms (UNITER), and USETI done in regard to the quality control and prevention of violations in conducting the testing sessions. Non-governmental organizations (NGOs), such as the Committee of Ukrainian Voters [Komitet izbiratelej Ukrainy (KIU)], and OPORA network, will also serve as observers in prospective students' testing, and this activity will be sponsored in part by the international donors, including the Renaissance Foundation, UNITER, and USETI. NGOs involvement in monitoring the testing process is neither the Ukrainian government's decision nor is it a requirement by outside funders. It is the result of grass roots political activism, civic engagement and public participation that is so much needed but lacking in Ukraine. The observers will watch for violations during the testing, while their organizations will work on informing the public about the testing campaign.

The Executive Director of Vidrodzhennya, Evgeny Bystritsky said in 2008 that,

> The importance of involving representatives of independent civil organizations and networks as observers in the testing campaign is in that it will become obvious this year whether clear testing procedures will be able to withstand the wish to corrupt them along with the only democratic reform realized by the Orange political forces. (Zatestirovaniem abiturientov. *Newsru.ua*, April 22, 2008)

Bystritsky also said that NGOs will spend $150,000 on this campaign. According to the representative of the KIU, Natalya Linnik, independent observers will focus their attention on such potential threats as intentional interruptions into the testing process, members of the administration and representatives of HEIs helping test-takers, and violations on the side of test-takers (Za testirovaniem abiturientov. *Newsru.ua*, April 22, 2008). Clearly, representatives of Vidrodzhennya and other NGOs worry about possible violations during the testing sessions, which would jeopardize the credibility of the testing and put the test results in doubt.

The major breaking point in the testing campaign is not in problems and violations in the testing and the need for independent observers. The very concept of testing and admissions criteria is still being argued over by the Ministry of Education and other interested parties, including international agencies. Tabachnik wants the system where results of tests, high school grades, and the university mark are given consideration in admissions decisions. He alleges that the US wants Ukraine to denigrate to the "debilitating level of equatorial countries":

> American advisors tell us all the time that a university should not have a say. The US Ambassador visits me practically every month. He is very excited and agitated by the fact that Ukraine is trying to reach out to the world experience of running university admissions. Maybe it is because one would want us to roll down to the grey third world, to the level of debilitating equatorial countries. There is not a single university among US's several thousand HEIs, including Princeton, Yale, Harvard, Georgetown, which would not have a say in selection of prospective students. Why are you, Mr. Ambassador, trying to debilitate Ukrainian, Russian, Belarusian University, et cetera? They should also have the right (SSHA hotyat, chtoby Ukraina. *Newsru.ua*, May 31, 2011).

Perhaps the Ukrainian government and even more so faculty and administrators of Ukrainian HEIs feel that the tests are being imposed on them from the outside, specifically by the US representatives. Clearly, they do not like the results of standardized tests to serve as the exclusive or major criterion in making the admissions decisions. The role of Ukrainian universities in making admissions decisions appears to be the apple of discord between Minister Tabachnik and Ambassador Tefft. As Edelman (1988) once observed, "...social situations and discourses create political arguments that cannot be finally verified or falsified. As a society, multiple realities and relative standards are all we ever achieve." (p. 111) Such may be the case with the debate over standardized testing in Ukraine.

The US Embassy in Ukraine denies Tabachnik's words about the wish to "debilitate" Ukrainian HEIs. It reacted to the interview promptly, saying that it is ready to continue its effort in strengthening the system of education in Ukraine despite accusations made by the Minister of Education and Science. The Embassy wants to dismiss certain misinterpretations regarding the relations between Dmitry Tabachnik and John Tefft, who met twice. According to the Embassy, the statements made by Tabachnik are "inaccurate." The US Embassy says that starting in 2006 the US proudly supports the efforts of the Ministry of Education of Ukraine and the UCEQA in creating the system of external independent assessment with the goal of opposing corruption in the process of admissions to HEIs. In the old system of oral and written examinations administered by HEIs, prospective students paid bribes in order to gain admission. Representatives of the US Embassy also noted that Ukrainian citizens have been complaining for a long time about the need to give bribes in order to get enrolled in a university:

> We were in agreement with the old suggestion of Minister Tabachnik that admission decisions should give the weight of 75 % to the testing results and another 25 % to grade point average (GPA) on the high school diploma. Experts think that this formula allows taking into consideration additional criteria in the admissions process, while not undermining the honesty of the process. We have not advocated that the external independent testing was the sole criterion, nor did we comment on the new proposition of the Minister regarding the role of the universities themselves in the recruitment process. Public opinion polls in Ukraine indicate that up to 80 % of Ukrainians support the ZNO and consider it a fair and just system of admission to HEIs and a serious indicator of success in education. Less than one percent of the respondents say that they faced corruption in the ZNO since it was introduced nationwide and made required for all prospective students in 2008. We are proud of the support they have given to Ukraine in the sphere of education, and are willing to cooperate with the Government of Ukraine in the future if the call for help will continue... Strengthening the system of education in Ukraine remains a common goal of the Government of Ukraine and the Government of the United States of America (Amerikanskoe posol'stvo otritsaet. *Newsru.ua*, June 1, 2011).

This is the most extensive media commentary on the role of international organizations in Ukraine's testing initiative. Here, the US Embassy is seen as a force of external influence similar to a major international organization, even though the US Embassy is certainly not an international organization. The US appears to be an important policy actor when it comes to implementing the standardized test in Ukraine.

The statement about the US's intent to "debilitate" Ukrainian higher education's future that comes from the Minister of Education is no surprise. Unlike in the 1990s, when foreign involvement in Ukraine was much welcomed, in the 2000s and beyond foreign agencies are treated with a bit of hostility. The global influences on Ukrainian locales are frequently met with opposition. The national media picks up this trend, including in its reporting on events and activities in the realm of higher education. One media report is entitled "Student actions are paid for by western funds, says Tabachnik," even though it does not mention the standardized test (Studencheskie aktsii proplachivayutsya. *Newsru.ua*, May 25, 2011). This headline gives a good idea about the perceptions of international donors or so-called "Western activities" in regard to education in Ukraine.

The Minister of Education also dismisses corruption in admissions to HEIs as the exclusive or even major reason for the introduction of standardized testing. Tabachnik said in particular that,

> The Order of Yanukovich was entitled 'On measures to increase the quality of education.' Only extremely unintellectual people and people with extreme prejudice can represent testing as a measure aimed exclusively against corruption (Tabachnik zayavil. *Newsru.ua*, March 23, 2010).

Tabachnik says that the US Ambassador

> repeats weighted diplomatic instructions that testing is a very transparent way that eliminates corruption. I respond that if prospective students would enter our HEIs based on recommendation letters, as it happens in the US, then I would not survive even in an armored vehicle. Imagine, took two letters from MPs of Verkhovna Rada and entered Kyiv University, took three letters and entered Kyiv Institute of International Relations (SSHA hotyat, chtoby Ukraina. *Newsru.ua*, May 31, 2011).

While foreign agencies are persistent in placing an emphasis on the eradication of corruption in admissions to HEIs as the major task of external independent knowledge evaluation, the Ukrainian officials do not assign corruption such a high place on its priorities list.

The rhetoric of educators and public officials in regard to the ZNO develops based on its own logic. Initially, the media highlighted the project of standardized testing along with the project of introducing educational vouchers. Later, the idea with the vouchers failed, and they were immediately taken off the media's menu. Instead, the major focus was on the idea of the ZNO confronting corruption in education. Later, it became obvious that the ZNO itself is not free of corruption. This facilitated a discussion about possible improvements and modernization of the ZNO. Finally, an obvious trend of reduction of state-funded scholarships in higher education programs gave way to the discussion of the necessity of educational loans. Despite all the opposition that the ZNO faces among leading educators and legislators, including The Chairman of Verkhovna Rada and numerous other members of the Ukrainian parliament and rectors of HEIs, the government continues implementation of the reform. Even though the ZNO is not likely to solve the problem of corruption in education, its full scale country-wide implementation is now completed with further development and improvements pending and appearing to be a matter of experience accumulated in the future.

The disputes such as those between the Minister of Education and the US Ambassador regarding the need for a swift further advancement of the test do not contribute much to the understanding of real changes that take place in the Ukraine's education sector. Corruption being a major point of the discussion on the agenda of foreign agencies is not so prevalent when it comes to Ukrainian media reports. The major point of discontent, the admissions criteria, creates a lot of buzz for both test-lovers and test-haters, but the real major criterion will be the size of the wallet, not the test score on the ZNO.

13.7 Conclusion

It is quite possible that media shapes public opinion more than it reflects on it. By doing so, media sets public discourse. Corruption, a form of unethical and indeed illegal behavior, normally attracts a lot of public attention. On one hand, corruption prefers to stay in the shade; on the other hand, people want to know about someone else's shady dealings. When individuals' personal interests are at stake, which is the case for many in Ukraine when it comes to entering HEIs and receiving higher education, media reports on educational corruption become a significant issue in public discourse. Naturally, the standardized test becomes a subject of national public discourse, conveyed through the media outlets. In light of Ukraine's orientation toward the European Union and adoption of the Bologna Declaration in its higher education sector, a good argument in support of the test would be positive Western experiences with standardized testing, including those in European countries. However, this does not seem to be the case with Ukrainian media. A most surprising finding is that the media does not mention virtually any international organizations in its reporting on standardized testing. This absence appears even more surprising when considering a significant role that foreign agencies have played in the testing initiative in Ukraine since its very inception.

The level of corruption in admissions to higher HEIs in Ukraine is not likely to decline significantly with the introduction of the national test. Instead, access to corruption will broaden with the shift from higher education to secondary education. HEIs will prefer to continue taking part in the selection process. Perhaps, a certain compromise will be found in the near future. Undoubtedly, college faculty will retain at least partial discretion over the admissions procedures and decisions and hence the access to higher education. Here, the role of international organizations is hidden from the readers' view by the media. As follows from the media reports, the national test has experienced numerous problems so far and will likely have even more problems in the future. Moreover, its predicted successes in fighting corruption in admissions are either overstated or dubious. However, the old system of admissions that used university-based entry examinations was morally outdated and had to be replaced. One should not exclude the chance that since implemented nationwide for several years, accumulated experience and improvements, and become a predominant form of admissions to higher education rather than the exclusive criterion, the national test will be more successful than it has been so far.

References

Amerikanskoe posol'stvo otritsaet slova Tabachnika o zhelanii "debilizirovat'" ukrainskie vuzy [US Embassy denies Tabachnik's words about the wish to "debilitate" Ukrainian HEIs]. *Newsru.ua*, June 1, 2011. http://rus.newsru.ua/ukraine/01jun2011/debillu.html

Bazhal, A. (2008, August 23). Mark Zelman: "Universitetam vazhno ne to, skol'ko formul ili dat zapomnil chelovek, a to, naskol'ko on obuchaem" [Mark Zelman: "Universities look into an individual's scholastic abilities rather than how many formulas and dates he remembers]. *Dzerkalo tyzhnya*, 31. http://www.zn.ua/3000/3300/63824/

Chapman, D. (2002). *Corruption and the education sector*. Overview commissioned by the USAID and Management Systems International. http://pdf.usaid.gov/pdf_docs/PNACT874.pdf. Accessed 1 July 2012.

Drummond, T., & DeYoung, A. J. (2012). The new educational assessment regimes in Eurasia: Impacts, issues, and implications. *European Education: Issues and Studies, 44*(1), 7–26.

Drummond, T., & Gabrscek, S. (2012). Understanding higher education admissions reforms in the Eurasian context. *European Education: Issues and Studies, 44*(1), 27–45.

Edelman, M. (1988). *Constructing the political spectacle*. Chicago: University of Chicago Press.

Hallak, J., & Poisson, M. (2007). *Corrupt schools, corrupt universities: What can be done?* Paris: Institute for International Educational Planning.

Heyneman, S. (2004). Education and corruption. *International Journal of Educational Development, 24*(6), 637–648.

Heyneman, S. (2007). Three universities in Georgia, Kazakhstan and Kyrgyzstan: The struggle against corruption and for social cohesion. *Prospects: Quarterly Review of Comparative Education, 37*(3), 305–318.

Heyneman, S., Anderson, K., & Nuraliyeva, N. (2008). The cost of corruption in higher education. *Comparative Education Review, 52*(1), 1–26.

Johnson, V. (2008). Corruption in education: A global legal challenge. *Santa Clara Law Review, 48*(1), 2–78.
Kovalchuk, S., & Koroliuk, S. (2012). The introduction of standardized external testing in Ukraine: Challenges and successes. *European Education: Issues and Studies, 44*(1), 46–71.
Litvin prognoziruet, chto Ukraina vernetsya k ekzamenatsionnoj sisteme otsenivaniya znanij [Litvin says that in the future Ukraine will return back to examinations]. *Newsru.ua*, December 17, 2008. http://rus.newsru.ua/ukraine/17dec2008/litv123.html
Orkodashvili, M. (2010). Higher education reforms in the fight against corruption in Georgia. *Demokratizatsiya: The Journal of Post-Soviet Democratization, 18*(4), 357–374.
Orkodashvili, M. (2011). Corruption, collusion, and nepotism in higher education and the labor market in Georgia. *European Education: Issues and Studies, 43*(2), 32–53.
Orkodashvili, M. (2012). The changing faces of corruption in Georgian higher education: Access through times and tests. *European Education: Issues and Studies, 44*(1), 27–45.
Osipian, A. (2007a). Corruption in higher education: Conceptual approaches and measurement techniques. *Research in Comparative and International Education, 2*(4), 313–332.
Osipian, A. (2007b). Higher education corruption in Ukraine: Opinions and estimates. *International Higher Education, 49*, 20–21.
Osipian, A. (2008a). Political graft and education corruption in Ukraine: Compliance, collusion, and control. *Demokratizatsiya: The Journal of Post-Soviet Democratization, 16*(4), 323–344.
Osipian, A. (2008b). Corruption in higher education: Does it differ across the nations and why? *Research in Comparative and International Education, 3*(4), 345–365.
Osipian, A. (2008c). Corruption and coercion: University autonomy versus state control. *European Education: Issues and Studies, 40*(3), 27–48.
Osipian, A. (2009a). “Feed from the service”: Corruption and coercion in the state—University relations in Central Eurasia. *Research in Comparative and International Education, 4*(2), 182–203.
Osipian, A. (2009b). Vouchers, tests, loans, privatization: Will they help tackle corruption in Russian higher education? *Prospects: Quarterly Review of Comparative Education, 39*(1), 47–67.
Osipian, A. (2009c). Investigating corruption in American higher education: The methodology. *FedUni Journal of Higher Education, 4*(2), 49–81.
Osipian, A. (2009d). Corruption hierarchies in higher education in the former Soviet Bloc. *International Journal of Educational Development, 29*(3), 321–330.
Osipian, A. (2009e). Corruption and reform in higher education in Ukraine. *Canadian and International Education Journal, 38*(2), 104–122.
Osipian, A. (2009f). *The impact of human capital on economic growth: A case study in post-Soviet Ukraine, 1989–2009*. New York: Palgrave Macmillan.
Osipian, A. (2010a). Le Bourgeois Gentilhomme: Political corruption of Russian doctorates. *Demokratizatsiya: The Journal of Post-Soviet Democratization, 18*(3), 260–280.
Osipian, A. (2010b). Corruption in the politicized university: Lessons for Ukraine's 2010 presidential elections. *Innovation: The European Journal of Social Science Research, 23*(2), 101–114.
Osipian, A. (2010c). Corrupt organizational hierarchies in the former Soviet Bloc. *Transition Studies Review, 17*(4), 822–836.
Osipian, A. (2010d). Korruptsiya v poslediplomnom obrazovanii [Corruption in doctoral education]. *Terra Economicus, 8*(3), 48–63.
Osipian, A. (2012a). Grey areas in the higher education sector: Legality versus corruptibility. *Brigham Young University Education and Law Journal, 1*(1), 140–190.
Osipian, A. (2012b). Loyalty as rent: Corruption and politicization of Russian universities. *International Journal of Sociology and Social Policy, 32*(3/4), 153–167.
Osipian, A. (2012c). Education corruption, reform, and growth: Case of post-Soviet Russia. *Journal of Eurasian Studies, 3*(1), 20–29.
Osipian, A. (2012d). Economics of corruption in doctoral education: The dissertations market. *Economics of Education Review, 31*(1), 76–83.
Osipian, A. (2012e). Who is guilty and what to do? Popular opinion and public discourse of corruption in Russian higher education. *Canadian and International Education Journal, 41*(1), 81–95.

Osipian, A. (2013a). Corrupt organizations: Modeling educators' misconduct with cellular automata. *Computational and Mathematical Organization Theory, 19*(1), 1–24.

Osipian, A. (2013b). Recruitment and admissions: Combating corruption and fostering transparency on the path to higher education. In Transparency International (Ed.), *Global corruption report: education*. New York: Routledge.

Osipian, A. (in press). Transforming university governance in Ukraine: Collegiums, bureaucracies, and political institutions. *Higher Education Policy*.

Petrov, G., & Temple, P. (2004). Corruption in higher education: Some findings from the states of the former Soviet Union. *Higher Education Management and Policy, 16*(1), 82–94.

Pottroff, V. (2009). *External independent knowledge testing in Ukraine from a historical and social perspective*. Master's thesis, Kansas State University. Accessed at http://krex.k-state.edu/dspace/bitstream/2097/1433/1/ViktoriyaPottroff2009.pdf.pdf

Round, J., & Rodgers, P. (2009). The problems of corruption in post-Soviet Ukraine's higher education sector. *International Journal of Sociology, 39*(2), 80–95.

Rumyantseva, N. (2005). Taxonomy of corruption in higher education. *Peabody Journal of Education, 80*(1), 81–92.

Shamatov, D. (2012). The impact of standardized testing on university entrance issues in Kyrgyzstan. *European Education: Issues and Studies, 44*(1), 71–92.

Shkol'niki uzhe mogut registrirovat'sya dlya prokhozhdeniya vneshnego otsenivaniya [Pupils can already register for independent testing]. *Newsru.ua*, December 1, 2008. http://rus.newsru.ua/ukraine/01dec2008/otsinyuvannya.html

Silova, I., Johnson, M., & Heyneman, S. (2007). Education and the crisis of social cohesion in Azerbaijan and Central Asia. *Comparative Education Review, 51*(2), 159–180.

SSHA hotyat, chtoby Ukraina skatyvalas' k "debilizmu ekvatorial'nykh stran", schitaet Tabachnik [US wants Ukraine to denigrate to "debilitating level of equatorial countries," says Tabachnik]. *Newsru.ua*, May 31, 2011. http://rus.newsru.ua/ukraine/31may2011/tabtefft.html

Street, J. (2011). *Mass media, politics & democracy* (2nd ed.). New York: Palgrave Macmillan.

Studencheskie aktsii proplachivayutsya zapadnymi fondami, uveren Tabachnik [Student actions are paid for by western funds, says Tabachnik]. *Newsru.ua*, May 25, 2011. http://rus.newsru.ua/ukraine/25may2011/sbnhyue.html

Tabachnik zayavil, chto ukrainskie shkol'niki i studenty smogut vybirat' yazyk obucheniya [Tabachnik said that Ukrainian pupils and students will be able to choose the language of instruction]. *Newsru.ua*, March 23, 2010. http://rus.newsru.ua/ukraine/23mar2010/tabach.html

Timoshenko protiv "eksperimentov na detyakh", a Yushchenko sovetuet vzglyanut' im v glaza [Timoshenko is against "experiments on children," while Yushchenko suggests to look them in the eyes]. *Newsru.ua*, April 21, 2008. http://rus.newsru.ua/ukraine/21apr2008/vlipli.html

Transparency International. (2011). *Corruption Perceptions Index (CPI)*. Retrieved December 10, 2011, from http://cpi.transparency.org/cpi2011/results/

Ukraina stavit "eksperiment" na detyakh. Nachinaetsya massovoe testirovanie [Ukraine sets "an experiment" with children. Mass testing has begun]. *Newsru.ua*, April 22, 2008. http://rus.newsru.ua/ukraine/22apr2008/testir.html

Vmesto vstupitel'nykh ekzamenov – sertifikat [A certificate instead of entry examinations]. *Newsru.ua*, October 1, 2008. http://rus.newsru.ua/press/01oct2008/testy.html

Vstupitel'naya kampaniya-2009 – istoriya bolezni ukrainskogo obshchestva [The admissions season 2009, – A history of illness of Ukrainian society]. *Dzerkalo tyzhnya, 33*(761), September 5–11, 2009. http://www.zn.ua/3000/3300/67078/

Waite, D., & Allen, D. (2003). Corruption and abuse of power in education administration. *The Urban Review, 35*(4), 281–296.

Za testirovaniem abiturientov budut nablyudat' i nepravitel'stvennye organizatsii [Non-governmental organizations will also serve as observers in prospective students' testing]. *Newsru.ua*, April 22, 2008. http://rus.newsru.ua/ukraine/30apr2009/test.html

Zarubezhnye eksperty dovol'ny testirovaniem ukrainskikh vypusknikov [Foreign experts are satisfied with the testing of Ukrainian graduates]. *Newsru.ua*, May 25, 2008. http://rus.newsru.ua/ukraine/25may2008/zabulionis.html

Part III
Toward a Theory of Collaboration

Chapter 14
Can There Be Real Collaboration Between Donors and Developing Countries in Educational Policy? Conclusions and Recommendations

Carolyn A. Brown

Abstract This chapter summarizes the main points and perspectives of all the contributors to this volume and attempts to integrate their points of view on the literature about Western donor educational policies. In addition, this chapter looks at several alternative perspectives on partnerships and cooperative arrangements with developing countries to examine what a collaborative theory might look like.

Throughout the world, educational policy formation tends to be, largely, the purview of government. This process of policy formation is often not informed by research as much as by political and economic factors, and scholars are frequently omitted from debates that influence educational policy. In developing countries, local scholars are particularly marginalized from the discussion because policy is often established through agreements between government officials and outside experts. These experts are generally connected to donor agencies and/or Western institutions of research or higher education. While input from local scholars is rarely solicited, in fact, their views are often drowned out by the voices of Western "experts" and the those who set the political or economic agendas of governments – both local and international. The purpose of this book was to enlist scholars from developing countries to address the question: What impact does international donor policy and international donors have on educational policy formation in your country or region? A call for chapters elicited a response from diverse geographical regions and from the perspectives of primary, secondary, and tertiary educational scholars. Surprisingly, the perspectives of the contributors to this book were quite varied.

C.A. Brown (✉)
Associate Professor, Educational Leadership, Administration, and Policy,
Graduate School of Education, Fordham University, New York, NY 10023, USA
e-mail: carolyn@cabrownassociates.com

C.A. Brown (ed.), *Globalization, International Education Policy and Local Policy Formation,* Policy Implications of Research in Education 5,
DOI 10.1007/978-94-007-4165-2_14

Some of the contributors had researched specific areas such as implementation of technology in education in Cambodia (Richardson, Nash, Chea & Peou). Others had conducted extensive interviews with government officials and had consulted documents to substantiate the changes in educational policy in their country over years or decades (Lolwana for South Africa; and Baldeh & Manion for The Gambia). Still others expressed views derived from their experiences or research on educational policy in their country.

This book is meant to highlight the perceptions of those local scholars who have followed or studied educational policy in their country or region but whose voices are seldom included in the discussions that transpire between international agencies and government officials as well as in the arena of international research publications.

14.1 The Search for Common Themes

As I sought common themes for this final chapter, I found as much variation in points of view as commonality. In spite of the purported international consensus on the value of education and the various world conferences on collaboration in educational policy formation at Jomtien, Thailand; Dakar, Senegal; Accra, Ghana, and Paris, there was no unanimous agreement by the contributors on any one theme. Only three themes were common across a majority of the contributors. The themes that emerged among the greatest number of contributors were (a) a stated or implied belief in the value of education for development, (b) the diversity of needs in education within regions, and (c) the influence of Western thought paradigms on educational policy formation.

14.1.1 Education as Necessary for Development

Although a belief in the value of an effective publicly funded educational system from primary through tertiary education as a structure for economic and political development was stated or implied in many of the chapters, two authors specifically noted that formal education should not, in fact, be a priority in their societies. In the Marshall Island, the Western paradigm of formal education does not meet the cultural or even the human capital needs of the population. Sauer asserts, "…many [Marshallese] stakeholders are unclear about what the purpose of education should be for Marshall Islanders" (p. 8). Uribe-Roldán in his chapter on Latin America advocates for tertiary education as a priority over basic (K-12) education in the southern countries of South America. He is critical of the formal structures of education, as advocated by donors for development. He asserts that research has not tied development directly to formal education and that a new paradigm is needed for tertiary education policies to meet the human capital needs of developing countries.

14.1.2 Diversity Among and Within Regions

The contributors who framed their discussion within the context of a region, such as Latin America or Africa, generally agreed that diversity among countries within a region was a factor that was seldom considered in international educational policy. Uribe-Roldán; Edwards, Martin & Victoria (El Salvador); and Wilhite, Geo-JaJa & Vuzo (Tanzania) particularly emphasized the variation among countries, even among sub-regions within countries, and the inability of international donor policy to meet the diverse needs of the countries within their region by applying a one-size fits all model. Uribe-Roldán and Wilhite et al. were strongly critical of donor policies that see Africa or Latin America as having more commonality than difference and fail to consider the vast regional differences in culture. Edwards et al.'s focus on El Salvador pointed out how the post-conflict situation in their country differentiated their educational support needs from other Latin American countries.

14.1.3 Influence of Western Education Paradigms on Local Policy

Another of the most common themes to emerge was the recognition that to a greater or lesser degree the paradigms that underlie international donor policy originate in the West. These Western models for formal education, arguably, have a substantial influence on local policy formation but often have limited applicability in practice in the context of developing countries. These Western education forms included test-based accountability, a priority on basic (K-12) education over tertiary/adult education and youth employment development, and the requirements of "contingencies" in countries that accept donor funds.

The West's emphasis on test-based accountability was addressed in two chapters – one dealing with primary education and one with admission to higher education. In Park and Ahmed's discussion of the effects of high- stakes testing on primary education in Bangladesh, they directly attributed the policy decision to the Bangladeshi government, but their final conclusion asserts that the policy formation can be traced to pressure from international donors. While the authors acknowledged that primary school testing acted as a motivator for schools to focus on a standard content for all students, the authors bemoaned the lack of teacher preparation for understanding how to best use these tests. Park and Ahmed were critical of these tests for their questionable reliability and validity. In addition, they objected to the high- stakes emphasis that labels students and schools as failing while the government lacks the needed resources for effective teaching and learning. The authors also questioned the pedagogical wisdom of using high-stakes testing as an assessment strategy at the primary school level, a controversial issue in the developed West that is, nevertheless, being imposed on the developing world.

Osipian (The Ukraine) also centered his chapter on the issue of test-based accountability but at the tertiary level. He analyzed the popular discourse around the value of recently implemented admission testing for higher education through media analysis. In his conclusions, he found that the public viewed the examinations more as a vehicle for corruption in maintaining the practice of admitting only children of the elite and well-connected to higher education, and that they were, essentially, a failure in their stated purpose of equalizing access to higher education in the Ukraine. Osipian is particularly critical of the United States policy of pressing for the test as a contingency for support for aid.

14.1.4 The Appeal for Tertiary Education as a Donor Priority

Several chapter authors viewed tertiary education as a vehicle for meeting a rapidly emerging need for human capital development to facilitate growth in developing countries. Attention to and funding of tertiary education and youth and adult training program are only recently, and to a limited degree, being addressed by donor countries. While Baldeh and Manion, generally, agreed that donor policy is most often aligned with the goals of local stakeholders, they acknowledged that a misalignment occurs in the donors' failure to recognize the need for tertiary education and youth development and employability. Uribe-Roldán discusses at length the struggle of South American countries to develop human capital without the support for tertiary education by donor agencies and developed countries. In his analysis of popular discourse in the Ukraine on the value of admissions testing for universities, Osipian implies that support for tertiary education is strong within the country and that its support is not dependent on donor funds.

14.1.5 Contingencies in Funding

Several chapters (Wilhite et al.; Edwards et al.; and Uribe-Roldán) discussed the use of "contingencies" in donor policy, that is, the overt or implied demands that are placed on the recipient countries in exchange for donor funds. Wilhite et al. were particularly concerned with contingencies in their chapter on African education and Tanzania in particular. They were critical of the donors' expectations that recipient countries would adopt neo-liberal policies, (i.e., tuition-based secondary schools) or require that funding be linked to schools using English as a medium of instruction rather than indigenous language and culture. Wilhite et al. were focused on the failure of international donors to meet the needs of developing Africa because of a lack of sensitivity to the advantages of indigenous language instruction and culturally and economically relevant curriculum and pedagogy. They used this extensive critique as a frame for their discussion of the Nordic countries as exceptions to these "post-colonial" and "imperialistic" practices. According to Wilhite et al., to Nordic countries (Norway, Sweden, and Denmark) had few if any contingencies attached to their bilateral funding and took a collaborative approach to educational programming in Africa, specifically Tanzania. While the authors are critical of post-colonial models for donor funding, their praise of the Nordic countries omits mention that none of these countries were involved in the colonialization in Africa.

Edwards et al. also discussed the expectations by Western donors that education policy would reflect a neo-liberal perspective. While the authors acknowledged that political support for current education policy and the formation of the policy in El Salvador has been accomplished by the government, they emphasizes that implementation by the Ministry of Education was achieved from a "position of vulnerability" since funding for policy implementation was largely dependent on international aid.

The issue of education policy implementation being dependent on international aid emerged in several other chapters. Park and Ahmed placed the responsibility for the policy on primary testing on the Bangladeshi government but implied that this policy is, in part, implemented under pressure from donors. Baldeh and Manion in The Gambia credited the international agencies and bilateral donors with providing the funds for the implementation for much of the educational programs. While Osipian was critical of the policy for university admissions testing in the Ukraine, he credited the pressure by USAID funding for policy implementation, even while criticizing the media for failing to adequately cover the involvement of the bilateral funding in the policy. Finally, Sauer attributed funding of educational program (as well as accountability measures) entirely to the United States because of the "protectorate" status of the Marshall Islands. In other chapters, the need for international funds to implement policy was often implied if not discussed directly.

14.1.6 Impact of Research and Reports on Policy

The influence of reports issued by donor organizations such as the World Bank and USAID was mentioned in several articles as having a direct impact on local policy formation. Baldeh and Manion; Edwards et al.; and Uribe-Roldán asserted that reports produced by the World Bank, OECD, and American think tanks were influential in shaping the debate on the formation of education policy in their countries. Edwards et al., in El Salvador, saw the influence of international research on education policy as having an impact on government policy formation within the Ministry of Education. Caride, in his analysis of policy formation on gender in Argentina, Chile, and Uruguay, credited international research with influencing the public discourse on gender that helped inform policy formation. Baldeh and Manion asserted that UNESCO's *Education for All* acted as a framework for developing educational policy in The Gambia and was generally well aligned with the country's goals and needs. Lolwana attributed some of the education policy formation in South Africa to the borrowing of ideas from Western countries, particularly the United States, through exposure of South African policy actors to research and traveling abroad for observation.

14.1.7 Minor Themes

Baldeh and Manion (The Gambia) and Caride (Chile, Argentina, and Uruguay) mentioned the role of non-governmental organizations in the formation of education. Caride credited women's non-governmental organizations with actively setting the discourse for gender education, and Baldeh and Manion mentioned non-governmental organizations as important partners with the government in the formation and implementation of education policy. Park and Ahmed's study of primary school testing in Bangladesh was conducted entirely within schools that were operated by a local non-governmental organization. While the non-governmental organization was operating the schools, the authors were clear that these schools were under the same policy mandates from the government as the state schools. So, in this study, the non-governmental organization was seen as implementers of policy rather than influencers of policy.

In other chapters, the influence of non-governmental organizations may have come into play in the development of policy through "borrowing" strategies where non-governmental organizations may have acted as conduits between Western ideas and local policy, but these were not specifically discussed.

Borrowing emerged as a theme in a few chapters. One example is Lolwana's investigation of education policy formation in post-apartheid South Africa. Most striking is that the discussion centers around the claim that the South African government developed education policy documents for the "new" South Africa from ideas and strategies that had been borrowed from Western countries and not under any pressure from donor agencies or countries. The author is adamant that South Africa has remained in control of its donor funding and educational policy formation throughout the post-apartheid era. Government officials responsible for education policy traveled abroad both before and after the fall of apartheid and brought back education policy ideas. The chapter concludes, that "while foreign countries wanted to encourage South Africa in its democracy trajectory, in relation to specific education policies, the education transformation discourse was shaped more by internal forces" (Lolwana). South Africa borrowed ideas from the West, but the decisions to codify these into policy were entirely a local decision.

14.2 Variations in Views of Donor Policy

Again, no common theme emerged across all chapters, even when the criteria for "implied theme" were applied. The authors tended to fall along a continuum between "donor as the all-knowing and demanding perpetuator of post-colonial domination" on one extreme, and "developing country as fully responsible for the setting, implementation, and success or failure of education policy" on the other. An interesting and potentially influential factor in these perspectives may lie in the extent of the exposure of the authors to the Western rhetoric on education and international policy formation.

Nearly all the authors received, at least, their graduate education in Western universities. Some were finishing their doctorates at the time that they wrote their chapters and others were serving in academic positions in the United States or Europe. The rhetoric of post-colonial imperialism in policy development seemed to emerge more often among those authors who were closest to Western educations, that is, those completing their doctorates or who were academics in Western universities. Those who were working within their own country (authors from Bangladesh, The Gambia, Latin America and South Africa) indicated a more balanced view of donor participation in educational policy formation and implementation.

In addition, in the chapters where the authors used interviews with local government officials and others involved in the policy formation and implementation process to gain their perspective on donor involvement in education policy, the authors tended to view international donors as partners in educational policy development rather than adversaries that demanded policies that were out of step with local needs. However, as a number of authors pointed out, "one size does *not* fit all". It is possible that the experience of the authors with donor policy, demands, and funding varied because of substantial variation in educational needs and requirements from region to region or country to country within a region. For instance, while asserting the same ideology, the three contributors who wrote about Latin America came to quite different conclusions about how effective donor policy was on the formation of local funding.

The contributors to this book did, overall, agree that each country has its own individual needs and goals and that what works in one context can be very dysfunctional in another. Baldeh and Manion in their chapter on The Gambia fell on one end of a continuum by agreeing that donor policy and expectations were vital for significant improvement in education, while Wilhite et al. in the chapter on Tanzania took the opposite end of the spectrum in arguing that the international donors acted as "post-colonial" and demanded contingencies that did not meet the needs of the local populations. The views of the other contributors fell along the "donor as benefactor – donor as oppressor continuum" to varying degrees.

The chapters on Bangladesh (Park and Ahmed), Cambodia (Richardson, Nash, Chea, & Peou), and South Africa (Lolwana) focused less on the role and demands of international and bilateral funding agencies and placed more emphasis on the role of local policymakers in the development and implementation of education policy. However, Park and Ahmed, in their discussion of primary school testing policy in Bangladesh, implied that these policies, while implemented by the Bangladeshi government, were at least an indirect result of the *Education For All* policy and pressure from international and bilateral donors. Richardson et al. in their chapter about educational technology development in Cambodia were explicitly critical of the Cambodian government for incomplete implementation of technology; even as, the role of the international community emerged as providing funding and technical support for the formation of the written technology plan. Lolwana, in the chapter on South Africa, was alone in perceiving the international donors as nearly irrelevant in educational policy formation and implementation; however, South Africa stands apart from the other countries that are represented in the book because of its position in the international development world. South Africa is included with the group of countries referred to at BRICS (Brazil, Russia, India, China, and South Africa), which, as emerging economies, are both recipients and donors of international funds in various arenas. These emerging economies, while they continue to receive international aid, have a lesser dependence on this aid and, in some cases, act as donors to more developing countries.

Some of the variations in author view points on the impact of donor policy on their local educational policy formation was due to the funding institutions on which the authors focused. While many of the authors agreed that UNESCO and the World Bank were major players in the development of international education policy, Sauer and Osipian focused almost entirely on the role of the United States in setting policy demands in exchange for funding for basic education in the Marshall Island and higher education in the Ukraine.

Overall, it is possible to conclude from these chapters that international policy in education such as UNESCO's *Education for All* and the resulting funding policies and practices of international and bilateral donors do, to some extent, influence the development of local educational policy. The relationship of local policy formation to the *Education for All* policy framework tends to be indirect through the funding regulations of donor agencies and individual donor countries. The majority of authors focused on areas that are included with *Education for All* and are high priority for international policy developers and donors such as basic education, girls' education, and accountability.

While UNESCO's policy has certainly had an influence on the funding agendas for both international and bilateral donors, the voices of local governments in developing countries have been heard in recent years through the meetings in Jomtien, Dakar, Accra, and Paris where collaboration between donor and recipient countries was the focus. One example of the influence of local governments and stakeholders on international policy is the increased emphasis on and funding for tertiary education and adult training. Certainly, overall, international agencies and bilateral donors from the developing world continue to exert a significant influence on the development and implementation of educational policy throughout the developing world, though this may be changing.

14.3 Toward a Theory of Collaboration

There is evidence of some collaboration in education policy between donors and recipient countries, but is this movement toward collaboration authentic and sustainable or limited to a few areas? If I posed this question to this book's contributors, I suspect the answers would vary, although overall I would anticipate a tentative agreement that there is, indeed, some movement toward collaboration, particularly if compared to the donor/recipient relationships of a decade ago. Even the authors most critical of international policy, such at Wilhite et al., saw progress in collaboration with Nordic countries focusing in the cultural and economic requirements set by their African recipients.

A number of the authors were critical of the bureaucratic slow downs of World Bank funding, and several were critical of the United States funding policy, in particular, being unresponsive to the local context. These factors can make collaboration difficult or, at least, slow. We understand from the documents produced from the meetings in Jomtien, Dakar, Accra, and Paris, that donors are buying into an a higher level of efficiency by working together to coordinate educational funding efforts to reduce redundancy in programs and that as a result of this there has been a reduction of overall funds to some developing countries (Abetti et al. 2011).

However, increasing efficiency in funding and cooperation between donors is not synonymous with collaboration. In fact, it could be argued that this increase in efficiency and coordination, which is resulting in reduced funding, may be another form of self-interest on the part of the donor. So, to what extent are the developing countries that receive these funds having a voice? Overall, most of the authors from the countries represented in this book agreed on two fundamental precepts: a recognition that formal education has value; acknowledgment that while developing countries remain dependent on international donors for the implementation of education policy, policy formation is increasingly being created by local governments in collaboration with donors and, in some cases, with the participation of non-governmental organizations – both local and international.

Since 2000, the world meetings at Jomtien, Dakar, Accra, and Paris have brought to the attention of international donors and policy drivers (such as UNESCO) that collaboration with the recipient countries is needed in order to empower local stakeholders to move toward sustainable development in educational practice. These conferences have, arguably, met with more or less success, as the global policy agenda continues to be established largely by the Western countries (i.e., early childhood education outranked tertiary education on the agenda even though adult education and human capital issues have long been goals in parts of the developing world as we heard from the authors from Latin America and Ukraine). Also, as was mentioned by Baldeh and Manion, a Western focus on girls' education has obscured an understanding of the need for boys' education. Expanding enrollment for equity and access for all students remains an international priority, while the poorest countries continue to struggle with funding even the most basic educational services for the students who *are able* enroll.

What factors make a developing country a collaborator? A few of the authors directly addressed the limitations of their own governments in meeting the educational needs of their citizens. Osipian, in his discussion of higher education in the Ukraine, was forthcoming in recognizing that corruption among government and university officials significantly impacted how successfully the programs in higher education could be implemented. Lolwana ended her analysis of the development of education policy in post-apartheid South Africa with the dramatic statement, "The changes that came to be were a result of an extensive search by South Africans to reform.... South Africans have nobody to blame for the policy mistakes they have made but themselves" (p. 25).

Many of the chapter authors discussed and deconstructed the educational policy formation and, sometimes, the protracted implementation of these policies and their successes and failures. Other authors were gentler in their criticism of the relationship between the donors and their governments in the implementation of education policy. Richardson et al. credited international donors and non-governmental organizations with helping the Cambodian government to formulate a technology plan, albeit a flawed one. Few of the authors addressed the issue of how to maintain funding over a period of years for sustainable educational programs. Does this responsibility lie with the donor agencies and countries or ultimately with the governments of the developing world?

Arguably, to be a collaborator, developing countries must be able to find the resources from their own economy and human capital to support long-term and consistent education programs. Many of the authors mentioned that a substantial number of education programs are funded through international donors, and a few of the authors bemoaned the cutbacks in funding that have occurred in recent years. Many of the poorest countries have deep and intractable issues of government corruption and shortage of resources and professional capacity – either because of a resource poor environment or the skimming of resources for uses other than education. For a country to be a collaborator, these issues need to be resolved, and to echo Lolwana's sentiments – the countries need to take the lead on their own educational development. In the end, if there is to be an resolution of the tension between donor and recipients and between the developed and developing world in the area of education, true collaboration may mean reaching a point where recipient countries accept funds from donors on a short-term basis in order to 'jump start' programs that can be sustained by adequate local resources and efficient governments that buy into the beliefs shared by most of these scholars that widely available public education is fundamental to long-term development. Sustainability is a key factor in functional educational systems throughout the developing world.

14.4 An Analogy

In part, the relationship between the donor agency and the recipients country is one where the donor provides funds…either as loans or grants. Wilhite et al.'s discussion of contingencies touched on the unequal nature of this relationship and that often the decision of the donor to give or loan money has its genesis in the self interest of the donor country or in the Western countries collectively, who control the priorities of the World Bank. But, what if the loan or donation was given based on a plan developed solely by stakeholders in the recipient country, that is, government officials, scholars, educational administrators and teachers, not by donor agencies or countries? In this scenario, the recipient country would put forth a plan, much like an individual or business might present to a bank for a loan to build a facility. The recipient country would have two options: (1) to adopt a pre-conceived plan or template (such as might be set by the World Bank or UNESCO) and receive the technical assistance to complete the plan analogous to hiring a contractor to build a pre-designed facility, or (2) to design their own system based on their own goals and needs using their indigenous capacity analogous to hiring their own architect. In either case, the bank/donor would provide funding for the entire project (entire implementation of a comprehensive education plan) but only on the basis of the recipient countries ability to maintain the facility (program) once it is built. This is essentially the structure that is currently used, at least on paper, but often not in fact. Too often developing countries opt for (or have forced on them) projects for which they have a shortage of technical capacity to complete or sustain. These projects diminish or disappear once donor support has ceased.

Related to this analogy is the concept of "marketization" of education, that is, the development of institutions that can be economically self-sustaining. This is particularly discussed in this book and in the general research in reference to secondary and tertiary education where schools are established as tuition-based. The concept of a "marketized" or neo-liberal agenda (generally mentioned as less than desirable by the contributors) has, arguably, dominated the funding agendas of many donor countries and, and to some extent, the World Bank. "Marketization" of education is problematic at best because students do not generate a short-term profit and tuition-based schooling places formal education beyond the means of most citizens of developing countries; however, direct "marketization" of development is being practiced in a number of African countries, today, at least by China. While these projects do not, for the most part, involve institutions of formal education, it is interesting to think about how the Chinese model of development might impact education.

14.5 China – Collaboration and Development

Although Western countries have objected to the Chinese model of development as exploitive, some African countries are embracing Chinese business. The application of this Chinese model and its partnerships with governments is interesting, if only hypothetically applicable to education. The relationship between China and its partner governments in Africa is symbiotic but transparent, in the sense that the Chinese incursion into the developing world is almost entirely accomplished by private businesses with the approval, if not the direct support, of the Chinese government. These relationships are not donor relationships, nor are they intended to be. Chinese companies are clear in their intention is to make a profit for themselves, that is, unapologetically self serving. However, in order to reach their profit goals (from mining to refining to manufacturing), they have to build an infrastructure for the partner country. This infrastructure may include material infrastructure such as roads and harbors or it may include (and in a few cases does) direct development of human infrastructure such as adult training and youth employability programs or indirect development of human capital through, for instance, the sale to families of affordable solar panels that can provide electricity for charging cell phones, which are increasingly vital for local business transactions and for furthering education "because [children] have light for studying." (Rosenthal 2010, para 7). In the long run, the Chinese will take what they came for, and the partner country will be on its own to maintain and support the infrastructure (or not). Is this collaboration or exploitation? I assert that the answer is not entirely black and white. Western countries have long been accused of exploitation of the developing world. Even as China's methods are outside the Western paradigm, only time will tell how these partnerships may result in exploitation that leaves the countries stripped of resources without substantial improvement or result in sustained collaboration with government that facilitate long term development.

All this begs the question of how educational development is meeting or will meet the long-term goal of human capital development throughout the world in order to alleviate poverty and to stabilize societies. Surprisingly, none of the chapter authors directly addressed the issue of education as a vehicle for poverty alleviation or of social stabilization. We are left wondering: Are these goals too large? What do these goals mean to individual countries? Devoid of Western influence, how would developing countries view the role and purpose of education, and how would that impact policy formation? These questions may be explored best by the scholars within the developing countries, who possess the indigenous knowledge to truly understand and critique the development of education in their countries and regions.

In thinking about recommendations for further study that emerged from these chapters, I would advocate the expansion of the academic milieu to encourage scholars from developing countries to participate in the discourse of development from their own perspective. Too often, they are educated in Western universities where success is, if not dependent, at least facilitated by their willingness to adopt Western rhetoric toward both development and education. In an era where information can be posted instantaneously on the Internet and can be, in fact, if not in practice, available to everyone, there should not be a limitation on either access to information or access to the discussion. University students in Bangladesh should not be limited to the dated research available in their institutions, and experienced scholars from Africa should not be marginalized from mainstream academic journals and discourse because they do not live in the West or because they advocate an opinion or point of view that diverges from or is counter to that of the West. Authentic collaboration requires not just cooperation between funding sources and developing countries, but also collaboration on ideas about what education is and what is means to be educated and for what purpose. This kind of collaboration requires not only the meetings of government officials and funders but also the meeting of minds across all countries.

References

Abetti, P., Beardmore, S., Tapp, C., & Winthrop, R. (2011). *Prospects for bilateral aid to basic education Put students at risk. Fast Track Initiative*. Washington, DC: World Bank.

Rosenthal, E. (2010, December 24). In Kenya, huts far off the grid harness the sun. *New York Times*. Accessed from http://www.nytimes.com/2010/12/25/science/earth/25fossil.html?pagewanted=all&_r=0

Index

A

Accountability, 6, 19, 21, 26, 28–30, 34, 53, 63–66, 91, 99, 108, 110, 117, 211, 239–241, 244
Accra Agenda for Action, 9, 63, 64
Accreditation, 138–140, 205, 208, 211, 216
Active learning, 107, 118, 120–122, 124–126
Adult
  basic skills, 186
  education, 5, 101, 186, 239, 245
Africa, 11, 32, 33, 59, 81, 108, 162, 184, 238
Aid
  context, 60, 63, 99
  influence, 1, 183–199
Apartheid, 5, 184–199, 242
Argentina, 5, 143, 144, 146, 148–151, 154, 207, 241, 242
Assessment, 5, 28, 29, 34, 42, 43, 62, 73, 75, 94, 99, 107–127, 132, 136, 165–173, 190, 215, 216, 218–221, 229, 239

B

Bangladesh, 2, 3, 5, 107–127, 239, 241–243, 248
Basic education, 3, 5, 12, 16, 19, 20, 26–28, 32, 34, 59, 60, 64–66, 68–73, 75, 76, 84–87, 92, 96, 99, 112, 113, 116, 127, 152, 188, 192, 198, 244, 245
Benchmarks, 111, 136, 160, 191
Bilateral donors, 2, 4, 26, 27, 32, 241, 243, 244
Bilateral relations, 15, 69, 244
Borrowing, 15–16, 192, 196, 198, 199, 241, 242
Brazil, Russia, India, China, and South Africa (BRICS), 244
Bretton Wood agreement, 14

C

Cambodia, 5, 157–180, 238, 243, 246
Capacity, 17, 19–21, 27, 30, 44, 47, 63, 73, 76, 77, 83, 85, 87, 88, 91, 96, 99, 100, 110, 115, 123, 126, 127, 137, 139, 152, 158, 160, 165, 179, 180, 191, 198, 208, 220, 246
Case study, 39–55, 59–77, 89, 208
Central America, 11, 42
Centralization, 136
Chile, 5, 143, 144, 146, 150–151, 153, 154, 202, 205, 207, 213, 241, 242
China, 18, 32, 33, 49, 50, 93, 140, 212, 244, 247–248
Civil society, 31, 48, 51, 60, 63, 65–67, 69, 71–77, 98, 154, 220
Coercion, 15–16, 217
Collaboration, 4, 5, 30, 32, 50, 72, 73, 114, 163, 201–213, 237–248
Colonialism, 6, 15, 33, 133–134
Common World Educational Culture (CWEC), 62, 70, 71
Conditionalities, 44, 47, 48, 53, 81, 82, 84, 85, 87, 88, 90, 91, 95, 97, 98, 100, 102, 208, 210

C.A. Brown (ed.), *Globalization, International Education Policy and Local Policy Formation*, Policy Implications of Research in Education 5,
DOI 10.1007/978-94-007-4165-2

Contemporary aid context, 60
Content analysis, 67
Contingencies, 2, 5, 239–241, 243, 246
Conventions on the Rights of the Child, 10
Cooperation, 3, 14, 51, 96, 98–101, 111, 114, 123, 152, 194, 202, 203, 205, 245, 248
Corruption, 6, 29, 32, 160, 215–232, 240, 245, 246
Critical theory, 12, 13
CWEC. *See* Common World Educational Culture (CWEC)

D
Dakar Framework for Action, 64–66
Dakar, Senegal, 59, 70, 108, 238
Danish international development agency (DANIDA), 98–99, 194
Decentralization, 19, 43, 45–47, 54, 86, 113, 148, 207, 210, 211
Democracy, 45, 51, 53, 54, 93, 100, 135, 145–148, 151, 154, 192, 197, 199, 201, 242
Denmark, 82, 90, 94, 98–99, 196, 241
Developing countries, 1, 4, 6, 14, 18, 19, 27, 29, 32, 44, 55, 64–66, 82, 88, 95, 96, 102, 152, 160, 208, 237–248
Development, 2, 10, 25, 40, 59, 81, 109, 132, 143, 157, 183, 201, 216, 238
Document analysis, 76
Donor(s), 2, 26, 43, 59, 82, 109, 131, 183, 204, 216, 237
  countries, 2, 4, 44, 82, 103, 183, 185, 188, 198, 199, 240, 244, 246, 247
  education policy, 67
  priorities, 240

E
Economic development, 14, 17, 18, 69, 93, 160, 201, 209–212
Economy, 15, 17, 18, 21, 27, 34, 61, 62, 83, 87, 102, 112, 133, 134, 161–163, 178, 190, 196, 205, 208, 211, 244, 246
Education,
Educational infrastructure, 33, 89, 99, 102, 112, 135, 152, 158, 160, 161, 164–172, 177, 179, 199, 247, 248
Educational outcomes, 28, 29, 71, 90, 96, 100, 110, 125, 126, 154, 155, 158, 186, 189, 191–193, 199
Educational planning, 65, 67, 179
Educational technology, 176, 243
Educational values, 132
Education expansion, 5
Education for All (EFA), 1, 2, 4, 11, 19–21, 25–29, 32, 45, 59–77, 86, 87, 89, 90, 108, 109, 113, 115, 116, 123, 131, 152, 198, 213, 241, 243, 244
Education Plan Development Grant, 66
Education policy,
Education with community participation (EDUCO), 40, 43, 45–48, 53–55
EDUCO. *See* Education with community participation (EDUCO)
EFA. *See* Education for All (EFA)
El Salvador, 5, 39–55, 239, 241
Emancipation, 204
Enrollment, 3, 11, 12, 20, 31, 67, 69, 76, 86, 162, 163, 167, 211, 216, 228, 245
Equality, 16, 18, 20, 40, 43, 48–51, 53–55, 64, 70, 87, 90, 93, 96, 100, 149–152, 206, 212
Equity, 13, 16, 26, 43, 53, 71, 72, 85, 87, 93, 95, 96, 103, 107–127, 208, 210–212, 245
European Union (EU), 186, 188, 194, 216, 219, 221, 227, 231

F
Fast Track Initiative (FTI), 21, 59, 63, 64, 74, 76
Focus groups, 165, 166, 173–176
Formal education, 32, 98, 112, 149, 162, 163, 178, 190, 238, 239, 245, 247
FTI. *See* Fast Track Initiative (FTI)

G
The Gambia, 59–77, 238, 241–243
G8 countries, 159
Gender, 5, 16, 20, 26, 27, 40, 43, 48–51, 53–55, 64, 67, 69, 71, 72, 76, 82, 112, 115, 116, 143–155, 211, 241, 242
Gender equality, 16, 20, 40, 43, 48–51, 53–55, 64, 149, 152
German Agency for Technical Cooperation (GTZ), 51, 53–55, 194
Globalization, 4, 27, 55, 61–62, 76, 86, 204, 205, 207, 208, 210, 211, 213, 222
Globally structured agenda, 62, 70, 73

Global Partnership for Education (GPE), 21, 59–61, 63–67, 69–76
Goals, 2, 4, 11, 16–22, 25–29, 42, 51, 52, 60, 61, 63, 64, 66–68, 70–72, 75–77, 82, 86, 87, 91, 93, 95, 96, 98, 102, 112–115, 118–120, 123, 127, 134, 135, 137, 140, 145, 148–152, 154, 158, 160, 175, 177, 179, 180, 190, 192, 218, 220, 221, 225, 229, 230, 240, 241, 243, 245, 247, 248
Government officials, 2–5, 30, 52, 60, 67, 74, 75, 184, 186, 198, 204, 205, 207, 237, 238, 242, 243, 246, 248
Governments, 2, 10, 27, 40, 60, 82, 108, 131, 146, 158, 184, 204, 217, 237
GPE. *See* Global Partnership for Education (GPE)

H
Higher education, 2, 5, 6, 9, 16, 19, 70, 99, 114, 148, 163, 174, 176, 186, 188, 201–213, 215–223, 226, 227, 230–232, 237, 239, 240, 244, 245
Higher education institutions, 163, 174, 205, 210, 211, 215, 220
High-income countries, 10
High stakes examinations, 109, 121, 123
History, 4, 9–22, 29, 32, 52, 92, 93, 94, 131–134, 144, 146, 153, 184, 186, 198, 218
Human capital, 18, 27, 87, 92, 96, 206, 238, 240, 245–248
Human rights, 9, 10, 33, 49, 52, 82, 84, 85, 87–102, 148, 154, 199

I
Informal education, 177
Information communication technologies (ICT), 157–181
Institutional context, 201
Institutionalization, 12, 52, 59, 60, 63, 210, 220
Institutions, 14, 18, 20, 27, 28, 31, 32, 40, 42, 44–46, 48, 50, 52, 72, 83, 86, 90, 93, 95, 102, 113–116, 127, 139, 144–146, 148, 150, 152, 155, 163, 168, 174, 191, 205, 210, 211, 215, 219, 220, 237, 244, 247, 248
Integration, 72, 82, 91, 92, 96, 98, 102, 190, 193, 195, 199, 201, 202, 211, 212
Intergovernmental cooperation, 205
International Development Bank, 40, 69, 123, 159, 187
International education, 1–4, 9–22, 25, 26, 28, 49, 63, 157, 203–205, 209, 219, 221, 239, 244
International education policy, 1, 4, 9–22, 25, 26, 28, 63, 244
International influence, 25, 32–34, 39–55, 184, 195–198
Internationalization, 205, 208, 211, 212, 216
International organizations, 15–17, 19, 40, 44–46, 48, 53–55, 144–146, 151–155, 208, 211, 216, 219–226, 228–232
Interviews, 5, 41, 47, 48, 67, 72, 74, 76, 118, 119, 121, 124, 166, 184–186, 188, 222, 229, 238, 243

J
Jomtien, Thailand, 70, 75, 108, 113, 238

L
Language, 12, 14, 18, 22, 67, 84, 89, 90, 97, 99–101, 112, 113, 127, 134, 137, 138, 143, 155, 163, 168, 170, 172, 192, 205, 207, 218, 223, 224, 240
Language instruction, 240
Latin America, 5, 11, 45, 88, 143–155, 201–213, 238, 239, 243, 245
Legal frameworks, 220
Legislation, 143, 144, 146–149, 151, 154, 209
Local control, 102
Local institutions, 14, 42, 168, 220
Low-income countries, 15, 29, 59, 66, 81, 108–111, 126, 208

M
Marketization, 87, 89, 150, 204–205, 247
Marshall Islands, 5, 131–141, 238, 241, 244
Master plan, 67, 139, 157–159, 162–166, 168–169, 171, 173–176, 178–180
MDG. *See* Millennium Development Goals (MDG)
Media, 187, 216, 221–228, 230–232, 240, 241
Media analysis, 240
Millennium Development Goals (MDG), 2, 4, 11, 20, 22, 72, 93, 96, 102, 115, 211

Ministry of Education, 41, 132, 135–138, 141, 157, 221, 229, 241
Ministry of Education and Youth and Sport, 157
Mission, 94, 98, 119, 120, 134, 137, 158
Modernization, 12–14, 17, 18, 53, 231
Multi-lateral donors, 69, 72, 84

N
National education policy, 40, 42, 44, 55, 60–62, 67, 70–72, 76, 115, 118, 123, 186
National laws, 144, 149–151, 155
National Qualifications Framework (NQF), 186, 189–192, 195, 196, 199
Neo-liberalism, 31, 61, 84, 91, 208, 211
No Child Left Behind, 136
Non-governmental organizations (NGO), 2, 3, 5, 16, 20, 26, 31, 32, 41, 42, 48–50, 52–54, 60, 65, 66, 69, 72, 74, 76, 108, 109, 113–115, 117–126, 135, 144, 145, 151, 153–155, 159, 160, 178, 185–187, 193, 196, 221, 226, 228, 229, 242, 245, 246
Non-native language instruction, 138
NORAD, 99–100
Nordic aid, 81–103
North, 11, 14, 16, 17, 71, 86, 90, 93–96, 101, 102, 191, 192, 202–204
Norway, 82, 90, 93, 94, 96, 98–100, 241
NQF. *See* National Qualifications Framework (NQF)

O
OECD. *See* Organisation for Economic Co-operation and Development (OECD)
OECD-DAC, 83, 90, 94, 97, 100, 102
Open Institute, 158, 170, 176
Organisation for Economic Co-operation and Development (OECD), 21, 30, 60, 63, 64, 82–86, 89, 90, 93, 94, 97, 100–102, 152, 162, 193, 205, 209, 211, 241
Outcomes-based education, 186, 191–193, 196, 199
Ownership, 19, 21, 60–66, 68, 74–77, 82, 85, 90, 92, 95, 99, 100, 135

P
Paris Declaration, 4, 9–22, 63, 64, 85, 86, 93, 95, 98–100
Participation, 5, 12, 20, 27, 30, 40, 41, 45, 46, 49, 54, 60, 63–65, 67, 74–76, 89, 91, 97, 100, 102, 112–114, 133, 135, 137, 162, 178, 196, 205, 209, 228, 243, 245
Partnerships, 20–22, 31, 45, 59–61, 63–66, 70, 72–76, 82, 85, 98, 100, 101, 127, 132, 158, 176, 179, 219, 247, 248
Pedagogy, 87, 113, 122, 127, 158, 175, 240
Planning, 17, 19, 21, 28, 30, 65–67, 77, 107, 165, 173–180
Policy
  formation, 1–5, 25, 30, 39–55, 203, 206, 237–239, 241–246, 248
  implementation, 241
Political, 1–4, 12, 13, 16, 19, 20, 22, 26, 41, 42, 46, 48, 51, 52, 55, 61, 62, 64, 66, 70, 81, 83–87, 89, 90, 92–95, 97, 98, 100–103, 124, 133, 135, 144–150, 154, 158, 160, 179, 180, 185, 188, 192, 194, 196–198, 201–205, 207, 209, 210, 212, 213, 217, 218, 222, 228, 229, 237, 238, 241
Political context, 62, 144, 146–151, 198
Post-colonialism, 5, 241, 242, 243
Post conflict, 239
Poststructuralist, 145
Poverty reduction, 13, 70, 71, 82, 86, 88, 92, 93, 96, 97, 103, 111, 203, 211, 212
Primary education, 11, 19, 20, 26, 41, 64, 101, 107–127, 187, 239
Primary school enrollment, 3
Primary schooling, 98
Program Implementation Grant, 66
Public discourse, 215, 216, 222, 231, 241
Public opinion, 222, 223, 230, 231

Q
Qualitative research, 67

R
Reports, 26, 41–43, 46, 48, 52, 67, 68, 74, 87, 89–91, 95, 98, 110, 115, 131, 132, 135, 136, 138–141, 152, 159, 184, 193, 203, 208, 209, 221–227, 230–232, 241
Resources, 3, 15–19, 21, 33, 45, 48, 61, 70, 73, 81, 84, 95, 98, 99, 102, 115, 121–123, 126, 132, 137, 152, 153, 160, 162, 165, 166, 169, 172, 178, 180, 208, 210, 212, 239, 246, 248
Rhetoric, 5, 44, 84, 85, 92, 94, 153, 155, 231, 243, 248

S
School enrollment, 3, 11
Schooling, 11–19, 21, 22, 27, 29, 31, 32, 68, 71, 72, 83, 84, 86, 89, 92, 98, 99, 101, 133, 162, 191, 192, 247
Secondary education, 19, 32, 68, 71, 73, 115, 123, 137, 146, 152, 163, 176, 204, 232
SIDA. *See* Swedish International Development Cooperation Agency (SIDA)
Skills development, 18, 26, 27, 186, 188–190, 193–196, 198, 199
Social development, 32, 49, 82, 90–94, 103, 119, 161–165, 203, 210
Social development indicators, 161–165
Social inclusion, 95, 202, 211
South Africa, 5, 32, 65, 100, 183–199, 238, 241–246
Soviet Union, 18, 20, 217, 221
Stakeholders, 14, 26, 28, 42, 44, 60, 65, 66, 73–77, 84, 89, 102, 135, 154, 155, 160, 161, 173, 174, 201, 202, 204, 205, 211, 212, 238, 240, 244–246
Standardized testing, 215–232
Standards, 20, 84, 88, 91, 92, 98, 101, 103, 108, 109, 112, 126, 133, 134, 136, 137, 139, 140, 152, 154, 159, 191, 220, 221, 229, 239
Standards-based education, 108
Structural inequality, 18
Student
 assessment, 108–111, 117, 123, 125
 uprisings, 212
Survey, 85, 165, 175, 187
Sustainable development, 70, 82, 83, 85, 87, 88, 90, 92, 96, 97, 102, 103, 211, 212, 245
Sweden, 82, 90, 94, 96, 98, 100, 196, 241
Swedish International Development Cooperation Agency (SIDA), 100–102, 111, 123, 193

T
Tanzania, 5, 18, 81–103, 239–241, 243
Teacher
 change, 109
 professional development, 109
 reflection, 148, 179–180
 training, 30, 53, 66, 73, 75, 116, 127, 136–137, 139, 163, 173–175
Technical Vocational and Education and Training (TVET), 99, 101, 190
Technology, 5, 17, 18, 22, 94, 100, 154, 157–180, 206, 238, 243, 246
Tertiary education, 26–28, 32, 34, 202, 205, 206, 212, 237, 238, 240, 244, 245, 247
Training, 10, 14, 18, 19, 29, 30, 50, 53, 66, 69, 73, 75, 99, 101, 116, 127, 135–137, 139–141, 146, 149, 162, 163, 165, 166, 168–176, 178–180, 183–199, 218, 240, 244, 247
Transition, 87, 138, 146, 179, 185–188, 198, 199
TVET. *See* Technical Vocational and Education and Training (TVET)

U
Ukraine, 6, 215, 216, 218, 220, 221, 223, 224, 226–232, 240, 241, 244, 245
United Nations (UN), 9, 10, 17, 69, 82, 89–91, 95, 102, 132, 134, 185, 206
United Nations Children's Fund (UNICEF), 12, 19, 46, 48, 66, 69, 72
United Nations Education, Science and Culture Organization (UNESCO), 4, 11, 17, 21, 26, 28, 41, 46–48, 51–55, 64–68, 86, 115, 116, 131, 146, 152, 154, 158, 163, 205–207, 209–212, 241, 244, 245, 247
United States (US), 18, 21, 40, 42, 51, 94, 131, 132, 134–139, 185, 217, 219–221, 226–232, 240, 241, 243–245
United States Agency for International Development (USAID), 19, 26, 40–42, 45, 51, 53–55, 188, 219–221, 228, 241
Universal Declaration of Human Rights, 9, 89, 92, 98
Universal education, 3, 9, 11–13, 20, 21, 28, 29, 32, 62, 64, 70, 75, 76, 87, 89, 92, 94, 98, 112, 127, 146
Universal goals, 21
Uruguay, 5, 143, 144, 146–148, 151, 154, 241, 242
USAID. *See* United States Agency for International Development (USAID)
U.S. Foreign Policy, 82, 94–95, 99, 198

V
Values education, 43, 51–55

W

War, 5, 11, 13–15, 17, 18, 20, 33, 40, 41, 51–54, 61, 83, 86, 94, 97, 183, 185, 187, 210
Washington Consensus, 86, 87, 203, 207
WCEFA. *See* World Conference on Education for All (WCEFA)
West Africa, 60
Western, 2–4, 11, 12, 16, 17, 28, 32–34, 135, 137, 138, 140, 223–228, 230, 231, 237–243, 245–248
Western values, 131
World Bank, 4, 5, 18, 19, 21, 26, 40–42, 45–48, 53, 59, 60, 68, 69, 71, 74–76, 86, 87, 90, 92, 133, 152, 158, 159, 161, 162, 187, 204, 205, 207–212, 220, 241, 244–247
World Conference on Education for All (WCEFA), 19, 45, 49, 108, 113, 198
World culture theory, 12, 62

MIX
Papier aus verantwortungsvollen Quellen
Paper from responsible sources
FSC® C105338

If you have any concerns about our products,
you can contact us on
ProductSafety@springernature.com

In case Publisher is established outside the EU,
the EU authorized representative is:
Springer Nature Customer Service Center GmbH
Europaplatz 3, 69115 Heidelberg, Germany

Printed by Libri Plureos GmbH
in Hamburg, Germany